ROMAN POLITICS AND THE CRIMINAL COURTS
149-78 B.C.

ROMAN POLITICS AND THE CRIMINAL COURTS, 149-78 B.C.

ERICH S. GRUEN

HARVARD UNIVERSITY PRESS
CAMBRIDGE, MASSACHUSETTS

1968

Distributed in Great Britain by Oxford University Press, London

Library of Congress Catalog Card Number 68-29179
Printed in the United States of America

UXORI CARISSIMAE

ACKNOWLEDGMENTS

Acknowledgments are the happiest of the historian's chores. A number of scholars have generously contributed to the improvement of this work. Professors Herbert Bloch, G. W. Bowersock, and T. R. S. Broughton read and criticized portions of the manuscript in various early stages of preparation. The second and third chapters benefited particularly from the comments of Mrs. M. I. Henderson, whose recent untimely death was a great loss to the world of classical scholarship. My gratitude to Professor Mason Hammond is especially deep. Dealing with an earlier version of the book, he spent countless long hours laboriously checking footnotes and judiciously criticizing venturesome hypotheses. His thoroughness and perception eliminated numerous flagrant and embarrassing errors. Those that remain can only be ascribed to the author's obstinacy. Finally, I owe an incalculable debt to Professor E. Badian. His published works were an inspiration; his meticulous and penetrating criticism at every stage of the manuscript's development was invaluable; and his tireless encouragement is responsible for much of whatever merit lies in the final product.

Berkeley, California   Erich S. Gruen
March 1968

CONTENTS

ABBREVIATIONS

AbhLeipz	*Abhandlungen der Sächsichen Akademie der Wissenschaften, Leipzig*
AbhMünch	*Abhandlungen der Bayerischen Akademie der Wissenschaften, München*
AHR	*American Historical Review*
AJP	*American Journal of Philology*
AnnPisa	*Annali della R. Scuola Normale Superiore de Pisa, Sezione di Lettere*
AntCl	*L'Antiquité Classique*
AnzAlt	*Anzeiger für die Altertumswissenschaft*
AnzWien	*Anzeiger der Österreichischen Akademie der Wissenschaften, Wien, Phil.-hist. Klasse*
Arch. Stor. Pugliese	*Archivio Storico Pugliese*
Atti Accad. Napoli	*Atti della Accademia di Archeologia, Lettere, e Belle Arti, Napoli*
AttiVen	*Atti dell'Istituto Veneto di Scienze, Lettere ed Arti*
BonnJbb	*Bonner Jahrbücher*
Bull. Ass. Budé	*Bulletin de l'Association Guillaume Budé*
CAH	*Cambridge Ancient History*
CIL	*Corpus Inscriptionum Latinarum*
CJ	*Classical Journal*
ClMed	*Classica et Mediaevalia*
CP	*Classical Philology*
CQ	*Classical Quarterly*
CR	*Classical Review*
CRAI	*Comptes Rendus de l'Académie des Inscriptions et Belles Lettres*
CW	*Classical World*
EHR	*English Historical Review*
FGH	F. Jacoby, *Die Fragmente der Griechischen Historiker* (Berlin, 1923————)
FIRA	S. Riccobono, *Fontes iuris Romani ante-iustiniani* (Florence, 1940)
GRBS	*Greek, Roman, and Byzantine Studies*
HRR	H. Peter, *Historicorum Romanorum Reliquiae* (Leipzig, 1906-1914)
HZ	*Historische Zeitschrift*
ILLRP	A. Degrassi, *Inscriptiones Latinae Liberae Rei Publicae* (Florence, 1965)
ILS	H. Dessau, *Inscriptiones Latinae Selectae* (Berlin, 1892-1916)
Int. Rev. Soc. Hist.	*International Review of Social History*
Jahrb. Class. Phil.	*Jahrbücher für Classische Philologie*
JP	*Journal of Philology*
JRS	*Journal of Roman Studies*
LEC	*Les Études Classiques*
Mem. Acad. Roy. Belg.	*Académie Royale de Belgique — Mémoires*

ABBREVIATIONS

MRR	T. R. S. Broughton, *The Magistrates of the Roman Republic* (New York, 1951-1952)
MünchBeitr	*Münchener Beiträge zur Papyrusforschung und antiken Rechtsgeschichte*
NC	*Numismatic Chronicle*
Nuov. Riv. Stor.	*Nuova Rivista Storica*
ORF	H. Malcovati, *Oratorum Romanorum Fragmenta Liberae Rei Publicae*, 2nd ed. (Turin, 1955)
Par. Pass.	*La Parola del Passato*
PBSR	*Papers of the British School at Rome*
PCPS	*Proceedings of the Cambridge Philological Society*
Proc. Afr. Class. Ass.	*Proceedings of the African Classical Association*
RE	Pauly-Wissowa, *Real-Encyclopädie der klassischen Altertumswissenschaft*
REA	*Revue des Études Anciennes*
REL	*Revue des Études Latines*
RendIstLomb	*Istituto Lombardo di Scienze e Lettere, Rendiconti*
RendLinc	*Rendiconti della R. Accademia dei Lincei*
RendNap	*Rendiconti della R. Accademia di Archeologia, Lettere ed Arti, Napoli*
Rev. Gen. Droit	*Revue Générale du Droit de la Législation et de la Jurisprudence*
Rev. Int. Droit. Ant.	*Revue Internationale des Droits de l'Antiquité*
Rev. Univ. Brux.	*Revue de l'Université de Bruxelles*
RHist	*Revue Historique*
RhM	*Rheinisches Museum für Philologie*
Riv. di Filol.	*Rivista di Filologia e d'Istruzione Classica*
Riv. Ital. Scienz. Giurid.	*Rivista Italiana per le Scienze Giuridiche*
ROL	E. H. Warmington, *Remains of Old Latin* (London, 1958)
SBHeid	*Sitzungsberichte der Heidelberger Akademie der Wissenschaften*
SBWien	*Sitzungsberichte der Akademie der Wissenschaften, Wien*
Studi Storici	*Studi Storici per l'Antichità Classica*
TAPA	*Transactions and Proceedings of the American Philological Association*
WS	*Wiener Studien*
WürzJbb	*Würzburger Jahrbücher für die Altertumswissenschaft*
ZSav	*Zeitschrift der Savigny-Stiftung für Rechtsgeschichte, Romanistische Abteilung*

ROMAN POLITICS AND THE CRIMINAL COURTS
149-78 B.C.

INTRODUCTION

Politics is only in small part a public performance. More extensive and generally more important activities lie behind the scenes, closed to the view of contemporary and historian alike. Clandestine, private maneuvers are the genuine stuff of politics, but it is only their issue that stands on record. Most known political actions are in the public domain because it was designed that they be in the public domain. The rough drafts or dress rehearsals of official events remain concealed. The historian of politics thus labors under severe handicaps. Even where documentation is plentiful, the writing of history cannot altogether escape these limitations. Documents are by nature artificial and even memoirs are normally the product of image-makers. To penetrate the surface manifestations requires hypothesis. For students of ancient history the problems are multiplied, the solutions considerably less secure. Not only are the events behind the scenes obscure but the scenes themselves must often be reconstructed because of paucity of information. The character, interests, and prejudices of the sources more frequently provide frustration than enlightenment.

In view of this it will hardly provoke surprise that the nature of Roman politics in the Republic is much disputed. Scantiness of evidence has compelled scholars to fall back upon modern analogies that are hazardous and misleading. Political parties familiar to nineteenth- and twentieth-century observers were once ascribed to the Roman situation — a fruitless enterprise.[1] Republican politics comprised no elaborate organizations, no platforms, no "tickets", no official policies associated with particular groups. Eighteenth-century England seemed to provide a more illuminating parallel: family and personal connections, cemented by favors, benefits, and mutual interests, supplied the basis for political allegiance. The analogy

[1] The classic, of course, is T. Mommsen, *Römische Geschichte* (Berlin, 1903-1904), esp. Books IV and V. Mommsen has had innumerable conscious or inadvertent emulators.

spurred a whole new school of prosopographical research investigating marriage alliances, adoptions, *amicitiae,* and *clientelae* in order to reconstruct the groups that dominated Roman politics.[2] This process, however, is also subject to abuse. Adequate language fails the historian who seeks to convey the informal compacts that linked leading Roman families and their adherents. Hence, descriptions of aristocratic factions invariably, if inadvertently, bestow upon them a consistency and a pattern that they rarely possessed in fact. The existence of Roman "parties" has been piously disclaimed and then smuggled in through the rear door in the guise of "factions." Critics have found it easy to cite family splits, lack of cooperation among alleged *amici,* and the fluidity of any political groupings.[3] What remains? A more recent approach virtually denies all structure to Roman politics. Personal ties, family connections, and hereditary obligations existed but their role on the political scene was limited. Continuity is not to be assigned to any aristocratic groupings. According to this view, electoral campaigns were run on temporary alliances and ad hoc arrangements; potential supporters had to be wooed anew for each campaign rather than brought to the polls as a pre-packaged bloc. Patterns of division do not bear scrutiny because the ruling oligarchy was internally united. Minor hostilities and *inimicitiae* within the ranks rarely affected politics. Factional groupings would be divisive and therefore the aristocratic class discouraged them. Personal or hereditary obligations might influence a particular voter, but these were in no sense "political" influences. The nobility controlled affairs and the populace acquiesced.

---

[2] Much credit must go to M. Gelzer's *Die Nobilität der römischen Republik,* published in 1912 and now reprinted in Gelzer, *Kleine Schriften* (Wiesbaden, 1962), I.19-135, a sober and illuminating analysis of Roman politics. On prosopography, the pioneering enterprises of F. Münzer, through countless articles in *RE* and his major work, *Römische Adelsparteien und Adelsfamilien* (Stuttgart, 1920), stand as the foundation for all subsequent work. The techniques were applied to the period of the late Republic and early Empire by R. Syme in his *Roman Revolution* (Oxford, 1939), and to the years 220-150 B.C. by H. H. Scullard in *Roman Politics, 220-150 B.C.* (Oxford, 1951). For the interim period the names of two younger scholars stand out, E. Badian and E. Gabba, whose books and articles have provided indispensable guidance and will be cited frequently in the footnotes.

[3] Scullard's *Roman Politics* has been the most inviting target of this criticism, much of it justifiable. Whatever Scullard's intent, the result is often schematic and forced; see esp. the reviews of Gelzer, *Kleine Schriften,* I.201-210, and A. Heuss, *HZ,* 182 (1956), 593-597; and cf. also the remarks by A. N. Sherwin-White, "Violence in Roman Politics," *JRS,* 46 (1956), 1-2, and J. P. V. D. Balsdon, "Review of Gelzer, *Kleine Schriften,*" *Gnomon,* 37 (1965), 579-580.

Such is the view of the most recent and most effective critic of the prosopographical approach.[4]

The present state of the controversy does not promise swift resolution. But this last contribution, if pursued, would tend to derail inquiry altogether. Too often, analysis of an approach degenerates into criticism of a caricature. Even the old notion of political parties was more sophisticated than is usually admitted.[5] As for the prosopographical method, its use as a tool remains indispensable for any understanding of the Roman Republic. Attacks on the concept of senatorial factions and alliances have stressed the almost total absence of references in the sources to such alignments.[6] That, however, brings us back to the point noted at the outset of this introduction. The workings of back-stage maneuvers would not usually find their way into the works of extant authors. It hardly follows that Romans refrained from organizing for political purposes. There is abundant evidence for links among influential families and for clashes among them in a struggle for power within ruling circles. The evidence, as we shall see, requires interpretation at every step and conjectures are inevitable, but the historian's obligation remains that of making some sense out of even the most slippery of materials. Those who see no factional underpinnings in Roman politics have directed their attention primarily to two chronological periods. First, the century and a half before Ti. Gracchus: those years seem to show considerable solidarity among the ruling class. Petty squabbles at election time or on a few other occasions disturb the picture but little. The senate had a common purpose and a common spirit; there was no room and no desire for internal dissension. Second, the Ciceronian age: economic, military, and social forces created disruption, loyalties were scattered, and families were divided. As for factional patterns, there are still none discernible. That much, so it is argued, the two eras have in common. But what of the interim period? With neither Livy's history nor Cicero's letters as guides, the information is severely limited. Conclusions arrived at for the age of Scipio Africanus or for the age of Cicero have been too readily applied

---

[4] C. Meier, in a series of articles and reviews: see esp. "Review of Badian, *Foreign Clientelae," BonnJbb*, 161 (1961), 503-514; "Review of Carney, *A Biography of C. Marius," Gnomon*, 36 (1964), 64-70; "Review of A. Lippold, *Consules," AnzAlt*, 19 (1966), 127-131; and his major work, *Res Publica Amissa* (Wiesbaden, 1966).

[5] Cf. the defense of Mommsen by L. R. Taylor, *Party Politics in the Age of Caesar* (Berkeley and Los Angeles, 1949), 12, 192.

[6] Cf. M. I. Henderson, "Review of Scullard, *Roman Politics," JRS*, 42 (1952), 114-116; P. A. Brunt, "*Amicitia* in the Late Roman Republic," *PCPS*, 191 (1965), 1-20; and Meier (see note 4 above).

to the years 149-78 B.C. Yet it is precisely in that pivotal period when the most fundamental changes in the Roman constitution and in political behavior were taking place; it is the period of the Gracchi, of the Social War, of Marius and Sulla, of agrarian reform, foreign crises, growing violence, and sharp political innovation. It is a period that must be examined in its own light and independent of categories supplied by the Punic Wars or by the Ciceronian era. It is the purpose of this study to carry out that charge.

The structure of Roman politics remains difficult to grasp. Although it does not consist of neat, insulated, and consistent patterns, neither is it to be dismissed as a totally unsystematic, ad hoc set of arrangements. Aristocratic factions were indeed fluid and shifts of allegiance are certainly discernible. What these pages will attempt to show, however, is that the shifts and fluctuations were not haphazard nor are they unintelligible. Political movements or charismatic leaders might attract fresh adherents. Loyalties to family, class, and faction could break down under pressure of crisis. Tension created antagonisms or produced new alliances. A common threat might unite senatorial factions, but the disappearance of that threat would customarily revive old rifts, although the lines would now be drawn differently. In the course of this seventy-year period senatorial politics had to come to grips with new problems and new dangers, and it changed considerably in the process. The forceful expression of economic grievances, a growing cleavage among classes, the enhanced power of business elements, non-senatorial leaders, non-Roman Italians, and the disruptive chaos of civil and foreign wars all served to alter the structure of Roman politics. It would be foolish to say that it was the same in 78 as in 149; much more foolish to see it in the reflection of 220 or of 49. But the shifts were hardly random. It is possible to detect and to delineate sharp changes in traditional allegiances during critical periods. The Gracchan movement cut across old lines; some men were shaken out of previous lethargy, others retreated into stronger conservatism, or formed different groups. The fall of the Gracchi ended the influence of some families, enhanced the power of others. Similar shakeups occurred during the Jugurthine War and in reaction to demagogic agitation toward the end of the second century. Even more shattering was the series of convulsions following the Social War and stretching through the 80's, which witnessed a considerable realignment on the political scene.

In none of these instances can prosopography tell the whole story. But in every case it provides revealing information on the actions and attitudes of Rome's leaders. Given the nexus of associations among those in politics, analysis of the leaders reveals much. One will not find fixed and static groupings. If phrases like "Scipionic circle" or "Metellan *factio*" are employed, these must be understood for what they are: convenient and expedient terms to denote an assemblage of individuals and families cooperating for mutual political advantage. They do not necessarily imply strict continuity of policy and personnel. Indeed it is one of the purposes of this study to indicate how and why these groups fluctuated and to point out changes in associations. If any pattern emerges at all it is a rhythmic one. The senatorial aristocracy was in full control of the springs of power in 149 B.C., and, after the reforms of Sulla, it was in full control once more in 78. But the composition of that body and the security of its status had altered considerably over three quarters of a century. When Ti. Gracchus drew to himself some influential aristocrats and issued a serious challenge to the oligarchy's traditional supremacy in 133, the ranks of the senatorial majority closed against him. His brother met the same fate a decade later. But on each occasion, when the threat receded, rifts among the ruling classes reappeared, each time more sharply than the last, for old antagonisms had been exacerbated and new ones created. At the same time more men from non-noble and even non-senatorial families found their way into the centers of power. A similar pattern appears in the last decade of the second century. Ambitious leaders took advantage of factional strife within the nobility to promote new men and to effect constitutional and social change; once more the aristocracy congealed and the threat was dissipated. But the ruling class again emerged weaker, not stronger. Superficial tranquillity inspired a revival of internecine quarrels within the senate in the 90's — the same rhythm again. But this time senatorial myopia had unleashed forces with which its leaders could no longer cope; the demand of the Italians for franchise and power, the self-consciousness of the armies, the rise of military figures. Efforts were still made in the 80's to reassemble political coalitions along the old lines and with widened participation, but to no avail. When Sulla restored the "oligarchy," he did so by force of arms.

Prosopographical studies that seek to reconstruct political factions have generally concentrated on evidence from electoral results. That can, on occasion, be illuminating, but only rarely. Consular collegiality can seldom be used to argue political cooperation; too many instances occur of *inimici* sharing high office. Much less does succession in office prove collaboration, for the decisive influence of magistrates over succeeding elections, so often assumed, has never been satisfactorily demonstrated.[7] Electoral contests could be spirited, but seldom did they decide political

[7] The strongest case has recently been made out by L. R. Taylor, *Roman Voting Assemblies from the Hannibalic War to the Dictatorship of Caesar* (Ann Arbor, 1966), 104-105. But even she is skeptical about the use of successive names in the *fasti* to prove political cooperation; see p. 158, n. 47.

issues or rivalries. An Ap. Claudius or a Caecilius Metellus might on occasion lose an election. But it was unthinkable to keep him out of office for any length of time. To discern the course of politics better evidence is available: the criminal trial.

The criminal prosecution as a political weapon in the years under scrutiny occurs with such frequency and regularity that it may legitimately be regarded almost as an institution. To a surprisingly, perhaps alarmingly, large extent, the business of politics was carried out not in the *comitia* or in the *curia*, but in the courts. Students of Roman law have generally shied away from the criminal law. The reasons are easy to comprehend. Roman criminal law evades convenient, legalistic treatment. The elaboration of legal techniques and the evolution of judicial machinery were wrapped up in politics almost from the beginning and continued to be subject to the vagaries of politics throughout the period of 149-78. The first permanent criminal court and procedure in Rome was set up in 149, at least partially under political pressures. It rapidly provided a new platform for struggles within the aristocracy and also for contests between the more conservative *nobiles* and the men who posed, whether genuinely or not, as defenders of the populace. In the next seventy years the creation of other temporary and permanent courts, the further definition and clarification of criminal procedures, went on steadily. The development was on each occasion paralleled by rising temperatures in political conflicts. The dictatorship of Sulla set the seal on this development. Under his aegis, public *quaestiones* replaced for almost all purposes the old process of trial before the assembly. A systematic analysis of the struggle over the courts and of the lengthy series of criminal laws and prosecutions will do much to illuminate the course of politics.

The term "political trial" is ambiguous. It should not be taken to mean simply a trial on political charges. Accusations on the ground of "treason" were frequent, to be sure. But "treason" in Roman parlance implied more than aiding and abetting the enemy. It covered offenses as remote as losing a battle through poor generalship or violent behavior in the course of holding public office. A political trial may be defined independently of the charge involved: a criminal prosecution motivated by political purposes. In addition to treason, common charges were extortion, electoral bribery, judicial corruption, theft of public funds, and even homicide. Some trials doubtless were rigged. But the applicability of the term "political" does not entail that no offense was committed. Personal and political enemies could exploit offenses for their own purposes. Conviction or acquittal was more often an index of political power than a testimony to the effectiveness of legal argument. The court as a staging ground for politics could serve several functions. Criminal prosecutions

6

provided an avenue for young men to make a name at the bar and to launch a public career. They also served to air and often to aggravate personal rivalries. On occasion, constitutional and legal issues of the greatest significance turned on the outcome of a prosecution. And finally, the criminal trial was a common vehicle for factional struggles within the governing class, or indeed a means whereby to attack that class itself. These strands are not easily isolable in any particular case and frequently, of course, several strands overlap and converge. Demonstrable conclusions emerge only rarely. The historian is confronted with much confusion, with inadequate and inferior sources. Conjecture and hypothesis dog his steps throughout. But it is time for an examination of criminal prosecutions in their proper context: that of Roman politics.

Readers who anticipate a neat and tidy picture will find disappointment. What emerges most strikingly from a study of this period is the rapidity of change, the shifting and slippery nature of political events. Legislation was swiftly passed and as swiftly repealed. Control of the judiciary changed hands five times within the era under scrutiny. Power controlled by individuals, by factions in the senate, and by external groups was transferred back and forth at a dizzying pace. Generalizations about such a period are hazardous in the extreme. Yet two important conclusions, at least, may be drawn. First, struggles for power, though differing in form and motive, came more and more to be waged in the courts, or over the courts. And second, political conflicts gradually took on larger dimensions. The injection of issues that cut through the boundaries of traditional allegiances compelled senatorial factions to gear policy and action to the increased political awareness and interest of groups like the *equites, populus,* and *socii.* Politics and the courts met at almost every turn. Sulla's final reorganization of the *quaestio* system had the same purpose as the original *quaestio perpetua* of 149: control of the judiciary by the oligarchy. But the triumph was destined to be short-lived. The past seventy years had unleashed passions that could not readily be stilled by administrative reform. Within another generation the Republic itself was to fall a victim to the cleavages first opened in the years from the *lex Calpurnia* to the *leges Corneliae.*

I. POLITICS IN THE AGE OF SCIPIO AEMILIANUS

Rome's first permanent criminal court saw the light of day in 149 B.C. The year may be taken as opening an epoch in Roman legal history. Criminal procedures had not been unknown before that date, but they had been manifold and unsystematic. Offenders could be hauled before the assembly of the whole people by magistrates who were often driven by personal motives or external pressure. On other occasions senatorial decree or popular decision would institute a special investigation organized on a temporary basis to deal with a particular offense. Moreover, the state had not yet isolated public supervision of criminal matters from private action. The two existed side by side and at times in combination.[1] These various operations did not vanish overnight with the institution of the first *quaestio perpetua* in 149. The entanglement of private and public elements lingered, magisterial prosecutions before the assembly continued to occur, and special courts were still set up from time to time for another seventy years. But the process of establishing *quaestiones perpetuae* went on gradually and piecemeal during that time until Sulla organized the system as a whole in 81. The same years that witnessed the slow regularization of the criminal court structure, however, also saw its greater and greater involvement in Roman politics. As criminal prosecutions and legislation were profoundly affected by political exigencies, so politics were shaped and channeled by criminal statutes, by interpretations of public and private offenses, and, not least, by the men and groups who controlled the courts. Politics and judicial action had coincided more than once in Rome's past. The notorious trials of the Scipios in the 180's provide only the most conspicuous example. But the gradual installation of regular criminal procedures after 149 added a new

[1] See the forceful and illuminating remarks of W. Kunkel, "Untersuchungen zur Entwicklung des römischen Kriminalverfahrens in vorsullanischer Zeit," *AbhMünch,* 56 (1962), 37-42, 97-130; and *RE,* 47.721-731, *"quaestio."* The *lex repetundarum* of 123, line 11, implies the existence of both public and private procedures for criminal offenses; *FIRA,* I.87.

dimension and greatly expanded the opportunities for this unholy alliance.

Inquiry must begin with the *quaestio de rebus repetundis,* instituted as Rome's initial permanent court by the *lex Calpurnia* of 149.[2] Customary modern usage knows it as the "extortion court," a convenient if not altogether accurate phrase. The crime with which it was designed to deal was the mistreatment of provincials, foreigners, or subjects by Roman officers abroad, a mistreatment that normally involved the exaction of money in some form. It ought not to be imagined, however, that Rome awoke to the existence of these offenses only as late as 149. The great era of Rome's expansion in the first half of the second century was hardly her finest hour from the moralist's point of view. Crimes against provincials multiplied and punishments leveled against offenders are on record. The *lex Calpurnia* came as no bolt out of the blue. The background is significant and warrants investigation.

Satisfaction for those who had been sinned against abroad was possible in a number of ways. Recourse could be had through civil procedure in order to recover pecuniary damages. The medium here was a board of *recuperatores* selected by the praetor to assess loss and facilitate recovery. Origin of the institution is obscure, but it seems to have been designed to promote speed and despatch in suits that involved both Romans and citizens of other states.[3] If the affair possessed some notoriety, magisterial (usually tribunician) initiative could summon a hearing before the assembled *populus.* Otherwise, a special inquisitorial tribunal, a *quaestio extraordinaria,* might be constituted for the occasion; in its procedure the investigative and the judicial functions possessed no clear boundaries. None of these methods, however, proved entirely satisfactory. In the quarter century prior to the *lex Calpurnia,* Rome continued to act in a groping and fumbling manner with offenses against *socii* and *peregrini.* Some examples will illustrate the problem and illuminate the background of the *quaestio de repetundis.*

In 173 the Statielli in Liguria endured the unfortunate fate of having a ruthless Roman commander, M. Popillius Laenas, operating in their area. Popillius, consul in that year, provoked a battle, routed the reluc-

---

[2] For the sources, see *MRR,* I.459. Fullest discussion of the law, but one that must be read with caution, is that of A. W. Zumpt, *Das Criminalrecht der römischen Republik* (Berlin, 1868), II.1.1-54. For Zumpt, the *lex Calpurnia* did not set up a *quaestio* but simply defined the charge of *repetundae;* see pp. 6-10; cf. also Sherwin-White, *"Poena Legis Repetundarum," PBSR,* 17 (1949), 6. That seems decisively refuted by Cicero's explicit statement, *Brutus,* 106: *quaestiones perpetuae . . . Piso trib. pl. legem primus de pecuniis repetundis . . . tulit.*

[3] See the discussion in A. H. J. Greenidge, *The Legal Procedure of Cicero's Time* (Oxford, 1901), 47-49, 266-269.

tant foe, and, after accepting the *deditio* of the survivors, sold them into slavery and disposed of their belongings as well. The audacity of the victor did not cease there: he proceeded to describe his conquest in detail in a letter to the senate, characterizing heinous crimes as services to the state. Enemies at home and outraged citizens still concerned with Roman *fides* reacted strongly. In the following year two tribunes succeeded in persuading the senate to institute a special *quaestio* under the presidency of a praetor charged with an investigation and trial of Popillius. The people ratified the decree. But M. Popillius coolly maintained his scorn, secure in the knowledge of powerful support in Rome. His prognosis was accurate. A brother, C. Popillius, was consul in 172, and the praetor assigned to conduct the inquiry was overawed by the political pressure. Postponements ensued and the whole matter was dropped without issue.[4]

Spain also felt the fury of rapacious Roman officials at this time. Unscrupulous extortion of money induced a Spanish embassy in 171 to demean itself before the senate and to plead for restitution. A board of *recuperatores* was selected to hear charges against three Roman officials and to estimate the damages. Provincials could not themselves argue their cases, but had to select Roman *patroni* to represent them. The results were inconclusive and unsatisfactory. Adjournments delayed matters; eventually one defendant secured acquittal, the other two enjoyed voluntary exile in Latium. On the question of the recovery of money the evidence is silent. The existence of *recuperatores* implies a civil proceeding. What induced the exile of the two offending magistrates is uncertain; perhaps fear of bankruptcy, or possibly the threat of a tribunician prosecution before the assembly. The whole affair, in any case, possessed a bad odor. The Roman *patroni* had not exerted themselves in the cause of the provincials, and the presiding praetor had choked off further action.[5] It is evident that Romans were still groping for a method to deal with extortion cases. The use of civil procedure to handle what was basically a criminal offense brought satisfaction neither to Rome nor to the *socii*.

The year 170 brought more of the same from other parts of the world. C. Cassius Longinus, consul in 171, had indulged himself in Gaul, ravaging the countryside and enslaving its inhabitants. Gallic envoys appealed to the senate and received a courteous but evasive response: there could

---

[4] Livy, 42.7-10, 42.21-22; cf. *ORF,* 92.

[5] Livy, 43.2; Ps-Asconius, 203, Stangl; *ORF,* 59. The conjecture of a fear of bankruptcy was made by T. Mommsen, *Römisches Strafrecht* (Leipzig, 1899), 707-708; threat of tribunician prosecution was suggested by J. L. Strachan-Davidson, *Problems of the Roman Criminal Law* (Oxford, 1912), II.3-4. See also Zumpt, *Criminalrecht,* II.1.17-19; W. W. Buckland, "Civil Proceedings Against ex-Magistrates in the Republic," *JRS,* 27 (1937), 40-41.

be no proceedings against Cassius *in absentia,* but the matter might be reopened when he returned. Cassius delayed that return sufficiently and no record survives of any action against him. Similar offenses had been committed in the East against the Chalcidians by a praetor of 171, C. Lucretius Gallus. Once more representatives of the aggrieved provincials brought their complaints to the Roman senate, in whose charge lay the conduct of foreign affairs. On this occasion, however, senatorial dilatoriness failed to satisfy two aggressive tribunes who took the initiative away from the *curia.* Lucretius faced trial before the popular assembly, which pronounced him guilty and levied a stiff fine of one million asses.[6] Senators with foresight may already have recognized the ominous signs. Tribunes were playing a larger role in mobilizing popular outrage. The unsystematic and haphazard nature of treating offenses against the provincials might eventually threaten senatorial control of external affairs.

Events on the foreign scene remained relatively quiet for a time thereafter. There is no reason to believe that Roman officials behaved themselves in a more seemly fashion during the succeeding years, but since Livy's text breaks off after 167 B.C., it is no longer possible to follow the violations in detail. The epitomator of Livy, lest there be any doubt, reports that prosecutions for misdemeanors abroad continued in the 150's, and even indicates some convictions.[7] On occasion there is an isolated and revealing notice. L. Cornelius Lentulus Lupus, consul in 156, was prosecuted and convicted of *repetundae* sometime around 154. Nature of the crime and place of origin are unknown; little conjecture can be built upon the compressed evidence. But one item is noteworthy. Lentulus suffered condemnation by virtue of a *lex Caecilia.* The likelihood is strong that the measure was initiated by a tribune.[8] Whether conviction came as a result of trial by the assembly or by a special *quaestio* author-

---

[6] For the case of Cassius, see Livy, 43.5; for that of Lucretius, Livy, 43.7-8: *multamque deciens centum milium aeris dixerunt.*

[7] Livy, *Per.* 47: *Aliquot praetores a provinciis avaritiae nomine accusati damnati sunt.*

[8] Val. Max. 6.9.10: *L. Lentulus consularis lege Caecilia repetundarum crimine oppressus;* also Festus, 360, L. The *lege Caecilia* is frequently emended to *lege Calpurnia* and the trial dated after 149; Zumpt, *Criminalrecht,* II.1.25-26; Mommsen, *Strafrecht,* 708, n. 3; Sherwin-White, *PBSR,* 17 (1949), 6; F. Pontenay de Fontette, *Leges Repetundarum* (Paris, 1954), 26. But Lentulus, who was consul in 156, would probably not have had the opportunity to commit acts of extortion in the 140's. Emendation is unnecessary. G. Niccolini, *I Fasti dei Tribuni della Plebe* (Milan, 1934), 409, conjectured a tribune Caecilius in the 150's, whom Broughton plausibly identifies with Q. Caecilius Metellus Macedonicus, consul in 143; *MRR,* I.450, 451, n. 2.

ized by the *lex Caecilia* cannot be determined. But the consequences of this general development were becoming clearer. Romans were gradually acknowledging extortion as a criminal offense, not readily handled through civil procedure. And the only institution that possessed some permanence as a criminal court was the *comitia*. Many aristocrats must have come to the conclusion that senatorial control over provincial governors was in danger of being undermined.

This analysis of *repetundae* cases brings us to the eve of the *lex Calpurnia*. And it is no accident that that measure was directly preceded by a real *cause célèbre*. The wars in Spain had resumed in 154. Lack of convincing success swiftly caused frustration, impatience, and short-sightedness in the field. Rome's brutal and often senseless management of Spanish affairs in these years made the question of how to check provincial governors a particularly acute one. Ser. Sulpicius Galba was pro-praetor in Further Spain in 150, a man of great wealth and among orators incontestably the most outstanding of his day. A hostile tradition, however, reports that he was also insatiably greedy and would stoop to deceit and perjury for personal gain. He had once before betrayed his own commander and had roused troops against that commander out of rage at a scanty distribution of booty.[9] In 150 came his most notorious act of perfidy: he enticed and disarmed the Lusitanians by treacherous promises, then murdered a large number of them, and enslaved the rest.[10] Conduct of so scandalous a nature could not pass unnoticed. Once more a triumphant return home was upset by criminal proceedings instituted by an enterprising tribune. L. Scribonius Libo in 149 denounced Galba in scathing terms in the forum and proposed a bill to the assembly providing for a special *quaestio* on the affair. One detail of the measure is preserved: the prospective defendant would be allowed to select a number of his own jurors, subject to challenge by the opposition. Scribonius mustered powerful support for his efforts. Among other spokesmen, the venerable Cato the Censor vented his moral wrath and warmly advocated Scribonius' bill. Matters looked grim for Galba, but he possessed his own resources. The distinguished *consularis* Q. Fulvius Nobilior spoke up in his behalf and cash may also have been used. But most effective was a *coup de théâtre:* Galba resorted to tears and entreaties, parading before the populace his two small sons and the orphan son of his *propinquus* Sulpicius Galus who had been committed to his care. Oratory and histrionics proved successful. The people forgot about the merits of the

[9] On Galba's eloquence, see esp. Cic. *Brutus,* 333: *Galba fuit inter tot aequalis unus excellens,* 82; *De Orat.* 1.40; on his character, Appian, *Iber.* 60; his attack on his commander, Livy, 45.35-39; Plut. *Aem. Paul.* 30-31.

[10] Sources in *MRR,* I.457.

12

issue and defeated Scribonius' proposal out of *misericordia.* The case never came before a *quaestio.*[11]

The *lex Calpurnia* was passed in the same year as the abortive indictment of Sulpicius Galba. The connection is definitive. A tribune in 149, L. Calpurnius Piso, a historian, an orator, and a stern moralist, lent his name to the measure. Rome was to have her first permanent criminal court, the *quaestio de rebus repetundis.* Exact terms of the law do not survive. Its import, however, is clear. Makeshift arrangements for dealing with those who exploited Rome's subjects could now be dispensed with; a specific standing *album* of *iudices* was instituted from which a designated magistrate would draw for every case of extortion to be heard in the future. The law also, no doubt, defined the offense and detailed the procedure. What was the motive? Sympathy for the provincials has often been urged as the explanation. There is, however, little sign of it, either before or after. The affair of 171, discussed above, shows that at that time the *socii* had to depend upon Roman patrons to plead the cases that they were barred from arguing. The *lex Calpurnia,* it appears, made no change in that requirement. It provided for the *legis actio sacramento,* a procedure open, so far as our evidence goes, only to those who possessed Roman citizenship.[12] Moreover, sentiment for the victims of in-

[11] The affair was notorious and the sources numerous. That Scribonius' bill was designed to institute a *quaestio* is clear from Cic. *De Orat.* 1.227: *L. Scribonio quaestionem in eum ferente; Brutus,* 89: *L. Libone tribuno plebis populum incitante et rogationem in Galbam privilegi similem ferente;* cf. Val. Max. 8.1.2. Later sources wrongly regarded Galba's escape as an actual trial and acquittal: Livy, *Oxyr. Per.* 49; Tac. *Ann.* 3.66; Fronto, *Ad M. Caes.* 3.20, N; Gellius, 1.12.17. Selection and challenge of *iudices* is noted by Cic. *De Orat.* 2.263. Nobilior's speech is mentioned by Livy, *Per.* 49, Cato's by many authors: Cic. *Brutus,* 89; *Pro Mur.* 59; *Div. in Caec.* 66; Livy, 39-40; *Per.* 49; Val. Max. 8.1.2; Quintilian, 2.15.8; Plut. *Cato,* 15.4; Gellius, 1.12.17, 13.25.15; Ps-Asconius, 203, Stangl; *Vir. Ill.* 47.7. The fragments of Cato's speech, *Contra Ser. Galbam ad Milites* (Gellius, 1.23.1), however, are almost certainly to be assigned to 167 rather than to this case; C. Cichorius, *Römische Studien* (Leipzig-Berlin, 1922), 91-96; *ORF,* 67-68. Appian, *Iber.* 60, putting the worst construction on the events, affirms that Galba escaped through bribery. See also Scullard, *Roman Politics,* 234-236; H. Simon, *Roms Kriege in Spanien* (Frankfurt, 1962), 60-67.

[12] *Lex repet.,* line 23 (*FIRA,* I.90): [*lege Calpu*]*rnia aut lege Iunia sacramento actum siet.* On this see F. Serrao, "Appunti sui patroni e sulla legittimazione all' accusa nei processi *repetundarum,*" *Studi De Francisci,* 2 (1956), 473-479. The rhetoric of Cicero, expressed in a case eighty years later when he had an obvious point at stake, is not to be taken literally: *tota lex de pecuniis repetundis sociorum causa constituta; Div. in Caec.* 17-18. There are some, however, who feel that the senate acted out of a sense of real responsibility toward its subjects; E. Badian, *Roman Imperialism in the Late Republic* (Pretoria, 1967), 10-11.

justice, if it played any role in 149, cannot have endured long. Only a quarter century later the extortion court had to be reformed on the grounds of mismanagement and prejudice. And one might add a point often overlooked: the author of the *lex Calpurnia,* whatever his virtues, was not a man to be moved by sentiment or feelings for the foreigner.[13] A recent suggestion views the law as designed to promote greater equity in the hearing themselves. When jurors were selected for special *quaestiones* the choice would be subject to the personal friendships and enmities within the senatorial aristocracy; with a fixed list of jurors, that eventuality was eliminated. Yet it is clear that equity was not one of the products of this measure. The *lex Calpurnia* provided that *iudices* would be drawn exclusively from the senatorial order, and the interplay of aristocratic power struggles continued to plague the judiciary.[14] Administrative convenience may have played a role. Many no doubt felt the need to replace confused ad hoc measures with a permanent procedure. But that does not tell the whole story. Politics provided a decisive impetus.

The Galba fiasco drove home a lesson that no senator could have missed. A quarter century of *repetundae* trials lay behind it. Now senatorial control of provincial governors and of external policy generally was more clearly in jeopardy than ever before. Aggrieved *socii* who had been in the habit of appealing to the senate for remedy were finding that decisions rested rather more frequently with tribunes and with the assembly. An obvious and admitted offender like Galba could not even be brought to trial because the populace was moved more by pity than by justice. As long as each prosecution required a special investigation and a special court, proceedings themselves often depended upon individual votes of the *comitia* instead of the deliberations of the aristocracy. In the case of Galba it appears that even if that *quaestio* had been organized, its composition would have been determined not by the senate but by a system of proposal and challenge between prosecutor and defendant. The law of Calpurnius Piso, by organizing a permanent *quaestio* staffed by members of the senate to hear all future extortion cases, obviously aimed at resolving the problem in the interests of that body. Tribunician bills and decisions of the assembly could thereafter be bypassed. Offenses by

[13] On the character of Piso, cf. the anecdote in Val. Max. 2.7.9; also Frontinus, *Strat.* 4.1.26.

[14] The suggestion was made by Kunkel, *AbhMünch,* 56 (1962), 95-96; and *RE,* 47.736-737, "*quaestio*." That the *lex Calpurnia* did provide for senatorial jurors is evident from the fact that C. Gracchus later transferred the court from the senate to the *equites;* Appian, *BC,* 1.22. The law need have made no change in the selection of *iudices* for civil cases, probably drawn from both senatorial and non-senatorial groups; P. Fraccaro, *Opuscula* (Pavia, 1957), 2.263.

14

magistrates in the field would now be prosecuted regularly before a standing tribunal, and a permanent control over those magistrates could be exercised by what was in essence a committee of the senate.[15]

Whether the extortion tribunal as organized by the *lex Calpurnia* was really a criminal or a civil court is basically a matter of juristic semantics. Evidently the earlier recuperatory procedure was not abandoned altogether. Civil elements endured. The *praetor peregrinus,* in all probability, sat as presiding officer with his *consilium.* Continuation of the *actio sacramento* indicates that civil procedure for recovery damages was still part of the extortion law of Piso. When C. Gracchus later passed a new measure, it provided, among other things, for a double restitution; the implication is that the *lex Calpurnia* demanded only simple repayment. Without the assessment of punitive damages, therefore, it would hardly be proper to regard the *lex Calpurnia* as a criminal law pure and simple. On the other hand, the framers of legislation had before them not only the civil procedures of the earlier actions for *repetundae,* but also the previous series of *iudicia publica,* the special courts organized on an ad hoc basis to deal with avowedly criminal acts. Both played a role in their thinking. It is noteworthy that jurors in extortion cases are no longer referred to as *recuperatores* after 149, but as *iudices.* Terms like *quaestio* and *quaesitores,* now associated with the court, are terms of the criminal law. The *lex Calpurnia* was a hybrid. But its institution foreshadowed what was to become a full-scale system of permanent criminal courts.[16]

No dissent on the *lex Calpurnia* is recorded within the Roman oligarchy. It was a measure that promised to benefit the *ordo senatorius* as a whole. A decade would pass before the *quaestio repetundarum* began to

---

[15] A further point made long ago by W. S. Ferguson, "The *Lex Calpurnia* of 149 B.C.," *JRS,* 11 (1921), 86-100, warrants mention in this connection. Although no new provinces had been added to Roman territory since 200, both the Macedonian and Carthaginian affairs were coming to a head in 149 and two additional provinces could already be contemplated. The senate doubtless desired to guarantee its control of these prospective appendages to the empire.

[16] Opinions on the *lex Calpurnia* have ranged widely. A few of the more important deserve mention. The incorporation of civil elements has been stressed by Zumpt, *Criminalrecht,* II.1.19-21; Mommsen, *Strafrecht,* 705-710; Strachan-Davidson, *Problems,* II.1; and Sherwin-White, *PBSR,* 17 (1949), 6; the criminal character by E. Blum, "L'Origine des *leges repetundarum,*" *Rev. Gen. Droit,* 46 (1922), 119-135, 197-206; Buckland, *JRS,* 27 (1937), 37-47; D. Daube, "The Peregrine Praetor," *JRS,* 41 (1951), 66-70; and Serrao, *Studi De Francisci,* 2 (1956), 485-492. More circumspect in their judgments are Greenidge, *Legal Procedure,* 415-416; Pontenay de Fontette, *Leges Repetundarum,* 26-31; and Kunkel, *AbhMünch,* 56 (1962), 11-14. For the double restitution in the Gracchan law, see *lex repet.,* line 59 (*FIRA,* I.96).

serve as an instrument of politics within the ruling aristocracy. It will be of value now to attempt to identify the leading figures and groups around whom senatorial politics seem to have revolved in the 140's and 130's.[17] The schematic character that many historians have ascribed to the Roman political scene may serve on occasion as a useful index but rarely corresponds to reality. Connections among individuals and families did not always endure over long periods of time and one generation could seldom answer for the next. Combinations were made and remade under pressure of events; individuals could succumb to expediency or to principle. Change and fluctuation are the most conspicuous hallmarks of Roman politics, especially from the mid–second century and, with increased rapidity, after the Gracchi. Reconstruction is difficult where sources are few and behind-the-scenes manipulations are concealed. But some patterns are discernible. The course of politics is not altogether hidden.

Students at all familiar with Roman history will know of the momentous clash between the Fabii and the Scipiones over strategy and power while the Hannibalic War was raging. But both those powerful houses faded from the limelight in the succeeding generation, particularly after the trials of the Scipios in the 180's. Old rivalries were forgotten. The lineup of hostile groups in 200 bore no resemblance to the situation a half century later. One may glance with profit at the renowned consul of 168, L. Aemilius Paullus, conqueror of Perseus and hero of the third Macedonian War. Paullus laid the foundations for a new coalition through a judicious choice of adoptive parents for his two sons. One was taken by the Fabii, the other by the Cornelii Scipiones: Q. Fabius Maximus Aemilianus and P. Cornelius Scipio Aemilianus respectively. Close and devoted to one another, the two brothers symbolized the reconciliation of those two great families. Both were to reach the consulship in the mid-140's. A new generation this was indeed. There had been no more bitter or effective opponent of the Scipios than Cato the Censor. That hardened ex-farmer and professional moralist had been the man chiefly responsible for the attacks on Scipio Africanus and his associates in the 190's and 180's that eventually brought about the retirement and eclipse of Hannibal's conqueror. Yet in old age Cato abandoned previous enmities. The attraction of Aemilius Paullus was a catalyst here as well. Cato's son

---

[17] The excellent book of A. E. Astin, *Scipio Aemilianus* (Oxford, 1967), appeared when this study was already in manuscript. Agreements and disagreements in details will be noted in the appropriate places. But, in general, it is gratifying to know that Astin's approach and his judgments closely parallel many of the conclusions reached in the first two chapters of the present work.

served with Paullus at the battle of Pydna and, after impressing his commander, was given Paullus' daughter in marriage. When the dashing young Scipio Aemilianus grew into manhood, Cato became one of his warmest admirers. That Aemilianus' adoptive grandfather Africanus had been the Censor's greatest enemy was a fact now buried in oblivion. Cicero's dialogue *De Senectute* depicts Cato in old age as counselor and friend of Scipio Aemilianus, relations that are almost certainly historical.[18]

Revival of Scipionic influence is evident by the mid–second century, centered upon the most prestigious figure of the era, P. Scipio Nasica Corculum. Twice consul, in 162 and 155, censor in 157, Nasica gained access to the highest secular and religious offices in the gift of Rome: in 150 he was named *pontifex maximus* and in 147 the censors elevated him to the post of *princeps senatus*. Lofty moral principles were his trademark, and scorn for the masses, not an unusual combination. Nasica's place in history was assured by his renowned series of debates with Cato on the wisdom of yet another Roman war with Carthage. The differences expressed were differences over foreign policy and the relative moral effect on Rome of the survival or destruction of Carthage. They did not affect Cato's attitude toward Scipio Aemilianus. When young Aemilianus distinguished himself as military tribune in Carthage in 149, Cato quoted Homer in his praise.[19] Aemilianus brought to a successful conclusion the war that Cato had inspired but whose issue he did not live to see.

When Nasica perished ca. 142, Scipio Aemilianus, already the toast of Rome, became the central figure in the Scipionic clan. Like his adoptive grandfather, he had reached the consulship *ante tempus* through conspicuous ability, had crushed Carthage, and had earned the appellation of "Africanus." He was only forty-two years of age when he secured

[18] The evidence for cooperation between Cato and Aemilianus has been carefully assembled and analyzed by Astin, "Scipio Aemilianus and Cato Censorinus," *Latomus,* 15 (1956), 159-180; and *Scip. Aem.,* 280-281. See also K. Bilz, *Die Politik des P. Cornelius Scipio Aemilianus* (Stuttgart, 1935), 11, n. 22; D. C. Earl, "Terence and Roman Politics," *Historia,* 11 (1962), 480-482. On the closeness between the two sons of Aemilius Paullus, see Polyb. 31.28.3; Cic. *De Amicit.* 69; Plut. *Aem. Paul.* 39.5; the adoptions, Plut. *Aem. Paul.* 5.3.

[19] Plut. *Cato,* 27.4. There is no reason to doubt that Scipio Aemilianus and Cato were in agreement on the need and justification for a war on Carthage; Bilz, *Politik des Scipio,* 19-20, 31-34; Astin, *Latomus,* 15 (1956), 159-180; contra: E. Lincke, *P. Cornelius Scipio Aemilianus* (Dresden, 1898), 13-20. On the moral nature of the controversy between Cato and Nasica, see Gelzer, *Kleine Schriften,* II.39-72. W. Hoffman, "Die römische Politik des 2. Jahrhunderts und das Ende Karthagos," *Historia,* 9 (1960), 309-344, even doubts that there was any such controversy. See Astin, *Scip. Aem.,* 276-280. On Nasica's character, see Livy, *Per.* 48; Val. Max. 2.4.2.

election to the coveted censorship. But Scipio represented more than a military hero and a political leader. A generous and charismatic personality attracted men to him from an early age, and admiring writers dwelled on his virtues, minimizing and obscuring his faults. Whatever the truth of Polybius' lavish praise and Cicero's idealized portrait, they are testimony to the magnetic appeal of the man who dominated the Roman scene for two decades.[20] Intellectuals, philosophers, and literary men found Scipio's company congenial or profitable. His father had brought home from Macedon the library of Perseus for the edification of his sons, and more important, Polybius himself was one of the spoils of war. The Achaean statesman and historian, so he himself reports, became tutor, friend, and constant companion of Scipio. Other cultured luminaries joined the set for stimulation or for patronage: philosophers like Panaetius, literary figures like Lucilius and Terence, jurists like M'. Manilius and the Scaevolae, budding young orators and writers like C. Fannius, Rutilius Rufus, and Aelius Tubero. How much of this "culture" rubbed off on Scipio himself it would be rash to conjecture. His actions in the political and military arenas show unmistakable signs of fierce ambition, ruthlessness, and cruelty. But the number and quality of the individuals who were at one time or another associated with the circle of Scipio and his bosom friend C. Laelius demonstrate the power and influence of that group.[21]

Prosopographical investigation reveals a number of important individuals associated with Scipio. The *factio* of which he was the center was

[20] On Scipio's qualities as a young man, see Polyb. 31.23-30. Cicero's idolatry is best seen in the dialogues *De Republica* and *De Amicitia*. On the date of Nasica's death, see Münzer, *Röm. Adelsp.*, 251. On the personality of Aemilianus generally, see the references collected and the sound analysis of Astin, *Scip. Aem.*, 12-34.

[21] See Cic. *De Amicit.* 69 (Laelius speaking): *Saepe enim excellentiae quaedam sunt, qualis erat Scipionis in nostro, ut ita dicam, grege.* Most of the individuals involved are noted in the *De Amicitia* and the *De Republica*. Scipio's cruelty can be illustrated by his treatment of fugitives after the destruction of Carthage; they were thrown to the wild beasts; Val. Max. 2.7.13; Livy, *Per.* 51. When four hundred young Spaniards were surrendered to him, Scipio had their hands lopped off; Appian, *Iber.* 94. Recently, H. Strasburger, "Der 'Scipionenkreis,'" *Hermes*, 94 (1966), 60-72, has challenged Cicero's notion of the Scipionic circle, regarding it as a fabrication modeled by Cicero on his own youthful experience with the circle of the Scaevolae, Crassus, and Antonius in the 90's. But although Strasburger can legitimately question the genuineness of the intellectual influence on Scipio, the personal contacts are historical, many of them solidified through familial ties. The political stature of Scipio is sufficient to explain his following; Cicero need not have invented that. See also Astin. *Scip. Aem.*, 294-306, on the Scipionic circle.

18

conspicuous in high office and in political activity during the 140's and 130's. Two men were closest to him, his brother Q. Fabius Aemilianus and C. Laelius. Fabius reached the consulship in 145, the year following Scipio's triumphant conquest of Carthage; his governorship of Spain in that year is one of the few that showed some military success and refrained from staining Roman honor. Laelius, the intellectual and patron of the arts, friend of Terence and intimate of Panaetius, was Scipio's inseparable confidant. Genial, self-controlled and cultured, Laelius was rated above even Scipio by the admiring Cicero, in oratory and in matters of the mind. He fought under Scipio at Carthage in 147, and served in Spain probably with Fabius Aemilianus in 145. In 140, after one failure, he reached the consulship.[22] An older man than Laelius, M'. Manilius, a jurist, appears in the *De Republica* as an *amicus* of Scipio. That can be documented further. As consul in 149, Manilius was in charge of military operations in Africa; Scipio was attached to him as *tribunus militum*.[23]

The consul of 142, Q. Fabius Maximus Servilianus, is of particular interest. An author and a student of pontifical law who nonetheless exhibited unmitigated cruelty when dealing with enemies in the field, he exemplified that combination of intellectual leanings at home and barbarity abroad characteristic of so many Roman aristocrats in this period. Servilianus was born a Servilius Caepio, a family unfriendly, we shall have reason to see, to the Scipios. Historians have generally placed him in a hostile camp.[24] Yet his adoption by the Fabii Maximi made him brother of Fabius Aemilianus. Adoptive ties in this instance appear to have been stronger than blood. When Servilianus campaigned in Spain in 141 he secured elephants and cavalry through personal request to Micipsa, king of Numidia. His connection with the house of Scipio and its patronage of Numidian royalty doubtless facilitated the transaction. Another item is even more revealing. Lack of military success induced Servilianus to conclude a treaty with the Spanish leader Viriathus. His successor in Spain, however, the consul of 140, denounced the agreement as faint-hearted and unworthy of Roman dignity, and reopened the war.

[22] On Laelius' career and personality, see Münzer, *RE*, 23.407, "Laelius," n. 3. The service in Spain, not specifically dated, is noted by Cicero, *Brutus*, 84; *De Off.* 2.40. On Fabius' activities in Spain, see esp. Appian, *Iber.* 65; Vell. Pat. 2.5.3.

[23] For the *amicitia*, see Cic. *De Rep.* 1.18, 3.17; the service in Africa, *MRR*, I.458-459. A link is suggested also with Polybius; Polyb. 36.11.

[24] Münzer, *Röm. Adelsp.*, 245-247; Scullard, "Scipio Aemilianus and Roman Politics," *JRS*, 50 (1960), 67; D. C. Earl, *Tiberius Gracchus: A Study in Politics* (Brussels, 1963), 100. On Servilianus' paradoxical character, see esp. Val. Max. 2.7.11; cf. Astin, *Scip. Aem.*, 111.

That consul was Q. Servilius Caepio, natural brother of Servilianus himself. No clearer evidence can be imagined for the political allegiance of Fabius Servilianus.[25]

Other names in the consular *fasti* of the 140's and 130's suggest links with the Scipios. C. Livius Drusus, consul in 147 and colleague of Scipio Aemilianus, was himself son of an Aemilianus. The family of Aemilius Paullus had stretched its connections intelligently and widely. It seems to have encompassed the Livii Drusi. And one may perhaps tentatively add the Calpurnii Pisones, a clan that provided four consuls between 148 and 133. L. Calpurnius Piso, as seen above, was responsible for the measure that instituted the *quaestio repetundarum*. That bill had important connotations which went well beyond petty factional squabbles. Yet, coming when it did, the *lex Calpurnia* was an unmistakable slap at Sulpicius Galba and his disgraceful escape at the hands of an emotional assembly. Possibly it is not irrelevant that Galba as a military tribune in 167 had turned on his own commander, Aemilius Paullus, the father of Scipio, and sought to deny him a triumph with bitter speeches before the soldiers and the *populus*.[26] It is prudent not to press these conjectures too far. Overt cooperation of the Drusi and the Pisones with Scipio Aemilianus is not attested. But other younger men do show direct contact with the Scipionic group. P. Scipio Nasica Serapio, the future assassin of Ti. Gracchus, reached the consulship in 138; he was Aemilianus' cousin by adoption. L. Furius Philus serves as one of the interlocutors in the *De Republica*. A disciple of Carneades and a friend of Terence, Furius was evidently an active member of the cultural coterie sponsored by Scipio and Laelius. But he was also politically active; his consulship came in 136. A similar background applies to the learned jurist P. Mucius Scaevola, who had close friends in this circle and whose cousin married

[25] Appian, *Iber*. 70: οὐ μὴν ἐπέμεινεν οὐδ' ἐς βραχὺ τὰ συγκείμενα. ὁ γὰρ ἀδελφὸς Σερουιλιανοῦ τοῦ ταῦτα συνθεμένου Καιπίων διάδοχος αὐτῷ τῆς στρατηγίας γενόμενος διέβαλλε τὰς συνθήκας καὶ ἐπέστελλε Ῥωμαίοις ἀπρεπεστάτος εἶναι. That event is overlooked by Astin, who regards all the Servilii Caepiones, including Fabius Servilianus, as political associates of Scipio; *Scip. Aem.*, 82-83, 315-316. On Fabius' securing of Numidian reinforcements, see Appian, *Iber*. 67. It is also suggestive that C. Fannius, an adherent of the Scipionic circle, served as military tribune under Fabius in Spain; Appian, *Iber*. 67.

[26] On Galba's betrayal of Paullus, see above, note 9. On Livius Drusus and the connection with the Aemilii, see the arguments of Münzer, *Röm. Adelsp.*, 235-237. Astin lists the Calpurnii Pisones as among the enemies of Scipio, on the grounds that the latter roundly criticized and replaced L. Piso Caesoninus in Spain in 147; *Scip. Aem.*, 61, 71, 91, 319. But Appian, *Lib*. 115-116, records no direct criticism of Piso by Scipio. Further evidence for Astin's hypothesis is lacking.

into the family of C. Laelius. He was consul in 133. P. Rupilius secured election to that office for the following year with the express and open assistance of Scipio Aemilianus.[27] Friends of Scipio and associates of his group obviously played prominent roles in the decade and a half between the *lex Calpurnia* and the tribunate of Ti. Gracchus. The men who reached the consulship attract immediate attention; the voices of the *consulares* carried in the debates of the Roman senate. But there are still other men who show connections with the Scipionic group, as will appear upon examination of the political events of that period.

Scipio was not without his enemies and his *factio* not without its challengers. The glory that accompanied the conquest of Carthage might impress the *populus,* but it would also inspire envy and resentment among ambitious colleagues. As so often in Roman history, the removal of external threat brought a reaction against the conquering hero and an intensification of internal struggles. Although patterns in the consular *fasti* are more frequently in the mind of the historian than in the objective situation, the electoral results in the latter half of the 140's show a striking number of victors whose hostility to the Scipios is demonstrable through independent testimony. There is at least *prima facie* evidence for a reaction to the meteoric rise of Scipio Aemilianus. The name of Sulpicius Galba crops up once more in this connection. His enmity toward Scipio is abundantly clear, attested by his violent attacks on Aemilius Paullus in 167. Cato the Censor, friend and admirer of Scipio, opposed Galba on that occasion and opposed him once more in the affair of 149. It may be noted also that Galba's son was soon to marry a daughter of P. Licinius Crassus Mucianus, a central figure in the Gracchan movement of the late 130's. Galba had escaped official condemnation for his acts in Spain, but his humiliating behavior in 149 had had its effect. Seven years elapsed between praetorship and consulship. Not until 144 did he occupy the highest magistracy.[28]

But Galba's character and his career did not equip him for effective leadership. Of the opponents of Scipio Aemilianus two men stand out conspicuously in the sources, the heads of two powerful houses, plebeian

---

[27] On Scipio Nasica Serapio, see Münzer, *RE,* 8.1501-1504, "Cornelius," n. 354; on Furius, see Cic. *De Rep. passim; De Orat.* 2.154; and Münzer, *RE,* 14.360, "Furius," n. 78. On Scaevola, see below, pp. 51-52. For Rupilius' election, see Cic. *De Amicit.* 73. His relationship to this group is further illustrated by the marriage of his daughter to the son of Fabius Servilianus; Appian, *Iber.* 67; Val. Max. 2.7.3.

[28] Analysis of the consular lists for the late 140's in Münzer, *Röm. Adelsp.,* 245-247. On Cato's speeches against Galba, see *ORF,* 67-69, 79-80. For the marriage alliance with Crassus Mucianus, see Cic. *De Orat.* 1.239; *Brutus,* 98, 127.

and patrician: Q. Caecilius Metellus Macedonicus and Ap. Claudius Pulcher, the consuls of 143. Macedonicus had earned his name as praetor in 148 with his successful recovery of Macedon from the pretender Andriscus. The benefits of his victory, however, did not help him immediately at the polls. Twice he failed in the consular elections before success came in 144. Macedonicus was not one to cultivate popularity among the masses, but opposition by the Scipios may also help to explain the delay. His battles with Scipio Aemilianus became renowned in the tradition. Although heated and frequent they were never personal. On that point Cicero is specific: *fuit inter P. Africanum et Q. Metellum sine acerbitate dissensio.* After perhaps two decades of *inimicitia* on a political plane, Macedonicus could nonetheless mourn Scipio's death in 129 and assign his own sons as pallbearers. But if he was a noble opponent, he was also a formidable one. He not only outlived Scipio, but survived to witness four sons reach high office in the public service.[29] Ap. Claudius Pulcher possessed equal *dignitas.* Heir to the ancient traditions of the patrician Claudii, he yielded to none of his ancestors in fierce pride. Before his career saw its end he had held the titles of consul, censor, and *princeps senatus.* A victory over the Salassi during his consulship of 143 entitled him, so he felt, to a triumph. Not everyone felt the same way. A tribune, suborned by Appius' enemies, vetoed the proceedings and even sought to remove him forcibly from the triumphal chariot. Nothing daunted, Appius saw himself as well served by his children as was Macedonicus by his: a daughter, a Vestal Virgin, climbed aboard

---

[29] The quote from Cicero is in *De Off.* 1.87; also *De Amicit.* 77: *propter dissensionem autem, quae erat in republica, alienatus est a collega nostro Metello.* Cf. Vell. Pat. 1.11.6: *acris innocentisque pro re publica cum inimicis contentiones.* The double failure at the polls is recorded by Val. Max. 7.5.4; Livy, *Oxyr. Per.* 52; *Vir. Ill.* 61.3. For Macedonicus' action at Scipio's funeral, see Val. Max. 4.1.12. Opposition between the two men is noted also in Pliny, *NH,* 7.144fi and Plut. *Apophth. Caec.* 3. Scipio's views of the Metelli may be reflected in the caustic comments of Lucilius, V.232-234, XXVI.637 (*ROL,* 3.27, 204); see F. Marx, *Lucilii Carminum Reliquiae* (Leipzig, 1904), xxxiv-xxxv, xlvii, 87, 247; C. Cichorius, *Untersuchungen zu Lucilius* (Berlin, 1908), 87-88, 134, 137-140, 278-279; cf. also what may be an attack on Macedonicus' son-in-law, C. Servilius (Vatia?), in Lucilius, 849-850 (*ROL,* 3.274); Cichorius, 154-157. Moreover, it was said, Lucilius attacked Metellus precisely to please Scipio; Schol. on Horace, *Sat.* 2.1.72. Cicero, *De Amicit.* 77, quoted above, suggests that Scipio and Metellus had once been friends but had had a falling out over politics. It would seem futile to attempt to date this estrangement. Astin puts it ca. 139 or 138 and regards the Metelli as staunch backers of the Scipios prior to that date; *Scip. Aem.,* 85-86, 110, 311-315. But all of the (very considerable) evidence on their relations refers to political opposition. The whole point of Cicero's statement is that political dissension broke their friendship, not that a shattered friendship caused them to split politically.

the chariot with him and the triumph went on as scheduled.[30] The hassle over the triumph was probably a manifestation of his equally notorious clash with Scipio. In the same year the two men stood in direct confrontation in the censorial elections. The electoral campaign was marked with mutual mud-slinging. Scipio's victory at the polls called forth acrid comments about pandering to the mob.[31] Appius had to wait until the ensuing elections before he reached the censorship in 136. Metellus Macedonicus and Ap. Claudius: these were the spearheads of opposition to Scipio and his compatriots. That the two men were linked in anything beyond that opposition eludes documentation. It would be rash to package them into a single "faction." But many of the individuals who stood against the Scipionic coalition in that generation show ties to one or the other of these two families.

Four men in the *fasti* of the late 140's can be directly associated with Metellus Macedonicus. His brother L. Metellus Calvus, consul in 142, requires no further comment. Not only the familial tie, but political cooperation between the brothers is attested, as will be seen below. The political allegiance of L. Aurelius Cotta, consul in 144, is demonstrable from a prosecution later at the hands of Scipio Aemilianus; among Cotta's *advocati* in that case was Metellus Macedonicus. Still another trial, this one in 139, witnessed collaboration among the Metelli brothers and two other brothers, the consuls of 141 and 140, Cn. Servilius Caepio and Q. Servilius Caepio. On the other side was a former associate of Scipio Aemilianus.[32] Q. Servilius Caepio we have met before. It was he who had the senate tear up the Spanish treaty his own brother had concluded; but that brother was the one who had been adopted by the Fabii, a family friendly to the Scipios.[33] The pattern of hostility to Scipio Aemilianus and of an assemblage around Metellus Macedonicus seems consistent.

A previous generation had witnessed political cooperation among the patrician Claudii, the Fulvii, and the Aemilii Lepidi. It would be wrong to make an *a priori* assumption of continuity for those relations. But there is corroborating evidence. Ap. Claudius Pulcher, the *inimicus* of Scipio, after his failure at the polls in 143, arrived at the censorship finally

[30] Cic. *Pro Cael.* 34; Val. Max. 5.4.6; Dio, fr. 74; Suet. *Tib.* 2; Orosius, 5.4.7; Macrob. *Sat.* 3.14.14.

[31] Plut. *Aem. Paul.* 38.3-4; *Apophth. Scip. Min.* 9; *Praec. Reip. Ger.* 14.12. Cf. Plut. *Apophth. Scip. Min.* 10, with Astin, *Scip. Aem.*, 112-113, 253. The enmity between Appius and Scipio is noted also by Cic. *De Rep.* 1.3.1; *Pro Scauro*, 32.

[32] On these trials and the connections, see below, pp. 34-38. Cf. also Badian, *Studies in Greek and Roman History* (New York, 1964), 36-37, who suggests that Cotta in 144 may have been responsible for the successful election of Macedonicus after his two previous failures.

[33] See above, pp. 19-20.

in 136. His colleague in that office was Q. Fulvius Nobilior. More important, it was Fulvius who awarded Claudius that most prestigious of titles, *princeps senatus*. It may be no coincidence that two Fulvii Flacci reached the consulship in the two succeeding years of 135 and 134. And Fulvius Nobilior warrants still another mention. He had conducted disastrous campaigns against the Spaniards in the late 150's for which Cato the Censor had often lacerated him verbally in the senate. And in 149 when Cato attacked another unsuccessful veteran of the Spanish Wars, Ser. Sulpicius Galba, the enemy of Scipio, Fulvius Nobilior came to Galba's defense.[34] The Aemilii Lepidi fit into this picture as well. The death, in 152, of that family's leading figure, M. Aemilius Lepidus, the *pontifex maximus* and *princeps senatus,* opened the way for the transfer of those offices to Scipio Nasica Corculum. The next generation witnessed another Lepidus of prominence, the consul of 137, M. Aemilius Lepidus Porcina, an orator of note often coupled by Cicero with Sulpicius Galba. One item from his consulship reveals much: Porcina vigorously opposed a tribunician measure advocated by Scipio Aemilianus.[35] Ap. Claudius, Fulvius Nobilior, Aemilius Lepidus, Sulpicius Galba: once more a pattern emerges of powerful individuals linked in *amicitia* and in hostility to the Scipios.

Two other families can be added. P. Licinius Crassus Mucianus, future consul of 131, was an orator and a jurist of real distinction. But in both areas he courteously yielded superiority to Sulpicius Galba, a friend and counselor and the man to whose son Crassus betrothed his daughter. When Crassus stood for the aedileship ca. 143 Galba was in attendance, lending moral and political support. Connection with this group is further demonstrable. Crassus Mucianus was married to a Clodia, almost certainly sister of Ap. Claudius Pulcher himself. In the late 130's, as will be seen below, cooperation between the two men in the Gracchan program and against the Scipionic *factio* became manifest and crucial.[36] A

[34] Livy, *Per.* 49: *Q. Fulvius Nobilior ei* [Cato], *saepe ab eo in senatu laceratus, respondit pro Galba.* For Nobilior's campaigns in Spain, see Appian, *Iber.* 45-47. On the censorship of 136, see *MRR,* I.486.

[35] Cic. *Brutus,* 97. For Porcina as an orator, mentioned with Sulpicius Galba, see Cic. *Brutus,* 95, 295, 333. Connections among the Claudii, Fulvii, and Aemilii Lepidi, stretching back for generations, are brilliantly elucidated by Münzer, *Röm. Adelsp.,* 237-245; cf. Scullard, *Roman Politics,* 36-38, 61-65, 177-189.

[36] For the marriage link and mutual admiration of Galba and Crassus, see esp. the anecdote in Cic. *De Orat.* 1.239-240: *cum aedilitatem P. Crassus peteret, eumque maior natu, etiam consularis, Ser. Galba assectaretur, quod Crassi filiam Gaio filio suo despondisset;* cf. *Brutus,* 97, 127. Crassus was also a linguist, a master of five Greek dialects; Val. Max. 8.7.6; Quintilian, 11.2.50. On his ties with Ap. Claudius, see Münzer, *Röm. Adelsp.,* 270-275.

relative of Mucianus, C. Licinius Crassus, conforms to the pattern. Little is known of that man but it is enough. As tribune in 145 he catered to the *populus* and sought to open priestly offices to popular election; the effort was stifled by Scipio's *amicus,* C. Laelius.[37] Finally, there is the consul of 138, D. Junius Brutus Callaicus. Overt hostility to the Scipios is unrecorded, but the familial relationships leave no room for doubt. Brutus was related by marriage to Aemilius Lepidus Porcina, and was himself married to a Clodia, the widowed sister of Ap. Claudius. A tie with Crassus Mucianus was also close enough so that later sources could confuse the two men when speaking of C. Gracchus' father-in-law.[38]

The prudent historian eschews dogmatism or slavish adherence to a schema. Yet the foregoing discussion undeniably reveals a strikingly consistent structure of political alliances for the 140's and 130's. In any case three major groups can be discerned gathered about Rome's leading political figures. The heroics and appeal of Scipio Aemilianus had attracted a large and significant following: names like Laelius, Fabius, Manilius, Drusus, Scaevola, Rupilius. But envy bred opposition. The Metellan clan, headed by Macedonicus, secured cooperation from the Cottae and the Caepiones. More formidable was the alliance of families around Ap. Claudius, including representatives of the Fulvii, Lepidi, Galbae, Crassi, and Bruti. No one can claim that these three factions exhaust the Roman political scene.[39] Indeed, other individuals appear who play significant roles but whom no evidence links to any of these groups. But the factional structure of senatorial politics admits of no doubt.

Illustrations of struggles within the aristocracy abound for this period. Some examples will indicate the trend. External affairs had preoccupied Rome in the first half of the decade of the 140's, but after the simultaneous fall of Carthage and Corinth in 146, internal contests were renewed with vigor. A propaganda campaign against Scipio Aemilianus is already discernible in 146. L. Hostilius Mancinus was consul-elect in that year,

---

[37] Cic. *De Amicit.* 96; *popularis lex de sacerdotiis C. Licini Crassi videbatur . . . religio deorum immortalium nobis defendentibus facile vincebat.*

[38] The relationship with Aemilius Lepidus: Appian, *Iber.* 80; with Ap. Claudius: Cic. *Ad Att.* 12.22.2; cf. Münzer, *Röm. Adelsp.,* 241-242; the confusion of Brutus and Cassius: Plut. *Ti. Gracch.* 21.1. Münzer, *RE,* 19.1024-1025, "Junius," n. 57, suggests that Plutarch's error may imply a marriage of Brutus to Crassus' widow.

[39] Cf., e.g., the Postumii Albini. They do not figure prominently in the political contests of the 140's and the 130's, nor are their political associations readily recoverable. But hostility to the Scipionic *factio,* at least, is demonstrable from attacks upon them by Polybius and Lucilius: Polyb. 39.1.1; Lucilius, 931-933, 1196-1208 (*ROL,* 3.300, 390-392); cf. Astin, *Scip. Aem.,* 65-67, 91-92.

a man who had also served against Carthage and had even temporarily seized the city before Scipio finished the job. Mancinus, upon return, naturally sought to dim the glory of Carthage's conqueror by advertising his own role in the capture of the city. Much to Scipio's chagrin, Mancinus displayed in the forum a representation of Carthage and of his part in its fall. The propaganda effort bore fruit. Mancinus' reputation was enhanced both for contemporaries and for posterity. He secured election to the consulship in 145 and the non-Polybian tradition awards him a large hand in the African victory. Scipio may even have had some brief difficulty in celebrating his own triumph. In any case he had to deliver a speech outlining his military campaigns.[40]

More senatorial infighting is evident in 145. That was the year of C. Crassus' tribunician bill to transfer priestly elections from the college of pontiffs to the people. Some will label this as "progressive" legislation, and so it was, no doubt, advertised. But it is perhaps of relevance that the recently named *pontifex maximus* was P. Scipio Nasica, whose appointment followed the end of the long tenure of M. Aemilius Lepidus. Crassus' measure may have been another side-swipe at the Scipionic faction. That at least was the view of C. Laelius, who took the lead in quashing the attempt, waxing eloquent on the traditions of the priestly orders.[41] Laelius was active in another connection as well. He sponsored a proposal for agrarian reform, but when senatorial opposition was voiced he swiftly withdrew the motion. That hasty retreat, so it was said, won him the nickname of *Sapiens*. The date of this event escapes record, but 145, the year of Laelius' praetorship, is suitable. The need for large scale demobilization after the African and Achaean wars provides a natural setting for the bill. But no more than Crassus' proposal should this be regarded as "liberalism" or "reformism." It was inevitable that the Scipionic group should desire to win credit for resolving the demobilization problem, especially since many of the veterans came from Scipio's own troops of the African campaign. It was inevitable also that there would be resistance. The oligarchy was not prepared to risk the unpleasant implications of agrarian reform for the social structure. Laelius had made his point and had no intention of pressing the matter. "Liberalism" is not a phrase that can readily be ascribed to any of the aristocratic factions

[40] Mancinus' propaganda in Pliny, *NH*, 35.23. The Livian tradition records his African successes; Livy, *Per.* 51; Florus, 1.31.10; Ampelius, 32.1. Appian, drawing on Polybius, stresses instead his rashness and his subsequent salvation at the hands of Scipio; *Lib.* 113-114; cf. Astin, *Scip. Aem.*, 71. On Scipio's speech after his return from Africa, see *ORF*, 124; cf. Scullard, *JRS*, 50 (1960), 66.

[41] See above, note 37; also Cic. *Brutus*, 83; *De Rep.* 6.2.2; *De Nat. Deor.* 3.5, 3.43.

who dominated Roman politics in this era.[42]

Jockeying for position within the ruling class continued along these lines. We have seen reason already to reckon Ser. Sulpicius Galba and L. Aurelius Cotta among the *inimici* of Scipio. They need, of course, have had no love for one another. If previous analysis carries any conviction, the two appear linked respectively to the Claudian and Metellan factions (if one may employ such designations). A pertinent event in 144, the year in which those two men shared the consulship, rounds out and confirms this picture. The Spanish command, fraught with danger though it was, still appears to have been regarded as a prize plum. Galba and Cotta both coveted it and carried their quarrels into the senate, where the house solicited the *sententia* of Scipio to make a choice between them. Scipio's response was sharp and definitive: "neither of them will do; the one has nothing, and for the other nothing suffices." It is not difficult to identify those references. The greed and unscrupulousness of Galba has been noted before; it requires no further elucidation. As for Cotta, a verse of Lucilius, client and friend of Scipio, portrays him as indebted and corrupt. Scipio's influence was sufficient to have both consuls passed over for the Spanish job. The result was a prorogation of the commands of men already in the field. It is, of course, no coincidence, that those men happened to be Scipio's brother Q. Fabius Aemilianus and his closest associate C. Laelius.[43] The pattern continues. In 143, as we have seen, Ap. Claudius found stiff resistance to his celebration of a triumph. The

---

[42] For Laelius' proposal and his withdrawal, see Plut. *Ti Gracch.* 8.4: ἐπεχείρησε μὲν οὖν τῇ διορθώσει Γάιος Λαίλιος ὁ Σκιπίωνος ἑταῖρος ἀντικρου-σάντων δὲ τῶν δυνατῶν φοβηθεὶς τὸν θόρυβον καὶ παυσάμενος ἐπεκλήθη σοφὸς ἢ φρόνιμος. Cf. G. Tibiletti, "Ricerche di storia agraria romana," *Athenaeum*, 28 (1950), 234-235. For a summary of views on the date, see Scullard, *JRS*, 50 (1960), 62-65, who plausibly argues for 145. More recently, Taylor, "Forerunners of the Gracchi," *JRS*, 52 (1962), 24, opted for 151, and Earl, *Ti. Gracchus*, 75-76, for 140. On the bill generally, see the account of Astin, *Scip. Aem.*, 307-310, who leans toward 140. Scullard, who sees Scipio as a moderate reformer, regards Laelius' measure as exemplary of Scipionic "liberalism." But there is little other evidence for liberal tendencies on Scipio's part, and a good deal of evidence to the contrary; cf. Earl, *Historia*, 11 (1962), 477-485.

[43] The anecdote is in Val. Max. 6.4.2: *"neutrum,"* inquit, *"mihi mitti placet, quia alter nihil habet, alteri nihil est satis"* . . . *quo dicto ut neuter in provinciam mitteretur obtinuit.* On Cotta, see Lucilius, XI.440-442 (*ROL*, 3.138): *Lucius Cotta senex, crassi pater huius, Paceni, magnus fuit trico nummarius, solvere nulli lentus.* See Marx, *Luc. Carm. Rel.*, 155; Cichorius, *Unt. zu Luc.*, 308-310. For Cotta's indebtedness, see also Val. Max. 6.5.4. On the prorogation of the previous commands, see Appian, *Iber.* 65; Cic. *De Off.* 2.40; *Brutus*, 84; cf. Lincke, *Scipio Aemilianus*, 22; Bilz, *Politik des Scipio*, 40-41; Scullard, *JRS*, 50 (1960), 67.

decemviri in charge of the Sibylline books conveniently found a provision requiring sacrifice in enemy territory before a campaign against Gauls, something Claudius had apparently neglected. The latter was not the only one to clash with the *decemviri* in that year. M. Aemilius Lepidus Porcina, whom other evidence has linked to Claudius, challenged them on behalf of Q. Marcius Rex and the Marcian aqueduct.[44] The year 143 also witnessed the bitter censorial contest between Scipio and Ap. Claudius, from which the former emerged victorious. A censorship too could be a political instrument. Scipio's was a harsh one, an advertisement for a restoration of the old morality. Among those who received a censorial *nota* at Scipio's hands were a P. Sulpicius Galus and Ti. Claudius Asellus. Asellus was reviled for excessive profligacy and stripped of his equestrian status. Galus' effeminacy was his downfall; Scipio pointed out that he used perfume, dressed before a mirror, plucked his eyebrows and beard, and, worst of all, wore a tunic that covered his arms. Choice of the victims was probably no accident. Galus, it may be surmised, was a relative of Sulpicius Galba, and the fact that Asellus was a Claudius was doubtless a relevant consideration.[45] Too much ought not to be made out of any one of these incidents. But the cumulative effect is potent and persuasive. The Scipionic faction was engaged in an almost incessant contest for supremacy within the ruling class, especially against the groups associated with Ap. Claudius and Metellus Macedonicus.

In light of this political constellation the criminal trials of the period

[44] On Claudius' triumph, see above, pp. 22-23. For the role of the *decemviri* in that affair, see Obseq. 21; Dio, fr. 74.1. For their objection to the Marcian aqueduct, on the grounds that the Sybilline books forbade the bringing of water to the capitol, see Frontinus, *De Aqued.* 1.7; cf. Livy, *Oxyr. Per.* 54; *Per.* 53. See esp. on all this the illuminating remarks of Münzer, *Röm. Adelsp.*, 239-241. The objections of Astin, *Scip. Aem.*, 94, 106-110, are unconvincing. It is difficult to see how the oracular pronouncement would serve Claudius' cause.

[45] For sources on the censorship, see *MRR*, I.474; the demotion of Asellus from the ranks of the *equites* to that of the *aerarii* is in Cic. *De Orat.* 2.268; Gellius, 3.4.1; Festus, 362, L; on Gallus, see Gellius, 6.12.4-5; cf. Fraccaro, "Studi nell' età Graccana," *Studi Storici*, 5 (1912), 373-374. Fragments of Scipio's censorial speeches are collected by Astin, *Scip. Aem.*, 253-257. Asellus was restored to his former status by Scipio's colleague L. Mummius Achaicus. The dispute between Scipio and Mummius ought not to be stressed. It was a disagreement on how to conduct a censorship, and not a political quarrel; cf. Val. Max. 6.4.2; *Vir. Ill.* 58.9; Dio, fr. 76; Bilz, *Politik des Scipio*, 42-43. Mummius' brother, Sp. Mummius, was, in any case, a good friend of Scipio; Cic. *De Rep.* 1.18; *De Amicit.* 69, 101. The famous story of Scipio's closing of the *lustrum* (Val. Max. 4.1.10) is probably a falsification; Marx, "Animadversiones Criticae in Scipionis Aemiliani Historiam et C. Gracchi Orationem adversus Scipionem," *RhM*, 39 (1884), 65-68. On the censorship generally, see Astin, *Scip. Aem.*, 115-124.

take on great significance. The 140's on the whole reveal few prosecutions. That is due in part to the skimpiness of available source material, but not entirely. Senatorial rivalries had not yet focused on the courts as a central arena for battle. Only one criminal trial is known for the mid-140's and it may be swiftly dealt with. C. Plautius, praetor in 146, had the misfortune of engaging the shrewd guerrilla leader Viriathus in Spain, for whom he proved no match. Viriathus lured him on with feigned flight and destroyed four thousand Roman legionaries. The hapless Plautius capped his disgrace with cowardly flight. That meant escape from Viriathus but certain doom in Rome. In the following year he was prosecuted for damaging the majesty of the Roman people. That charge would mean *perduellio*, treason, and a trial before the *populus*. Conviction was inevitable and Plautius spent the remainder of his days in exile.[46] It would be hazardous to read political implications into this case. No one is recorded as having come to Plautius' defense and he shows no association with Rome's major senatorial families. The condemnation was simply the outcome of indignation at defeat and cowardice. Failures in foreign policy were more palatable if one could find a scapegoat.

A second trial appears to belong in a similar category: once again the victim was notoriously guilty, the outrage universal, and the evidence of political manipulation scanty. L. Hostilius Tubulus, as praetor in 142, had sat as presiding officer on the *quaestio de sicariis*. That role was too tempting for the man whom Cicero, with characteristic hyperbole, referred to as the most criminal and audacious individual within memory. In the following year Tubulus underwent prosecution for bribery and corruption. The very existence of a murder court as early as 142 deserves a brief pause. Was it, as has often been asserted, a *quaestio perpetua,* established on the model of the extortion tribunal? If so, of course, it must have been of most recent vintage, and no evidence survives on the date of its institution. In the year 138, when murders were committed in the forests of Sila, a special *quaestio* had to undertake the task of investigation and prosecution. That would indeed be strange if a permanent court on homicide were standing by idly. It is more than likely that the tribunal over which Hostilius Tubulus presided in 142 was a *quaestio extraordinaria*. Be that as it may, Tubulus compromised himself in that capacity and suffered for it after the expiration of his office. In this instance the

---

[46] On Plautius' Spanish campaign, see Appian, *Iber.* 64; cf. Orosius, 5.4.3; Livy, *Per.* 52. Trial and conviction are recorded in Diod. 33.2. The charge is usually translated as *imminuta maiestas;* Münzer, *RE,* 41.9, "Plautius," n. 9; *MRR,* I.466. *Maiestas* is probably what Diodorus intended with his ἐπὶ τῷ τεταπεινωκέναι τὴν ἀρχήν. It is, however, anachronistic. The charge of *maiestas* was not written into Roman law until later. Plautius was doubtless accused of *perduellio;* Zumpt, *Criminalrecht,* I.2.345.

evidence is clear that prosecution came before a court organized for the occasion. The tribune P. Mucius Scaevola moved a *rogatio* to place the investigation in the hands of the senate, which then commissioned a consul to conduct the inquiry. Criminal procedures were still primitive and ad hoc. Judicial corruption obviously was an offense that the assembly did not normally hear and for which no standing court existed. Tubulus acceded to the inevitable and elected to leave Rome before proceedings began. Tradition transformed him into a veritable *exemplum* of iniquity.[47] Tubulus' ultimate fate was a grisly one. Asconius reports that he was recalled from exile in order to be killed in prison, but forestalled his executioners by taking poison. The story is puzzling. No parallel can be found in Republican history for the recall of an exile for a retrial or to face a new charge. Rome would have no jurisdiction over an *exul* strictly speaking, that is, one who had accepted citizenship of another state. That she could summon one who had not been accepted elsewhere is also incapable of documentation. It demands extraordinary credulity to believe that Tubulus would have answered a summons that he knew would involve imprisonment and execution. Asconius' statement incorporates too great a legal anomaly to be accepted at face value.[48] Doubtless, as was customary, the *plebs* passed a decree of *aquae et ignis interdictio* following Hostilius' voluntary departure. The exile was forbidden to return upon pain of death. If there is any truth to Asconius' tale, it would appear that Tubulus returned to Rome in defiance of the decree, was seized and sentenced to execution, and swallowed poison.

Were there political connotations in that trial? At best one can offer only cautious conjecture. The Hostilii Mancini, as we have seen, had no

[47] The key passage is Cic. *De Fin.* 2.54: *An tu me de L. Tubulo putas dicere? qui cum praetor quaestionem inter sicarios exercuisset, ita aperte cepit pecunias ob rem iudicandam, ut anno proximo P. Scaevola tribunus plebis ferret ad plebem velletne de ea re quaeri. Quo plebiscito decreta a senatu est consuli quaestio Cn. Caepioni; profectus in exsilium Tubulus statim nec respondere ausus; erat enim res aperta;* also *De Fin.* 4.77; *De Nat. Deor.* 1.74; cf. *Ad Att.* 12.5b.3. For Cicero's opinion of Tubulus, see esp. Asconius, 23, Clark: *unum ex omni memoria sceleratissimum et audacissimum;* cf. Lucilius, 1138-1141 (*ROL*, 3.370); Gellius, 2.7.20. For the notion that the *quaestio inter sicarios* of 142 was a *quaestio perpetua,* see Mommsen, *Strafrecht,* 612-616; J. Lengle, *Untersuchungen über die Sullanische Verfassung* (Freiburg, 1899), 36-40; Greenidge, *Legal Procedure,* 420; rightly denied by Zumpt, *Criminalrecht,* II.1.55; Strachan-Davidson, *Problems,* I.227, n. 6. The murder investigation of 138 is given in Cic. *Brutus,* 85.

[48] Asconius, 23, Clark: *Is propter multa flagitia cum de exsilio arcessitus esset ut in carcere necaretur, venenum bibit.* Mommsen, *Strafrecht,* 71, n. 1, 197, n. 2, 633, n. 4, conjectured that Hostilius was summoned to answer a second charge on an offense committed while he lived in exile, a most implausible suggestion. Cf. H. Siber, "Anologie, Amtsrecht, und Rückwirkung im Strafrechte des römischen Freistaates," *AbhLeipz,* 43 (1936), 48-53.

love for the Scipios. Whether the same can be said of the Hostilii Tubuli is uncertain. But the praetor of 142 was the first of his family in the *fasti* for almost three quarters of a century, and he succeeded in a decade when the Hostilii Mancini reached real prominence with three men in curule office. One should add that the man who moved the prosecution was P. Scaevola, of a family associated with the Scipionic circle. Political implications ought not to be stressed: Tubulus' crimes were open and blatant. But the case fits appropriately into a period of political fencing between Scipio's friends and rivals.[49]

The harshness of Scipio's censorship in 142 came back to haunt him in a prosecution later. Ti. Claudius Asellus, whom Scipio had demoted from the ranks of the *equites,* was reinstated in that same year, and in 140 turned up again as tribune of the plebs. As one might expect, he sought vengeance on his *inimicus.* Asellus succeeded in hauling Scipio before the assembly and brought an accusation, pointing out the *infelicitas* of the latter's censorial *lustrum.* Specific basis for the charge is obscure; but the penalty proposed was simply a fine. Scipio's speeches in his own behalf were devastating. He made the most of the prosecutor's unfortunate *cognomen,* "little-ass." He also managed to turn the accusation around nicely, lambasting the prosecutor for profligacy and vice. No source records the outcome of this trial, but conjecture is safe. Had Scipio Aemilianus been convicted, we would surely have heard of it.[50] Personal, not political, considerations doubtless predominated. Asellus was anxious for vengeance and self-vindication. But the hypothesis of a connection with the Claudian group would not be rash. Not only did Asellus conduct a public attack on Aemilianus; he also sought to prevent the departure of the consul Servilius Caepio for Spain and had to be frightened off by a show of force.[51]

In this aggregation of maneuver and counter-maneuver in the 140's, one element is conspicuous by its absence. The *quaestio de rebus repetundis* had not provided a stage for factional conflict. Indeed, close to a decade elapsed after the passage of the *lex Calpurnia* before the first recorded instance of a *repetundae* offense. That may be accident or a gap in

[49] See E. S. Gruen, "The Political Allegiance of P. Mucius Scaevola," *Athenaeum,* 43 (1965), 322-323.

[50] References to and quotations from Scipio's speech form the source of our information on the affair; fragments collected in *ORF,* 127-129, and Astin, *Scip. Aem.,* 257-258. On the charge, see Cic. *De Orat.* 2.268: *Asello Africanus obicienti lustrum illud infelix;* Gellius, 6.11.9: *P. Africanum pro se contra Tiberium Asellum de multa ad populum;* cf. Scullard, *JRS,* 50 (1960), 69. The trial, so far as the evidence allows, is fully discussed by Fraccaro, *Studi Storici,* 5 (1912), 375-382. Astin ascribes more importance to this case than is perhaps warranted; *Scip. Aem.,* 127, 175-177.

[51] Livy, *Oxyr. Per.* 54.

the sources. But the affair itself, when it comes, is most suggestive. So far were the Romans from utilizing the extortion court for political purposes that this case never even reached the bench. The machinery of the *quaestio repetundarum* remained rusty and unused. The facts may be briefly stated.

D. Junius Silanus, praetor in Macedon in 141, had despoiled that province and spent his time in exacting money from the provincials. After his return to Rome and loss of his magisterial immunity in 140, envoys from the victimized Macedonians arrived in Rome to lodge their complaints before the senate. By all rights, the case ought to have been turned over to the *quaestio de rebus repetundis*. But Silanus' natural father, T. Manlius Torquatus, intervened. Silanus, born into the patrician Manlii, had been adopted by the Junii, one of the very rare instances of adoption from a patrician into a plebeian family. Manlius expected no less of his son for all that. The old man, consul a quarter of a century before, never ceased to remind contemporaries of his ancient lineage. He literally lived among his ancestors; effigies and images of previous Manlii glared down at every visitor to his entrance foyer. Silanus had been an unforgivable disgrace to the family name. When the Macedonians listed his son's crimes, Manlius Torquatus begged leave of the senate to pursue his own investigation. Permission was granted. The proud and uncompromising patrician held an inquiry behind closed doors, pronounced his son guilty, and banished him from his sight. On the following night, Silanus did what the family code required: he hanged himself. While the funeral was celebrated, Manlius sat at home unmoved, conducting his customary business of advising clients on points of law.[52]

The case is clearly unusual, perhaps unique. On the surface, it is disconcerting for the historian. At least one scholar has argued from it that the *lex Calpurnia* never really set up an extortion court at all: the grievances of provincials against oppressive governors continued, after the law as before, to be brought before the senate as a body that retained discretion as to how the issue was to be handled; in this instance, the case was turned over to Manlius to be treated in the form of a domestic tribunal.[53] The argument, however, cannot stand. A domestic tribunal, in a strictly legal sense, had no acknowledged existence.[54] The verdict of Tor-

[52] The story is given in full by Val. Max. 5.8.3; also Livy, *Per.* 54; *Oxyr. Per.* 54; Cic. *De Fin.* 1.24.

[53] Zumpt, *Criminalrecht*, II.1.21-24.

[54] See E. Volterra, "Il preteso tribunale domestico in diritto romano," *Riv. Ital. Scienz. Giurid.*, 2 (1948), 103-153; *contra:* Kunkel, "Das Konsilium im Hausgericht," *ZSav,* 83 (1966), 219-251.

quatus cannot have had binding legal force, nor was it intended to represent a condemnation recognized by public law. Banishment from the house of a father was, of course, never a penalty incorporated into the Roman criminal code. The suicide of Silanus was the outcome of disgrace and despair, not of a capital conviction. To be sure, the Macedonian embassy appeared before the senate. That is only to be expected. The senate did supervise foreign policy, a practice reaffirmed and reinforced by the *lex Calpurnia* itself. Moreover, the jury of the extortion court had to be staffed from the ranks of the senate in any case. By yielding to the request of Manlius Torquatus, the senate did not abrogate the powers of the *quaestio repetundarum*. Valerius Maximus makes it clear that there was no intention that Manlius' inquiry be a substitute for judicial decision. Manlius simply requested the senate and the legates of Macedon to delay the trial until he could have an opportunity to ascertain the facts: *ne quid ante de ea re statuerent quam ipse Macedonum filiique sui causam inspexisset.* The request was filled out of courtesy to the *dignitas* of an ancient patrician house. Formal trial would doubtless have followed Manlius' inquiry, but was forestalled by the suicide of Silanus. The affair does not indicate that the *quaestio de repetundis* was in abeyance, but it does suggest that men had not yet come to look upon it as a political instrument. The *lex Calpurnia* had been designed to secure aristocratic control of foreign policy, not to serve as a staging-ground for internal quarrels. It can be imagined, however, that the case of Silanus, striking and notorious, caused a stir of some proportions. In a very short time rival senatorial groups would be making use of the extortion court for their own purposes. As a vehicle for political warfare, the courts could be far more effective and damaging than consular elections or censorial *nota*.

Events in Spain have been alluded to on more than one occasion. The wars in that area had been resumed in 154 and continued without cease for over twenty years. Guerrilla warfare on rugged terrain against tenacious enemies wasted Rome's resources, frustrated her people, and brutalized her leaders. Triumph-hunting had for some time been a favorite sport among Roman generals. But genuine victories were hard to come by in Spain. Commanders instead substituted deceit and murder and contracted flimsy treaties that were overturned at home by jealous and vindictive rivals. The allegation that Spaniards were by nature faithless was made an excuse for Roman perfidy and ruthlessness.[55] Spain seems to have brought out the worst in Romans who campaigned there. We have

---

[55] Cf. Appian, *Iber.* 60: ἀπιστίᾳ μὲν ἄρα ἀπιστίαν μετιών, οὐκ ἀξίως δὲ 'Ρωμαίων μιμούμενος βαρβάρους. On the course of the war, see Simon, *Roms Kriege, passim.*

had reason already to note the crimes of Sulpicius Galba that directly precipitated the passage of the *lex Calpurnia*. The intense competition for triumphs and the struggle waged by each commander to eclipse his predecessor are no better illustrated than by one brother's renunciation of a treaty concluded by another.[56] In 139 the unspeakable events in the Iberian peninsula began to have direct effect on the history of criminal prosecutions.

The proconsul in Hither Spain in that year, Q. Pompeius, was an extraordinary individual whose peculiar career is baffling and almost unfathomable. A *novus homo,* with no illustrious ancestors on whom to call, he gained the highest offices open to any Roman aristocrat and opened the way to a string of distinguished descendants. Another *novus homo,* two generations later, reserves the highest praise for him as a man of supreme courage, prudence, and wisdom.[57] But *novi homines* could rarely make it to the top without powerful support. Pompeius came up through the magisterial ranks as a protégé of Scipio Aemilianus. Yet when time came for a consulship he had sufficient confidence in his ability and his established connections to defy the Scipionic *factio*. After promising support for Laelius' canvass in 142, he double-crossed his associates and sought the consulship himself. Through personal soliciting and to the surprise of his former friends, Pompeius was successful and Laelius had to wait another year. Pompeius had run an independent and effective campaign, greeting voters by name and making himself everywhere conspicuous. Scipio could laugh off the whole affair but others in his circle were furious.[58] Scholars have puzzled and debated Pompeius' subsequent status, conjecturing either a reconciliation with the Scipios or an adoption by opposing *factiones*.[59] In

[56] On Galba, see above, pp. 12-13. On the Caepio's rejection of his brother's agreement, see above, pp. 19-20.

[57] Cic. *De Rep.* 3.28: *si ratio, consilium, prudentia, Pompeius antistat; Pro Mur.* 16: *Q. Pompeio, novo homine et fortissimo viro.* He was also an orator of no mean ability; Cic. *Brutus,* 96: *Q. enim Pompeius non contemptus orator temporibus illis fuit.*

[58] See esp. Plut. *Apophth. Scip. Min.* 8: ἀγανακτούντων δὲ τῶν ἄλλων, ὁ Σκιπίων γελάσας, 'ἀβελτερία γε,' εἶπεν, 'ἡμῶν καθάπερ οὐκ ἀνθρώπους μέλλοντες ἀλλὰ θεοὺς παρακαλεῖν πάλαι διατρίβομεν αὐλητὴν ἀναμένοντες; also Cic. *De Amicit.* 77; Rutilius Rufus, fr. 7 (*HRR,* I.88): *Pompeius elaboravit, uti populum Romanum nosset eumque artificiose salutaret.*

[59] For the argument that Pompeius' break was minor and reconcilable, see Münzer, *Röm. Adelsp.,* 248-249; Fraccaro, *Opuscula,* 2.267-268; Scullard, *JRS,* 50 (1960), 69; that he came under the wing of Scipio's enemies, Bilz, *Politik des Scipio,* 59, n. 153; Astin, *Scip. Aem.,* 85, 121-122, 311-312. Earl's discussion of Pompeius is the most comprehensive and the best; *Ti. Gracchus,* 98-103. But, because his account rests on a rather static idea of Roman factions, he leaves himself in the unhappy position of explaining Pompeius' "fantastic career" as impelled by "forces, obscure but powerful."

fact, schematic interpretations clearly will not do. Enmities aroused by a career that was promoted by the Scipionic group lingered beyond 141. One source reports that Metellus Macedonicus deliberately handed over his troops in Spain to Pompeius in an undisciplined and chaotic fashion. The hostility of the Metellan *factio* toward Pompeius is well documented, as we shall see. By the same token, friendships made in those early years need not all have vanished in the electoral campaign of 142. The resentment of Laelius was doubtless keen and Pompeius, we know, could henceforth count on the relentless *inimicitia* of L. Furius Philus.[60] But the Scipionic circle was not a monolith. Pompeius' career is sufficient to demonstrate that. Private friendships and associations made in early years did not always follow "party" lines. Elements hidden to the researcher's eye may play a larger role than is customarily conceded. Roman politics were often more complex than any modern account can legitimately delineate.

Whatever Pompeius' capacities and background, his experience in Spain is distressingly familiar: a series of blunders and defeats, treachery, cowardice, and finally a degrading treaty with the enemy.[61] A return home in 139 was eagerly awaited by the many *inimici* of that mercurial character. The senate immediately declared the treaty invalid and announced that the war would proceed. Such action was by now customary and expected. But matters proceeded to a more serious decision. A proposal was mooted to salvage Rome's corporate honor by singling out Pompeius and sending him back to the Numantines in chains. Details of the senatorial debate, unhappily, are not preserved, but it appears that Pompeius could still reckon on a reservoir of strength in the *curia*. His *gratia* sufficed to defeat the motion.[62] Full explanation for Pompeius' escape is difficult, probably impossible. It is especially striking that in a precisely parallel situation three years later C. Hostilius Mancinus was in fact surrendered to the Numantines through a measure brought by the consuls. Perhaps it would not be out of place to suggest that in 139 Pompeius could count on the consuls. Cn. Calpurnius Piso must have chaired the senate meeting that discussed Pompeius' fate. His consular colleague, M. Popillius Laenas, was already in Spain. There is some evidence for links between the Popillii and the Scipiones, and it has been suggested above that a Piso had also found himself cooperating against an enemy of Scipio in

[60] On Macedonicus' actions in Spain, see Val. Max. 9.3.7. The account is obviously exaggerated, and contradicted by Appian, *Iber.* 76; cf. Miltner, *RE*, 42.2058, "Pompeius," n. 12. On the attitude of Laelius and perhaps Scipio, see Cic. *De Amicit.* 77; on Furius Philus, Val. Max. 3.7.5; Dio, fr. 82.

[61] See esp. Appian, *Iber.* 76-79; other sources in *MRR*, I.477, 480; cf. the account in Simon, *Roms Kriege*, 108-116.

[62] Vell. Pat. 2.1.5: *sed Pompeium gratia impunitum habuit;* also Cic. *De Off.* 3.109; *De Rep.* 3.28; Appian, *Iber.* 79.

149.[63] Possibly these men were among the older friends who had not abandoned Pompeius. It would be foolhardy to speculate further on that matter. What is of importance is the outcome of this affair.

The fact that Q. Pompeius got off scot-free in his senatorial hearing seems to mark a turning point. His enemies, frustrated and furious, turned to a new avenue of attack, the extortion court. Formal charges of *res repetundae* were now filed against Pompeius and four distinguished consulars brought testimony against him. Their identities suggest strongly that this was the working of a political faction: Q. Metellus Macedonicus, L. Metellus Calvus, Q. Servilius Caepio, and Cn. Servilius Caepio. One can hardly ascribe it to righteous indignation at Pompeius' deeds. Macedonicus was a known *inimicus* of Pompeius; he had already shown resentment toward him in 141, before the latter's campaigns had even begun. As for Q. Caepio's testimony against Pompeius, no better example can be imagined of the pot calling the kettle black. That despicable individual had torn up his own brother Fabius Servilianus' treaty in order to conduct warfare against the Spaniards. It was Q. Caepio who was responsible for the demise of the Spanish chieftain Viriathus. That, however, was an act of pure treachery: Caepio bribed three friends of Viriathus to murder their leader in cold blood. Such were the witnesses for the prosecution; clearly they were not acting as champions of Rome's honor and *dignitas*.[64] The trial has all the earmarks of a political prosecution. For the first time, to our knowledge, the *quaestio de repetundis,* originally designed to protect the interests of the senate against encroachments by tribunes and assembly, was employed as an instrument by a particular senatorial faction. The trial is customarily dated in 138. More likely it occurred shortly after the rebuff in the senate in 139. Hostile Numantine envoys were in Rome at the time; Pompeius' enemies would doubtless have made use of their testimony. But the combined weight

[63] The cases of Pompeius and Mancinus are frequently linked in the sources; Cic. *De Off.* 3.109; *De Rep.* 3.28; Vell. Pat. 2.1.5. On possible connections between Popillii and the Scipionic group, see Earl, "M. Octavius, trib. pleb. 133 B.C., and his Successor," *Latomus,* 19 (1960), 657-666. It should be noted that Lucilius does take a swipe at M. Popillius; 714 (*ROL,* 3.228). But the contrast between Popillius and Scipio there expressed is a reference to their respective failure and success in Spain. On Piso, see above, p. 20.

[64] The trial of Pompeius is reported by Cic. *Pro Font.* 23 and Val. Max. 8.5.1. For the enmity between Macedonicus and Pompeius, see Val. Max. 9.3.7: *Q. Pompeium consulem inimicum suum;* cf. 3.7.5; Dio, fr. 82. On Caepio's cowardly slaying of Viriathus, see Appian, *Iber.* 74; Livy, *Per.* 54; *Oxyr. Per.* 54, 55; Vell. Pat. 2.1.3; Val. Max. 9.6.4. There are also suggestions of hostility toward Caepio from Ap. Claudius and from M. Popillius; see Astin, *Scip. Aem.,* 144-145.

of the luminaries of the Metellan *factio* and the evidence of the Numantines were insufficient. Or more accurately, they backfired. The jurors
feared the reproach of their contemporaries if they appeared to convict a
man because of the prestige and influence of his accusers. Q. Pompeius
led a charmed life; he escaped once again.[65]

The lesson of this affair was not lost on Scipio Aemilianus. The Metelli
and their friends had utilized the extortion tribunal to attack a man who
had been a protégé of the Scipionic circle and who was (perhaps) still a
friend of Scipio himself. But two could play at that game. It can be no
coincidence that in the year 138 Scipio brought a charge of *repetundae*
against L. Aurelius Cotta. We have met the latter before, an unsavory
character. Frequently in debt, he had hoped to hide behind his tribunician
immunity ca. 154 and ignore his creditors, but in vain. During his consulship of 144, the senate had been unwilling to appoint him to a Spanish
command because of the arguments and influence of Scipio. Now in 138
he faced an extortion charge.[66] The offense cannot have been a recent
one. Cotta had held the consulship six years before and there is no evidence for a subsequent and extraordinary provincial assignment. Some
have conjectured that the delay was due to Scipio's career: though anxious
to eliminate Cotta, he had no opportunity until 138. But the suggestion
does not suffice. Even if Scipio were on an embassy to the East between
140 and 138, and even if he would not have undertaken a prosecution
during his censorship of 142, there is no reason for him not to have
accused Cotta in, say, 143 or 141. Moreover, Cotta no doubt had other

---

[65] Cic. *Pro Font.* 23: *qui Cn. et Q. Caepionibus, L. et Q. Metellis testibus
in Q. Pompeium, hominem novum, non crediderunt, quorum virtuti, generi,
rebus gestis fidem et auctoritatem in testimonio cupiditatis atque inimicitiarum
suspicio derogavit;* Val. Max. 8.5.1: *non abrogata fides absoluto Pompeio,
sed ne potentia inimicum oppressisse viderentur occursum est.* The date of
138 is given, probably wrongly, by Miltner, *RE,* 42.2057, "Pompeius," n. 12;
Cichorius, *Unt. zu Luc.,* 139; *ORF,* 140. The Numantine legation was in
Rome in 139; Appian, *Iber.* 79.

[66] The date is specified by Livy, *Oxyr. Per.* 55. Cicero at one point refers
to Scipio as conqueror of Numantia in connection with this trial, which
would put it after 133; *Pro Mur.* 58. That reference has led some scholars
astray; A. W. Zumpt, *Der Criminalprocess der römischen Republik* (Leipzig,
1871), 469; *Criminalrecht,* II.1.24-25; Klebs, *RE,* 4.2485, "Aurelius," n. 98.
It was, however, over-exuberance on Cicero's part. Elsewhere he is more
accurate; Scipio was simply "twice consul and censor" at the time of Cotta's
trial; *Div. in Caec.* 69; cf. *ORF,* 129-130. Val. Max. 8.1.11 wrongly states
that the trial was heard *apud populum.* The evidence is otherwise clear that
this was a *repetundae* charge heard by senatorial jurors; Cic. *Pro Mur.* 58:
sapientissimi homines; cf. *Div. in Caec.* 69; *Pro Font.* 38; Appian, *BC,* 1.22;
and see Appendix C.

inimici who were not preoccupied during those intervening years.[67] The explanation lies elsewhere and fortifies the conclusions hitherto expressed. Cotta's prosecution must be seen in connection with that of Pompeius, which preceded it by a short interval. The *quaestio de rebus repetundis* was not meant as a battleground for internal senatorial warfare. So far as our evidence goes it had seen no use since its inception in 149, though the Spanish wars, among others, could have provided innumerable opportunities. But once Pompeius had been hauled before the extortion court by the Metellan group, the "gentlemen's agreement" collapsed. Scipio would then have ransacked the events of recent history for a suitable instance with which to confront his *inimicus*. It is, of course, no accident, therefore, that Cotta was defended in his trial by Metellus Macedonicus, who had been one of the principal accusers of Pompeius. Jurors were once more in a quandary. The case was adjourned seven times before Cotta at last heard the verdict of acquittal. Again, so the sources report, the *iudices* were reluctant to convict, lest the decision appear to have been dictated by the presence of a prestigious *accusator*. Connection between the cases of Pompeius and Cotta seems abundantly clear.[68]

[67] For the suggestion that Scipio could not prosecute until 138, see Badian, *Studies*, 105-106. On Scipio's eastern embassy, a disputed subject, see Marx, *RhM*, 39 (1884), 68-71; Lincke, *Scipio Aemilianus*, 24-25; Bilz, *Politik des Scipio*, 44-46; *MRR*, I. 481, n. 2; Astin, "Diodorus and the Date of the Embassy to the East of Scipio Aemilianus," *CP*, 54 (1959), 221-227; Scullard, *JRS*, 50 (1960), 69.

[68] Cic. *Pro Mur.* 58: *Noluerunt sapientissimi homines qui tum rem illam iudicabant ita quemquam cadere in iudicio ut nimis adversarii viribus abiectus videretur;* also Val. Max. 8.1.11; Livy, *Oxyr. Per.* 55. There is no need to believe that bribery was employed to sway the jurors; Appian, *BC*, 1.22. C. Gracchus may have made this charge in 122, but this is hardly impartial testimony. On Macedonicus' defense, see Cic. *Brutus*, 81. On the case, see further Fraccaro, *Studi Storici*, 5 (1912), 383-385. One other trial took place in 138, a murder inquiry conducted by the consuls against some *publicani* through a special *quaestio;* Cic. *Brutus*, 85-88. No politics ought to be read into this affair. Scullard's suggestion that the Scipionic group was seeking the support of the *equites* is indefensible; *JRS*, 50 (1960), 70. If that were so, why should C. Laelius have handed over the case to Sulpicius Galba, an enemy of the Scipios? In the same year, a soldier, C. Matienus, was condemned for desertion, scourged, and sold into slavery; Livy, *Per.* 55. That was probably not a genuine trial. Although Livy says that Matienus was accused before the tribunes, such offenses were normally punished under magisterial *coercitio*. Mommsen is probably right in surmising that the victim appealed for tribunician *auxilium*, but that the conviction and sentence were imposed by his commanding officer; *Strafrecht*, 43, n. 2. Matienus was only one of many deserters sold into slavery in that year; Livy, *Oxyr. Per.* 55; cf. Frontinus, *Strat.* 4.1.20.

Double acquittal had produced frustration. Aristocratic leaders were now prepared to employ the extortion court to settle private feuds or to wage political battle. But the jurors had not cooperated and the results were inconclusive. There were, however, other avenues. Scipio was not popular in all quarters of the aristocracy, but he could still hope to tap the reservoir of good feeling among the *populus,* who had elevated him to lofty honors in the past. An important event in 137 becomes at once illuminated when seen at least partially in the light of the preceding discussion. A tribune of that year, L. Cassius Longinus Ravilla, sponsored a measure to institute secret ballots for all trials held before the people except those for high treason. Cassius earned wide reputation and popularity as a man of incorruptible integrity and uncompromising severity. He was later much sought after as a judge for those very qualities. This venture was his first prominent appearance on the public stage and he could claim to be in the mainstream of progressive legislators. Two years before, the secret ballot had been established for magisterial elections. But Cassius' action was more than a simple bid for popular favor. The measure received the overt support of Scipio Aemilianus and his influence proved sufficient to induce an interposing tribune to withdraw his veto, thus assuring passage into law. Does this make the Scipionic *factio* Rome's "liberal party"? Hardly. The appellation does not well suit a group that had, a few years earlier, opposed popular election for the priestly colleges. Senatorial politics lies in the background; the consul, M. Aemilius Lepidus Porcina, from a family traditionally tied to the Claudii and Fulvii, had attempted in vain to block the bill in 137. More important, the events of the preceding year lie in the background. If Scipio could not count on the senatorial jurors of the extortion court to convict his enemies, he might have better luck with the popular assembly, especially if the ballot were secret. Because of the primitive and uncertain state of Roman criminal law it would be as easy to manufacture a charge that could be brought before the *populus* as to tailor one for the jurisdiction of the extortion court.[69]

The operation of the new law came with astonishing swiftness and with a certain amount of poetic justice. Lepidus Porcina, the same man who had so vigorously and vainly opposed the bill, proceeded to carry out his

[69] Sources on Cassius' *lex tabellaria* are collected in *MRR*, I.485. See esp. Cic. *Brutus*, 97: *L. Cassius . . . homo non liberalitate, ut alii, sed ipsa tristitia et severitate popularis, cuius quidem legi tabellariae M. Antius Briso tribunus plebis diu restitit, M. Lepido consule adiuvante; ea res P. Africano vituperationi fuit, quod eius auctoritate de sententia deductus Briso putabatur.* On Scipio's popularity with the people, consciously cultivated, see Astin, *Scip. Aem.*, 26-34, 182-184.

stint as military commander in Spain. The customary pattern in that area can be discerned again. Lepidus did not want to return home without material for a triumph. When no enemy offered, he provoked hostilities himself, rousing new foes for Rome, and encountering defeat and disaster at the siege of Pallantia. For similar transgressions Q. Pompeius had been prosecuted before the *quaestio de repetundis*. But a new path had been opened by Cassius' *lex tabellaria*. Lepidus was charged before the assembly, convicted, and saddled with a heavy fine. The sources record no prosecutor, but it is not unreasonable to see this as the work of the Scipionic group. Not only had the accusers bypassed the *quaestio de repetundis;* they had also elected to avoid a capital charge. Can one doubt that this was precisely because the *lex Cassia* did not apply to the capital crime of *perduellio?* It should be added also that Scipionic hostility toward Lepidus appears in the mocking verse of Scipio's friend Lucilius on Lepidus, that "bald-headed unwarlike warrior who botched the Pallantine campaign."[70]

When senatorial feuds received expression in political trials, bitterness deepened and the lines between factions hardened. Scipio Aemilianus claimed more than one victim in 136. Lepidus could consider his fate a mild one when compared with that of his consular colleague of 137, C. Hostilius Mancinus. It will be recalled that Mancinus' cousin L. Hostilius had earned Scipio's resentment by exaggerating his own credit for the fall of Carthage. The younger Mancinus had the misfortune of being another in that lengthy string of blundering Roman commanders in Spain. On the whole, the sources are not unkind to him: a man of modesty, uprightness and honor, but the most unfortunate of Roman generals.[71] After humiliating defeat at the hands of the Numantines, Mancinus concluded an ignominious agreement in order to extricate himself and other survivors. The mobilization of opponents at home had now become almost a reflex action and Mancinus knew what to expect when he returned. He appealed to the case of Q. Pompeius, who for equally disgraceful deeds had escaped punishment three years before. But Pompeius, it

---

[70] Lucilius, 1123 (*ROL,* 3.362): *Calvus Palantino quidam vir non bonus bello;* see Cichorius, *Unt. zu Luc.,* 36, 265. On the trial of Lepidus, see Appian, *Iber.* 83; Livy, *Per.* 56; Orosius, 5.5.13-14. The account of Val. Max. 8.1.damn.7 confuses the trial in 136 with a censorial *nota* imposed on Lepidus, once again by his enemy Cassius Longinus Ravilla; cf. Vell. Pat. 2.10.1. For the date, see Livy, *Per.* 56; *MRR,* I.488, n. 4. It was probably in this same year that Scipio delivered his speech *de imperio D. Bruti; ORF,* 131. Despite Fraccaro, *Studi Storici,* 5 (1912), 386, the speech was more likely opposed to rather than in behalf of the extension of Brutus' command in Spain.

[71] Cic. *De Rep.* 3.28; Plut. *Ti. Gracch.* 5.1; cf. Cic. *De Off.* 3.109; *De Orat.* 1.181; Vell. Pat. 2.1.5.

seems, had had support within the chief magistracy at that time. Mancinus saw no friendly faces there in 136. Of the consuls, one was L. Furius Philus, an intimate member of the Scipionic circle. The other, Sex. Atilius Serranus, has left no mark in history. One preserved item, however, is relevant: either he or a relative had served as commander of Scipio's fleet in Africa in 147 and the man whom he replaced and dismissed at that time was Mancinus' cousin.[72] Mancinus could expect no sympathy from those consuls. In 136 they successfully promoted the very measure that had failed to pass when aimed at Pompeius in 139. The unhappy Mancinus dropped resistance and was handed over, stripped and in chains, to the Numantines. Appeasement of the gods would be effected by the rendering of a sacrificial victim. The Spaniards, it is gratifying to report, showed more human decency than their enemies: they refused to mistreat Mancinus and sent him back to Rome unharmed. The Romans would have to confront divine wrath without utilizing the Numantines as intermediaries.[73] The Scipionic *factio,* however, had gained two striking political successes in 136: the conviction of Lepidus on the basis of the *lex Cassia* and the disgrace of Mancinus through the rejection of his treaty and the personal humiliation inflicted upon him.

This grisly affair had more far-reaching consequences than a mere temporary political triumph. Mancinus' quaestor in Spain had been young Ti. Sempronius Gracchus. From an illustrious family with a long record of public service, Gracchus had early demonstrated qualities that commended him to his contemporaries and promised a career of extraordinary merit. The flattering biography of Plutarch depicts him as temperate, gentle, austere, and modest, fearless in the face of the

---

[72] On Mancinus' appeal to the precedent of Pompeius, see Appian, *Iber.* 83; cf. L. Pareti, *Storia di Roma* (Turin, 1953), III.261-262. On Serranus and Scipio in 147, see Appian, *Lib.* 114; rightly pointed out by Earl, *Ti. Gracchus,* 71.

[73] Sources in *MRR,* I.484. In addition, a line of Lucilius may also refer to the fate of Mancinus; 1218-1219 (*ROL,* 3.396); see Cichorius, *Unt. zu Luc.,* 37-39. In general on Mancinus' campaign and his fate, see Simon, *Roms Kriege,* 145-159. The debate over Mancinus' status after the Numantines returned him reveals further strife between the Scipionic group and its enemies; Gruen, *Athenaeum,* 43 (1965), 323-324. When L. Furius succeeded to the Spanish command he took along two bitter *inimici,* Q. Pompeius and Metellus Macedonicus; Val. Max. 3.7.5. Despite Münzer, *Röm. Adelsp.,* 250-252, and Earl, *Ti. Gracchus,* 101-102, the reasons were surely not political. After the successive failures of Pompeius, Mancinus, and Lepidus, Furius' main concern would have been to avoid giving grounds for future prosecution, a motive specifically noted by Dio, fr. 82. Furius' caution is indicated by the fact that he seems to have engaged in little combat during his term of command; *MRR,* I.486.

41

enemy, just with inferiors, and incorruptible with public trust. The Latin tradition is no less favorable: blameless in personal life, of brilliant intellect and absolute integrity, equipped with every virtue that nature or training could bestow.[74] Here was a young man well worth cultivating. Scipio Aemilianus was not blind to his talents and his connections. Scipio's aunt, by adoption, was Cornelia, the mother of the Gracchi, and he himself strengthened the tie by marrying Sempronia, Tiberius' sister. Tiberius first put his qualities on public notice when he served under Scipio at Carthage, sharing his general's tent and taking pride in being the first to scale the wall of the besieged city. But the two men drifted apart thereafter. Perhaps close personal contact had undermined the public image. Scipio's marriage to Sempronia proved to be an unfortunate mismatch. By 143 Tiberius had been welcomed with open arms into the family of Scipio's great enemy Ap. Claudius Pulcher, whose daughter became Tiberius' wife.[75] That the young man should next turn up as quaestor to another of Scipio's enemies, C. Hostilius Mancinus, now falls into place. Mancinus' treaty with the Numantines was, in fact, largely the work of Gracchus, who alone held the confidence of the Spaniards because of good will left by his father forty years before. The senate's rejection of the treaty was, above all, a slap in the face to the proud aristocrat, for whom it remained a source of the greatest indignation. Scipio's friends, as we have seen, were chiefly responsible for the humiliation of Mancinus. The political victory secured, Scipio could afford to be magnanimous and spare his *adfinis* Gracchus; Mancinus was the only one who had to be turned over to the Spaniards. This lenity won Scipio no credit with Ti. Gracchus. Observers bitterly censured Scipio for degrading Mancinus and for allowing the treaty of his brother-in-law to be scrapped. Gracchus would not forget; the clash in 136 foreshadowed the great political struggle and the reform movement of 133.[76]

[74] Plut. *Ti. Gracch.* 2.2-4, 3; Vell. Pat. 2.2.1-2.

[75] On Tiberius' early career, see Plut. *Ti. Gracch.* 4.1-5; the marriage between Scipio and Sempronia, Appian, *BC,* 1.20; for the date of Tiberius' marriage, see Fraccaro, *Studi sull' età dei Gracchi* (Citta di Castello, 1914), I.42; Münzer, *Röm. Adelsp.,* 268-269; Astin, *Scip. Aem.,* 319-321; contra: Earl, *Ti. Gracchus,* 67-69.

[76] On Scipio's role in the affair, see Plut. *Ti. Gracch.* 7.3: δοκεῖ δὲ καὶ Σκιπίων βοηθῆσαι μέγιστος ὢν τότε καὶ πλεῖστον δυνάμενος Ῥωμαίων. ἀλλ' οὐδὲν ἧττον ἐν αἰτίαις ἦν ὅτι τὸν Μαγκῖνον οὐ περιέσωσεν, οὐδὲ τὰς σπονδὰς ἐμπεδωθῆναι τοῖς Νομαντίνοις ἐσπούδασε δι' ἀνδρὸς οἰκείου καὶ φίλου τοῦ Τιβερίου γενομένας. Cf. Astin, *Scip. Aem.,* 131-133, 179, 181-182. For the impact on Tiberius, see Cic. *Brutus,* 103; *De Har. Resp.* 41, 43; Vell. Pat. 2.2.2; Orosius, 5.8.3; Dio, fr. 82.2.

Scipio's opposition to any peaceful negotiation with the Numantines was in line with his earlier imperialist policy on Spain and Carthage. It was Scipio also who was, in the long run, the principal beneficiary of all this. After two more years of sluggish and unproductive conduct of the Numantine War, Rome was prepared at last to turn again to her military hero. In 134 the law was suspended. Scipio secured a second consulship, and took supreme command of the war effort. Senatorial enemies made one last gasp: they obstructed the levy and cut off military funds. It was all to no avail. Private recruitment and financing sufficed to promote the venture and men from all groups hastened to join the ranks.[77] It was a personal and political triumph for the Scipionic faction. It also proved an incalculable boon to Rome, who within a year was finally rid of the devastating war that had plagued her for two decades.

The imposing figure of Scipio Aemilianus dominated the era here under discussion. But his path was not always smooth in the tangled thicket of aristocratic politics. Analysis of the 140's and 130's reveals at least three major groups who contended for supremacy within the ruling class. The *factio* of Aemilianus had to endure harassment from the Metelli, Caepiones, and Cottae on the one hand, the Claudii, Lepidi, Fulvii, and Mancini on the other. Paucity of information forbids understanding of the details, but the outlines emerge with some clarity. Electoral campaigns played but a small role in the tests of power. It was the war in Spain that cast a continuous shadow over Roman politics almost every step of the way, from its impact on the *lex Calpurnia* to the final commission of Scipio Aemilianus. The real struggles came over the Spanish commands, the desperate search for triumphs in the Iberian peninsula, and the embittered repercussions in Rome after each fruitless campaign. Foreign warfare in this period brutalized Roman character and poisoned relations within the aristocracy to an extent rarely, if ever, experienced before. The same period also presaged the enormous role that the judicial process was soon to play on the political scene. Failures in military and foreign policy had loosened senatorial control of affairs abroad. It was to restore and affirm that control that the first permanent criminal court was instituted in 149. But as rivalries and feuds within the oligarchy became more intense it was inevitable that that tribunal should begin to be utilized

[77] Sources in *MRR*, I.490; cf. Bilz, *Politik des Scipio*, 61-65. On the politics of the Spanish war generally, the view of A. Schulten, *CAH*, VII.313, that Scipionic supporters were in charge throughout the period of 143 to 134 has been sufficiently refuted; see Münzer, *Röm. Adelsp.*, 245-257. Rome's foreign policy has been discussed, in his usual intelligent fashion, by Astin, *Scip. Aem.*, 137-160.

as a weapon of political warfare. The signs are already recognizable in the trials of 139 and 138. Not only the extortion court but also the popular assembly could be a setting for political trials. The secret ballot measure of 137 facilitated that development. Politics and the judiciary can no longer be seen in isolation.

Ch. 2 Page 45

Ch. 3 Page 79

II. TI. GRACCHUS AND THE GRACCHAN *FACTIO*

Ti. Sempronius Gracchus was not a lonely, isolated figure. Nor was his tribunate of 133 a startling new thrust, suddenly ushering in a whole new era of Roman history. Behind it lay a tradition of dissent, a gradual increase in tribunician activity and authority, a growing self-consciousness on the part of men engaged in business and of those for whose economic plight the state had demonstrated little concern. Something had gone wrong in Rome and Italy. From the comfortable distance of a century, Sallust could describe it with confidence: prosperity bred arrogance and avarice; external security produced internal strife; success proved to be more cruel than adversity.[1] That is hindsight and, perhaps, oversight. But the Gracchan era possessed its own acute and perceptive analysts of contemporary malaise. Polybius observed the effects of affluence upon an aristocracy that had ceased to be conquerors had become consumers.[2] L. Calpurnius Piso, statesman, historian, and intellectual, could even fix a date for the onset of decline — 154 B.C.[3] The choice was surely not fortuitous. In 154 began two decades of brutal combat in the Spanish peninsula. Hence perhaps it was not peace or complacency that caused degeneracy of character, but war, specifically the conflict in Spain, lengthy, frustrating guerrilla warfare. The cost was heavy in manpower and resources, even heavier in prestige and *fides*. War provoked Roman ruthlessness and treachery in the provinces, and severe political conflict at home. Piso was not content to carp from the sidelines. His name is on the measure that set up Rome's first criminal court to deal with provincial exploitation.

No single issue can suffice to explain the conditions and motivation behind the Gracchan program. Much called for redress and reform. Decline

[1] Sallust, *Iug.* 41.3-5.

[2] Polyb. 31.25; cf. 6.57.5-8.

[3] Pliny, *NH,* 17.244. Others, of course, might select different dates: 187 or 168, or, later, 146; Livy, 39.6; Polyb. 31.25; Sallust, *Cat.* 10.1; *Iug.* 41.1-2; *Hist.* 11-12, Maur.

45

in moral character, a favorite theme among Roman writers and thinkers, did not come only with the fall of Carthage. A sumptuary law was passed in 182, but had to be supplemented in 161 and again in 143. Legislation, obviously, could not correct private morals. Nor did the Gracchan and post-Gracchan eras have a monopoly on electoral corruption. It was prevalent at least as early as 181 when the first *ambitus* law was passed. Once more the inadequacy of legislation is clear: in 159 a new measure on the subject was required. The actions of pro-magistrates and military leaders in Spain, as noted earlier, comprise one of the darkest chapters of Roman official behavior. The moral degeneration of a whole people, however, eludes documentation. It might be argued that the callousness of public conscience contributed to the situation that Ti. Gracchus faced. But he did not portray himself as a *curator morum*.[4]

The agrarian problem has exercised the attention of most students of the Gracchan reforms, ancient and modern.[5] Our most extensive sources, Appian and Plutarch, portray conditions of grave economic inequality: public land, thrown open to "squatters" after the Hannibalic War, was gradually absorbed by the wealthy; money, persuasion, and force squeezed out the small farmer; vast tracts fell into the hands of a few who cultivated their holdings through the use of slave labor. The picture is probably exaggerated, influenced in part by a pro-Gracchan tradition. But, in its essentials, it is unquestionably correct.[6] Roman land was still good in the second century and cereal cultivation had not been abandoned.[7] But it is revealing that Cato's contemporary treatise on agriculture places the growing of grain sixth in his order of preferences.[8] Farming was already looked upon as a source of profit, not subsistence. Deforestation and overpasturage had made many areas, notably southern

[4] On the sumptuary laws, see *MRR*, I.382, 443, 472; *ORF*, 55-56. For the *ambitus* measure of 181, see *MRR*, I.384; of 159, see Livy, *Per.* 47.

[5] The most important recent work, with full bibliography, may be found in G. Tibiletti, "Il possesso dell' *ager publicus* e le norme *de modo agrorum* sino ai Gracchi," *Athenaeum,* 26 (1948), 173-236; 27 (1949), 3-41; *Athenaeum,* 28 (1950), 183-266; "Lo sviluppo del latifondo in Italia dall' epoca graccana al principio dell' Impero," *Relazioni del X Congresso Internazionale di Scienze Storiche* (Rome), 2 (1955), 237-292. Drawing heavily on Tibiletti is the valuable but often repetitive and tedious analysis by A. J. Toynbee, *Hannibal's Legacy: The Hannibalic War's Effects on Roman Life* (London, 1965), II.155-210, 286-312.

[6] Appian, *BC*, 1.7; Plut. *Ti. Gracch.* 8.1-3. A recent study of the subject, that of Earl, *Ti Gracchus,* 16-40, unnecessarily minimizes the agrarian question.

[7] Cf. T. Frank, *An Economic Survey of Ancient Rome* (Baltimore, 1933), I.158-160. Toynbee, *Hannibal's Legacy,* II.228-235.

[8] Cato, *De Re Rust.* 1.7.

Italy, totally unsuited to the production of grain. Olive orchards and the vine were becoming more prevalent, as Cato's tract clearly demonstrates. After the second Punic War, the senate commissioned a translation of Mago's agricultural treatise, a work dealing with the large vine and oil plantations surrounding the city of Carthage.[9] Even more important was the increase of large ranches, the proliferation of grazing. For these operations much capital was required and slave labor was convenient and practical. How far the decline of the small farm had gone by the 130's no man can say. The free peasant farmer, to be sure, had not vanished, nor had vast *latifundia* absorbed the Italian countryside. But in viticulture, olive-growing, and ranching the small peasant could not compete, and, for the absentee landlord, slave labor possessed advantages that free workers did not afford.[10] The evidence for growth of slavery is plentiful and consistent.[11] The slaves were profitable, but also dangerous. A serious revolt erupted in Etruria in 196 and another in Apulia in 185. In 135 came the most violent and widespread servile insurrection in Sicily. To be sure, conditions in that island do not necessarily reflect the Italian situation, but the event doubtless created a vivid impression in Rome.[12] It is not entirely coincidental that Ti. Gracchus secured the passage of agrarian reform while slave revolt raged to the south of Italy.

The rural problem was also an urban problem. Men who lost their farms through usurpation or debt or prolonged absence abroad found their way to Rome. Signs of heavy immigration can already be seen early in the second century.[13] The city had its attractions. For those who had done military service in the east amidst the ancient towns of Greece and Asia Minor a return to the Italian countryside may have been unappealing, even if they did not feel an economic pinch. Lucrative wars of the early 140's brought a surplus of cash to the capital. An increased building program meant that employment opportunities were high and the urban population unquestionably swelled. A period of inflation, however, was

[9] Pliny, *NH,* 18.22; Varro, *De Re Rust.* 1.1.10.

[10] Cf. the excellent accounts of C. Yeo, "The Overgrazing of Ranch-Lands in Ancient Italy," *TAPA,* 79 (1948), 275-307, and esp. "The Development of the Roman Plantation and Marketing of Farm Products," *Finanzarchiv,* 13 (1952), 321-342, neglected by most scholars.

[11] W. L. Westermann, *The Slave Systems of Greek and Roman Antiquity* (Philadelphia, 1955), 57-65. The casual or seasonal free laborer, however, continued to exist; cf. Cato, *De Re Rust.* 5.4, 13.1, 66-67, 144-146; Varro, *De Re Rust.* 1.17.2; Toynbee, *Hannibal's Legacy,* II.302-310.

[12] Cf. Appian, *BC,* 1.9. On the revolt of 196, see Livy, 33.36.3; of 185, Livy, 39.29; of 135, Diod. 34.2ff. In general, see Toynbee, *Hanibal's Legacy,* II. 313-331.

[13] Livy, 39.3, 41.9.

succeeded by depression in the 130's, and by decreased public spending, owing to lengthy and expensive foreign wars that brought no tangible rewards. For the urban population unemployment and economic dislocation were made acute by a grain shortage while the island of Sicily was engulfed in a servile rebellion.[14] The influx of new city dwellers from the countryside meant increased participation in the political process by men still registered in the rural tribes. In the *comitia tributa,* where thirty-one of thirty-five tribes were rural, their votes were powerful and disruptive.[15]

Connected with this depopulation of the countryside was a burgeoning crisis in the military. For more than half a century since the Hannibalic War the vast commitment of Roman arms abroad was a constant drain on manpower resources. Wars in the east may have been profitable, but Spain was dangerous and deadly. Conscription was limited to property holders and their numbers were decreasing in the second century. It is not beyond imagination that some practical individuals voluntarily abandoned their holdings and moved to Rome in order to evade the levy. Other more hardy souls returned from extended service to find their farms in disrepair and their families in debt.[16] Still others, of course, did not return at all. Wars claimed many lives, and discontent and social conditions reduced the numbers of those eligible for the wars. Mutinous activity in the ranks emerged as early as the 190's and continued sporadically for the next half-century.[17]

The consequences are reflected in our demographic evidence. The cessation of Latin colonies after 181 shows Roman reluctance to lose any more citizens, that is, to lose potential recruits for foreign service. Census figures, recorded in the Livian tradition, reveal a steady decline from 164 to 136 B.C. Military losses account for much of this.[18] If the

[14] On all this see the illuminating remarks of H. C. Boren, "The Urban Side of the Gracchan Economic Crisis," *AHR,* 63 (1958), 890-902, and "Numismatic Light on the Gracchan Crisis," *AJP,* 79 (1958), 140-155.

[15] Cf. T. F. Carney, "Rome in the Gracchan Age," *Theoria* (1960), 38-42. Of course, it was theoretically possible for censors to re-register immigrants from the countryside into urban tribes. But virtually no evidence attests to this practice; cf. L. R. Taylor, *The Voting Districts of the Roman Republic* (Rome, 1960), 23, 280-282, 294.

[16] Sallust, *Iug.* 41.8: *Interea parentes aut parvi liberi militum, uti quisque potentiori confinis erat, sedibus pellebantur.* Cf. Val. Max. 4.4.6 on Regulus in the first Punic War. The story, like so many about Regulus, may be apocryphal, but the description would fit many veterans of foreign wars.

[17] Earl, *Ti. Gracchus,* 30-40, rightly stresses the significance of the military crisis in the mid second century. But it is an artificial distinction to isolate this from the agrarian situation.

[18] Frank, *Econ. Surv.,* I.109-110.

figures refer only to men with registered property, rather than all adult male citizens, the decline may also suggest the gradual depopulation of the countryside.[19] That members of the aristocracy felt a deepening concern is clear from Metellus Macedonicus' censorial speech of 131 urging increased reproduction of the species in the interests of the state.[20]

All of these elements hang together. Wars drew off small farmers and kept many of them so long they could not maintain their property upon return. Urban employment and attraction brought the adventuresome and the desperate into the city. There they were at the mercy of the fluctuations of the economy, and became a potential menace to the traditional social and political order. The grisly nature of the Spanish War drove others to seek the immunity of a propertyless status, a development that both swelled the urban proletariate and reduced the pool of legionary recruits. Booty found its way into the pockets of a wealthy class interested in increasing its agricultural holdings and cultivating the land with profit-making crops. The growth of slavery went on unchecked. Slaves were not only economically practical; they were ineligible for the military.[21]

Ti. Gracchus was not the first to agitate for change. Secret ballot, introduced for elections and for popular trials in 139 and 137, indicates a more active and perhaps more independent voting populace.[22] The unpopularity of conscription for the Spanish Wars induced unwilling victims to appeal to the tribunes. On more than one occasion between 152 and 138, tribunes sought to block the levy, not stopping short even of imprisoning the consuls.[23] Gracchus' boldness in 133 then must have drawn some comfort from increased tribunician activity in the previous decades.

[19] On the meaning of the census figures, total agreement among scholars will probably never be secured; cf. F. Bourne, "The Roman Republican Census and Census Statistics," *CW*, 45 (1952), 129-135; E. Gabba, "Ancora sulle cifre dei censimenti," *Athenaeum*, 30 (1952), 161-173; Earl, *Ti. Gracchus*, 35-37; Toynbee, *Hannibal's Legacy*, I.438-479; Astin, *Scip. Aem.*, 335-338. A substantial rise in numbers by 125, however, does seem to indicate that agrarian reform had produced more men eligible for military service. Certainly no widespread extension of the franchise had intervened.

[20] *ORF*, 107-108.

[21] Cf. Appian, *BC*, 1.10. On all these matters, see the judicious and sober examination by Astin, *Scip. Aem.*, 161-174.

[22] *MRR*, I.482, 485. On voting procedure, see Taylor, *Roman Voting Assemblies*, 34-58.

[23] Taylor, *JRS*, 52 (1962), 19-27. Miss Taylor argues plausibly that the *leges Aelia et Fufia* were passed ca. 150 to check tribunician obstructionism. Astin, "Leges Aelia et Fufia," *Latomus*, 23 (1964), 421-445, on other grounds, puts them a few years later. The arguments of G. V. Sumner, *"Lex Aelia, Lex Fufia,"* AJP, 84 (1963), 337-358, for 132 will not hold in view of Cic. *In Pis.* 10.

Of course, obstructionism, even if successful, could not resolve the deeper issues. The agrarian measure of C. Laelius was undoubtedly a step in the right direction. But when that effort failed to secure senatorial endorsement, Laelius withdrew his proposal and the friends of Scipio Aemilianus took no further interest in land reform.[24]

The situation then was eminently ripe for another to promote change. What Ti. Gracchus' personal motives were is a well-worn but fruitless controversy. The influence of Greek philosophy and Hellenistic ideas has often been invoked.[25] Greeks like Blossius and Diophanes were Tiberius' companions and teachers. But intellectual tendencies in the tribune remain obscure and speculation has been excessive.[26] Wounded pride, the insult to his *dignitas* that Tiberius suffered as a consequence of the Mancinus affair in 137, brought fierce resentment and a desire to redress the balance.[27] This motive however, although it may account for the stirring of Tiberius' adrenalin, does not explain the following he amassed. The agrarian law, in any case, might have cured several connected maladies. An upper limit of five hundred *iugera* to holders of public land would still allow scope for wine and oil plantations, as well as moderately large ranches for the absentee landlord and investor. Distribution of the surplus would relieve the overcrowdedness of the city, stock the pool of eligible military men, and perhaps ease the moral consciences of the aristocracy. (The provision that made distributed land inalienable was surely designed to short-circuit further evasion of the draft.) The tendency can be described as conservative rather than revolutionary: prudent reform in the interests of restoring an older, more stable situation.[28]

But there is more to it than that. The affair can take its rightful place in the context of factional politics.[29] In 133 Scipio Aemilianus was in Spain, reestablishing Rome's military reputation, if not her *fides,* and

[24] Plut. *Ti. Gracch.* 8.4.

[25] E.g., S. Katz, "The Gracchi: An Essay in Interpretation," *CJ,* 38 (1942), 65-73; T. S. Brown, "Greek Influence on Tiberius Gracchus," *CJ,* 42 (1947), 471-473; F. Smuts, "Stoic Influences on Tiberius Gracchus," *Acta Classica,* 1 (1958), 106-116; T. Africa, "Aristonicus, Blossius, and the City of the Sun," *Int. Rev. Soc. Hist.,* 6 (1961), 110-124; C. Nicolet, "L'inspiration de Tiberius Gracchus," *REA,* 67 (1965), 142-158.

[26] Cf. the sensible remarks of D. R. Dudley, "Blossius of Cumae," *JRS,* 31 (1941), 92-99.

[27] Cf. esp. Cic. *Har. Resp.* 43; *Brutus,* 103; Vell. Pat. 2.2.1; Orosius, 5.8.3.

[28] This, of course, has been noted by many scholars. See, most recently, Meier. *Res Pub.,* 95-100, 107-110, 128-131.

[29] The political links are discussed by Münzer, *Röm. Adelsp.,* 257-270, and, more recently, by Earl, *Ti. Gracchus,* 1-15. In both instances, however, there is heavy reliance on connections allegedly formed two generations previously. Given the fluctuating character of senatorial politics, that evidence, such as it is, is not worth much.

further enhancing his own status. With him were several prominent figures connected with his *factio*.[30] A counter-stroke on the domestic front by the enemies of Scipio should cause no surprise. The personnel of the group behind Ti. Gracchus and the timing of his move can leave no doubt that the political advantages of reform received consideration. Agrarian reform in 133 was especially appropriate and politically pointed. With the Numantine War drawing to a close, it would be Scipio's own veterans who would find benefits coming from Ti. Gracchus and his *factio*. The opposition of Scipio to Gracchus is often said to have involved disavowal not of the latter's aims but of his methods. The evidence is silent on any such distinction, and, from a political point of view, it may be irrelevant. The earlier "reforms" sponsored by the Scipionic group in 145 and 137 were also, in part, political maneuvers. Other progressive acts sponsored by the enemies of Scipio had met with tenacious opposition.[31] When reform seemed imminent, it was important that the right group gain the credit for it. If this proved impossible, the common tactic was to discredit the proposals, by denouncing aims, methods, or the reformers themselves. What Scipio's real feelings were on the issues raised by the Gracchan movement is beyond knowing. The exigencies of the political situation, in any event, dictated overt opposition.

Ti. Gracchus' marriage into the family of the Claudii brought powerful support, and perhaps inspiration to his project. The sources identify his most prominent backers as Ap. Claudius Pulcher, P. Licinius Crassus Mucianus, and P. Mucius Scaevola.[32] Ap. Claudius, the *princeps senatus,* was Tiberius' father-in-law and a long time opponent of Scipio Aemilianus.[33] Licinius Crassus Mucianus, as his name shows, had been adopted

[30] Scipio's legate was his brother Q. Fabius Maximus Aemilianus (Appian, *Iber.* 90), his quaestor probably his nephew Q. Fabius Allobrogicus (Appian, *Iber.* 84; Val. Max. 8.15.4; Cichorius, *Unt. zu Luc.,* 317-318). Others included P. Rutilius Rufus, the literary figures Lucilius and Polybius, and the young soldiers who first made their military names, C. Marius and Jugurtha. It was not, however, an all-Scipionic venture. Glory was to be attained and men like C. Gracchus, C. Metellus Caprarius, and C. Memmius were also included in the retinue, though they were hardly loyal followers of the Scipionic group.

[31] Earl, *Historia,* 11 (1962), 477-485.

[32] Plut. *Ti. Gracch.* 9.1; Cic. *Acad. Prior.* 2.13.

[33] Plut. *Ti. Gracch.* 4.1. Earl, *Ti. Gracchus,* 8-10, seeks to push back for several generations the connections between the Claudii and the Sempronii. But the only evidence adduced is consular collegiality and he must dismiss as "exceptions" the instances of clear opposition between members of their families. No occasions of prior cooperation are recorded. Similarly, Earl can point to no express testimony on cooperation with the Scaevolae and Crassi in earlier generations (pp. 10-11).

by the Licinii Crassi, whose opposition to the Scipionic group had been most strikingly demonstrated by the clash between C. Crassus and Laelius in 145. Married to a Clodia, Mucianus was probably the brother-in-law of Ap. Claudius, and his daughter Licinia married C. Gracchus at about this time. Connections with the Claudian group were therefore close and multiple. Mucianus himself was to serve later on the Gracchan triumviral commission, as did Ap. Claudius, and to oppose Scipio overtly in 131.[34] His brother, P. Mucius Scaevola, an eminent jurist, is a more ambiguous figure. Cultural and intellectual interests had brought him and his cousin Q. Scaevola into association with the Scipionic literary circle. As late as 136 he appears to have acted on behalf of Scipio's interests by opposing the reinstatement of Hostilius Mancinus.[35] Acquaintance with Ti. Gracchus may have come while both were traveling in Scipionic society. By the mid-130's Gracchus was firmly in the Claudian camp. P. Scaevola seems to have moved in the same direction, doubtless under the influence of his more vigorous and active brother Mucianus, who pursued the policies of his adopted house, the Licinii Crassi, against the prior connections of the Mucii Scaevolae. A transfer of allegiance proved somewhat awkward for the cautious jurist. Cicero reports that though Crassus Mucianus was an overt adherent of Ti. Gracchus, P. Scaevola preferred to remain in the background.[36]

The sources do not specify other backers of Tiberius. But it is clear that the Fulvii, adhering to their old allegiance, also supported him. Plutarch mentions two Fulvii as friends of Gracchus in the course of his turbulent tribunate. One of these is described as the "consular Fulvius" who appealed to Tiberius to avoid violence and to submit his proposals to the senate, a piece of advice followed by the tribune.[37] Identity of the ex-consul cannot be precisely determined, for there were four Fulvii who had held the consulship since 159. Associated with Fulvius in this appeal is another ex-consul referred to by Plutarch as Μάλλιος. He is usually identified as M'. Manilius, a renowned jurist and

[34] On the marriage links, see Münzer, *Röm. Adelsp.*, 270-275.

[35] Q. Scaevola was married to the daughter of Laelius, and more than one item associates the Scaevolae with the friends of Scipio. See the references collected by Münzer, *RE*, 31.425-428, "Mucius," n. 17, and Gruen, *Athenaeum*, 43 (1965), 321-324.

[36] Cic. *Acad. Prior.* 2.13: *P. Crassum et P. Scaevolam, aiunt Ti. Graccho auctores legum fuisse, alterum quidem, ut videmus, palam, alterum, ut suspicamur, obscurius.*

[37] Plut. *Ti. Gracch.* 11: Μάλλιος καὶ Φούλβιος, ἄνδρες ὑπατικοί, προσπεσόντες τῷ Τιβερίῳ καὶ χειρῶν ἁπτόμενοι καὶ δακρύοντες ἐδέοντο παύσασθαι... ἐπιτρέψαι δὲ τῇ βουλῇ κελεύοντες καὶ δεόμενοι συνέπεισαν.

consul in 149.[38] But Μάλλιος could mean Manlius rather than Manilius, and the consul of 149 was a personal friend of Scipio Aemilianus, who served under him in Spain in that year.[39] He is not the most likely man, therefore, to have given advice to Ti. Gracchus. The last Manlius to reach the consulship was A. Manlius Torquatus in 164. Though an old man in 133, it is not impossible that he is referred to here by Plutarch. In that event, the Fulvius may be the consul of 159 or of 153.[40] A second Fulvius, described simply as a senator, warned Tiberius of the plot on his life in late 133. This is probably M. Fulvius Flaccus, the future consul of 125, firm friend and closest supporter of C. Gracchus. The connections of the Fulvii, Claudii, and Licinii Crassi with the Gracchan movement are therefore amply demonstrated. Whatever the deep-seated motives for reform among some individuals, the factional nature of this struggle cannot be gainsaid.[41]

Tribunician *intercessio* had long been a weapon of the oligarchy to checkmate potentially disruptive proposals. When the tribune M. Octavius rose to interpose his veto of Ti. Gracchus' agrarian bill, he was acting on behalf of the *possessores,* so the ancient testimony reports.[42] That would be a natural conjecture. It is possible that Octavius had in mind also the interests of the Scipionic *factio,* who would not welcome the resurgence of the Claudii through their young protégé. There are slight indications of familial ties between the Octavii and the Popillii Laenates that may suggest a link with Scipio.[43] P. Popillius Laenas was to take bitter revenge on the Gracchans in the following year. The alle-

---

[38] A. Schäfer, "Miscellen," *Jahrb. Class. Phil.,* 107 (1873), 71-72; Fraccaro, *Studi sull' età dei Gracchi* (Citta di Castello, 1914), 105; Babba, *Appiani, Bellorum Civilium Liber Primus* (Florence, 1958), 35-36; Earl, *Ti. Gracchus,* 85.

[39] For Manilius' friendship with Scipio, see Cic. *De Rep.* 1.18, 3.17; for his service in Spain, see *MRR,* I.459.

[40] Cf. Astin, *Scip. Aem.,* 348. Another senior senator, T. Annius Luscus, consul in 153, played an active role in this year. There is some evidence, for what it is worth, for cooperation between Manlii and Fulvii in the early second century; Livy, 37.47.7; Scullard, *Roman Politics,* 179, 184; Earl, *Ti. Gracchus,* 13.

[41] For Flaccus' warning to Tiberius, see Plut. *Ti. Gracch.* 18. Later, in 130, he received appointment to the agrarian commission; *MRR,* I.503. Cf., on the backers of Tiberius, Münzer, *Röm. Adelsp.,* 257-270; Fraccaro, *Studi Gracchi,* 79-82; Bilz, *Politik des Scipio,* 68-70; Earl, *Ti. Gracchus,* 8-15; Astin, *Scip. Aem.,* 190-201. Meier, *Res Pub.,* 98, in defiance of the evidence, denies all factional considerations to the Gracchan program. Few will follow him.

[42] Appian, *BC,* 1.12; Plut. *Ti. Gracch.* 10.2, 10.5.

[43] Earl, *Latomus,* 19 (1960), 657-666.

giance of Octavius, however, ought not to be pressed. It was not the Scipionic faction alone, as we shall see, that provided opposition. Tiberius took it upon himself to effect a suspension of all public business. And worse yet, Octavius was removed from office in order to secure passage of the agrarian law. The deposition of Octavius, engineered by Tiberius, raised constitutional issues of momentous proportions.[44] Was a tribune a mere passive organ of the popular will who could be removed if the populace saw fit? Could the mood of a particular meeting of the people represent itself as the "popular will"? One did not have to be a friend of Scipio to find the implications of Gracchus' actions objectionable. The evidence shows that a large number of important senators registered their objections and made their presence felt.

The senior consular Q. Metellus Macedonicus, who had earned his *cognomen* by crushing the revolt of the Macedonian Andriscus, delivered a blistering speech against Ti. Gracchus, comparing him unfavorably with his father.[45] Macedonicus was also, it has already been noted, a formidable enemy of Scipio Aemilianus. It is no accident that he was the object of attack by the poet Lucilius, a friend and client of Scipio.[46] Macedonicus' leadership here presaged an increased role and importance for the powerful alliance centered about the family of the Metelli.[47]

[44] Whether a tribune could legitimately declare a *iustitium,* a suspension of public business, is a matter of dispute; see, e.g., J. Carcopino, *Autour des Gracques* (Paris, 1928), 17-23; Gelzer, "Review of Carcopino, *Autour des Gracques,*" *Gnomon,* 5 (1929), 649-650; R. Thomsen, "Erliess Tiberius Gracchus ein *Iustitium?*" *ClMed,* 6 (1944), 60-71; Astin, *Scip. Aem.,* 346-347. The tribune elected to succeed Octavius has been variously given as Mucius (Plut. *Ti. Gracch.* 13.2), Q. Mummius (Appian, *BC,* 1.12), or Minucius (Orosius, 5.8.3). A case has been made for Minucius, associating him with C. Minucius Augurinus, a *monetalis* in the Gracchan period; Earl, *Latomus,* 19 (1960), 666-669; cf. E. A. Sydenham, *Coinage of the Roman Republic* (London, 1952), 54, n. 463.

[45] The speech was recorded by the contemporary historian C. Fannius and known to Cicero; *Brutus,* 81. A fragment probably survives in Plut. *Ti. Gracch.* 14.3; cf. Fraccaro, *Studi Storici,* 5 (1912), 335-336; *ORF,* 107.

[46] For Lucilius' lines see Schol. on Horace, *Sat.* 2.1.63ff. The poet's attacks on the sanctity of marriage are plausibly connected with an attack on Macedonicus' famous censorial speech in 131; Marx, *Luc. Carm. Rel.,* 246-250; Cichorius, *Unt. zu Luc.,* 133-140.

[47] K. Ziegler, "L. Caecilius Metellus Diadematus," *Gymnasium,* 63 (1956), 483-486, makes the attractive suggestion that Macedonicus' son L. Metellus Diadematus received his *cognomen* in this year. The diadem offered to Ti. Gracchus by the Pergamene envoy Eudemus was a fruitful source of hostile propaganda; Plut. *Ti. Gracch.* 14, 19; cf. Florus, 2.7.7; *Vir. Ill.* 64.6. It may be Diadematus who is to be identified with the L. Metellus attacked in a speech by C. Gracchus; *ORF,* 194.

Another ex-consul, Q. Pompeius, denounced Gracchus' aggrandizement and declared his intention of prosecuting the tribune once his term of office came to an end.[48] Pompeius' checkered career shows no consistent pattern. An earlier link with the Scipionic group had been strained, if not severed, when he double-crossed Laelius in 142. Men hostile to Scipio, including Metellus Macedonicus, had promoted Pompeius' prosecution in 139, but he also had personal enemies in the Scipionic faction, like L. Furius Philus. Pompeius' stance in 133 defies categorization within a factional nexus. His was an independent but influential voice.[49]

The implementation of Pompeius' threat had to await the expiration of Ti. Gracchus' tribunate. But judicial machinery as a means of checking the tribune was invoked in 133. The elderly senator T. Annius Luscus, who had held the consulship twenty years earlier, challenged Tiberius to a ὁρισμός to determine the validity of the deposition of a sacred tribune.[50] This ὁρισμός is, apparently, the Greek translation for the Latin *sponsio,* a judicial wager, generally followed, if accepted, by reference to a *iudex* for settlement. The procedure, usually employed in civil cases, could, it seems, be used to determine points of public law as well.[51] The affair is odd, but there is no reason to discount Plutarch's evidence. Prosecution of a tribune while in office was not, of course, possible, and Annius may have hit upon this unusual procedure to bring Tiberius before a court without violating constitutional practice. The challenge, Plutarch implies, was not taken up, but Tiberius retaliated in kind by attempting to initiate a prosecution of Annius before the people. The nature of the charge is unknown.[52] Interference with tribunician activity is quite possibly what Tiberius sought to claim. But whatever the formal charge, the trial never materialized. Annius' pointed and embar-

---

[48] Plut. *Ti. Gracch.* 14.3; Orosius, 5.8.4; cf. Appian, *BC*, 1.13. On the question of immunity from prosecution for members of the agrarian commission, see Appendix A.

[49] For the enmity with Furius, see Val. Max. 3.7.5; Dio, fr. 82; Cic. *De Off.* 3.109; *De Rep.* 3.28; in general, Earl, *Ti. Gracchus,* 98-103.

[50] Plut. *Ti Gracch.* 14.5; cf. Livy, *Per.* 58.

[51] The word is so translated by A. H. J. Greenidge, *History of Rome During the Later Republic and Early Principate* (London, 1904), 131, and Fraccaro, *Studi Storici,* 5 (1912), 331; *Studi Gracchi,* 143. Cf. its use in Plut. *Alex.* 6; *Cato Maior,* 17.5-6; and see also Strachan-Davidson, *Problems,* I.61-66.

[52] Plut. *Ti Gracch.* 14.5: τὸν Ἄννιον ἀχθῆναι κελεύσας ἐβούλετο κατηγορεῖν; Livy, *Per.* 58. Fraccaro, *Studi Gracchi,* 144, conjectures that since Annius' *sponsio* would have meant a judicial decision of some sort, Tiberius charged him with seeking to bring a tribune to court while in office. The constitutional problems here are, unfortunately, too obscure to allow of any certainty on this score.

rassing questions left Tiberius no alternative but to dismiss the assembly rather than have the doubtful legality of his actions submitted to judicial scrutiny, even by the people.[53] It was perhaps at this time also that an attack was launched on Scipio's close friend and protector of his interests in Rome, C. Laelius. All that remains of that now are three fragments of a speech by Laelius *pro se ad populum*. Date and circumstances are nowhere reported and conjectures are at best tentative. But the maneuvers of 133 provide a plausible setting. That an actual trial took place is uncertain, but charges and countercharges before the *populus* seem to have been the order of the day. Laelius, in any case, survived to play a major role in the following year.[54] Recourse to judicial procedure had thus proved a failure on all sides, and the path was open to more drastic measures.

The program of Ti. Gracchus roused greater opposition than the Claudian faction had bargained for. How far his proposals and actions went beyond the plans laid by his supporters cannot be discerned. His father-in-law, Ap. Claudius Pulcher, was named to one of the triumviral posts on the agrarian commission, and P. Licinius Crassus Mucianus was later appointed to fill the vacancy left by Tiberius' death. They may be presumed to have stood by him, as did M. Fulvius Flaccus and his own brother C. Gracchus.[55] Others may have had second thoughts. The deposition of a tribune was reason enough. But Tiberius also conducted personal negotiations with a representative of the kingdom of Pergamum. The funds willed to the Roman people by the Pergamene monarch were to be utilized to finance the agrarian program.[56] Ti. Gracchus was now threatening to short-circuit the traditional senatorial con-

[53] Plut. *Ti. Gracch.* 14.7-9. A fragment of Annius' speech has been preserved; *ORF*, 106. It is impossible to say whether this is part of the senatorial address or the remarks in the forum. The phrase *imperium . . . abrogatum est* led Fraccaro to argue that the reference cannot be to the deposition of Octavius since tribunes did not possess *imperium; Studi Storici*, 5 (1912), 331-334. L. R. Taylor has recently suggested that Annius referred to a bestowal of *imperium* on the Gracchan triumvirs; "Was Tiberius Gracchus' Last Assembly Electoral or Legislative?" *Athenaeum*, 41 (1963), 66, n. 31.

[54] For the fragments, see *ORF*, 119. The affair has been variously placed: after Laelius' praetorship in 145 by Fraccaro, *Studi Storici*, 5 (1912), 349-350; during his consulship of 140 by L. Lange, *Römische Alterthümer* (Berlin, 1876), 2.591; or during the period 131-129 by Meyer (See Fraccaro, *Studi Storici*, 5 (1912), 349-350).

[55] On Claudius, cf. Earl, *Ti. Gracchus*, 91; on Flaccus, see below, pp. 62-63.

[56] Plut. *Ti. Gracch.* 14; Livy, *Per.* 58; *Vir. Ill.* 64; *Orosius*, 5.8.4; cf. E. Badian, *Foreign Clientelae, 264-70 B.C.* (Oxford, 1958), 173-174.

trol of finance and foreign affairs. The utilization of foreign *clientelae* in domestic politics was an ominous sign. Moderate or faint-hearted sympathizers, like P. Scaevola, may have found it prudent to withdraw their support.[57]

Efforts to gain a second consecutive tribunate appear to have been Ti. Gracchus' undoing. It is reported also that the group behind Tiberius sought two other offices in 133, success in either of which would have been a constitutional anomaly: a tribunate for young C. Gracchus, though he had not yet held even the quaestorship, and a second consulship for Ap. Claudius Pulcher, though this was forbidden by law.[58] That report is evidence for anti-Gracchan propaganda, not fact.[59] Some of Gracchus' contemporaries spread reports of a prospective tyranny and perhaps even genuinely feared one; a dynastic control of the higher magistracies may well have been rumored. That the three alleged candidates already controlled the agrarian commission would have made the rumor plausible.[60]

A second tribunate for Tiberius, however, was definitely in the works.[61] It is possible that this attempt was in violation of Roman law.[62] It was

[57] Astin unduly minimizes the revolutionary character of Tiberius' actions: *Scip. Aem.*, 201-226. But his lengthy and intelligent discussion rightly stresses what most modern accounts overlook: a growing number of constitutional violations in previous years preceded and prepared the way for Tiberius' actions (pp. 175-189). Not the least of them were the two extraordinary consulships of Scipio Aemilianus himself.

[58] Livy, *Per.* 56, reports the ban on iteration of the consulship. One cannot rule out the possibility that this is a late annalistic fiction, but, in any case, a second consulship would be unusual and menacing. Similarly, age qualifications for the tribunate and the point at which one held that office were probably not fixed rigidly. But few would look kindly upon the absentee candidacy of a twenty-one-year-old.

[59] The story is conveyed by a single source; Dio, fr. 83: ἐπεχείρησε καὶ ἐς τὸ ἐπιὸν ἔτος μετὰ τοῦ ἀδελφοῦ δημαρχῆσαι καὶ τὸν πενθερὸν ὕπατον ἀποδεῖξαι, μηδὲν μήτ' εἰπεῖν μήθ' ὑποσχέσθαι τισὶν ὀκνῶν. It is almost certainly tendentious, although accepted now by Earl, *Ti. Gracchus,* 112-113, and, more cautiously, by Astin, *Scip. Aem.* 351.

[60] Cic. *De Rep.* 6.8; Plut. *Ti. Gracch.* 19.3: ὁ δὲ Νασικᾶς ἠξίου τὸν ὕπατον τῇ πόλει βοηθεῖν καὶ καταλύειν τὸν τύραννον. Cf. H. C. Boren, "Tiberius Gracchus: The Opposition View," *AJP*, 82 (1961), 358-369.

[61] Cic. *Cat.* 4.4; Appian, *BC,* 1.14-16; Plut. *Ti. Gracch.* 16-19; Livy, *Per.* 58; Orosius, 5.9.1: Dio. fr. 83; cf. Florus, 2.2; *Vir. Ill.* 64.

[62] Such, in any case, is the implication of Appian, *BC,* 1.14; οὐκ ἔννομον εἶναι δὶς ἐφεξῆς τὸν αὐτὸν ἄρχειν; cf. *BC,* 1.21; Gabba, *App. BC Lib. Prim.,* 45, 71-72; Taylor, *Athenaeum,* 41 (1963), 56-57; Astin, *Scip. Aem.,* 351-352; contra: A. H. M. Jones, "De Tribunis Plebis Reficiendis," *PCPS,* 186 (1960), 35-39; Earl, *Ti. Gracchus,* 103-104.

certainly in violation of constitutional precedent. A tradition persists that Tiberius sought to introduce fresh legislation, possibly in order to smooth the path to reelection.[63] The assembly that he called prior to his assassination may well have been a legislative rather than an electoral *comitia,* but the bills reported by the sources look suspiciously like doublets of those later offered by C. Gracchus. An alleged judiciary measure is of special relevance to this study. Plutarch asserts that Tiberius sought to institute mixed juries of senators and *equites,* Dio that he transferred the courts wholesale to the equestrian order. These remarks doubtless reflect confusion with the later measures of his brother. To be sure, Scipio Aemilianus delievered an oration *contra legem iudiciariam Ti. Gracchi,* and it has been taken as confirmation of the tradition on Tiberius' judicial measure.[64] But Scipio was in Spain in 133 and could not have spoken against a bill of Ti. Gracchus. Moreover, the phrase *lex iudiciaria* implies a law, not a mere proposal that failed to pass. Tiberius had promulgated a measure that supplemented his *lex agraria* and awarded judicial power to the agrarian commission.[65] Scipio's speech was obviously directed against this piece of legislation and was part of his anti-Gracchan campaign of 129. That Tiberius thought in terms of the judiciary is extremely unlikely. The desire for a second tribunate, primarily to evade prosecution, is, in any case, clear. That brought matters to a head.

Ti. Gracchus represented a terrifying menace to the traditional structure of Roman politics. Land reform might have been acceptable, but not in the face of adverse senatorial opinion. Laelius had politely dropped his efforts when he failed to carry a majority in the *curia.* Such a move, one may presume, was standard procedure in that august body. But Tiberius had pressed on and was now threatening to make the urban populace and the small peasants his personal *clientelae.* This threat aroused vigorous and swift reaction. It also presented the Scipionic group with an issue to use against their political enemies. The most conspicuous Scipionic leader present in Rome was P. Scipio Nasica Serapio, *consularis* since 138, and *pontifex maximus* since 141. A fierce oligarch, he inherited his father's contempt for the masses, a contempt unashamedly

[63] Plut. *Ti. Gracch.* 16.1; Dio, fr. 83.7; Vell. Pat. 2.2; Ampelius, 26.1; cf. Appian, *BC,* 1.2. The validity of this tradition is forcefully argued by Taylor, *Athenaeum,* 41 (1963), 51-69; "Appian and Plutarch on Tiberius Gracchus' Last Assembly," *Athenaeum,* 44 (1966), 238-250; contra: Earl, "Tiberius Gracchus' Last Assembly," *Athenaeum,* 43 (1965), 95-105.

[64] Macrob. *Sat.* 3.4.6; accepted by Taylor, *Athenaeum,* 41 (1963), 55, n. 7.

[65] Livy, *Per.* 58: *Promulgavit et aliam legem agrariam, qua sibi latius agrum patefaceret, ut iidem triumviri iudicarent, qua publicus ager, qua privatus esset.* Cf. Gabba, *App. BC Lib. Prim.,* 39-40.

expressed in the forum as well as the senate. Nasica had already sought to emasculate the agrarian commission. He had sponsored a senatorial resolution to slash its budget to an absurd minimum.[66] Now, shortly before the tribunician elections, he urged the consul to present a motion declaring a national emergency and to take steps against Ti. Gracchus. The consul was P. Scaevola. It is likely that Scaevola had already become disenchanted with Tiberius and he made it clear that he frowned on the tribune's demagogic tactics.[67] But Scaevola did not relish the role of executioner. He refused to put the question, declaring that he could not sanction the execution of a Roman citizen without trial.[68] A special tribunal was not, of course, mooted, for Ti. Gracchus was still tribune and no proceedings could therefore be brought against him. Extra-legal proceedings remained as an alternative. Nasica, though a *privatus,* led a crowd of rioters against the Gracchani and in the resultant melee the tribune was lynched.[69]

Ti. Gracchus and his supporters were not the sole victims; Roman judicial procedures had been ignored and subverted. The normal practice would have been a prosecution after the close of Tiberius' tribunician office, as Pompeius had in fact threatened. This avenue, however, seemed closed to his opponents. Election to a second tribunate would have forestalled prosecution, and no one could then predict what magisterial office might follow. But even if Tiberius were to become a *privatus,* prosecution would presumably be for *perduellio,* which would have to be heard by the *populus,* who were very unlikely to convict him. Recourse could still be had to the declaration of the tribune as a *hostis.*

[66] Plut. *Ti. Gracch.* 13.3. On Nasica's offices, see *MRR,* I.478, 479, n. 2; Münzer, *Röm. Adelsp.,* 251, 260. On his character, see esp. Cic. *De Off.* 1.109; *Brutus,* 107; Val. Max. 3.7.3, 7.5.2.

[67] Plut. *Ti. Gracch.* 19.3: εἰ μέντοι ψηφίσαιτό τι τῶν παρανόμων ὁ δῆμος ὑπὸ τοῦ Τιβερίου πεισθεὶς ἢ βιασθείς, τοῦτο κύριον μὴ φυλάξειν.

[68] Plut. *Ti. Gracch.* 19.3: ἀποκριναμένου δὲ πράως ἐκείνου βίας μὲν οὐδεμιᾶς ὑπάρξειν οὐδὲ ἀναιρήσειν οὐδένα τῶν πολιτῶν ἄκριτον; Val. Max. 3.2.17: *Scaevola negavit se quicquam vi esse acturum;* G. Plaumann, "Das sogennannte *Senatus Consultum Ultimum,* die Quasidiktatur der späteren römischen Republik," *Klio,* 13 (1913), 359-361, argues that the *s.c.u* was actually passed but that the consul Scaevola decided the time was not ripe to act upon it. This interpretation is contradicted by Cic. *Cat.* 1.3-4; cf. *Phil.* 8.14; see Fraccaro, *Studi Gracchi,* 179, and Gruen, *Athenaeum,* 43 (1965), 326.

[69] Plut. *Ti. Gracch.* 19; Appian, *BC,* 1.16; Val. Max. 3.2.17; Cic. *Pro Planc.* 88; *Tusc. Disp.* 4.5.1; *Cat.* 1.3; *Phil.* 8.14; *De Domo,* 91. Astin, *Scip. Aem.,* 220-224, goes too far in denying that Nasica had any intention of lynching Tiberius and argues that matters simply got out of hand. This view involves the scrapping of almost all the evidence as *post eventum* fabrications.

P. Scaevola declined that act, but Nasica took the responsibility into his own hands. Thus, new and ominous means had been found to deal with objectionable demagogues. The *quaestio* that followed was even more insidious, for it preserved the semblance of legality without its substance.

Special *quaestiones* were not a novelty in 132. But those set up simply on the basis of a senatorial decree and without express popular sanction appear only rarely in the sources. Of these the best known is the tribunal designed to investigate the Bacchanalian conspiracy in 186. Apart from it there is mention only of a poisoning case in 180 and the murder investigation against the *publicani* in 138.[70] In 132 this method was resorted to once again, but for the first time with serious political implications. The earlier instances of a court established in consequence of a senatorial decree seem to have been justified by the need for swift and decisive action to provide adequate police protection. There is no reason to believe that there was any popular disapproval of the measures taken in 186, 180, and 138. In 132, however, Ti. Gracchus' followers were prosecuted for a political crime: pursuance of Gracchan policy.[71]

The moment was a triumphant one for the Scipionic group. Others had objected to Ti. Gracchus; some of his own supporters had abandoned him. But it was the Scipionic *factio* that had seized the reins of leadership. The tide seemed to be running in their direction. Weighty political implications could be drawn from actions like the deposition of a tribune and the administration of funds from a foreign principality, and opinion appears to have turned against the sympathizers of Tiberius. Even a significant portion of both the rural and urban *plebs* seems to have defected.[72] Enemies of Tiberius had put pressure on their *clientelae*. No proceedings were undertaken in 133 against Scipio Nasica for his deed. P. Scaevola, in fact, sponsored senatorial resolutions to honor the assassin.[73] The consular posts for 132 went to P. Popillius Laenas and P. Rupilius, who presided over the investigatory tribunal of that year.[74] Since Rupilius was later in the year despatched to Sicily to take charge of the slave war, the trials before their commission must have taken place early, before hostility to the Gracchan movement could die down.

[70] On the Bacchanalian case, see *FIRA*, I.240-241; Livy, 39.8-19. For the case in 180, see Livy, 40.37; cf. R. L. Calvert, "M. Claudius Marcellus, cos. II, 155 B.C.," *Athenaeum*, 39 (1961), 11-23. For the case of the *publicani*, see Cic. *Brutus*, 85-88.

[71] Val. Max. 4.7.1: *qui cum Graccho consenserant.*

[72] Plut. *Ti. Gracch.* 16.2; Appian, *BC*, 1.14; cf. Earl, *Ti. Gracchus*, 115-117.

[73] Cic. *De Domo*, 91; *Pro Planc.* 88. Astin, *Scip. Aem.*, 228, has no warrant for throwing out this evidence.

[74] Val. Max. 4.7.1; Vell. Pat. 2.7.4; cf. Sallust, *Iug.* 31.7.

Rupilius was a Scipionic protégé; he owed his consulship to the support of Scipio. Rupilius' daughter married a Q. Fabius, probably the son of Q. Fabius Maximus Servilianus, also a Scipionic adherent. The younger Fabius then served with his father-in-law in Sicily in that year. Connections between the Popillii and the Scipionic group are more difficult to demonstrate but not unlikely.[75] The two consuls, we are told, relied heavily on the advice of C. Laelius, and also, apparently, on the assistance of Scipio Nasica, who served either as inquisitor or prosecutor.[76] It is clear that the prosecution of Gracchus' followers was largely a Scipionic venture.

So far as we can tell, the men hauled before the tribunal of 132 were not Romans of any real stature. The most noteworthy was Tiberius' tutor C. Blossius of Cumae, who was summoned before the *quaestio*. Blossius sought to implore pardon through a private interview with Laelius. But friendship for Ti. Gracchus would hardly have counted as mitigating circumstances to Laelius' mind. Evidently realizing this, Blossius fled to Asia rather than appear before the tribunal.[77]

Beyond Blossius few names are known. Plutarch asserts that Diophanes the rhetorician was summarily executed and that a certain C. Villius received the punishment of the sack. Many others were banished without trial and still others simply seized and slain.[78] This account is almost certainly exaggerated. We know from the affair of Blossius that legal process was carefully followed, whatever the unconstitutionality of the tribunal itself. That some rioting in the streets may have led to unwarranted murders is not to be denied, but is unconnected with the judicial commission. Banishments were surely pronounced, and, in a strict sense, without trial, but these were doubtless decrees of *interdictio* following what must have been numerous voluntary exiles, to which Blossius himself had recourse. The punishment of Villius, an unknown personality,

[75] For Rupilius and the slave war, see *MRR*, I.498. On Scipionic support for his consulship, see Cic. *De Amicit.* 73: *ut Scipio P. Rupilium potuit consulem efficere;* cf. *De Amicit.* 69. For the marriage alliance with Fabius Servilianus, see Val. Max. 2.7.3. For associations between Popillii and the Scipiones, see Earl, *Latomus,* 19 (1960), 657-666.

[76] For Laelius, see Val. Max. 4.7.1: *Laelium, cuius consilio praecipue consules utebantur;* and Cic. *De Amicit.* 37: *aderam Laenati et Rupilio consulibus in consilio* (Laelius speaking). For Nasica, see Plut. *Ti. Gracch.* 20.

[77] Cic. *De Amicit.* 37; cf. Val. Max. 4.7.1. Plut. *Ti. Gracch.* 20 offers a variant version that Blossius actually underwent prosecution and was cross-examined by Scipio Nasica.

[78] Plut. *Ti. Gracch.* 20: τοὺς μὲν ἐξεκήρυττον ἀκρίτους τοὺς δὲ συλλαμβάνοντες ἀπεκτίννυσαν. Cf. also Orosius, 5.9.3, who speaks of two hundred supporters killed, doubtless an excessive figure.

indicates that he was convicted of parricide, and that Plutarch has inadvertently included him among the victims of political persecution. Diophanes, of course, was one of Ti. Gracchus' tutors, and would have been pursued on that account. The commentary of Plutarch may suggest that he was slain in the rioting and not executed as the result of judicial investigation. Whatever the truth of this matter it appears that the victims of the Popillian commission were largely small fry and non-Romans. The explanation for this choice of victims may not be simply that the Scipionic group feared to attack the more prominent individuals behind Ti. Gracchus, but that it represents part of the propaganda campaign to associate Tiberius' power grab with essentially non-Roman ideas and supporters.[79]

On this basis, we may perhaps associate with this witch-hunt C. Gracchus' defense of his friend Vettius, a defense that first made Gaius' reputation.[80] Plutarch seems to date the trial not long before C. Gracchus' election to the quaestorship in 127. But his reputation had been made well before that time, and his previous public appearances had included a famous speech in 131. The trial of Vettius probably occurred not long after Gaius' return from his service in Spain. In that event, nothing stands in the way of identifying the prosecution with one of those under the Popillian tribunal.[81] Vettius, therefore, may be one of the Italian clients of Tiberius, now attacked, among others, in order to scatter Tiberius' non-Roman support. It was possibly this same Vettius who was satirized by Lucilius, a conjecture that, if true, fits nicely with the Scipionic prosecution of Tiberius' followers.[82] No further victims of the tribunal of 132 are known to us.

Perhaps the eloquent testimony of C. Gracchus on behalf of Vettius began to stem the tide. His speech, we are told, was the talk of the town.[83] In any event, the Scipionic group had done its worst. The elements of a crisis were no longer in the air, and the death of Tiberius may already have taken on some of the aura of martyrdom. In late 132 the sup-

[79] The U.S. House Un-American Activities Committee provides an instructive parallel. On Diophanes as Tiberius' tutor, see Cic. *Brutus,* 104; Strabo, 13.617.

[80] Plut. *C. Gracch.* 1.3: δίκην τὲ τινι τῶν φίλων φεύγοντι βεττίῳ συνειπών τοῦ δήμου συνενθουσιῶντος ὑφ' ἡδονῆς καὶ βακχευόνος περὶ αὐτόν, ἀπέδειξε τοὺς ἄλλους ῥήτορας παίδων μηδὲν διαφέροντας.

[81] Münzer, *RE,* 16.1843-1844, "Vettius," n. 2; *ORF,* 177-178.

[82] Quintilian, 1.5.56: *Taceo de Tuscis et Sabinis et Praenestinis quoque . . . eorum sermone utentem Vettium Lucilius insectatur.* See Cichorius, *Unt. zu Luc.,* 348-349. That he was a Vettius Sabinus, however. as Cichorius suggests, cannot be proved.

[83] Plut. *C. Gracch.* 1.3.

porters of the Gracchi began to regain courage. The obvious target was
Scipio Nasica. M. Fulvius Flaccus provides a thread of continuity. Scion
of the noble house of Fulvii Flacci who had long cooperated with the
Claudii, he had been with Tiberius at the end and had warned him of
impending danger. Now he initiated a prosecution against Tiberius'
assassin.[84] Tensions were high and it was not easy to produce impartial
jurors. Even the learned jurist P. Scaevola, proposed by Flaccus, was
rejected by Scipio Nasica.[85] His reputation for strict adherence to justice
had been tarnished by ambiguity and vacillation in the previous year.
Details of the proceedings defy reconstruction. The selection of jurors
shows that the case was not to be heard before the people; Cicero's
account makes it clear that the jurors were being chosen from the ranks
of the senate. The evidence is insufficient to determine whether it was a
special tribunal or a standing court. A standing court on murder does
not seem to have existed as recently as 138, and we have no indication
of a change before 132.[86] A special *quaestio,* however, would presumably have been in the charge of the consuls, who were hardly likely to
befriend the Gracchan cause. Feeling, in any case, was bitter against
Scipio Nasica. His friends in the senate avoided further embarrassment
by appointing an embassy to Asia of which Nasica was conveniently
made a member. He lived out the brief remainder of his life in Pergamum.[87]

Nasica's departure was an admission of defeat by the Scipionic group,
and a significant victory for their opponents. The victory was rapidly
enhanced. Nasica seems to have died within the year, and his successor
as *pontifex maximus* was P. Licinius Crassus Mucianus, the first man
not of the Scipionic faction to hold the office in twenty years. Mucianus,
now the acknowledged leader of the Claudian bloc, along with Ap.
Claudius Pulcher, was elected to the consulship of 131, defeating the
Scipionic candidate L. Rupilius, brother of the consul of 132, in the
process.[88] Moreover, the two censors of 131 represent a clear setback
for the Scipionic group. One was Q. Metellus Macedonicus, a long-

---

[84] Plut. *Ti. Gracch.* 21; Cic. *De Orat.* 2.285.

[85] Cic. *De Orat.* 2.285; *cum ei M. Flaccus, multis probris obiectis P.
Mucium iudicem tulisset, "Eiero," inquit, "iniquus est;" cum esset admur-
muratum, "Ah", inquit, "P.C., non ego mihi illum iniquum eiero, verum
omnibus."*

[86] See above, Chapter I, note 68.

[87] Plut. *Ti. Gracch.* 21; Val. Max. 5.3.2; *Vir. Ill.* 64.9; Cic. *Pro Flacco,* 75;
Pliny, *NH,* 7.120; cf. Strabo, 14.1.38; *ILS,* 8886.

[88] On the pontifical succession, see *MRR,* I.499. On the elections for 131,
see Cic. *De Amicit.* 73; *Tusc. Disp.* 4.40.

standing enemy of Scipio. His censorship was duly attacked by Lucilius.[89] The other was the mercurial Q. Pompeius, once a protégé of the Scipionic bloc, but quarrels with men like L. Furius Philus and C. Laelius had announced his independence. The process may be further illustrated. Metellus and Pompeius named a new *princeps senatus* in 131 to succeed Ap. Claudius Pulcher, who died at about that time. Their choice was L. Cornelius Lentulus Lupus, consul in 156, who, it can be shown from the fragments of Lucilius, was a bitter enemy of Scipio.[90] The lines of a new alliance may perhaps already be discerned — in the next generation Pompeius' son or grandson, the consul of 88, was to be a strong adherent of the Metellan group — but it still lay in the future. In 131 the Scipionic faction faced severe challenge. The Gracchani were prepared to capitalize on the martyrdom of Tiberius and on the political issues raised in the past few years.

Scipio Aemilianus had returned to Rome, probably in late 132, to celebrate a triumph over the Numantines.[91] His attitude toward the death of Ti. Gracchus had already been registered while he was in Spain: "So perish all who do likewise." [92] Scipio's enemies did not lose the opportunity. The Gracchan movement had attracted some young aristocrats with a taste for progressive reform and with an inclination towards the battles of the forum. Among them was a vigorous, eloquent, and charming orator, C. Papirius Carbo, a contemporary of Ti. Gracchus.[93] Carbo was tribune in 131 and also a member or about to become a member of the Gracchan commission.[94] He now sought to lay the groundwork for further reform by proposing a bill for iteration of the tribunate. The measure was vigorously supported by C. Gracchus, but opposed by C.

[89] Cf. A. Berger, "A Note on Gellius, *N.A.* I.6," *AJP*, 67 (1946), 320-328.

[90] Horace, *Sat.* 2.1.63ff and Schol. Perseus *Sat.* 1.114; Lucilius, Bk. I, *passim;* XXVIII.805-811, 1131, 1138-1141 (*ROL*, 3.2-18, 260, 366, 370); Marx, *Luc. Carm. Rel.*, xxxv-xl, 276-277; Cichorius, *Unt. zu Luc.*, 58, 77-86, 225-226, 346-347; cf. *MRR*, I.501, n. 1. This choice for *princeps senatus* must have been particularly galling to Scipio, the only other living patrician ex-censor.

[91] Livy, *Per.* 59; cf. Cic. *Phil.* 11.18; Eutrop. 4.19.

[92] Plut. *Ti. Gracch.* 21: ὡς ἀπόλοιτο καὶ ἄλλος ὅ τις τοιαῦτα γε ῥέξοι; the quotation is from Homer, *Odyssey*, 1.47.

[93] On Carbo's oratorical gifts and personality, see Cic. *Brutus,* 105-106.

[94] The tribunate of Carbo has sometimes been dated to 130 on the basis of Cicero's remark in *De Amicit.* 96, dramatic date 129, that it was *nuper;* so Fraccaro, *Studi Storici,* 5 (1912), 440; *MRR*, I.503, n. 1. This is hardly convincing testimony. Val. Max. 6.2.3 indicates that the tribunate followed shortly after the return of Scipio from Spain, and the date of 131 seems to fit the historical events more easily. Cf. Niccolini, *Fast. Trib. Pleb.*, 154; Münzer, *RE*, 36.1017-1018, "Papirius," n. 33.

Laelius and by Scipio himself.[95] In the course of debate on the measure, Carbo utilized the occasion to embarrass Scipio before the populace by questioning him again on the fate of Ti. Gracchus. The answer was a repetition of his statement made in Spain the previous year: *iure caesum videri*. Velleius prefaces Scipio's answer with the conditional clause *si is occupandae rei publicae animum habuisset*.[96] But if Scipio's response was a hedge it was not a successful one. An uproar ensued, and Scipio told the crowd what he thought of it: *quorum noverca est Italia*.[97] There is no ambiguity here. Scipio Aemilianus washed his hands of the mob demonstrating on behalf of the Gracchan movement. Carbo's bill was, in fact, defeated, but the defeat is not to be taken as a personal triumph for the Scipionic group. Iteration of the tribunate was an issue that had turned a large segment of public opinion against Tiberius in 133 and the same sentiment seems to have carried the day against Carbo in 131. That Scipio's position vis-à-vis the supporters of the Gracchi was not enhanced is demonstrated by the passage of another of Carbo's measures in that year, a bill for secret ballot in legislative *comitia,* and, more important, by the fact that Scipio failed to secure the prize military plum of the year, command against the rebel Aristonicus in Asia.[98]

It is in connection with this latter event that the only judicial case known to us in 131 occurred. The consuls, P. Crassus Mucianus and L. Valerius Flaccus, both coveted the Asian command. But Crassus, who doubled as *pontifex maximus,* checked his colleague by imposing a fine upon him and warning him not to desert the sacrifices. It was a convenient stroke of fortune for Crassus that Flaccus happened to be *Flamen Martialis.* Flaccus appealed to the popular assembly, which, though remitting the fine, stood by the consul and ordered the *flamen* to remain in Rome. That Flaccus was acting in Scipionic interests cannot be maintained, since Scipio himself desired this command. The decision was left to the tribal assembly, and the measure of Scipio's

---

[95] Livy, *Per.* 59; fragments of Gaius' speech are collected in *ORF,* 178-179.

[96] Vell. Pat. 2.4.4.

[97] Vell. Pat. 2.4.4; Val. Max. 6.2.3; *Vir. Ill.* 58.8; Plut. *Apophth. Scip. Min.* 22; Polyaenus, *Strat.* 8.6.5. The argument of Fraccaro, *Studi Storici,* 5 (1912), 390-393, that this fragment belongs to 129 rather than to the context of Carbo's bill has been successfully refuted by A. E. Astin, *"Dicta Scipionis* of 131 B.C.," *CQ,* 10 (1960), 137-139.

[98] For the measure on secret ballot, see Cic. *De Leg.* 3.35. Astin, *CQ,* 10 (1960), 138, makes the attractive suggestion that Carbo's first bill was defeated through aristocratic control of clients' votes and that the second was proposed for the purpose of checking this control. For the command against Aristonicus, see Cic. *Phil.* 11.18.

decline in popularity may be read in the vote of thirty-three tribes for Crassus and two for Aemilianus.[99]

The Scipionic faction continued to lose ground. Scipio Nasica had been induced to seek refuge in Asia, where he perished. Scipio Aemilianus himself, conqueror of Carthage and Spain, was denied a command against Aristonicus. The consular elections for 130 continue to illustrate the trend. L. Cornelius Lentulus Lupus was elected to one of the posts, and M. Perperna, possibly associated with the Claudii,[100] secured the other. On the death of Lentulus in the year of his consulship, he was succeeded by Ap. Claudius Pulcher, probably a cousin of Ap. Claudius Pulcher the father-in-law of Ti. Gracchus.[101] In the same year, Crassus Mucianus perished in the war against Aristonicus, but the coveted office of *pontifex maximus* went to Mucianus' brother, P. Scaevola.[102] Men hostile to the Scipionic bloc thus completely dominated all the higher magistracies of Rome in 131 and 130.

The Gracchan movement had obviously caused a serious reconsideration of political allegiances. In this respect the tribunate of Tiberius marks a real watershed. The once proud and powerful alliance that centered on Scipio Aemilianus was breaking up. Motives are not easy to disentangle. Some may have found idealistic reform appealing; others were perhaps repelled by intransigence and the violence of reaction against Ti. Gracchus. Capable and influential figures like P. Scaevola and Q. Pompeius had already severed ties with the Scipios. Younger men too, men of talent and promise, were looking elsewhere. C. Carbo was probably never connected with the Scipionic circle. He had learned his oratory at the feet of M. Aemilius Lepidus and Ser. Sulpicius Galba.[103] But C. Porcius Cato, Scipio Aemilianus' nephew,[104] was also captured by the glamor and excitement of Ti. Gracchus. Their friendship was close and when Tiberius set out upon a program of reform, Cato, along with Carbo and C. Gracchus, followed him loyally and unstintingly.[105] C. Fannius, in his early career and background, was a Scipionic adherent

---

[99] Cic. *Phil.* 11.18. On the legal powers of the *pontifex maximus* over subordinate religious officials, see Mommsen, *Strafrecht*, 559.

[100] See Münzer, *Röm. Adelsp.*, 95-97.

[101] *MRR*, I.502; Münzer, *RE*, 6.2667-2668, "Claudius," n. 11.

[102] Sources in *MRR*, I.503.

[103] Cic. *Brutus*, 96; cf. *De Orat.* 1.40, 2.9.

[104] Miltner, *RE*, 43.105, "Porcius," n. 5.

[105] Cic. *De Amicit.* 39: *At vero Ti. Gracchum sequebantur C. Carbo, C. Cato, et minime tum quidem Gaius frater, nunc idem acerrimus.* By contrast, another nephew of Scipio, Q. Aelius Tubero, broke a friendship with Tiberius when the latter shook the equilibrium of the republic; Cic. *De Amicit.* 37: *Tiberium quidem Gracchum rem publicam vexantem a Q. Tuberone aequalibusque amicis derelictum videbamus.*

if ever there was one. A personal friend of Aemilianus and a student of
Panaetius, he was a member of the philosophical Scipionic circle. In 146
he was a legate of Scipio at Carthage, and in 141 he served in Spain
under Q. Fabius Servilianus, another Scipionic supporter.[106] His marriage
to the younger of C. Laelius' two daughters cemented the allegiance
with family ties.[107] By 123, however, he was the choice of C. Gracchus
for the consulship of the following year.[108] The old coalition had lost
another member.

The Claudio-Fulvian alliance of the 140's and 130's had also lost
stature in the ranks of the aristocracy. Factional politics was one thing;
association with a revolutionary tribune quite another. If one may judge
from M. Fulvius Flaccus, consul in 125, the Fulvii continued to support
the Gracchan cause. But the defection of P. Scaevola no doubt brought
others in its wake. Evidence on specific individuals eludes research.
Death, in any event, removed the foremost spokesmen for the group.
By 129, Ti. Gracchus, Ap. Claudius, and Crassus Mucianus had all
perished. Leadership had to pass into the younger and less experienced
hands of C. Gracchus, M. Fulvius Flaccus, and C. Carbo.

Another *factio* emerged from these turbulent years with renewed
vigor and influence. Q. Metellus Macedonicus, the conspicuous and
active censor of 131, boasted a distinguished war record and a reputation for severity.[109] He had managed to pursue a line independent of the
Scipiones and the Gracchani, and now spearheaded a growing and powerful coalition. The Servilii Caepiones and the Aurelii Cottae show consistent links with the Metelli in the 130's and later. The Cornelii Lentuli
provided two consecutive *principes senatus* between 131 and 115.
Enemies of the Scipiones, they too may owe their success to a connection with the Metellan *factio*. As so often, the astute P. Mucius Scaevola
serves as a weathervane. He had abandoned both the Scipionic circle
and the Gracchan movement; but in 130 he reached the exalted post of
pontifex maximus and turns up in overt cooperation with Metellus
Macedonicus. As Cicero reports in a revealing and significant passage,

[106] On his involvement in the Scipionic circle, see Cic. *De Rep.* 1.18;
Brutus, 101; and cf. Fannius' role generally as a participant in the dialogues
De Republica and *De Amicitia*. For his service in Carthage, see Plut. *Ti.
Gracch.* 4.5; in Spain, Appian, *Iber.* 67.

[107] Cic. *Brutus*, 101; *De Amicit.* 8. That this man is also the historian C.
Fannius is uncertain because of Cicero's own confusion as well as hopeless-
ness in the text of *Ad Att.* 16.13.2. See Münzer, *RE*, 13.1987, "Fannius," n.
7; "Die Fanniusfrage," *Hermes* 55 (1920), 427-442; Fraccaro, *Opuscula*,
2.103-123; D. R. Shackleton Bailey, *Cicero's Letters to Atticus* (Cambridge,
Eng., 1966), V.400-403.

[108] Plut. *C. Gracch.* 8.2, 11.2.

[109] On his censorship, see *MRR*, I.500.

the enemies of Scipio Aemilianus had once been marshalled by Ap. Claudius and Crassus Mucianus, but by 129 the leaders of the opposition worthy of mention are Metellus and P. Scaevola.[110] This was a new era.

An opportunity still remained to resuscitate the falling fortunes of the Scipionic group. The death of Ti. Gracchus had not entailed the repeal of his *lex agraria*. Even the Roman oligarchy acknowledged the necessity of land reform and Tiberius' measure, if not his methods, could be represented as conservative or as a safety-valve. At least one member of the oligarchy boasted of his role in restoring *ager publicus* from the *pastores* to the *aratores*.[111] Opposition to the Gracchani was political, not economic.[112] The work of the triumviral commission had gone on. But the task was a difficult and disruptive one. Much of the *ager publicus* had been acquired several generations earlier; few of the *possessores* could have produced any deeds. The passage of time and the transfer of titles made it very difficult to ascertain what was public land and what private. Every disputable effort to confiscate provoked a legal wrangle.[113] Especially troublesome was the problem of distinguishing *ager publicus* from land in the possession of allied communities and guaranteed to them by treaty. Boundaries were unclear and encroachment had been wide, probably on both sides. The *socii* now maintained that their rights and treaties were being violated by the agrarian commission. Scipio Aemilianus did not allow the occasion to pass, and proclaimed himself the champion of Rome's allies in Italy.[114] This maneuver was good propaganda and

[110] Cic. *De Rep.* 1.31: *obtrectatores autem et invidi Scipionis initiis factis a P. Crasso et Appio Claudio tenent nihilo minus illis mortuis senatus alteram partem dissidentem a vobis auctore Metello et P. Mucio;* see Gruen, *Athenaeum,* 43 (1965), 330-331.

[111] *ILS,* 23. The author of this famous *elogium* from Polla is anonymous. It may be Popillius Laenas (A. Degrassi, "Un nuovo miliario calabro della Via Popillia," *Philologus,* 99 [1955], 259-265) or T. Annius Luscus (V. Bracco, "L'*Elogium* di Polla," *RendNap.* 29 [1954], 5-38; and "Ancora sull' *elogium* di Polla," *RendNap,* 35 [1960], 149-163). Both were opponents of Ti. Gracchus. T. P. Wiseman, *"Viae Anniae,"* PBSR, 32 (1964), 21-37, has recently suggested T. Annius Rufus, praetor ca. 131. F. T. Hinrichs, "Der römische Strassenbau zur Zeit der Gracchen," *Historia,* 16 (1967), 162-176, falsely reports the inscription as including the name of Popillius Laenas. In any case, the oligarchy clearly was prepared to claim credit for land reform.

[112] See Val. Max. 7.2.6: *Par illa sapientia senatus. Tib. Gracchum tribunum plebis agrariam legem promulgare ausum morte multavit. Idem ut secundum legem eius per triumviros ager populo viritim divideretur egregie censuit. Siquidem gravissimae seditionis eodem tempore et auctorem et causam sustulit.* Cf. Plut. *Ti. Gracch.* 21.1.

[113] Appian, *BC,* 1.18.

[114] Cic. *De Rep.* 1.31, 3.41: Appian, *BC,* 1.19; Schol. Bob. 118, Stangl. There is no need to deny, of course, that Scipio felt some genuine sympathy for Italian claims.

effective. It need not imply that all classes of Italians sought redress. The large landowners would have been most affected by the agrarian legislation and they may have lobbied in Rome, though it is not unlikely that the idea originated with Scipio himself rather than being forced upon him by Italian laments.[115]

The outright abolition of the triumviral board would have been risky and probably fruitless. Scipio proposed the compromise solution that whenever objection arose to seizure of a particular plot of land the dispute be referred not to the commissioners themselves but to the consuls. Such a move would, in effect, abolish the judicial functions of the agrarian triumvirs.[116] The Gracchan *factio* was thrust onto the defensive. M. Fulvius Flaccus and C. Gracchus headed a bitter and spirited opposition to Scipio's efforts.[117] Discussion seems to have taken place both in the senate and in the assembly, but the measure passed.[118] This was a significant victory for Scipio. We are told that he was triumphantly escorted home by his supporters.[119]

There is an odd element in Scipio's measure that has not aroused

[115] There is no space here to go into the vexed question of whether Ti. Gracchus' measure allowed for distribution of land to Italians as well as Romans. One might point out, however, that there is no evidence to suggest that Italians were complaining in 129 about ineligibility for land grants. We hear only of neglect of the *foedera;* Cic. *De Rep.* 3.41. Appian's account is clear and consistent on the fact that Ti. Gracchus was much concerned with the *socii.* For this view of the measure, see Gabba, *App. BC Lib. Prim.,* 59; contra: Fraccaro, "Review of Carcopino, *Autour des Gracques,*" *Athenaeum,* 9, (1931), 294; A. Bernardi, "La Guerra Sociale e le lotte dei partiti in Roma," *Nuov. Riv. Stor.,* 28-29 (1944-45), 65; Badian, *Foreign Clientelae, 264-70 B.C.* (Oxford, 1958), 169-173; Earl, *Ti. Gracchus,* 20-21.

[116] Appian, *BC,* 1.19. A fragment of Scipio's speech is preserved by Macrob. *Sat.* 3.14.6; cf. Fraccaro, *Studi Storici,* 5 (1912), 393-400; *ORF,* 133-134. Whether this bill removed the commission's judicial authority only in cases involving allies, as was long ago suggested (E. G. Hardy, "Were the *Lex Thoria* of 118 B.C. and the *Lex Agraria* of 111 B.C. Reactionary Laws?" *JP,* 31 [1910], 272-273) or altogether (Bilz, *Politik des Scipio,* 74, n. 208) cannot be determined with any certainty.

[117] Orosius, 5.10.9: *P. Scipionem Africanum pridie pro contione de periculo salutis suae contestatum, quod sibi pro patria laboranti ab improbis et ingratis denuntiari cognovisset;* Polyaenus, 18.6.5; Plut. *C. Gracch.* 10.4; *Apophth. Scip. Min.* 22-23.

[118] Cic. *De Amicit.* 12: *senatu dimisso;* Orosius, 5.10.9: *pro contione.* That the measure secured passage is expressly stated by Appian, *BC,* 1.19: ᾧ δὴ καὶ μάλιστα ἔπεισεν εἶναι δοκοῦντι δικαίῳ. The doubts of R. M. Geer, "Notes on the Land Law of Tiberius Gracchus," *TAPA,* 70 (1939), 30-36, cannot get around this testimony.

[119] Cic. *De Amicit.* 12. That he was accompanied by a crowd of senators, people, and allies, however, is an obvious exaggeration. On Scipio's last year, see the lucid account of Astin, *Scip. Aem.,* 238-241.

curiosity. The bill gave to the consul authority on judicial matters connected with land distribution. Yet of the two chief magistrates in 129, one, M'. Aquillius, was off in Asia, and the other, C. Sempronius Tuditanus, deliberately avoided the new functions assigned to him by going off to war against the Iapydes.[120] Their absence makes nonsense of the modern conjecture that the consuls were Scipionic supporters.[121] Was Scipio deceived or misled? It would be perverse to believe that the measure was designed to be effective for only a single year. Scipio may already have had in mind the consular elections for 128. It is revealing, in any event, that the successful candidates turned out to be Cn. Octavius and T. Annius Rufus. The former was probably the elder brother of M. Octavius, who as tribune in 133 had sought to block the efforts of Ti. Gracchus by *intercessio*.[122] Rufus was doubtless a relative of the T. Annius Luscus who had clashed with Tiberius and was on the verge of being prosecuted by him.[123] These were men who could be relied upon to hamstring the activities of the agrarian commission.

Feelings now ran high on both sides. The claim that Scipio was aspiring to a dictatorship was doubtless made, but there is no reason to ascribe any substance to this charge.[124] It was not long before Scipio was found dead one morning, the tablet for an unwritten speech to the assembly at his bedside.[125] The ancient sources have preserved a bewildering variety of explanations for this death. It is beyond our scope to investigate in detail the scattered suggestions of assassination, suicide, or natural death. Suffice it to say that the most important fact about the aftermath of this affair is that no investigation was undertaken.[126] In view of the bitter hostility in the air, this failure would be inexplicable, had there been so much as the slightest hint of murder. The flames of suspicion would have been fanned, not extinguished, by Scipionic supporters. The funeral

[120] Appian, *BC,* 1.19.

[121] As proposed by W. Schur, *Das Zeitalter des Marius und Sulla, Klio Beiheft* (Leipzig, 1942), 29; Pareti, *Storia di Roma,* III.344-345; cf. also Münzer, *RE,* 4(2).1441-1442, "Sempronius," n. 92. It is worth noting that Tuditanus took with him as legate D. Junius Brutus Callaicus, a man associated with the Claudian group; Livy, *Per.* 59; *MRR,* I.505.

[122] The consul of 128 was son of a Gnaeus, therefore probably the eldest son. The date of his consulship also indicates, of course, that he was older than M. Octavius.

[123] See above, pp. 55-56.

[124] Plut. *Apophth. Scip. Min.* 22-23; Cic. *De Rep.* 6.12; cf. 1.31. Münzer, *Röm. Adelsp.,* 100, takes this report much more seriously than is warranted. Cf. Bilz, *Politik des Scipio,* 77. On the extreme tension at this time, see Obseq. 28a, with Astin, *Scip. Aem.,* 240-241.

[125] Appian, *BC,* 1.20.

[126] Cic. *Pro Mil.* 16; Livy, *Per.* 59; *Vell. Pat.* 2.4.6; Plut. *C. Gracch.* 10.4.

oration, written by C. Laelius, and delivered, apparently, by Scipio's nephew Q. Fabius Maximus Allobrogicus, clearly refers to death by natural causes. That opponents of the Gracchi would stir up all forms of rumor later is only to be expected. Every possible candidate is named: not only Carbo, but C. Gracchus, Fulvius Flaccus, Cornelia, and Sempronia! None of this can count as decisive evidence for homicide.[127] The measure of Scipio's unpopularity with the people is demonstrated by their refusal to bestow upon him a public funeral.[128] The Gracchan movement had brought the *plebs* onto the political scene with a vengeance. Factional politics could no longer operate without taking them into consideration. Scipio Aemilianus, once so popular with the people that they had voted him two irregular commands against Carthage and Numantia and had elected him to the censorship, concluded his career as their bitter enemy.

The death of Scipio did not entail the immediate dissolution of the group that had claimed him as its spokesman and had pursued his policies. Political factions do not usually disappear overnight.[129] Growing defections and the demise of its leader weakened its influence. But the cancellation of the agrarian commission's judicial powers had been a telling victory and may have rallied a significant number of senators (and their clients) behind the group. Anti-Gracchan consuls reached office in 128, and, of those who succeeded them, one was the stern and exacting L. Cassius Ravilla, whose earlier career had shown overt cooperation with Scipio Aemilianus.[130]

The distribution of land, Appian reports, was slowed.[131] The slow-

---

[127] On the funeral oration, see Schol. Bob. 118, Stangl: *eo morborum temovit et in eodem tempore periit;* Cic. *Pro Mur.* 75; *ORF,* 121-122. The divergent account in Cic. *De Orat.* 2.341 that the speech was delivered by Q. Aelius Tubero, another nephew of Scipio, may be an error; cf. Fraccaro, *Studi Storici,* 5 (1912), 357-358; *ORF,* 121. Carcopino, *Autour des Gracques,* 88-121, presents a persuasive case for natural death, stressing the funeral speech of Laelius and the unlikelihood of any of the persons named by the sources as possible assassins. Cf. also Badian's review of *ORF* in *Studies,* 249. Contra: M. Renard, "L'Assassinat de Scipion Emilien," *Rev. Univ. Brux.,* 37 (1932), 483-498.

[128] Appian, *BC,* 1.20; Pliny, *NH,* 10.123.

[129] Cf. the speech of C. Gracchus against Scipio's nephew Q. Aelius Tubero which denounces *inimicorum meorum factio; ORF,* 194. In 123, another nephew of Scipio, Q. Fabius Allobrogicus, received senatorial censure for his activities in Spain on C. Gracchus' motion; Plut. *C. Gracch.* 6.2.

[130] See above, pp. 39-40. The political connections of Ravilla's consular colleague L. Cornelius Cinna are unknown and do not repay conjecture.

[131] Appian, *BC,* 1.21: τὴν δὲ διαίρεσιν τῆς γῆς οἱ κεκτημένοι καὶ ὡς ἐπὶ προφάσεσι ποικίλαις διέφερον ἐπὶ πλεῖστον; cf. Appian, *BC,* 1.27.

down may be exaggerated,[132] but there can be no doubt that distributions ran into difficulties when dealing with Italian land. The consuls of 128 and 127 would have seen to that. Scipio Aemilianus had raised the matter of the Italian allies and turned it into a significant political issue. The large Italian landowners were the chief beneficiaries, but many poor Italians who depended for livelihood upon the pasture lands held in common by Italian states would also have approved.[133] The Italian question had now entered the arena of Roman politics, and the Gracchan group was swift to utilize this fact for its own purposes. M. Fulvius Flaccus, a friend of the Gracchi, had matured as a politician during the turbulence of the past decade. Although an orator of only moderate gifts, he brought to the forum the equipment of a writer and an intellectual.[134] He was capable of seeing the Italian issue in a broader context. Older than either Carbo or C. Gracchus, Flaccus seems to have assumed leadership of the Gracchan *factio*. As consul in 125, he sought to allay Italian misgivings about land distribution by offering in return Roman citizenship or, for those who preferred, *provocatio* against Roman magistrates.[135] This proposal was already in the air in 126 and is to be connected with the law of M. Junius Pennus expelling aliens from Rome.[136] The latter measure was surely a counter-stroke on the part of conservatives who were prepared to play upon Italian sentiment for political advantage but not to countenance their presence in Rome on behalf of the Gracchani. The importance of Pennus' measure is underscored by the violence of C. Gracchus' speech against it.[137] The Italians now became a political football among Roman senatorial factions. The revival of Scipionic influence had been due to the raising of this issue, and now the Gracchan group had snatched it up with considerable embarrassment to the opposing *factio,* compelled to demonstrate its real feelings about Italian aims. It may be of significance that an Aemilius Lepidus, of a family long hostile to the Scipios, was consul in 126, and his colleague,

[132] Cf. the statements of Dio, fr. 83.2, and Livy, *Per.* 59, perhaps also exaggerated on the other side. The rise in census figures by 125 indicates that the work of the agrarian commission had been substantial; Livy, *Per.* 60.

[133] Such is the view of Bernardi, *Nuov. Riv. Stor.,* 28-29 (1944-45), 68-72.

[134] Cic. *Brutus,* 108.

[135] The connection of Flaccus' bill with the agrarian problem is expressly asserted by Appian, *BC,* 1.21.

[136] Cic. *Brutus,* 109; *De Off.* 3.47. The connection is acutely pointed out by Badian, *For. Client.,* 176-178.

[137] Festus, 388, L (*ORF,* 180): *eae nationes cum aliis rebus per avaritiam atque stultitiam res publicas suas amiserunt;* cf. Fraccaro, *Studi Storici,* 6 (1913), 76-78. The view of Bernardi, *Nuov. Riv. Stor.,* 28-29 (1944-45), 70, that the bill was never passed is refuted by Cic. *De Off.* 3.47: *male etiam, qui peregrinos urbibus uti prohibent, eosque exterminant, ut Pennus apud patres nostros, Papius nuper.*

L. Aurelius Orestes, was perhaps not unsympathetic to the Gracchan cause.[138] Flaccus was doubtless elected for 125 on the basis of his proposal, but the majority of the senate was hostile. His consular colleague, M. Plautius Hypsaeus, was no friend of the Gracchi, and appears to have led senatorial opposition against Flaccus.[139] The proposal was dropped, but not willingly. The senate eased the problem by sending the consul on a military mission to Massilia.[140]

The dangers of the Gracchan movement must now have impressed conservative senators more than ever. Not only agrarian reform but Italian enfranchisement was in the air; the senate's traditional control of its *clientelae,* a fundamental prop of the oligarchy, was in grave jeopardy. Senatorial leaders chose the path of reaction and repression. The revolt of Fregellae was ruthlessly crushed by the praetor L. Opimius, whose taste for violence and cruelty was to be demonstrated on more than one occasion.[141] The censorship could also be utilized as an instrument of conservatism and preservation of the status quo. The two censors of 125, Cn. Servilius Caepio and L. Cassius Longinus Ravilla, whatever their relations with one another, were united in their opposition to the Gracchani. The aged P. Cornelius Lentulus Lupus was named *princeps senatus* by these censors. An ardent foe of the Gracchi, Lentulus did not allow advanced years to dampen his enthusiasm for violence in 121.[142] It was a censorship in the old style, apparently, of stern and rigid adherence to traditional standards. Extravagance and ostentation were not to be tolerated.[143] The opportunity was soon at hand to attack C. Gracchus himself.

[138] Orestes selected C. Gracchus as his quaestor in that year; *MRR,* I.508. Plutarch's statement, *C. Gracch.* 1, that Gaius' despatching pleased his enemies neglects the fact that the Gracchi had ancestral connections in the island and that Gaius probably welcomed the post; cf. Badian, *For. Client.,* 166, 180.

[139] Val. Max. 9.5.1. A fragment of one of C. Gracchus' speeches against a Plautius has been preserved; Val. Max. 9.5.ext.4; *ORF,* 195. The identification with the consul of 125 is plausible; Lange, *Röm. Alterth.,* 3.43; Carcopino, *Autour des Gracques,* 195. The date and occasion of the speech are beyond knowing.

[140] Appian, *BC,* 1.34; that Flaccus was not cowed by senatorial opposition is demonstrated by Val. Max. 9.5.1: *Flaccus in totius amplissimi ordinis contemnenda maiestate versatus est.* Cf. Badian, *For. Client.,* 177-178. On Flaccus' activities in Gaul, cf. Fraccaro, "Un episodio delle agitazioni agrarie dei Gracchi," *Studies Presented to D. M. Robinson,* 2 (1953), 884-892.

[141] Sources in *MRR,* I.510.

[142] On Lentulus' appointment, see *MRR,* I.501, n. 1; cf. I.510. For his activities in 121, see below, p. 97.

[143] Ravilla would have taken special pleasure in imposing a fine on his old foe of 137, Lepidus Porcina; Vell. Pat. 2.10.1; Val. Max. 8.1.damn.7; Cic. *Brutus,* 97.

Gaius was young in years, but mature in judgment, and, to the oligarchy, dangerous and formidable. The martyrdom of his brother was a persistent theme, acutely exploited to focus attention upon himself.[144] Our own age has witnessed the capital to be made by an astute politician from the death of an elder brother in public service. Gaius was not a novice to the contests of the forum. Service on the agrarian commission since its inception had hardened him to controversy. The defense of Vettius evoked widespread admiration. In a hostile atmosphere he had spoken with vigor and courage for iteration of the tribunate and against summary expulsion of aliens from the city. In Sardinia he paraded ancestral connections on that island as well as in Numidia.[145] C. Gracchus was a man of both talent and industry. Eloquent, fiery, and emotional on the rostra, he could reduce even unfriendly listeners to tears. His personality was high-strung and his public appearances perhaps designedly theatrical.[146] But the orations were more than emotional outbursts; they were marked by elevated diction and informed by intellect and perception. Cicero rated him as unrivaled by his contemporary orators and judged his death a loss not only to the state but to Latin literature.[147]

C. Gracchus, aware of rapidly hardening senatorial hostility, could not afford a longer stay in Sardinia, where he and his commander had been twice prorogued on senatorial orders. He returned home in late spring or early summer 124 in order to recover lost ground.[148] He was immediately brought before the censors and charged with abandoning his commander before his term of duty was up.[149] This was not, of course, a criminal prosecution, for the censors had no judicial powers. It has been suggested that the censorial deliberation at which Gracchus was charged involved either the question of seating him in the senate or that of depriving him of his public horse.[150] But nothing is reported of an effort to exclude him from the senatorial lists, and after 129 all new senators seem to have been required to surrender the *equus publicus*.[151]

[144] Cic. *Brutus*, 126.

[145] For Gaius' actions abroad, see Plut. *C. Gracch.* 2.3.

[146] Cic. *De Orat.* 3.214; Plut. *Ti. Gracch.* 2.2.

[147] Cic. *Brutus*, 125-126.

[148] Fraccaro, *Studi Storici*, 6 (1913), 84, n. 1.

[149] Plut. *C. Gracch.* 2.4-5: κατηγορίας αὐτῷ γενομένης ἐπὶ τῶν τιμητῶν.

[150] For the senate seat, see Fraccaro, *Studi Storici*, 6 (1913), 80. For the question of the public horse, see *ORF*, 181; C. Nicolet, *L'Ordre Equestre a l'Epoque Republicaine, 312-43 av. J.C.* (Paris, 1966), 107-108.

[151] Cic. *De Rep.* 4.22; H. Hill, *The Roman Middle Class in the Republican Period* (Oxford, 1952), 105-106; contra: Nicolet, *L'Ordre Equestre*, 103-111. Of course, one cannot even be sure that Gaius was a senator by 124.

Censors, in reviewing the morals of the citizen body, did not require a special occasion to investigate the actions of a particular individual. During the review of his case, the issue of his early departure would naturally have been brought up. That he left without the permission of Sardinia's governor, Aurelius Orestes, is usually stated in modern works, but nowhere mentioned by the ancient sources. His enemies would nevertheless have thrown up his early departure to him. There is no warrant here for speaking of an "acquittal." No trial had taken place. That he could have warded off a censorial rebuke is most unlikely in view of the hostility of the censors. Plutarch tells us that Gracchus gave a ringing and impressive speech, but not that he convinced the censors.[152] A censorial *nota* is further indicated by the fact that he was compelled to defend his actions once more, this time at a *contio,* in order to assure his followers of his good character.[153]

A more serious charge was brewing. C. Gracchus' plans for a tribunate in the following year must have been known or certainly suspected. It was imperative for the opposition to remove him now, something that could be accomplished by a capital conviction, but not by a censorial *nota.* Gracchus was to be prosecuted for stimulating and abetting the revolt of Fregellae.[154] The charge must have been *perduellio* and would therefore have to be heard before the *populus.* This fact illuminates the events that immediately preceded the trial. Since the people had many reasons for sympathy with the Gracchan cause, the oligarchy sought to damage Gaius' character with a preliminary censorial *nota.* That effort also explains why Gaius felt obliged to defend his actions at a *contio,* prior to the formal filing of charges. That the trial itself actually took place has been doubted.[155] But Plutarch, though hardly precise, does indicate that accusations were brought and that the defendant cleared himself.[156] The fragment of Gaius' speech *pro se* almost certainly belongs to this trial.[157] The senatorial effort failed. Gaius escaped conviction,

---

[152] Plut. *C. Gracch.* 2.4. This account seems to imply, in fact, that Gaius did receive a censorial *nota,* much to the indignation of his audience: μετέστησε τὰς γνώμας τῶν ἀκουσάντων ὡς ἀπελθεῖν ἠδικῆσθαι τὰ μέγιστα δόξας. Two fragments of his speech *apud censores* are preserved; *ORF,* 181; Fraccaro, *Studi Storici,* 6 (1913), 80-81.

[153] Gellius, 15.12.1-4; Fraccaro, *Studi Storici,* 6 (1913), 81; *ORF,* 180-181.

[154] Plut. *C. Gracch.* 3: ἐκ τούτου πάλιν ἄλλας αἰτίας αὐτῷ καὶ δίκας ἐπῆγον ὡς τοὺς συμμάχους ἀφιστάντι καὶ κεκοινωνηκότι τῆς περὶ Φρέγελλαν ἐνδειχθείσης συνωμοσίας.

[155] Badian, *For. Client.,* 180, n. 3.

[156] Plut. *C. Gracch.* 3.1: αἰτίας αὐτῷ καὶ δίκας ἐπῆγον . . . ὁ δὲ πᾶσαν ὑποψίαν ἀπολυσάμενος καὶ φανεὶς καθαρός.

[157] Fraccaro, *Studi Storici,* 6 (1913), 87-88; *ORF,* 183.

and was forthwith elected to the tribunate for 123. A throng from the rural areas of Italy poured in to shout approval from roof-tops and tilings. But the continued balance of factional influence among the people is demonstrated by the fact that he stood only fourth on the list of tribunes returned for that year.[158]

Criminal trials, if investigated with care, often reveal much that remains obscure in a cursory examination. One case, the prosecution of M'. Aquillius, exposes and elucidates major issues faced in Rome on the eve of C. Gracchus' tribunate and possesses far-reaching implications for the political contests of the succeeding decades. The Gracchan era witnessed the acquisition of real power by men of business and money outside the ranks of the senatorial order. The number and influence of men engaged in financial operations had been expanding gradually for half a century or more. Areas shunned by many in the aristocracy as beneath their dignity were systematically exploited by enterprising and adventuresome Romans. Commerce and banking received powerful stimulus from Roman expansion abroad in the third and second centuries.[159] But more important and profitable, then as now, were state contracts. Organization, maintenance, and supervision of public works, in an era of building boom, provided not only work for the unemployed but profit for the contractor. Public property in Italy and abroad, saltworks, mines, forests, fisheries were also under the supervision of private hands for the convenience of the state. Of growing significance were the revenues from dependent territories farmed out to companies of taxgathers, the *publicani*. These *societates* eventually involved not only the big financiers but large numbers of individual investors and shareholders.[160] The considerable acquisition of provincial areas in the second century increased the scope of these operations in a dramatic fashion. Political developments of the Gracchan period were bound to affect the interests of the *publicani* profoundly. Distribution of *ager publicus* under Ti. Gracchus' legislation meant loss of income to the public coffers and reduction of profit to the tax-farmers who had administered these revenues. It is likely that business interests, if they took any part, were ranged in opposition to the Gracchan *factio*.[161] But the absorption of

[158] Plut. *C. Gracch.* 3.1-2. It is possible, however, that C. Gracchus had arranged election with a group of friendly colleagues. He does not seem to have had any tribunician opposition in 123.

[159] The usurer was already a familiar figure by the time of Cato the Elder, *De Re Rust.* pr. 1; cf. Hill, *Roman Middle Class,* 49-50.

[160] Polyb. 6.17; see Frank, *Econ. Survey,* I.148-157; corrected by P. A. Brunt, "The *Equites* in the Late Republic," in *2nd Int. Conf. of Econ. Hist. 1962* (Paris, 1965), I.138-141. Cf. Toynbee, *Hannibal's Legacy,* II.341-373.

[161] For opposition of the *equites* to Ti. Gracchus in 133, see Vell. Pat. 2.3.2; Livy, *Per.* 58; cf. Hill, *Roman Middle Class,* 103.

76

the fabulously wealthy province of Asia put a whole new aspect on the situation. That was the task of M'. Aquillius.

Aquillius, consul in 129, had stamped out the last resistance to Rome in Asia and had organized the province with the assistance of a ten-man senatorial commission. He returned to a triumph in November of 126.[162] At some time after that date, he underwent prosecution on a charge of extortion.[163] The year was probably 124.[164] It would be a mistake to see this trial simply in terms of factional politics. Aquillius' accuser, P. Cornelius Lentulus, belonged to a family hostile to the Scipios, but the *subscriptor* to the charge, C. Rutilius Rufus, was presumably a cousin or brother of P. Rutilius Rufus who had close connections with the Scipionic circle.[165] Personal, rather than political, grudges may be involved here. But political implications of the first magnitude, perhaps unforeseen by the prosecutors at the outset, rapidly emerged in this case.

A *lex Aufeia* apparently provided for the new Asian arrangements proposed by Aquillius and the senatorial commission. C. Gracchus spoke up in sharp opposition.[166] A decade had passed since the passage of his brother's *lex agraria*. He knew that the support of the *publicani* and business interests was worth winning for the Gracchan *factio*.[167] What the provisions of the *lex Aufeia* were is not specified in the sources, but no doubt the rich agricultural tithe was to be farmed out in the province under the watchful eye of the senatorial governor. It was precisely this practice that C. Gracchus, eliciting the approbation of the *publicani*, was to upset in 123, by having the contracts farmed out in Rome.[168] The formal charge against Aquillius was *repetundae;* imputation of bribery by Mithridates V was also made, but, in view of C. Gracchus' proposed

[162] Sources in *MRR*, I.504, 509.

[163] Cic. *Div. in Caec.* 69; *Pro Font.* 38; Appian, *Mithr.* 57; *BC*, 1.22; the charge is specified by Ps-Asconius, 204, Stangl: *Hic M'. Aquillius de pecuniis repetundis accusatus est.*

[164] Badian, *For. Client.*, 183, n. 9. Cic., *Div. in Caec.* 69, speaks of his prosecutor, Cornelius Lentulus, as *princeps senatus*. Lentulus' appointment came through the censors of 125. The bill to ratify Aquillius' *acta* doubtless followed his trial, and was opposed by C. Gracchus, who did not return to Rome before 124.

[165] For C. Rutilius Rufus, see Cic. *Div. in Caec.* 69; on P. Rutilius Rufus, see below, pp. 120-121.

[166] Gellius, 11.10; *ORF*, 187-188. That the *lex Aufeia* is a paleographic error for *lex Aquillia* has been argued; Hill. "The So-Called *Lex Aufeia*," *CR*, 62 (1948), 112-113; *MRR*, I.515, n. 3. This is unnecessary and unlikely; cf. Niccolini, *Fast. Trib. Pleb.*, 163-164; Badian, *For. Client.*, 183, n. 9.

[167] This is not to deny that Gracchus had other motives in mind as well. Provincials might be expected to benefit from a check on the hitherto unlimited power of senatorial governors; Badian, *For. Client.*, 184-185; *Roman Imperialism*, 41-45.

[168] Hill, *Roman Middle Class,* 67.

legislation, it must soon have become clear that the whole future of Aquillius' settlement, and, with it, senatorial control of taxation in that province was at stake.[169] Condemnation of Aquillius, even though on charges not directly linked with the new financial arrangements, might easily have been used as a pretext to overthrow the settlement of the ten-man senatorial commission. The oligarchic opposition to the Gracchan *factio* must have seen what political capital could be made by C. Gracchus out of the condemnation of Aquillius. Extensive pressure was then exerted and the defendant, though notoriously guilty, secured acquittal.[170] As it turned out, C. Gracchus was able to take advantage of the situation in any case. By turning his fire on the injustice of senatorial judicial decisions he would succeed in transferring the courts to the equestrian order, and could then cap his victory by the passage of the *lex de provincia Asiae*. The trial of Aquillius had landed the senate in a dilemma that worked perfectly to the advantage of the Gracchan group.

The advent of the Gracchi had significantly altered the political scene at Rome. Issues like land reform, judicial corruption, and provincial organization now became hotly debated and cut sharply across old factional lines. The senatorial groups of the 140's and 130's were barely recognizable in 123. A more fluid and shifting political structure was the order of the day. Perhaps the most striking feature of the age, graphically illustrated in the decade between Tiberius' and Gaius' tribunates, was instability, and the rapidity of change both in public opinion and political power. The traditional categories of politics became complicated by the injection of new issues and the emergence of men motivated by principle as well as (and sometimes in defiance of) factional allegiance. To see this simply in terms of *optimates* and *populares* is to cut away a large segment of the era's complex structure. The Gracchi began as supporters of a senatorial faction and ended as molders of their own faction. As they attracted support on the grounds of family as well as principle, so opposition was marshalled on both these counts by various and differing groups. The succeeding decades were to see greater, not less, complexity; more rapid and radical shifts, not greater stability; issues and political stands became more ill-defined, not neatly demarcated. Politics was never the same again after the Gracchi.

---

[169] For the formal charge, see Ps-Asconius, 204, Stangl; for the imputation of bribery, see Appian, *Mithr.* 57; *BC*, 1.22.

[170] Appian, *BC*, 1.22: ὅτι Αὐρήλιος Κόττας καὶ Σαλινάτωρ καὶ τρίτος ἐπὶ τούτοις Μάνιος Ἀκύλιος, ὁ τὴν Ἀσίαν ἑλών σαφῶς δεδωροδοκηκότες ἀφεῖτο ὑπὸ τῶν δικασάντων.

III. GRACCHAN LEGISLATION AND LEGACY

Ti. Gracchus had produced revolution. It was not his intent at the outset. Agrarian reform for the purpose of reviving the countryside and revitalizing the military stock can be described as essentially conservative: an effort to restore an earlier, more rurally-oriented society. C. Gracchus' horizons were far wider. The problems of a swelling urban population required more imaginative solutions; the constitutional and legal issues raised by Tiberius' tribunate and the factional contests that succeeded it had to be faced; a class of businessmen and entrepreneurs had claims of their own on state protection and support; Italians without the benefit of Roman political privilege had caught a glimpse of their potential influence on Roman internal struggles; even the state of the countryside and the health of the military remained insecure as long as wars continued abroad and conscription of property owners stocked the service.

The legislation of C. Gracchus demonstrates that the tribunate of his brother had raised many more problems than it had solved. Gaius' program addressed itself to a society that had become much more complex in the past decade. The chronology of Gaius' bills, despite numerous discussions, is hardly less obscure today than it ever was.[1] But the breadth of his scope is undeniable. A plague of locusts that ruined the African grain crop in 125 had dramatized the insecurity of a large urban populace dependent upon imported corn.[2] Gracchus' *lex frumentaria* put the state for the first time in the business of stabilizing the market price and removing it from the province of unscrupulous profiteers. A reen-

---

[1] See esp. H. Last, *CAH*, IX.49-91; Fraccaro, "Ricerche su Gaio Graccho," *Athenaeum*, 3 (1925), 76-97, 151-180; Badian, *For. Client.*, 299-301. Badian's statement, p. 181, that the year 123 "produces the impression of a lull," is, in any case, seriously misleading; cf. Obsequens, 31. And see the acute remarks of Brunt, *2nd Int. Conf. of Econ. Hist., 1962* (Paris, 1965), I.146-148.

[2] Livy, *Per.* 60; Orosius, 5.11; Obsequens, 30.

actment of his brother's law presumably revived the judicial functions of the triumviral commission and provided for more efficient land distribution. But he saw beyond the immediate situation. Individual allotments might run into difficulties again; colonization was a better solution. Colonies in Italy were no longer a strategic necessity, but surplus population could be attracted to new foundations and selection of maritime sites would appeal to growing commercial interests. An increased network of secondary roads in the peninsula would draw the support of commercial interests as well as stimulate greater participation in the political process over a wider area. Economic hardships produced by conscription and meager military pay could not be eliminated overnight, but Gracchan legislation at least spared the very young from the levy and provided soldiers' clothing at public cost. Constitutional measures also reflected a newer and more liberal atmosphere, stirred by events of the past few years. Iteration of the tribunate, apparently, had been sanctioned. Senatorial jurisdiction over the selecting of provincial assignments was now altered. Other efforts were less successful but kept pressure on the oligarchy: a threat to debar deposed magistrates from holding further offices and a bill to have the order of voting in the *comitia centuriata* subject to the lot instead of to the priority of wealth. Flaccus' espousal of Italian enfranchisement had been thwarted. But C. Gracchus was more circumspect: Roman franchise for the Latins and Latin rights to the Italians.[3] It was a program of imagination and breadth, designed both to confront contemporary needs and to build the strength of his faction. Men of all walks of life were to be seen in constant attendance upon the tribune; C. Gracchus was as skillful and diplomatic in business transactions and social intercourse as he was effective and persuasive on the rostra.[4]

Nothing in Gaius' program, however, is of greater significance than the judiciary legislation with which he was very deeply concerned and which is the special concern of this study. It is no accident that among the first measures of his initial tribunate in 123 was a famous law guaranteeing protection for the people against special inquiries organized by senatorial decree.

This measure was, of course, directed against the revival of such

---

[3] For the sources on Gracchan legislation, see *MRR*, I.513-514, 517-518; on the program generally, see Greenidge, *History of Rome*, 198-235; for iteration of the tribunate, see Appian, *BC*, 1.21; on the Italian proposals, cf. Badian, *For. Client.*, 185-186. See also R. J. Rowland, "C. Gracchus and the *Equites*," *TAPA*, 96 (1965), 361-373.

[4] Plut. *C. Gracch.* 6.4.

quaestiones as the hated tribunal of Popillius Laenas in 132. The bill was of momentous consequence both for Roman criminal law and for Roman politics. Its precise form is not easy to discern. Plutarch says merely that it forbade any magistrate from banishing a Roman citizen without trial.[5] This restriction can hardly have been the substance of the measure. The banishments of 132 came as the consequence of an organized tribunal before which pleadings could be heard and sentences passed. Despite the cries of partisan propaganda that obscure the real proceedings, there is no reason to believe that anyone was banished without trial. Greater precision is to be found in the comments of Cicero. The Gracchan law, he says on more than one occasion, provided that no citizen could be tried on a capital charge without the sanction of the people.[6] The phrase *iniussu populi,* however, does not have its meaning clearly stamped on its face. Interpretations have been numerous and varied. Some have believed that the *lex Sempronia* outlawed senatorial declaration of a Roman citizen as a *hostis.*[7] But Cicero specifically contrasts *hostes* with *cives* and asserts that the *lex Sempronia* concerned itself only with the latter.[8] Moreover, as an analysis of the events of 133 and 132 has shown, neither Ti. Gracchus in 133 nor his followers in 132 had officially been declared enemies of the state by the senate. The normal explanation of Gracchus' law is that it was a *lex de provocatione* that secured the right of appeal to the people in any capital trial.[9] The theory possesses apparent plausibility. It is certainly true that the tribunal of Popillius Laenas had not allowed appeal to the *comitia,* which would have been fatal to its own ends. It is also true that Cicero, in an emotional outburst on the "sweet name of liberty," links the *leges Semproniae* with the *lex Porcia,* which we know to have been a law on *provocatio.*[10] Yet Ciceronian rhetoric ought not to be confused with historical accuracy.

The proper explanation is surely that Gaius' bill forbade the institution of any special *quaestiones* without the passage of a law by the

[5] Plut. *C. Gracch.* 4: εἰ τις ἄρχων ἄκριτον ἐκκεκηρύχοι πολίτην κατ' αὐτοῦ διδόντα κρίσιν τῷ δήμῳ.

[6] Cic. *Pro Rab. Perd.* 12: *iniussu vestro;* Cat. 4.10: *iussu populi;* Schol. Gronov. 2.289, Stangl: *iniussu populi.*

[7] So Greenidge, *Legal Procedure,* 323.

[8] Cic. *Cat.* 4.10: *legem Semproniam esse de civibus Romanis constitutam; qui autem rei publicae sit hostis eum civem esse nullo modo posse.*

[9] Cf., e.g., Zumpt, *Criminalrecht,* I.2.71-78; Mommsen, *Stafrecht,* 42, 163, 258; Siber, *AbhLeipz,* 43 (1936), 9-11; Fraccaro, *Opuscula,* 2.268-270.

[10] Cic. *Verr.* 2.5.163: *O nomen dulce libertatis . . . O lex Porcia legesque Semproniae!*

assembly.[11] If the Gracchan measure were simply a *lex de provocatione,* then one is hard pressed to explain the novelty or the necessity of it. *Provocatio* laws had been on the books for a long time prior to 123 B.C.[12] But they do not seem to have affected *quaestiones extraordinariae.* Special tribunals not subject to *provocatio* had existed prior to the Popillian tribunal; and, what is more to the point, they continued to be established after the *lex Sempronia* was passed.[13] The difference, of course, is that after 123 no special court was instituted except on the basis of a specific law, passed by the assembly.[14] This fact can be no accident. Tribunals established pursuant to senatorial decree were acceptable and unquestioned until they were employed overtly for political purposes. In the eyes of the Gracchan *factio,* political maneuvering was the intolerable aspect of Popillius' tribunal. Since it is clear that Gaius' bill was specifically directed against any repetition of the events of 132, this explanation fits neatly into the historical context. *Quaestiones extraordinariae* were not outlawed; nor was there any thought of securing *provocatio* against them. But henceforth, no such *quaestio* could be set up merely on the basis of a *senatus consultum.* Only an act of the people could guarantee legitimacy.[15]

The first victim of this new law, not surprisingly, was P. Popillius Laenas himself. Factional vengeance was involved, of course, but, more important, the trial of Popillius was a crucial test case for the efficacy of the *lex Sempronia.* P. Rupilius, Popillius' consular colleague and fellow *quaesitor* in 132, would doubtless have been prosecuted as well;

---

[11] So, rightly, Strachan-Davidson, *Problems,* I.237-245, not buttressed by sufficient arguments, but endorsed now by the *auctoritas* of Kunkel, *Abh-Münch,* 56 (1962), 28, n. 89. Kunkel argues generally that *provocatio* laws are not connected with trials before the assembly, but simply developed as a check on magisterial *coercitio* (pp. 24-33).

[12] On the *provocatio* laws, see Greenidge, *Legal Procedure,* 307-323.

[13] For the pre-Popillian tribunals, see above, p. 60. For later occasions, see below, pp. 142-143, 162-163.

[14] Some might urge as an exception the actions of Opimius against the Gracchani in 121. But those actions can hardly be classified as judicial proceedings; see below, note 90.

[15] This is also the most natural translation and interpretation of *iniussu populi.* E. A. Yarnold's attempt to identify the tablet from Bantia with this law ("The Latin Law of Bantia," *AJP,* 78 [1957], 163-172) can only be conjectural, as are all previous attempts at identifying the fragmentary inscription. Cf. Mommsen, *CIL,* I.2.441; H. Stuart Jones, "A Roman Law Concerning Piracy," *JRS,* 16 (1926), 170-171; G. Tibiletti, "Le leggi *De Iudiciis Repetundarum* fino alla Guerra Sociale," *Athenaeum,* 31 (1953), 57-73; E. Schönbauer, "Das Problem der beiden Inschriften von Bantia," *Rev. Int. Droit. Ant.,* 2 (1955), 311-363.

but Rupilius, it is reported, died of grief when his brother L. Rupilius failed to secure the consulship, probably for 131 and certainly before the death of Scipio Aemilianus in 129.[16]

The type of court at which charges were leveled against Popillius is not stated explicitly in the sources. It has been suggested that he was tried either by a special *quaestio* or perhaps by a standing *quaestio de sicariis*.[17] But as was shown, there is no conclusive evidence for a standing murder court at this date,[18] and it is unlikely that C. Gracchus, who had just limited the *quaestiones extraordinariae*, would have instituted one himself, even through the assembly, against Popillius. Plutarch, in fact, states explicitly that any offender against C. Gracchus' law is to be called to account before τῷ δήμῳ.[19] The bill obviously was retroactive and aimed at Popillius. Involvement of the assembly can be supported from preserved fragments of C. Gracchus' speeches. The tribune delivered an oration against Popillius *pro rostris,* probably at the preliminary *anquisitio*.[20] Of course, it might have been an informal denunciation of Popillius, perhaps identical with the fiery address lamenting the fate of Tiberius.[21] But there are also fragments of a Gracchan speech *De P. Popillio Laenate circum Conciliabula*. Such a speech suggests that Gaius was making the rounds of rural villages near Rome in order to drum up support for his prospective accusation.[22] It is probable that dwellers in the *conciliabula* and elsewhere were sought as voters in a popular trial. C. Gracchus, as tribune, was in a perfect position to initiate such proceedings.[23]

Popillius did not await trial. Conviction was certain and he wisely chose the alternative of voluntary exile.[24] His partisans did not miss the

[16] Cic. *Tusc. Disp.* 4.17.40; *De Amicit.* 73. Vell. Pat., 2.7, wrongly records a trial of both Popillius and Rupilius. The error is obvious and intelligible.

[17] Siber, *AbhLeipz,* 43 (1936), 11; Kunkel, *AbhMünch,* 56 (1962), 29. Vell. Pat., 2.7.4, does use the phrase, *iudiciorum publicorum,* but this ought not to be pressed in a technical sense. His account is otherwise erroneous; see previous note.

[18] See above, p. 29.

[19] Plut. *C. Gracch.* 4.

[20] *ORF,* 184.

[21] Plut. *C. Gracch.* 3.2-3.

[22] So Fraccaro, *Studi Storici,* 6 (1913), 93, without specifying the implications. Fragments in *ORF,* 184-185.

[23] Gaius' role as tribunician prosecutor before the people is implied by Cic. *De Leg.* 3.26: *tribuniciaque vis in me populum, sicut Gracchus in Laenatem . . . incitasset;* cf. *Pro Cluent.* 95; *Brutus,* 128.

[24] Plut. *C. Gracch.* 4.2: Ποπίλλιος μὲν οὐκ ὑποστὰς τὴν κρίσιν ἔφυγεν ἐξ Ἰταλίας.

opportunity to dramatize his martyrdom. Weeping and prayers by a multitude of friends and relations accompanied him to the city gates.[25] Following the withdrawal, the normal decree of *aquae et ignis interdictio* was passed by the *plebs*. The exile was forbidden return upon pain of death.[26] Popillius' removal was a significant victory for the Gracchan group, as well as a milestone in Roman legal history. No other individual is ever again known to have been convicted under this law. The example was a deterrent: no further tribunals were instituted on the basis of a senatorial decree alone. But there was another consequence, unforeseen and ominous. Emergency situations could not await the cumbersome procedure of comitial gathering and action by the whole *populus*. The elimination of senatorial *quaestiones* opened the way to the *senatus consultum ultimum* and presaged the demise of C. Gracchus himself.[27]

The problems surrounding Gracchus' law on special courts pale into insignificance beside those on the most obscure of his measures, the so-called *lex ne quis iudicio circumveniretur*. As so often happens, the paucity of evidence bears a relationship in inverse proportion to the number of conjectures offered. Testimony on this law is confined to a few phrases in Cicero's *Pro Cluentio,* and one incidental reference, with no elucidation, in the *Brutus*. We know it simply as a measure on judicial corruption of some sort under which A. Cluentius was tried in 66 B.C., after its incorporation into Sulla's *lex de sicariis et veneficiis*.[28] Beyond this, all is obscurity and confusion. The law's meaning and purpose, however, is not beyond recovery. The measure instituted no new permanent court, either on homicide or on judicial corruption.[29] Cicero pointedly contrasts the law as passed by C. Gracchus with the use made of it by Sulla in the establishment of a *quaestio*.[30] Connection with the aims and purposes of Gracchus' tribunate must be sought in order to place the measure in an intelligible context.

The *quaestio de repetundis* suggests itself. The alteration of its composition, described below, was a central element in Gaius' program. Yet

---

[25] Cic. *Post Red. in Sen.* 37; Diod. 35.26. It is possible that in this connection C. Gracchus delivered his speech *In Popillium et Matrones; ORF,* 185.

[26] Cic. *De Domo,* 82; *De Rep.* 1.3.6. On the institution of *interdictio* generally, see Mommsen, *Strafrecht,* 72-73.

[27] Cf. Kunkel, *AbhMünch,* 56 (1962), 89.

[28] Cic. *Pro Cluent.* 148, 151, 154; *Brutus,* 48; cf. *Inst.* 4.18.5; *Digest,* 48.8.1.

[29] For the former view, see Lange, *Röm. Alterth.,* 2.664; Siber, *AbhLeipz,* 43 (1936), 10; for the latter, Greenidge, *Legal Procedure,* 421; Strachan-Davidson, *Problems,* II.20.

[30] Cic. *Pro Cluent.* 151: *Postea L. Sulla . . . cum eius rei quaestionem hac ipsa lege constituerat.*

members of the equestrian order were not bound by the provisions of the *ne quis* bill.[31]   It is unthinkable that a measure on judicial corruption would exempt the very men who were now to sit on the juries. Hence, the *ne quis* law has been claimed as an early action of Gaius before he contemplated transferring the courts to the *equites*.[32] But that interpretation misreads the politician's line of attack. The failings of senatorial courts and juries were under assault on the grounds of scandalous acquittals such as the notorious one of M'. Aquillius.[33] They provided the motivation and justification for the new staffing of courts with members of the equestrian class. But the context and numerous specific statements of the *Pro Cluentio* show that the *ne quis* law was directed not against unjust acquittals but against conspiracy to condemn innocent men.[34] Moreover the acquittals that grieved C. Gracchus were acquittals on political grounds, and for those bribery would not usually have been necessary.[35] The change in jury personnel, apparently, is not to be associated with a measure on judicial corruption.

Another association is plausible and revealing. The *lex Sempronia* guaranteeing popular sanction for special tribunals discussed above affords the proper context. This theory, advanced long ago, has recently been revived and vigorously argued.[36] A measure directed against judicial

[31] Cic. *Pro Cluent.* 148-159.

[32] Last, *CAH*, IX.53-54, 70; E. Badian., *"Lex Acilia Repetundarum," AJP*, 75 (1954), 375-378; E. Gabba, "Osservazioni sulla legge giudiziaria di M. Livio Druso (91 a.C.)," *Par. Pass.*, 11 (1956), 367.

[33] Appian, *BC*, 1.22.

[34] Apart from the references given above, see Cic. *Pro Cluent.* 9, 30, 79, 90, 131, 145, 192. Despite Sherwin-White, "The Extortion Procedure Again," *JRS*, 42 (1952), 45-47, it appears that the *ne quis* provision could be used against the recipients of bribes as well as the briber; see *Pro Cluent.* 90: *qua de re Iunius causam dixerit; quemcumque rogaveris, hoc respondebit, quod pecuniam acceperit, quod innocentem circumvenerit.* Among those covered by the law was *falsumve testimonium dixerit; Pro Cluent.* 157. This was surely the bribee, not the briber. Nicolet, *L'Ordre Equestre*, 503-511, has recently argued that there is an echo of the Gracchan *ne quis* law in line 16 of the *lex repetundarum* (*FIRA*, I.89), which he restores as *queive merc [ede aliqua ac pretio corruptus siet].* The extortion measure thus excludes from the juries not only senators, but ex-senators expelled from the *curia* after being convicted of corruption. The hypothesis is undemonstrable and, on the face of it, implausible.

[35] U. Ewins, *"Ne Quis Iudicio Circumveniatur," JRS,* 50 (1960), 101-102.

[36] Mommsen, *Strafrecht*, 258; Fraccaro, *Opuscula*, 2.270-272. N. J. Miners, "The *Lex Sempronia Ne Quis Iudicio Circumveniatur*," *CQ*, 8 (1958), 241-243, reopened the subject and rightly endorsed the Mommsenian view. Since then, U. Ewins has produced what is easily the best and most thorough investigation of this difficult subject; *JRS*, 50 (1960), 94-107. See also Kunkel, *AbhMünch*, 56 (1962), 70, n. 263a.

conspiracy to condemn innocent men fits perfectly and naturally with Gaius' law against senatorially ordained *quaestiones*. Both would have been inspired by the tribunal of Popillius Laenas. The provision confining liability to senators now receives a natural explanation. Gaius was not concerned with the standing court, whose control he probably already contemplated transferring to the knights, but he did fear the revival of special *quaestiones* staffed by senators. It would not have been difficult to foresee that his own fate could be in the hands of another tribunal like that of Popillius.

The two measures are closely linked. Was the *ne quis* provision a clause in the *lex Sempronia* on senatorial courts?[37] It would seem not. The latter was still in effect in the Ciceronian period,[38] whereas the former had been absorbed in the Sullan legislation. The statute under which Cluentius was charged was once a *lex Sempronia* itself.[39] That measure had its own rationale. Cluentius was prosecuted for corrupting a jury, but Gracchus' original purpose was wider: *Qui eorum coiit, coierit, convenit, convenerit quo quis iudicio publico condemnaretur.*[40] The offense outlined is nothing less than judicial murder; that is why Sulla could legitimately encompass it in a homicide statute. Gracchus' ban on special courts without popular sanction did not close all the loopholes. Although no *senatus consultum* alone could thereafter institute a *quaestio,* it was perfectly possible for a court set up by a law of the assembly to be manned by members of the senatorial class. It was obviously in order to decrease the danger inherent in this contingency that Gaius' measure against conspiracy to condemn an innocent man was passed. C. Gracchus, from the experience of 132, was worried about senators, not *equites.* The puzzling fact, not explicable on other theories, that there are no certain recorded prosecutions[41] under this law until it became part of Sulla's murder law now becomes intelligible. Not only were there no further *quaestiones extraordinariae* established by senatorial decree after 123, but those that were instituted were staffed by non-senatorial jurors. C. Gracchus' law *ne quis iudicio circumveniretur* had an impact and influence for which he has never received due credit.

At some time during Gracchus' two tribunates, probably in 123, came the most renowned and, from a political point of view, the most signifi-

[37] That is the opinion of almost all who have perceived the connection. See previous note. Miss Ewins is the exception.

[38] Cic. *Pro Rab. Perd.* 12; *Cat.* 4.10.

[39] Cic. *Pro Cluent.* 151, 154.

[40] Cic. *Pro Cluent.* 148.

[41] The trial of Decius in 119 may have been on the basis of this law. See below, pp. 110-111.

cant of his measures. The literary sources describe it in a simple and straightforward manner: a judiciary law that transferred control of the *iudicia* from the senate to the *equites*.[42] The description may be misleading. It is well to remember that all the testimony is post-Sullan and written in a period when the system of several permanent *quaestiones* had long been well established. The concern of the sources is essentially a political one, and, from this angle, the change of composition is, of course, central. But the word *iudicia* need not imply that there was more than one *quaestio perpetua* in existence in 123. When employed properly *iudicium* means a single trial or a board of *iudices,* not a *quaestio perpetua*.[43] So far as one can tell, the *quaestio repetundarum* was the only permanent criminal court in Rome at the time of C. Gracchus' reforms.[44] Special *quaestiones,* of course, may have been considered.[45] *Equites,* as a matter of convenience, were employed to staff their juries after the passage of the Gracchan law, but there is no reason to believe that Gaius foresaw this development. The *lex ne quis iudicio circumveniretur* indeed demonstrates that he expected that special courts would continue to be staffed by senators. The new law, therefore, applied specifically and directly to the *quaestio de repetundis*.

Where does this measure fit into the Gracchan scheme? Two pieces of evidence have bedeviled and confused scholars. The Epitomator of Livy asserts that Gaius introduced six hundred *equites* into the senate, to yield a body of nine hundred in all. Plutarch's version is that Gaius combined three hundred *equites* with the senatorial order and made the courts a joint responsibility of the two groups.[46] The remainder of the evidence is unanimous and definitive that senators were excluded from the extortion court. Hence, it is widely believed, C. Gracchus evolved his bill only after an earlier false start: the testimony of Plutarch and the Epitomator records an original proposal, later abandoned when he

[42] Vell. Pat. 2.6.3, 2.13, 2.32; Tac. *Ann.* 12.60; Diod. 35.25; Appian, *BC,* 1.22; Florus, 2.1.6; Varro in Non. Marc. 728 L; Pliny, *NH,* 33.34.

[43] M. I. Henderson, "The Process *De Repetundis,*" *JRS,* 41 (1951), 82.

[44] Cf. Zumpt, *Criminalrecht,* 2.1.54-56; Fraccaro, *Opuscula,* 2.273-286. Brunt, *2nd Int. Conf. Econ. Hist., 1962,* I.143-144, believes that there may have been more. But there is no substantive evidence. Cicero's remark, *Brutus,* 160, in context, surely means that the institution of *quaestiones perpetuae* dated to 149, not that several *quaestiones* were constituted about that time. Brunt cites also Cic. *Pro Rab. Post.* 14, which suggests that proposals for *quaestiones* were familiar by the time of Glaucia at the end of the second century. But that proves nothing for 123.

[45] Such is the view of Kunkel, *AbhMünch,* 56 (1962), 96, n. 349, followed now by A. R. Hands, "The Political Background of the *lex Acilia de Repetundis,*" *Latomus,* 24 (1965), 231-233.

[46] Livy, *Per.* 60; Plut. *C. Gracch.* 5; *Compar.* 2.

determined to give the knights a monopoly.[47] It is time that that theory be laid to rest. The sources say nothing of proposals but refer to the measure as a duly promulgated law. That it was passed by C. Gracchus and then repealed by the same man within months is not only unreasonable in itself, but finds no support in the ancient evidence. Despite numerous references to C. Gracchus' reform of the juries, there is nothing that implies more than one measure. The point is that Livy and Plutarch themselves thought that they were talking about Gaius' final jury bill, not about an unsuccessful proposal, or a measure later to be repealed by the tribune himself. Either they are correct and the bulk of our evidence wrong, or they must be dismissed. No combination or compromise seems possible.

Two factors help to justify dismissal. Livy and Plutarch do not agree even with one another; the figure is six hundred in one and three hundred in the other, and the Epitomator does not even speak of a jury law, but simply a reform of the senate. Second, the similarity of this measure to that ascribed to M. Livius Drusus in 91 and to those of Sulla in 88 and 81 make it easier to understand how an error could have been made. Rejecting these two accounts clears away an obstinate barrier to the understanding of C. Gracchus' program. A shifting of gears midway in his tribunates lack documentation. Gracchus had his aims outlined in advance. Before he took office he had espoused the interests of the *equites* in debating the *lex Aufeia*. In all probability, he contemplated from the beginning a wholesale transfer of jury duty to that class.

The identification of the famous *lex repetundarum* on bronze tablets now in Naples and Vienna[48] with the Gracchan judiciary law may be accepted without serious reservation. Since there is no reason to postulate two Gracchan laws, one a *lex iudiciaria* and the other a *lex repetundarum,* the most significant obstacle to such acceptance disappears. Mention of a *lex Rubria* helps to put the inscription in the period of C. Gracchus' tribunates.[49] The *lex Rubria,* sponsored by a tribunician col-

---

[47] E. G. Hardy, "Notes on the *Lex Iudiciaria* of C. Gracchus, the *Lex Servilia* of Caepio, and the *Lex Thoria,*" *JP,* 32 (1912), 96-99; Greenidge, *History of Rome,* 213; Last, *CAH,* IX.52-55; Hill, *Roman Middle Class,* 109. Others have argued even that the measure recorded by Plutarch and the Epitomator was actually passed and then replaced later by the law to exclude senators from the juries; Gelzer, "Review of Hill, *Roman Middle Class,*" *Gnomon,* 25 (1953), 319-320; Badian, *AJP,* 75 (1954), 375-378; A. H. M. Jones, "De Legibus Junia et Acilia Repetundarum," *PCPS,* 186 (1960), 39-42; Rowland, *TAPA,* 96 (1965), 364-365.

[48] *FIRA,* I.84-102.

[49] Cf. Mommsen, *CIL,* I.54-57.

league of Gaius, provided for a Roman colony at Carthage on Gaius' incentive.[50] The removal of all senators and relatives of senators and all magistrates even down to the minor offices makes it clear that this inscription is part of the Gracchan enterprise.[51]

No source speaks of a *lex Sempronia repetundarum*. The hypothesis suggests itself that a friend and colleague of Gracchus took the responsibility for guiding the extortion law through the *comitia*. That Gaius did not move personally all the legislation ascribed to him is proved by the *lex Rubria*. When speaking loosely, ancient authors could also describe it as a Gracchan law.[52] For the *lex repetundarum* a measure lies ready at hand: the *lex Acilia,* carried by M'. Acilius Glabrio long ago and doubtless correctly identified with the inscription.[53] Of the *lex Acilia* literary authorities preserve only the detail that under it a defendant could be heard either in a single sitting or in several sessions broken by adjournments.[54] The single sitting, according to Cicero, became a quite common procedure.[55] Frequent *ampliationes* had generally reflected stalling tactics, leading to unjust acquittals, as in the trial of Cotta in 138, a case cited by C. Gracchus as evidence for senatorial corruption.[56] The epigraphic *lex repetundarum* appears to fit this specification. It recognizes the practice of *ampliatio,* but discourages its use by imposing a fine on *iudices* who drag on proceedings beyond the second *ampliatio*.[57] It remains possible that the *lex Acilia* was a later measure, ratifying and reviving the Gracchan provision.[58] But the purpose of such a repetitive bill is difficult to imagine. Moreover the one other extant piece of evidence on the *lex Acilia* suggests that, among other things, it changed the

[50] Plutarch, *C. Gracch.* 10.2; *lex repet.* line 22; *lex agrar.* line 59 (*FIR*, I.90, 114).

[51] Two earlier measures *de repetundis* are mentioned in the inscription, the *lex Calpurnia* and the *lex Junia*. For the latter no other evidence survives beyond this single reference, which gives neither details nor description. See Appendix B.

[52] Livy, *Per.* 60; Plut. *C. Gracch.* 8; Vell. Pat. 2.7.

[53] T. Mommsen, *Gesammelte Schriften* (Berlin, 1904-1913), I.1-64.

[54] Cic. *Verr.* 2.1.26: *antea vel iudicari primo poterat vel amplius pronuntiari.* The scholiast on this passage, Ps-Asconius, 231, Stangl, has, unfortunately, misread it; cf. J. P. V. D. Balsdon, "History of the Extortion Court at Rome, 123-70 B.C.," *PBSR,* 14 (1938), 108-113.

[55] Cic. *Verr.* 2.1.26: *Aciliam legem restituo qua lege multi semel accusati, semel dicta causa, auditis testibus condemnati sunt.*

[56] Appian, *BC,* 1.22; see Appendix C.

[57] *Lex repet.* line 48 (*FIRA,* I.94).

[58] Fraccaro, *Opuscula,* 2.282-286; Tibiletti, *Athenaeum,* 31 (1953), 5-18; Serrao, *Studi De Francisci,* 2 (1956), 480.

composition of the extortion court by employing equestrian jurors.[59] If this is so, then identification with the Gracchan law seems the only reasonable solution. Results may be briefly summed up. The tablet at Naples records the *lex Acilia,* an integral part of the Gracchan movement. There is no question here of two or three different *leges,* but of a single piece of legislation, passed as part of Gaius' program by another tribune sympathetic to that cause.[60]

The major import of C. Gracchus' judiciary law, as justly emphasized by the literary authorities, was the transfer of judicial control from the senate to the knights. The equestrian class rapidly became a political force to be reckoned with.[61] Specification as *iudices* in the Gracchan law doubtless spurred an increased self-awareness and political consciousness.[62] *Equites* are at no point to be reckoned as a caste apart, with distinct interests, but there can be no question that the Gracchan reform made possible for future occasions a greater community and cooperation among those who qualified for equestrian rating.[63] That the *equester ordo* can be identified with the business interests, the *publicani,* or the "middle class" is manifestly false. Scholarly dispute will continue on the question of whether the rank of an *eques* was determined by a financial qualification or, more strictly, by formal censorial enrollment into the category of *equites equo publico.* There was certainly a juridical distinction between the senatorial and equestrian orders, the former identifiable as the office-holding class, the latter ranking just below it in *dignitas,* though not always in wealth. But beyond that the boundaries are fuzzy and not to be stressed. Senators too engaged in money-making activities; many *equites* were landed *possessores.* Social mobility between the two groups

[59] Cic. *Verr.* 1.51: *de pecuniis repetundis optimis iudiciis severissimisque iudicibus usus est.* This point is made by Badian, *AJP,* 75 (1954), 379.

[60] On this whole matter, see the judicious remarks, with full references, of Gabba, *App. BC Lib. Prim.,* 338-341. On the very vexed and unsettled question of the penalty under the Gracchan law, see Sherwin-White, *PBSR,* 17 (1949), 6-8; and *JRS,* 42 (1952), 43-55.

[61] This is not to say that the business classes exercised no influence in politics prior to this time. See Gabba, "Le origini della guerra sociale e la vita politica romana dopo l'89 a.C.," *Athenaeum,* 32 (1954), 53-61; Nicolet, *L'Ordre Equestre,* 347-350.

[62] Pliny, *NH,* 33.34: *Iudicum autem appellatione separare eum ordinem primi omnium instituere Gracchi, discordi popularitate in contumeliam senatus.* Cf. Cic. *Brutus,* 128.

[63] On the equestrian census, surely not defined for the first time by C. Gracchus as has often been thought, see the remarks of Nicolet, *L'Ordre Equestre,* 47-68. The *lex repetundarum* has an unfortunate lacuna where positive qualifications for jurors would have been noted. For an attempted restoration, see Nicolet, pp. 513-515.

grew steadily freer. Marriage links across the official lines are discernible; more and more *equites* sought senatorial careers in the late Republic, some senators even chose the *otium* of an *eques*. Although in the pages of this study *"equites"* is used frequently as a synonym for business classes, it is not to be imagined that this usage exhausts or defines the term. But our principal concern here is politics; and insofar as equestrian interests were marshaled on the political front in this period, it was the *publicani* and the leading *negotiatores* who tended to pull the strings and to play a predominant role in the struggle over the judiciary. It is not without reason that ancient authors often dissolved the distinctions: *publicani, hoc est equites Romani.*[64] The debate on the Asian arrangements had demonstrated how the interests of senate and *equites* could diverge, and control of the extortion court gave the business classes a base of political power from which to enforce their demands.[65]

The Gracchi had broken all the rules of traditional factional politics by appealing for support to extra-senatorial elements in what should have been, from the senatorial viewpoint, an internal struggle. Of course, Scipio Aemilianus himself was not above such tactics altogether. He had more than once appealed to the populace for military commands otherwise blocked by senatorial enemies, and even employed the grievances of the Italian allies to enhance his political position vis-a-vis opposing factions in 129. But Scipio knew where to stop. Reform proposals were useful only insofar as they could not be construed as damaging the prestige of the senate as a whole. The Gracchi had taken the significant and irreversible step beyond this attitude. Tiberius had professed to act in the name of the people as a whole, M. Fulvius Flaccus had sought support from the Italian allies of all classes, and C. Gracchus had called in the equestrian order to take sides in a factional struggle.

[64] Cic. *Verr.* 2.3.169; cf. *Pro Planc.* 23; Livy, *Per.* 70; Pliny, *NH,* 33.34. For the notion of *equester ordo* as referring strictly to *equites equo publico,* see the arguments of Nicolet, *L'Ordre Equestre,* 69-102, 163-176, 189-212. That the term covered a broader spectrum is maintained, e.g., by Hill, *Roman Middle Class,* 45-48, and Henderson, "The Establishment of the *Equester Ordo,"* JRS, 53 (1963), 61-72. On the contacts and social mobility between senatorial and equestrian orders, the comprehensive analysis of Nicolet is indispensable; pp. 253-464, esp. pp. 253-284.

[65] Varro in Non. Marc. 728, L: *bicipitem civitatem fecit, discordiarum civilium fontem;* also Florus, 2.5.3; cf. Appian, *BC,* 1.22. Varro's rhetoric, however, is not to be taken without qualification. Sharp antagonism between the *ordines* proved to be the exception rather than the rule; cf. Brunt, *2nd Int. Conf. Econ. Hist.* 1962, I.117-137; Meier, *Res Pub.,* 70-95; Nicolet, *L'Ordre Equestre,* 473-475. For possible Greek influence on C. Gracchus' reform, highly speculative, see Nicolet, pp. 517-527.

The effect of this appeal to extra-senatorial forces was that the Gracchan group was forced to attract assistance by condemning policy of the senate as a body.[66] This program did not eliminate factional politics but added a new dimension to it. It was, however, a slippery dimension. The *plebs,* the allies, and the *equites* were ranged temporarily on the side of the Gracchan group, but their interests were divergent and not readily controllable. As will appear, the equestrians emerge and vanish rapidly, more than once, from the political scene, and their support could never be claimed by a particular senatorial group for any length of time. The same is true, on a smaller scale, of the *plebs* and the Italians. Useful and significant political forces, they were never consistently loyal to particular senatorial factions.

Reliance on a policy that, at least in certain points, was highly critical of the senate as a body explains both the strengths and the weaknesses of the Gracchan position. To speak, in this period, of a "popular party" and a "senatorial party" is to render inexplicable the events of the succeeding years. Men of family and standing continued to wield great influence among their *clientelae* in the populace. Although on some issues C. Gracchus might convince the people of their common interest, a policy that threatened senatorial standing as a whole aroused concerted opposition which, when translated into the actions of *clientelae,* produced the downfall of Gaius himself. Opposition to the Gracchan faction rapidly took on major proportions in 123 and 122.

A friendly consul for 122 was a necessity, but it appears that this is precisely what the Gracchan group found itself unable to secure. The anti-senatorial or, at least, extra-senatorial measures proposed by Gaius in 123 ought to be explained by growing hostility in the senate, and not vice versa, as most modern accounts maintain.[67] The earliest known bills of the tribune were already markedly anti-senatorial. This fact suggests that the group faced strong aristocratic opposition and had to fight for its political life by appealing to other groups. M. Fulvius Flaccus had held the consulship in 125, but in the crucial succeeding years we find no adherent of the Gracchan *factio* in the *fasti.*

It is known that for the important consulship of 122, Gracchus sup-

[66] Another instance may be noted. Senatorial *patroni* for aggrieved provincials in extortion cases had been obligatory under the *lex Calpurnia.* In Gaius' law they were optional; *lex repet.* lines 9-12 (*FIRA,* I.87-88); Serrao, *Studi De Francisci,* 2 (1956), 480-484. The law may also for the first time have granted to Romans as well as provincials the right to initiate prosecutions and have extended the scope of *reus* from ex-magistrate to *senatorius* in a wider sense; Henderson, *JRS,* 41 (1951), 84-85.

[67] E.g., Last, *CAH,* IX.52-55; rightly criticized by F. B. Marsh, *History of the Roman World, 146-30 B.C.;* 3rd ed. rev. by H. H. Scullard (London, 1963), 53.

ported C. Fannius who, bolstered by this assistance, was returned.[68] The inner motivations of the enigmatic Fannius, however, remain elusive. It is naive to regard him simply as a representative of the Gracchan group. As shown earlier, Fannius' connections and associates had all been spawned by the Scipionic circle.[69] The marriage alliance with a daughter of Laelius, adviser to the anti-Gracchan tribunal of 132, dramatizes Fannius' political loyalties.[70] That he drifted away from the Scipionic faction in the 120's is eminently likely. He would not have been the first to do so. The death of Aemilianus in 129 deprived his followers of leadership and doubtless caused a shifting of allegiance for many. Fannius, it is noteworthy, was passed over by his father-in-law Laelius, who preferred Q. Scaevola, though a younger man, for a vacant position on the college of auspices.[71] This incident reveals personal animosity between Fannius and Laelius and may also have influenced Fannius' defection.

Yet an attachment to the Gracchan *factio* appears dubious. Fannius' hostile actions immediately upon taking office should put this beyond question. Two rapid turnabouts would be inexplicable. In the consular elections of 123, he was pitted against L. Opimius.[72] The fact that Gaius lent his weight to Fannius' candidature shows not the strength but the weakness of the Gracchan *factio* in the *comitia centuriata*. The Gracchani were at a loss for candidates. Fannius, apparently, appealed to them as a more reasonable prospect than the ruthless L. Opimius whose stand had already been demonstrated with vigor and certainty in his crushing of the Fregellan revolt of 125. Fannius had been more discreet and less conspicuous. The disappointment of C. Gracchus must have been keen when Fannius voiced his views at last in 122.[73]

As is well known, Fannius crippled the Gracchan proposals for Latin and Italian enfranchisement by a stirring address that played upon the selfish interests of the Roman *plebs*.[74] The aristocracy could not face the

[68] Plut. *C. Gracch.* 8.2, 11.2.

[69] See above, pp. 66-67.

[70] Cic. *Brutus,* 101; *De Amicit.* 8.

[71] Cic. *Brutus,* 101. Fannius did reach the augurate before 129; Cic. *De Amicit.* 8; Scaevola, obviously, some time earlier.

[72] Plut. *C. Gracch.* 11.2.

[73] Against the bulk of scholarly opinion, H. C. Boren, "Livius Drusus, T.P. 122, and his Anti-Gracchan Program," *CJ,* 52 (1956), 36, rightly argues that no close alliance between C. Gracchus and Fannius should ever be postulated. But Boren betrays addiction to a static notion of family politics in affirming that Gaius supported Fannius' candidature because the latter was of the Scipionic group. To assume that Gaius was cooperating with the Scipios is to render totally unintelligible the events of the previous decade.

[74] Cic. *Brutus,* 99; *De Orat.* 3.183. See the fragments of this speech in *ORF,* 143-145; cf. also the remarks of Fraccaro, *Studi Storici,* 5 (1912), 410-417.

prospect of swarms of new voters independent of the Roman nobility and not subject to the ties of clientage. But the citizen populace could also be made to see that a sharing of privileges entailed less advantage for each individual. The tactics of the Gracchi had been turned against them. The interests of the *plebs* could cut more than one way. Scipio Aemilianus was seven years dead but the anti-Gracchan policy he had pursued continued to weigh heavily on the events of the late 120's. It is striking to observe how many of the most vocal and active opponents of C. Gracchus show links with the conqueror of Carthage.

Fannius, as we have noted, grew up under the tutelage of the Scipionic circle. In addition to that consul, the spearhead of the opposition in 122 was the capable and energetic tribune M. Livius Drusus, a man of weight in both eloquence and influence.[75] His connections, it appears, were Scipionic. His father C. Livius Drusus had been consul with Scipio Aemilianus in 147 B.C. Conjunction of consulship is never of itself sufficient to show association, but it is noteworthy that the consul of 147 was son of an Aemilianus.[76] The conjecture that his father was born an Aemilius Paullus is not unreasonable. Connections between the Livii and the Aemilii Paulli in an earlier period can be demonstrated. The consuls of 147 may then have been first cousins.[77] This association did not die out in the succeeding generation. The tribune of 122 was married to a Cornelia. It is probably also his sister who was the Livia of remarkable longevity, the wife of P. Rutilius Rufus, another protégé of the Scipionic circle.[78] The two consuls who reached office for 121, when Gaius failed to secure a third tribunate, illustrate the political trend. One was the bitter anti-Gracchan L. Opimius, succeeding after a previous failure. The other was Q. Fabius Maximus Allobrogicus. Allobrogicus was a nephew of Scipio Aemilianus and had already crossed swords with C. Gracchus in 123.[79] Gaius' speech against another nephew of Scipio, Q. Aelius Tubero, would also fit in these years.[80] Opposition grew. The dignified and respected senior consular, L. Piso Frugi, spoke up against Gracchus. Piso, a historian and a scholar, had been responsible for

[75] Cic. *Brutus,* 109; Plut. *C. Gracch.* 8.4.

[76] A. Degrassi, *Fasti Capitolini* (Turin, 1954), 70-71 (on 147 B.C.).

[77] Münzer, *Röm. Adelsp.,* 235-237.

[78] For Drusus' marriage to Cornelia, see Seneca, *Ad Marc.* 16.4; Münzer, *Röm. Adelsp.,* 399, 403; Boren, *CJ,* 52 (1956), 29. For the wife of Rutilius Rufus, see Val. Max. 8.13.6; Pliny, *NH,* 7.158.

[79] Plut. *C. Gracch.* 6.2: τὸ περὶ τοῦ σίτου δόγμα . . . ὃν ἔπεμψε μὲν ἐξ 'Ιβηρίας Φάβιος ἀντιστράτηγος ἐκεῖνος δ' ἔπεισε τὴν βουλὴν ἀποδομένην τὸν σῖτον ἀναπέμψαι ταῖς πόλεσι τὸ ἀργύριον καὶ προσεπαιτιάσασθαι τὸν Φάβιον ὡς ἐπαχθῆ καὶ ἀφόρητον ποιοῦντα τὴν ἀρχὴν τοῖς ἀνθρώποις.

[80] *ORF,* 193-194.

instituting the extortion court under senatorial auspices over a quarter century earlier. He doubtless fought the transfer of judicial control to the *equites*, though the accident of survival records only opposition to the *lex frumentaria.* Piso dramatized his scorn by lining up himself for grain distribution and made a mockery of the Gracchan law.[81] He drew the fire of Gaius' fiercest invective.[82] Piso too may have had Scipionic connections in earlier days.[83] The elimination of Gracchan legislation began in 121, when the tribune M. Minucius Rufus moved the repeal of the *lex Rubria.*[84] Minucius' activities in these years are otherwise unknown, but in an earlier generation, for what that is worth, the Minucii Rufi had connections with the Scipionic group.[85] It is noteworthy that the Gracchan grain bill was eventually repealed, we do not know when, on the motion of a M. Octavius.[86] It was belated retaliation, of a sort, for the humiliation of an ancestor, the anti-Gracchan tribune of 133. Despite factional shifts and political upheaval, there is unmistakable continuity in the opposition to the Gracchi. The shadow of Scipio Aemilianus still hangs over the events of the late 120's.

The activities of Livius Drusus and C. Fannius show clearly how the tactics of the Gracchan group had altered the form of senatorial politics. Appeal for support now had to be made to large groups outside the senate itself. Fannius pointed out the special privileges of the Roman *plebs;* Drusus offered programs of colonization more extensive and more attractive than those of C. Gracchus. The Latins could be appeased and their interests utilized to preserve the status quo in Italy.[87] The success of the opposition in 122 demonstrates that no individual senatorial faction could claim the unswerving loyalty of any extra-senatorial class. The *popularis* party is a myth. The rules were different now but the game of factional politics continued to be played.

The death of C. Gracchus, like the activities of his life, marks a major

[81] Cic. *Tusc. Disp.* 3.48.

[82] Cic. *Pro Font.* 39; Schol. Bob. 96, Stangl; *ORF,* 186-187. The bitterness of the enmity here recorded makes it difficult to accept the hypothesis of Earl, "Calpurnii Pisones in the 2nd Century B.C.," *Athenaeum,* 38 (1960), 283-298, that Piso sympathized with Ti. Gracchus in 133. Cf. Astin, *Scip. Aem.,* 316-319.

[83] See above, p. 20.

[84] Sources in *MRR,* I.521. One fragment of C. Gracchus' speech against Minucius' law is extant; *ORF,* 193.

[85] Scullard, *Roman Politics,* 46, 104; Earl, *Latomus,* 19 (1960), 667.

[86] Cic. *Brutus,* 222; *De Off.* 2.72. The date of repeal may be sometime between 91 and 78; Niccolini, *Fast. Trib. Pleb.,* 426-427.

[87] For Drusus' tribunate and activities, see the sources in *MRR,* I.517. Cf. the excellent analysis of Badian, *For. Client.,* 187-191.

milestone in the history of Roman legal process. When riots ensued over the repeal of the *lex Rubria,* the senate had a pretext for vigorous action. Neither C. Gracchus nor M. Fulvius Flaccus held office in 121. Judicial prosecution was therefore possible, and, it would seem, to be expected. Yet the Gracchani were not tried. A declaration issued from the *curia.* For the first time in Roman history the senate had recourse to the notorious *senatus consultum ultimum:* the consul was empowered to take whatever steps he saw fit to save the Republic.[88]

In view of earlier discussion in this study, the reasons for bypassing a criminal trial and undertaking administrative action instead should hardly be a mystery. The prosecution of the Gracchani would require, as it did in 132, the establishment of a special *quaestio.*[89] But, of course, this is precisely what was forbidden by the Gracchan law of 123 specifying that such tribunals could only be authorized by popular decree. The populace was divided, but the likelihood of its sanctioning a *quaestio extraordinaria* directed against C. Gracchus was very slim. Since the senate could no longer legitimize such a tribunal on its own hook, the avenue of judicial attack was closed.[90] By a strange irony of fate, it was C. Gracchus' own law that sealed his end in 121, by compelling the senate to adopt extra-legal measures. A *senatus consultum ultimum* had also been mooted in 133, but it was suggested then because Tiberius was still tribune and therefore immune to criminal prosecution. It was used now not because Gaius was immune, but because potential prose-

[88] Cic. *Cat.* 1.3-4; *Phil.* 8.14; Plut. *C. Gracch.* 18.1; also *MRR,* I.520. Contra: Plaumann, *Klio,* 13 (1913), 359-363.

[89] A charge of *perduellio* was theoretically possible, but this would have been heard before the assembly, a risk the senate was not eager to take with the popular support that Gracchus could still command.

[90] This point was convincingly made against Mommsen by Strachan-Davidson, *Problems,* I.235-245. See also H. Siber, *"Provocatio,"* ZSav, 75 (1942), 380-390. The actions of Popillius in 132 and Opimius in 121 were of quite different forms from a constitutional point of view. There is, to be sure, a reference to *quaestiones* conducted by Opimius; Vell. Pat. 2.7.3: *Crudelesque mox quaestiones in amicos clientesque Gracchorum habitae sunt.* Velleius' phrase is generous and misleading. It would be wrong to put Opimius' actions in the category of formal judicial inquiry. After Gaius' death, his lesser sympathizers were seized, imprisoned, and summarily slain; cf. Sallust, *Iug.* 31.7: *Post C. Gracchi et M. Fulvi caedem item vostri mortales in carcere necati sunt. Utriusque cladis non lex verum lubido eorum finem fecit;* Orosius, 5.12.10: *Opimius consul sicut in bello fuit ita in quaestione crudelis. Nam amplius tria milia hominum suppliciis necavit, ex quibus plurimi ne dicta quidem causa innocentes interfecti sunt;* Appian, *BC,* 1.26; Plut. *C. Gracch.* 17.4-5; 18-1.

cution had been hamstrung by his own measure. In 133 the proposal to pass a *s.c.u.* was thwarted because the presiding consul, P. Scaevola, declined to get involved. In 121, however, the consul Opimius, familiar with the solution of the sword, had long been awaiting his opportunity.[91]

Once the *s.c.u.* was passed, the consul could undertake quasi-military operations. Short work was made of the Gracchani.[92] Among those who fell were both C. Gracchus and Fulvius Flaccus, and even Flaccus' young son, who had sought mediation in vain.[93] It was bitter irony that Opimius should rededicate the Temple of Concord after the massacre. "Discord produced this concord" was scribbled beneath his inscription.[94] Not just the heirs of the Scipionic circle, but other political groups and even former friends of the Gracchan *factio* were to be found on the side of "law and order" in 121. Q. Metellus Macedonicus, head of a large and powerful clan, had denounced Ti. Gracchus in 133, and now partook in the slaughter twelve years later. So also did the aged *princeps senatus,* P. Cornelius Lentulus, who had held the consulship over forty years before and was probably in his eighties. The doughty patrician marched up the Aventine against the Gracchani and was wounded in active combat.[95] The involvement of another patrician, of a younger generation, is also on record: M. Aemilius Scaurus. A humble and obscure background delayed his career, but his abilities were formidable; he was to dominate the Roman political scene for almost three decades. A late source reports that Scaurus acted as adviser to Opimius in 121.[96] The story may be doubted. Scaurus was only an *aedilicius* at this time and hardly in a position to exert significant influence. The fact that he did act in a similar capacity in 100 may be the origin of this story. That Scaurus played some role, however, is not unlikely. He and C. Gracchus had both served under L. Aurelius Orestes in Sardinia in the mid-120's and may have come to despise one another at that time. Gaius had delivered a speech boasting of his refusal to oppress Sardinian provincials and

[91] Plut. *C. Gracch.* 13.4: ὁ δὲ 'Οπίμιος ὥσπερ ἐνδόσιμον λαβὼν ... παρώ-ξυνε τὸν δῆμον ἐπὶ τὴν ἄμυναν; cf. Vell. Pat. 2.7.3. Opimius administered proceedings because his colleague Allobrogicus was in Gaul.

[92] For an account of the last days of the followers of Gracchus, see Greenidge, *History of Rome,* 248-258. Sources in *MRR,* I.520.

[93] The figure of three thousand slain is surely excessive; Orosius, 5.12.10; Plut. *C. Gracch.* 18.1.

[94] Plut. *C. Gracch.* 17.6.

[95] Cic. *Phil.* 8.14; Val. Max. 5.3.2f; cf. Cic. *Cat.* 3.10, 4.13.

[96] *Vir. Ill.* 72.9: *tantumque auctoritate potuit, ut Opimium . . . privato consilio armaret.* Cf. Cic. *Pro Sest.* 101: *qualis pater tuus, M. Scaure, fuit qui a C. Graccho usque ad Q. Varium seditiosis omnibus restitit.*

hinting darkly that there were others who did not resist the temptation.[97] M. Scaurus already revealed in 121 his ability to be on the right side at the right time.

The new loyalties of former Gracchan supporters could also be dramatized in 121. D. Junius Brutus Callaicus had close connections with the Claudian group. He had married the sister of Ap. Claudius Pulcher, adviser and father-in-law to Ti. Gracchus.[98] But in 121 Brutus led a cordon of troops against Gaius during the struggle.[99] More significant than defection of individuals is the fact that the *equites* (insofar as it is possible to speak of them as a unit), though beneficiaries of the Gracchan legislation, did not consider themselves bound by any enduring loyalty. The opposition had succeeded in showing shrewd businessmen that their interests did not coincide with those of an urban proletariate.[100] Opimius felt free to call upon them for assistance, and, it seems, they seized the opportunity to demonstrate their displeasure with Gracchan tactics.[101] It is symbolic of the breakup of the Gracchan *factio* that C. Gracchus' head was delivered to Opimius by an L. Septumuleius, once a close friend of Gaius and now an instrument of the opposition.[102]

The slaughter of the Gracchani entailed the final demise of the old Claudio-Fulvian group, once the most redoubtable senatorial coalition. The Sempronii Gracchi vanish from the pages of Republican history. The Fulvii never again held curule office in Rome. The proud patrician Claudii turn up again only as hangers-on of a more powerful political group.[103] The same is true of the Aemilii Lepidi. Others, like the Metelli, Servilii Caepiones, Aurelii Cottae, Licinii Crassi, and Junii Bruti either remained independent or severed connections early enough to protect their political careers. The same, as will appear, was probably true of the Papirii Carbones and the Sulpicii Galbae. The rout was widespread and a whole political faction was the victim.

[97] Gellius, 15.12.3. This is pointed out by E. Pais, *Dalle Guerre Puniche a Cesare Augusto* (Rome, 1918), 125-128.

[98] Cic. *Ad Att.* 12.22.2; Münzer, *Röm. Adelsp.,* 241-242.

[99] Orosius, 5.12.7; Ampelius, 19.4, 26.2.

[100] Sallust, *Iug,* 42.1: *nobilitas . . . per equites Romanos, quos spes societatis a plebe dimoverat, Gracchorum actionibus obviam ierat.*

[101] Plut. *C. Gracch.* 14: καὶ τῶν ἱππέων ἑκάστῳ παράγγελμα δόντος ἄγειν ἔωθεν οἰκέτας δύο καθωπλισμένους.

[102] For his friendship with Gaius, see Pliny, *NH,* 33.3.48; Val. Max. 9.4.3; *Vir. Ill.* 65.6. For his role in the murder of Gaius, see Plut. *C. Gracch.* 17; cf. Cic. *De Orat.* 2.269; Florus, 2.3.

[103] A Q. Claudius, son of an Appius, appears in a *consilium* of 129, but apparently never reached the higher magistracies; Taylor, *Voting Districts,* 203-204; R. K. Sherk, "The Text of the *Senatus Consultum De Agro Pergameno*," *GRBS,* 7 (1966), 368.

The most serious defection was that of C. Papirius Carbo. He had, of course, been a leading supporter of the Gracchi, an opponent of Scipio, and a member of the agrarian commission with C. Gracchus and M. Fulvius Flaccus.[104] But Carbo too sensed the drift of the tide and transferred allegiance to the opposition. His departure came late, but it was telling and obviously earned rich rewards. Carbo secured swift election to the consulship for 120 and was shortly to appear in defense of C. Gracchus' slayer. His colleague in the consulship, P. Manilius, bears a name that recalls yet another friend of Scipio Aemilianus.[105] Carbo's defection, which necessarily crippled the work of the agrarian commission, was the most significant gained by the opponents of the Gracchi. What his motives were, if there were any apart from political expediency, is beyond knowing. His character was not one to arouse admiration. Carbo was eloquent and persuasive, but a man ignorant of Roman legal traditions and unconcerned with the institutions bequeathed by the past.[106]

An important inscription from Carthage sheds light on the political situation in these years.[107] The stone lists what appears to be a three-man commission with the names Galba, Carbo, and Bestia. Identification is disputed. Since the only known Bestia of the period is L. Calpurnius Bestia, the future consul of 111, this identification seems reasonably secure. But there are three Papirii Carbones and two Sulpicii Galbae who qualify as possible candidates for the other two places. Galba is either Ser. Sulpicius Galba, consul in 108, or C. Sulpicius Galba, who was later to be tried by the Mamilian *quaestio* in 109. Since Bestia also fell victim to this tribunal, the conjunction favors the latter Galba as the one named in the inscription. Of the three Carbones, the consul of 120 remains the best candidate, given his experience on the Gracchan agrarian commission. Certainty is impossible.

The nature and purpose of the triumvirate recorded on this inscription have been much discussed.[108] Despite the repeal of the *lex Rubria* in 121, land distributions in Africa went on and were confirmed by the *lex agraria* of 111.[109] That this group was a land commission is not

---

[104] He is named on two Gracchan boundary stones; see Carcopino, *Autour des Gracques*, 237-238.

[105] Cic. *De Rep.* 1.18; cf. *MRR*, I.459.

[106] Cic. *De Orat.* 1.40.

[107] *ILLRP*, I.275, no. 475.

[108] Cichorius, *Röm. Stud.*, 113-116; Carcopino, *Autour des Gracques*, 244-266; Gelzer, *Gnomon*, 5 (1929), 656-657; H. Chantraine, *Untersuchungen zur römischen Geschichte am Ende des 2 Jahrhunderts vor Chr.* (Kallmünz, 1959), 15-26; Earl, "Sallust and the Senate's Numidian Policy," *Latomus*, 24 (1965), 535.

[109] *Lex agrar.* lines 45, 55, 59-60, 66 (*FIRA*, I.113-115).

specified on the stone, but is most probable. Plots were assigned in Africa and it is difficult to imagine what else a commission would be doing there. The commission presumably post-dates the repeal of the *lex Rubria*. It would therefore have been set up at the instigation of the opponents of the Gracchi. If the Carbo involved is the consul of 120, then the inscription can date no later than 119, the year of Carbo's death.

There is no reason to believe that the Gracchan commission was disbanded after the murder of C. Gracchus and Fulvius, any more than it had been after the death of Tiberius in 133. The task in Africa may well have been assigned to the old body of which Carbo was already a member or perhaps to a new group recruited for the purpose. In any case, the opposition would naturally have staffed it with men of their own liking. Carbo was a defector and experienced. Bestia's political allegiance was manifest: in 120 he sponsored the bill to recall the exile Popillius Laenas, persecutor and victim of the Gracchani.[110] The appearance of Galba in this company is an important piece of information. The Sulpicii Galbae had been closely connected with the Claudio-Fulvian group. C. Sulpicius was a brother-in-law of C. Gracchus, since both married daughters of P. Licinius Crassus Mucianus.[111] But Sulpicius, like Carbo, was drawn to greener pastures. The inscription suggests that he had deserted the Gracchan *factio* and reaped his reward. It indicates also, what has been noticed here before, that other senatorial groups had learned the lessons of the Gracchan clique. Land reform was not the province of a particular *factio*. The claims of extra-senatorial elements had to be appeased. Internecine warfare could no longer be fought out in the senate alone. Success in factional politics fell to that faction which could gain credit for measures appealing to external groups.

It is in this light that one must approach the series of three agrarian laws passed in the years following C. Gracchus' death and recorded in an unfortunately truncated manner by Appian.[112] That they were not merely illustrative of an anti-Gracchan "reaction," as Appian, obviously drawing here on a partisan source, portrays them, is now generally recognized.[113] The great bronze tablets recording the *lex agraria* of 111 are enough to show that the Gracchan land assignations were not wiped off the books, but were, on the contrary, largely confirmed.[114] By 111

[110] Cic. *Brutus,* 128; cf. *Post Red. in Sen.* 38; *Post Red. ad Quir.* 10-11.

[111] See above, pp. 21, 52.

[112] Appian, *BC,* 1.27.

[113] Cf. the judicious remarks on this score by Hardy, *JP,* 31 (1910), 268-286.

[114] *FIRA,* I.102-121. The most recent discussion of this measure is that of Hinrichs, "Die *lex agraria* des Jahres 111 v. Chr.," *ZSav,* 83 (1966), 252-307.

the agrarian commission had been abolished and there was little *ager publicus* remaining for distribution; yet there is no hint in the sources of popular unrest. Land hunger did not become a problem again until Marius opened the military to landless volunteers. Which group or groups were responsible for the agrarian laws is beyond knowing and does not warrant speculation. No names can be culled from the scanty evidence except that of the hopelessly obscure Sp. Thorius. But there is no reason to doubt that there was some factional infighting on each of these measures.

The identification and dating of these three bills has long stirred fierce controversy, and there is little point in adding fuel to the fire here. The first law, Appian says, was passed not long after the murder of C. Gracchus, and eliminated the inalienability of land holdings. This evidence should date it in 121 or 120. The measure need not be regarded as a reactionary move. Many small-holders would have been unable to farm successfully and doubtless welcomed the provision. Friends and political heirs of Scipio Aemilianus, their status enhanced in the senate with the crushing of C. Gracchus, may have sought to soften the blow and increase their *clientelae* among the populace. It should be repeated, however, that since neither proposer nor result is known, and date itself is uncertain, not much weight can be laid on this interpretation. The second law, passed by the much debated Sp. Thorius, eliminated further land distribution, confirmed *possessio,* and imposed a *vectigal* to be employed for the poor. Again, compromise and not reaction, seems to be the motive. The third law abolished the *vectigal* itself, possibly because of pressures by small land holders who could no longer afford it. Dating can only be conjectural. According to Appian, it was passed not much later than the second law and the whole series of measures fell within a fifteen-year period.[115] This dating might place the last law as late as 109 or 108, and the second a year or so earlier. If so, identification of the *lex Thoria* with the epigraphic law of 111 would become a natural as-

---

[115] Appian. *BC,* 1.27: καὶ νόμων πεντεκαίδεκα μάλιστα ἔτεσιν ἀπὸ τῆς Γράκχου νομοθεσίας ἐπὶ δίκιας ἐν ἀργίᾳ γεγονότες. That the "fifteen years" dates from the tribunate of C. Gracchus and not that of Ti. Gracchus seems clear from the context in Appian; cf. Gabba, *Appiano e la storia delle guerre civili* (Florence, 1956), 65-69; Niccolini, "Sp. Thorius *Tribunus Plebis* e la *Lex Agraria* del 111 a. Chr.," *RendLinc,* 28 (1919), 193-194; *Fast. Trib. Pleb.,* 182-183. For the opposite view, see, e.g., Carcopino, *Autour des Gracques,* 258-266; Pareti, *Storia di Roma,* III.398-400; E. D'Arms, "The Date and Nature of the *Lex Thoria,*" *AJP,* 56 (1935), 232-245; A. E. Douglas, "The Legislation of Spurius Thorius," *AJP,* 77 (1956), 376-395; "*Oratorum Aetates,*" *AJP,* 87 (1966), 304-306; and *M. Tulli Ciceronis Brutus* (Oxford, 1966), 246-250.

sumption.[116] But the first section of the *lex agraria* speaks of the removal rather than the imposition of *vectigal*.[117] The "fifteen-year" period may be an inexact estimate. It is surely not irrelevant that Sallust, under the year 111, can speak of a "fifteen-year" period of senatorial repression.[118] This partisan judgment is directly akin to that of Appian. The *lex agraria* of 111 is therefore more probably Appian's third law, whereas the *lex Thoria* falls a year or so earlier.[119] With the gradual ascendance of the Metellan *factio* in the decade after C. Gracchus' death,[120] it is possible that the latter two laws were sponsored by this group, though, again, little stress can be placed on this assumption. In any case, it should be clear that the laws represent continued efforts to attract support from elements of the population who would benefit and are not to be dismissed as "reactionary optimate policy."

By compelling the aristocracy to broaden its social and economic horizons, the Gracchi had performed a signal service. But the entanglement of judicial processes in politics had deepened. Nor were Gaius' hands clean in this development. Alteration of personnel in the extortion court set the stage for provincial exploitation and political contests unforeseen but ultimately provoked by Gaius himself. His judiciary laws had eliminated senatorial kangaroo courts and witch hunts under the guise of legal process; however, by hampering the government's authority to deal with emergencies, he had opened the door to more drastic procedures.

The constitutionality of the senate's "ultimate decree" did not go unchallenged. L. Opimius' term of office and his immunity expired in 120. A new tribune, P. Decius, described as reckless and undisciplined both in language and action, emerged to lodge prosecution against him

[116] This identification has been made, e.g., by Niccolini, *RendLinc*, 28 (1919), 189-194; *Fast. Trib. Pleb.*, 179-184; and by Badian, "From the Gracchi to Sulla (1940-1959)," *Historia*, 11 (1962), 211-213. Certainly the coupling of this second law with Cicero's *lex Thoria* (*Brutus*, 136) should no longer be doubted. The emendation of Appian's βόριος to θόριος is in-inevitable. See the vigorous arguments of Badian, *Studies*, 235-242. Recent objections of Douglas, *AJP*, 87 (1966), 304-306, do not persuade. Nor is there any warrant for emending Cicero, despite R. Seager, "Cicero, *Brutus*, 136," *CR*, 17 (1967), 12-13.

[117] *Lex agrar.* lines 19-20 (*FIRA*, I.107); cf. Gabba, *App. BC Lib. Prim.*, 94.

[118] Sallust, *Iug.* 31.2: *his annis quindecim quam ludibrio fueritis superbiae paucorum*. This is pointed out by Gabba, *Appiano*, 66.

[119] This persuasive solution has been most recently argued by Gabba, *Appiano*, 64-73; *App. BC Lib. Prim.*, 93-96.

[120] See below, Chapter IV.

102

before the people.[121] Was this a revival of the Gracchan cause? That is not easy to believe, for in 121 and 120 reaction had been complete and decisive. A hint survives, moreover, that Decius had had his differences with the now martyred Gracchan leader Fulvius Flaccus.[122] Motives for prosecution may have been personal. In the previous generation Q. Opimius, consul in 154, and a Decius were *inimici,* their hostility punctuated by a bitter, sarcastic exchange preserved by the sources.[123] The quarrelsome Decius had no difficulty in making powerful enemies in many camps. The scorn of Scipio Aemilianus is reflected in a probably slighting, though unintelligible, remark.[124] Later in 115 Decius had a violent interchange with the consul M. Aemilius Scaurus.[125] The attack on Opimius, then, may have been a personal vendetta, not the reemergence of a defunct political group. The constitutional issue, however, was novel and disputable. A good case could be made for the danger of Opimius' precedent and Decius could hope to convince the people of their interest on this count. The validity of Opimius' action in 121 was an issue long debated in Roman history and became a favorite topic in the rhetorical schools.[126]

Whatever Decius' motives, therefore, his hopes for success rested on convincing the populace that the constitutional issue represented a serious threat to liberty. The ground of the charge was obviously the execution of Roman citizens without trial.[127] According to Decius' argument this action was *contra leges.* The reference must be to the *lex Sempronia* of

[121] On Drusus' character, see Cic. *Brutus,* 108. For the trial, see Livy, *Per.* 61; Cic. *Brutus,* 128; *De Orat.* 2.106, 2.132, 2.170; *Pro Sest.* 140; *Part. Orat.* 106; cf. *ORF,* 154-156.

[122] Cicero's description of Decius as *Flacci aemulus* probably means "rival of Flaccus"; *Brutus,* 108.

[123] The evidence, fragmentary but consistent, was carefully pieced together by the keen eye of Münzer, "Anmerkungen zur neuen Livius-Epitome," *Klio,* 5 (1905), 135-139; Cic. *De Orat.* 2.253, 2.277; Livy, *Oxyr. Per.* 48; Val. Max. 6.1.10. His analysis is followed by Cichorius, *Unt. zu Luc.,* 310-318, and by Badian, "P. Decius P.f. Subulo," *JRS,* 46 (1956), 91-92.

[124] Cic. *De Orat.* 2.253: *Quid Decius? Nuculam an confixum vis facere?* The passage is taken from a poem of Lucilius.

[125] *Vir. Ill.* 72.6: *P. Decium praetorem, transeunte ipso* [Scaurus] *sedentem, iussit assurgere, eique vestem scidit, sellam concidit, ne quis ad eum in ius iret, edixit.* J. Heurgon, "Le préteur P. Decius et l'*imperium* de Marius," *REL,* 16 (1938), 161-168, argues, not very convincingly, that this incident occurred in 108 and involved the consul M. Aurelius Scaurus.

[126] Cic. *De Orat.* 2.106, 2.132, 2.165, 2.169; *Part. Orat.* 106.

[127] Cic. *Part. Orat.* 106; *De Orat.* 2.132, 2.106: *nihil de C. Gracchi nece negabat, sed id iure pro salute patriae factum esse dicebat.*

123, outlawing capital condemnation *iniussu populi,* which Decius sought to apply to this case. The comment of the Livian Epitomator that the charge was casting Roman citizens into prison without trial is incomplete but consistent with this interpretation. Imprisonment itself was not a legal penalty, but employed generally to detain condemned men prior to execution.[128] The defense of Opimius was handled by the consul, the renegade Gracchan C. Carbo.[129] It rested its case on the authority of the *senatus consultum ultimum.*[130] The facts were not in dispute; but the legitimacy of Opimius' action was. Details of the argument do not survive, but a case might have been made on the grounds that the *lex Sempronia* forbade judicial inquiry against *cives* without popular sanction, whereas the Gracchani had been executed not as *cives* but as *hostes* who were not covered by that law.[131]

The trial must have produced great tension and excitement. The oligarchy unquestionably placed concerted pressure upon their *clientelae.* Opimius secured acquittal, a result that probably owed more to political influence than to the legality of his action or the persuasiveness of his defense counsel.[132] The news had significant implications for another persecutor of the Gracchani, still languishing in exile. Cicero reports that Opimius did not press for the return of P. Popillius Laenas.[133] That statement should not mislead readers into assuming enmity between the two men. On the contrary, the implication is that Opimius was expected to advocate Popillius' recall. That he did not do so is doubtless due to the uncertainty of the situation in 121. If Popillius' recall had been blocked by the assembly, Opimius' own case would have been prejudiced. Once the Gracchani were eliminated and Opimius himself acquitted, the path was cleared for Popillius. A measure of L. Calpurnius Bestia secured the triumphant return of Popillius Laenas.[134]

Political pressure turned the trick, but Opimius' acquittal also entailed the settling of a momentous constitutional issue. The *lex Sempronia*

---

[128] Livy, *Per.* 61: *quod indemnatos cives in carcerem coniecisset;* cf. Mommsen, *Strafrecht,* 960-962.

[129] Cic. *De Orat.* 2.106, 2.165, 2.169-170.

[130] Cic. *De Orat.* 2.132: *Interfecit Opimius Gracchum. Quid facit causam? Quod rei publicae causa, cum ex senatus consulto ad arma vocasset. Hoc tolle, causa non erit.*

[131] Cf. Cic. *Cat.* 4.10.

[132] Livy, *Per.* 61; Cic. *Brutus,* 128; *Pro Sest.* 140. C. H. Brecht, "Perduellio," *MünchBeitr,* 29 (1938), 294, argued that acquittal came because the prosecution failed to produce an adequate precedent. But why was one needed? The Gracchan law had been passed but three short years before.

[133] Cic. *Post Red. ad Quir.* 10-11.

[134] Cic. *Brutus,* 128.

remained on the books. Special *quaestiones,* instituted by senatorial decree, were still forbidden and were no longer to be discerned in the Republic. The recall of Popillius did not repeal the *lex Sempronia.* The law that restored him would have repealed the *interdictio* passed by the assembly in 123 after his voluntary exile; the measure of Gracchus was not affected. But the *senatus consultum ultimum,* designed to circumvent this law by authorizing consular action against men declared *hostes* by the senate, had now been justified by Opimius' acquittal in a criminal trial. Precedent weighed heavily in Roman constitutional history. The *s.c.u.* was to be employed again and effectively on several occasions before it was challenged (unsuccessfully, as it turned out) more than sixty years later.

The Gracchan movement had left a considerable mark on both Roman judicial processes and Roman politics. Its legacy included new legal forms and new means of conducting political warfare. Criminal prosecutions in the past decade had been of particularly critical import. The lynching of Ti. Gracchus had its repercussions in the successful prosecution of Scipio Nasica, which once and for all outlawed the unauthorized use of force by a private citizen. The exile of Popillius Laenas confirmed the Gracchan legislation against senatorial use of *quaestiones extraordinariae* directed at political enemies. Gaius greatly widened the political stage. A self-consciousness of common interest was granted to groups like the *plebs,* the Italians, and the business classes. If extra-senatorial groups could be marshaled on tribunician initiative against the senate, that august body could swiftly be converted to a debating society. The answer was the *senatus consultum ultimum,* whose fate was decided at the crucial trial of L. Opimius. His acquittal sanctioned the newest and most ominous weapon in the senatorial arsenal, and the recall of Popillius reduced the efficacy of the *lex Sempronia.* For the next century, the *s.c.u.* menaced prospective reformers who might undermine senatorial prestige in the name of other groups. The outcome of Opimius' trial cleared the way for the revival of factional politics. The narrow oligarchic infighting of the pre-Gracchan period was a thing of the past, but a factional basis remained an integral part of the Roman political structure to the end of the Republic. The ranks of the senate had closed against Gaius as against Tiberius, but with the dissipation of the Gracchan group, new factions emerged, on a wider basis, and senatorial struggles held the stage once more in the succeeding decade.

IV. THE EMERGENCE OF METELLAN SUPREMACY

The elimination of the Gracchani and the derailing of the Gracchan movement considerably eased pressure on the aristocracy. The coalition that had been assembled to upset senatorial policy and shatter the prestige of the *curia* was now in disarray. The *equester ordo* saw that its control of the extortion court and the new financial arrangements in Asia went unchallenged by the oligarchy and abandoned C. Gracchus. The *plebs* recognized that a program of broad enfranchisement was inconsistent with its interests. The Latins could be appeased by greater political participation and the offer of *provocatio;* the Italians were less vocal and less troublesome. The Roman oligarchy seemed secure. As on more than one occasion, once external pressure was removed, the senate need no longer present a united front. The game of factional politics could be resumed.

It is not easy to discern political alignments in the decade of the 110's. The sources become tantalizingly fragmentary and elusive. Ancient commentators and historians tended to lose interest after the death of C. Gracchus. But the indications that survive warrant investigation and may provide more information than has hitherto been suspected.

An episode in 120 that has received scant attention perhaps provides a clue. As noted earlier, among those who had participated in the final assault on the Gracchani in 121 was the octogenarian *princeps senatus* P. Cornelius Lentulus, who sported a wound on his triumphant descent from the Aventine. In the following year, it is reported, public hostility against him for this action was so strong that he had to resort to the artifice used for Scipio Nasica and obtain from the senate a *legatio libera* to Sicily, where he spent the remainder of his days.[1] That is an item which no historian should have missed. In this same year and for this same offense L. Opimius was brought to trial and triumphantly acquitted,

[1] Val. Max. 5.3.2f. Münzer, *RE,* 4.1375, "Cornelius," n. 202, on no grounds, doubts this information.

and Popillius Laenas was recalled from exile. Yet the senate could not protect the venerable *princeps senatus,* who was forced to flee. Lentulus did not command the support that could be marshaled by Opimius. Both had been conspicuous in the crushing of C. Gracchus, but that problem had been disposed of. The affair suggests that divisions in the senate were evident again now that unity was no longer required.

The most vocal and aggressive leaders of the opposition to Gracchus had been M. Fannius, Livius Drusus, Minucius Rufus, L. Piso, and of course, L. Opimius. Hostility is attested also for Q. Aelius Tubero and Fabius Maximus Allobrogicus. The summoning of Popillius Laenas from banishment set a victorious seal upon the anti-Gracchan movement. As indicated earlier, most, if not all, of these men show a connection with Scipio Aemilianus or an earlier association with the Scipionic circle. Whether they should be lumped together and regarded as a political group is not subject to documentation. Yet friends and relatives of Scipio Aemilianus survived his death, and the elimination of the Gracchani would have appealed to some as vengeance for his premature demise. In any case, these individuals are to be distinguished from another *factio,* untarnished with Gracchan associations, but traditionally hostile to the Scipios, which had gradually been consolidated in the 120's. The four sons of Metellus Macedonicus had now reached political maturity and the adherence of families like the Servilii Caepiones and the Aurelii Cottae formed the nucleus of a powerful alliance. Metellus Balearicus had secured the censorship for 120, and the consuls of 119, Metellus Delmaticus and L. Cotta, were both members of this group. The violent and enraged passions of 121 had died down. The successors of Scipio could not trade forever on their successful demolition of the Gracchan group. With the "popular" menace removed, factional politics could once more be played out in the courts.

The most vulnerable aristocrat was obviously C. Papirius Carbo. His earlier Gracchan connections and attacks on Scipio in 131 doubtless assured him some enemies in the oligarchy. A renegade is never without suspicion among his new compatriots. Rumors of Carbo's involvement in the death of Scipio Aemilianus could also be used against him. His defense of Opimius dramatized the baseness of his treachery. Carbo was the logical point at which to launch a political attack.

The task was entrusted to a young man who made his first appearance before the bar in this case. L. Licinius Crassus, despite his youth, had extensive preparation and carried impressive credentials. He possessed oratorical gifts in abundance, but much more than that; he was a voracious student of the law, a scholar and an intellectual. No orator was more highly praised by Cicero. The combination of dignified presence, command of language, and lucidity of argumentation was unrivaled. Crassus was the future *fori princeps*.[2] His family was also distinguished and influential. The previous generation had seen opposition to the Scipionic bloc.[3] Connections of the Licinii Crassi with the Claudian group were doubtless severed during the 120's after the death of Crassus Mucianus. The family did not suffer in the Gracchan debacle. Crassus himself appears later as a close ally of the Metellan group,[4] and it is perhaps not unreasonable to see his maiden political appearance as activity on behalf of that group. It was also, of course, the beginning of a brilliant oratorical career.

Carbo was prosecuted probably near the beginning of 119 and convicted.[5] The charge on which he was brought to trial is nowhere recorded in the sources. That he was implicated in the death of Scipio was bound to be mentioned, in the expectation of playing on the prejudices of some of Carbo's would-be backers. But it is hardly likely that the murder of Scipio was the formal charge laid.[6] The ancients themselves, as discussed above, were thoroughly bewildered about the cause of Scipio's death. It is inconceivable that our sources would be so confused on this subject if Carbo had actually been convicted of Scipio's murder. That the charge was *maiestas* and was connected with the same offense on which Opimius had been prosecuted was long ago suggested and has often been reiterated.[7] But the charge of *maiestas* had not yet even been defined as a criminal offense. It is very difficult to believe, moreover, that, after the signal failure to convict Opimius in the previous year, the same accusation would have been attempted against Carbo. An important piece of information rules this conjecture out of court. Opimius, as was proper according to the terms of the *lex Sempronia*, was tried by the assembly, but Carbo's trial took place before *iudices*.[8] That a *quaestio extraordinaria* was instituted is nowhere recorded.[9] The trial

[2] Val. Max. 8.5.3; cf. Cic. *Brutus*, 143-145; and *De Orat. passim*.

[3] For the relationship of L. Crassus to the Crassi mentioned earlier (not very close), see the stemma in Münzer, *RE*, 25.247-248.

[4] See below, pp. 157-159, 201-202.

[5] Cic. *De Orat.* 1.40, 3.74; *Brutus*, 159; Val. Max. 3.7.6, 6.5.6; Tac. *Dial.* 34.

[6] As is believed by Carcopino, *Autour des Gracques*, 94-99. See Cic. *De Orat.* 2.170.

[7] Mommsen, *Röm. Gesch.*, 2.126; cf. Greenidge, *History of Rome*, 282; *ORF*, 240. *MRR*, I.526, still considers it a possibility.

[8] Cic. *Brutus*, 103: *se a severitate iudicum vindicavit*.

[9] It is usually assumed that Q. Fabius Maximus Eburnus sat on this case as praetor; Münzer, *RE*, 12.1797, "Fabius," n. 111; *MRR*, I.526. But Cic. *De Orat.* 1.121 need not refer to the trial of Carbo. Indeed, the description of Crassus as pale and terrified rather tells against it.

was very likely heard by a standing court, and, in all probability, since we know of no other *quaestiones perpetuae,* by the extortion court.[10] Since the important point was to ruin Carbo, his past would have been ransacked to provide a plausible charge. The affair probably grew out of a provincial assignment following Carbo's praetorship, though nothing of that praetorship is known. Conviction was, in any case, not dependent on the degree of Carbo's guilt. His new associates doubtless found Carbo's trial embarrassing and do not appear to have struggled in his defense. Their lack of support helps to explain the fact that Carbo committed suicide, although exile was, of course, open to him. Carbo must have been abandoned on all sides; suicide was the recourse of desperation.[11] The trial was the opening move in a series of criminal prosecutions reflecting an internal political struggle.

The friends of Opimius and of Carbo, his erstwhile defense counsel, seem to have sought retaliation against Opimius' prosecutor and *inimicus* P. Decius. Only accident preserves the two references that elucidate this obscure event. Among the rhetorical exercises popular in the schools, a typical illustration of the question of pure fact was *ceperitne pecunias P. Decius.*[12] Decius is too insignificant a character for this exercise simply to have been invented out of thin air. The incident must have some basis in fact. It is possible that he was accused of having been bribed by Opimius' enemies to undertake the prosecution in 120.[13] That Decius underwent a formal trial, probably in 119, is clear. Cicero gives two other illustrations in the same context with Decius' offense and both of these refer to actual criminal prosecution.[14]

What was the meaning of this affair? It has been argued that Decius' case was a *repetundae* trial, and that his acquittal, coupled with the conviction of Carbo, both by equestrian jurors, represents a reaction by the *equites* against the senatorial anti-Gracchan policy.[15] That is an over-simplification. The mood of the *equites* is elusive and difficult to

[10] So also Zumpt, *Der Criminalprocess der römischen Republik* (Leipzig, 1871), 470-471, who wrongly dates the trial to 118, and Fraccaro, *Studi Storici,* 5 (1912), 446-447.

[11] Cic. *Brutus,* 103; *Ad Fam.* 9.21.3. Crassus later repented of this prosecution; Cic. *Verr.* 3.1.3. He did so not, surely, on political grounds, but perhaps because he could not have foreseen the eventuality of suicide.

[12] Cic. *De Orat.* 2.135; *Part. Orat.* 104.

[13] Fraccaro, *Studi Storici,* 5 (1912), 444-445.

[14] Cic. *Part. Orat.* 104. The other two cases are the *maiestas* trial of Norbanus and the prosecution of Opimius; cf. Badian, *JRS,* 46 (1956), 92-95.

[15] Badian, *JRS,* 46 (1956), 92-95; reiterated in *Historia,* 11 (1962), 214-215. That Decius was acquitted seems certain from the fact that he went on to hold a praetorship in 115; *Vir. Ill.* 72.6.

follow. It would be most misleading to speak of *equites* as if they formed a compact unit with a consistent policy. Men of business and finance had no reason to maintain loyalty to the Gracchi in 119. Indeed, what little evidence survives on their activities in 121 shows that some at least had assisted Opimius against the followers of C. Gracchus.[16] Their control of the courts could discourage meddling with business activities abroad, but there is no reason to believe that they felt their interests directly involved in the fate of Carbo and Decius. To see the trials of 119 in terms of a struggle between the *boni* on the one hand and the *equites* as heirs of the Gracchi on the other would be to misconstrue the events of the past two years. A Gracchan faction after 121 is out of the question. Individual *populares,* of course, crop up sporadically, advocating various portions and extensions of the Gracchan program, but the *equites* can hardly be regarded as the heirs of this program. Their alliance with the Gracchi was rewarding but brief, as was their temporary alignment with the populace at the time of the Mamilian commission. Their condemnation of Carbo was the elimination of a man who had offended all elements of society and who was abandoned even by many of his own recent friends.

Of the case of Decius, it is worth reiterating that we know very little. It is not at all certain even that he was tried by a jury of *equites*. The evidence shows only that he was tried on grounds of accepting money for some purpose. That this charge represents bribery to accuse Opimius is not unlikely, but cannot be proved. Even if this hypothesis be accepted, however, it does not follow that the case would come before the *quaestio repetundarum.* Under the *lex Iulia repetundarum* of Julius Caesar, bribery for the purpose of *accusandum vel non accusandum* did fall within the purview of the extortion court,[17] but there is no warrant for reading this back into the Gracchan age. The extant portions of the *lex Acilia* make no mention of any such provision. Under the Sullan law the corruption of jurors was regarded as a *repetundae* offense,[18] but the corruption of jurors is not the same thing as bribery of an *accusator,* and, in any event, we have no reason to believe that Sulla adopted this provision from the Gracchan extortion law. If Decius were prosecuted for illegal collusion in the trial of Opimius, then the operative piece of legislation may well have been the *lex ne quis iudicio circumveniretur,* in which case Decius would have been tried by the *comitia* and not by a panel of equestrian *iudices.*[19] Be that as it may, the coalition of populace and knights had been dissolved two years earlier; there is no reason to

[16] Sallust, *Iug.* 42.1; Plut. *C. Gracch.* 14.
[17] *Digest,* 48.11.6.2.
[18] Cic. *Verr.* 1.38; *Pro Cluent.* 104, 114.
[19] On this law, see above, pp. 84-86.

resurrect it here. The trial of Decius reflects personal bitterness and factional contest. The senatorial leaders of 121 were being challenged. Carbo had been convicted and took his own life. The friends of Opimius (one presumes) failed to secure a condemnation of P. Decius. The Metellan *factio* was to be the gainer.[20]

The *equester ordo* merits another pause. This class has often been seen by modern historians as wooed and won by the Metellan group after the death of C. Gracchus.[21] Documentation is difficult and proof impossible. It is true that the Metelli formed a link with M. Aemilius Scaurus, the future *princeps senatus,* who had many connections among the business classes.[22] They also adopted as a client the promising *novus homo* C. Marius, who was, throughout his life, closely associated with equestrian interests.[23] These maneuvers indicate that the Metelli were bidding for equestrian support. As the people could no longer simply be ignored after the Gracchi, neither could the business classes. But to assume that the Metellan group had captured the *equester ordo* goes well beyond the evidence. As we have seen, the *equites* cannot, in any case, be considered an integrated unit with consistent common interests. Insofar as the ancient sources permit conjecture, an equally good case could be made out for the endeavor of other groups to conciliate business elements. Marius, after all, served under Scipio Aemilianus in 134, and was highly praised by him.[24] There may even have been ancient family bonds.[25] Overseas ventures in these years suggest greater state

[20] Q. Metellus Numidicus, the promising nephew of Macedonicus, appeared in his first criminal case probably in or around this year. It was the successful prosecution of a Valerius Messala; Gellius, 15.14.1; cf. R. Syme, "Missing Senators," *Historia,* 4 (1955), 70-71.

[21] G. Bloch and J. Carcopino, *Histoire Romaine,* II (Paris, 1940), 276-279; Pareti, *Storia di Roma,* III.388, 391-392; T. F. Carney, *A Biography of Marius, Proc. Afr. Class. Ass.,* Supp. No. 1 (Assen, Netherlands, 1961), 17-18.

[22] On the business connections, cf. *Vir. Ill.* 72.2; Pliny, *NH,* 36.116; Sallust, *Iug.* 15, 25, 28-30, 32, 40; G. Bloch, "M. Aemilius Scaurus," *Mélanges D'Histoire Ancienne,* 25 (1909), 21-24; Pais, *Dalle Guerre Puniche,* 112-118.

[23] Plut. *Marius,* 4.1, on the clientship; cf. Weynand, *RE,* Supp. 6.1369-1371, "Marius," n. 14. For Marius' equestrian connections, see esp. Sherwin-White, *JRS,* 46 (1956), 2-5; T. F. Carney, "Coins Bearing on the Age and Career of Marius," *NC,* 19 (1959), 79-82.

[24] Val. Max. 8.15.7: *forte inter cenam quidam Scipionem interrogasset, si quid illi accidisset, quemnam res publica aeque magnum habitura esset imperatorem . . . "vel hunc" dixerit.* So also Plut. *Marius,* 3.4. The story itself may be spurious, but it indicates friendly relations between the commander and his junior officer. Cf. E. Valgiglio, *Plutarco, Vita di Mario* (Florence, 1956), 15-16.

[25] Cf. Carney, *A Biog. of Marius,* 15.

concern with expanded economic opportunities. Activities like those of
Q. Metellus Balearicus, who cleared the Balearic Isles of piracy in 123,
and of L. Licinius Crassus, who advocated the foundation of Narbo,
may well have been designed to appeal to the business classes. But the
same can be said of the Gallic campaigns and foundations in the north
by Q. Fabius Allobrogicus and Cn. Domitius Ahenobarbus in 121-120,
neither of whom was connected with the Metellan *factio* and one of
whom was a nephew of Scipio Aemilianus. The evidence, such as it is,
shows, therefore, that the bidding for support among extra-senatorial
groups inaugurated by the Gracchi continued to be practiced by senatorial factions in the succeeding decade. But that either the people or
the *equester ordo* can be systematically linked to a single *factio* for any
length of time is nowhere suggested and is unreasonable in itself.

Labels such as "moderate" or "progressive" cannot legitimately be
stamped upon the Metelli, any more than upon the older Scipionic
group.[26] The Gracchan movement had left at least this heritage: political
success had to be grounded on a much wider base than the pre-Gracchan
oligarchy had ever required. Factional struggles went on after the death
of C. Gracchus, but the differences between factions did not always
rest on political conviction or principle.

Whatever the influence of the Metelli in the equestrian ranks, however,
a careful analysis of the decade of the 110's reveals that faction's gradual
rise to ascendancy within the aristocracy. The evidence of judicial prosecutions, although it must be treated with caution, is fundamental. In a
period where sources are few and fragmentary, criminal trials reveal
much of shifting political allegiances and the consolidation of power.

The first case that seizes attention is that of the distinguished jurist
and philosopher Q. Mucius Scaevola. Dignified but gracious in bearing,
he was the most learned of Romans in the civil law. Jurisprudence was
his specialty, but Scaevola, Cicero reports, was preeminent in every
sphere of wisdom.[27] Yet after a praetorship in 120 and a term as governor
of Asia, Scaevola returned in 119 and was promptly charged with extortion.[28]

Scaevola's political connections at this juncture are by no means easy

---

[26] Bloch-Carcopino, *Hist. Rom.*, 277, even refer to the Metelli as "Whigs."
No ancient evidence is cited for the "moderation" of the Metellan clique.
None can be.

[27] Cic. *Brutus*, 102, 145, 212.

[28] Cic. *De Orat.* 1.72, 2.281, 3.171; *Orator*, 149; *De Fin.* 1.9; *Brutus*, 102;
Persius. *Sat.* 1.115; Juvenal, *Sat.* 1.15.4; Apuleius, *Apol.* 66. Almost all, if
not all, this information derived from Lucilius' satire on this trial; II.53-93
(*ROL*, 3.18-31). For the date of Scaevola's praetorship, see Cichorius, *Unt.
zu Luc.* 88-89.

to make out. As a young man he had been closely linked with the philo-
sophic and literary coterie around Scipio Aemilianus. He had been
attracted by Stoicism and became a disciple of Panaetius.[29] Poseidonius
reckoned him, along with two others in the Scipionic group, Q. Aelius
Tubero and P. Rutilius Rufus, as the most genuine of the Roman Stoics.[30]
Scaevola's ties with the Scipionic bloc were further consolidated by his
marriage to the elder daughter of C. Laelius, and he was preferred by
him for the augurate over Laelius' other son-in-law, C. Fannius.[31]

Scipionic connections in the 140's and 130's, however, cannot be
taken as decisive for 119. Factional allegiance fluctuated and the Scipionic group had already lost its attraction for some men, like Q. Pompeius,
C. Cato, and C. Fannius, in the 130's and 120's.[32] The Scaevolae are
enigmatic. As has been seen, P. Mucius Scaevola, once a supporter of
Scipio, abandoned him to follow his brother Mucianus into cooperation
with the Licinii Crassi and the Claudio-Fulvian group. Need it be assumed that Q. Scaevola had joined his cousins in support of the Gracchi? [33] The evidence is not decisive. P. Scaevola, cautious and temporiz-
ing, had not backed Ti. Gracchus to the hilt and later praised his slayer.
There was a delay in Q. Scaevola's career; he reached the higher magisterial posts rather late.[34] That fact can cut both ways: Scaevola may
have failed to advance in the 120's either because he had supported or
because he had opposed the Gracchi.[35] The consular *fasti* cannot answer
the question conclusively either way. The period between 133 and 122
shows Gracchan and anti-Gracchan consuls alike, quite apart from the
fact that many names cannot be conclusively identified with one group
or another. A different piece of information, however, may provide some
enlightenment. In Cicero's *De Oratore* words are put into the mouth of
Scaevola denouncing the Gracchi as having wrecked the Republic. Of
course, the perspective of three decades may have altered Scaevola's

[29] Cic. *De Orat.* 1.43, 1.75. Scaevola was old enough to hear the lectures
of Carneades in that year; Cic. *De Orat.* 3.68. Hence, he was probably born
around 174, the year of his father's consulship.
[30] Athenaeus, 6.274.
[31] On the marriage, Cic. *De Orat.* 1.35, 1.58, 2.22, 3.45; *De Rep.* 1.18;
Brutus, 3, 26. On the augurate, Cic. *Brutus,* 101; G. Lepointe, *Q. Mucius
Scaevola* (Paris, 1926), 12-13.
[32] See above, pp. 66-67.
[33] As Kübler, *RE,* 31.432, "Mucius," n. 21; also, more cautiously, Münzer,
Röm. Adelsp., 277.
[34] If Scaevola was born in the late 170's, he was more than fifty when he
reached the praetorship.
[35] For the former view, see note 33 above; for the latter view, see M. van
den Bruwaene, "L'Opposition à Scipion Emilien après la mort de Tiberius
Gracchus," *Phoibos,* 5 (1950-51), 234-235; Hands, *Latomus,* 24 (1965),
226-228.

view of the Gracchan movement.[36] More significant is the fact that the year 121, which saw the assassination of C. Gracchus and the election to the consulship of C. Papirius Carbo, was also the year in which Q. Scaevola finally reached the praetorship for 120. It is in the highest degree unlikely that a follower of the Gracchi would have been elected in 121 and then receive the key post of Asia in 120 at the height of the anti-Gracchan reaction.

That Scaevola ever sympathized with the aims of the Gracchani is nowhere recorded and, considering the training and background of the conservative jurist, probably unlikely. It is noteworthy also that L. Septumuleius, who was involved in the murder of Gaius and was a friend of Opimius, expected to receive a post on Scaevola's staff in Asia. That fact certainly implies that Scaevola was not in the Gracchan circle. But though the jurist might support opposition to the Gracchi, he could not countenance illicit and unnecessary violence. Scaevola's reply to Septumuleius' petition was a rejection and severe rebuke.[37] He was doubtless indignant at the murder of C. Gracchus, the ruthless persecution of his followers, and the association with hired assassins and thugs like Septumuleius.

Earlier associations with the circle of Scipio were probably severed by Scaevola as by many others in the 120's. The poet Lucilius, a protégé of that circle, launched bitter attacks on Scaevola.[38] The jurist was a man of principle and independence. One daughter was married off to L. Licinius Crassus, the young prosecutor of Opimius, the other later to the former Gracchan tribune M'. Acilius Glabrio, author of the *lex Acilia*. Crassus' marriage had already taken place by the time of Scaevola's trial in 119 and since Crassus was only twenty-one years old in that year, his wedding cannot have been much earlier.[39] The harshness of the anti-Gracchan reaction had repelled Scaevola and the marriage

[36] Cic. *De Orat.* 1.38; *rempublicam dissipaverunt.* Dramatic date of the dialogue is 91.

[37] Cic. *De Orat.* 2.269: *ut noster Scaevola Septumuleio illi Anagnino, cui pro C. Gracchi capite erat aurum repensum, roganti ut se in Asiam praefectum duceret, "Quid tibi vis," inquit, "insane? tanta malorum est multitudo civium ut tibi ego hoc confirmem, si Romae manseris, te paucis annis ad maximas pecunias esse venturum."*

[38] Juvenal, *Sat.* 1.154: *quid refert, dictis ignoscat Mucius an non?*; Persius, *Sat.* 1.115: *secuit Lucilius urbem, te Lupe, te Muci:* Cic. *De Orat.* 1.72: *C. Lucilius . . . homo tibi subiratus;* cf. *Ad Herenn.* 2.19, with W. Barr, "Lucilius and Accius," *RhM*, 108 (1965), 101-103.

[39] For Crassus' age, see Cic. *De Orat.* 3.74. He is referred to as married in 119; Lucilius, II.86 (*ROL*, 3.28); cf. Marx, *Luc. Carm. Rel.*, 40. That the marriage alliance with Glabrio came later is indicated by the birth of his first son, the consul of 67, ca. 110. Münzer, *Röm. Adelsp.*, 275-279, has no warrant for dating Glabrio's marriage prior to that of Crassus.

link with Crassus must have come at about the time of the latter's prosecution of Carbo. Scaevola's cousin and fellow jurist P. Scaevola had already advertised his political association with Metellus Macedonicus a decade before.[40] The later activities of both Crassus and the Scaevolae show cooperation with the Metellan *factio*,[41] which continued to gain strength. For Q. Scaevola, the turning point may have come in 121.

The men who took the lead in the slaughter of the Gracchani might have expected the sanction and endorsement of Q. Scaevola. Had not his cousin P. Scaevola done as much for Scipio Nasica a dozen years earlier? But Quintus gave his answer to Septumuleius and his daughters to men who scorned violence and reaction. It is not impossible that resentment against the learned lawyer helped inspire a prosecution upon his return from Asia.

Political motivation perhaps ought not to be overstressed in this case. Scaevola's accuser T. Albucius had a personal grievance. A self-styled Hellenist, Albucius liked to flaunt his Graecisms; worse yet, he was a "perfect Epicurean." Scaevola, apparently, mocked him for his obnoxious Hellenic affectation.[42] Evidence for the trial comes almost exclusively from what remains of Book II of Lucilius' satires. There is no need to examine in detail the brief and generally baffling fragments.[43] Some points, however, merit discussion. That the prosecution pursued every avenue to secure conviction appears from the fact that, though the trial was for extortion,[44] intimations of homicide also seem to have been introduced. At one point during the trial, Albucius apparently charged Scaevola with deliberate assault on someone.[45] Indeed, Scaevola's enemies were so eager to convict him that they arranged a fake funeral and burial of a man who was not even dead. Scaevola was obliged to commission two members of his staff to exhume the coffin in order to establish his innocence.[46] That incident may suggest more than just a personal quarrel.

Cicero indicates that Albucius sought to use the evidence of the account books of Scaevola's quaester Albius against him. The loyal Albius rejoiced at Scaevola's acquittal despite the fact that it entailed the rejection of his own records, for which he was mockingly reproved by

[40] Cic. *De Rep.* 1.31.

[41] See below, Chapter VII.

[42] Cic. *De Fin.* 1.9; *Brutus,* 131.

[43] This has been adequately done by Marx, *Luc. Carm. Rel.,* 29-44; Cichorius, *Unt. zu Luc.,* 237-251.

[44] Cic. *Brutus,* 102: *Mucius autem augur, quod pro se opus erat, ipse dicebat, ut de pecuniis repetundis contra T. Albucium.* Cf. Lucilius, II.57 (*ROL,* 3.20).

[45] Lucilius, II.54 (*ROL,* 3.20).

[46] Lucilius, II.73-74 (*ROL,* 3.24); cf. Cichorius, *Unt. zu Luc.,* 242-244.

another friend of Scaevola, the herald Granius.[47] This episode is evidence for substantial influence being brought to bear on behalf of Scaevola. The account books of Albius apparently told against Scaevola, but acquittal came in spite of them. The equestrian jurors may not have ruled merely on the merits of the case.

The acquittal of Scaevola, who went on to hold the consulship in 117, suggests the decline of the extremists of 121. Drift from the old Scipionic group into the swelling alliance of the Metelli may be illustrated by more than one distinguished individual. Q. Lutatius Catulus, the future consul of 102, was also as a youth associated with the literary circle around Scipio, including Laelius, L. Furius Philus, and their philosophical friends from Greece.[48] His mother was a Popillia, doubtless of the Popillii Laenates, also connected with this group and associated with the harshest anti-Gracchan reaction.[49] Catulus was among the most cultured men of his day. He boasted the purest style of Latin diction and his mastery of Greek was acknowledged with admiration by Romans and Greeks alike.[50] He was a philosopher, a historian, and a poet.[51] Cicero can hardly find words glowing enough to describe him: *humanitate, sapientia, integritate antecellens.*[52] But Catulus seems to have abandoned his former associates at some time during this decade. The divorce of his first wife Domitia may mark the break.[53] His marriage to Servilia now linked him to the Servilii Caepiones, a family long connected with the Metelli. Another piece of evidence lends further credence. Catulus was a friend of L. Aurelius Cotta, tribune in 103 and member of another family with close Metellan ties.[54] In the *De Oratore,* Catulus appears as one of the chief interlocutors along with L. Crassus and M. Antonius, both of whom, it will be seen, were also members of this group. Q. Scaevola and Q. Catulus, men of the intellectual as well as the political world; both seem to have lent their talents to the Metellan coalition. A famous name of the next generation discloses a neglected link between

[47] Cic. *De Orat.* 2.281: *obiurgavit Albium Granius quod, cum eius tabulis quiddam ab Albucio probatum videretur, et valde absoluto Scaevola guaderet neque intellegeret contra suas tabulas esse iudicatum.* We may note that this same Granius was a friend of Scaevola's new son-in-law L. Licinius Crassus; Lucilius, XI.448-449 (*ROL*, 3.140); Cic. *Brutus,* 160, 172.

[48] Cic. *De Orat.* 2.154-155.

[49] Cic. *De Orat.* 2.44.

[50] Cic. *Brutus,* 132; *De Orat.* 2.28, 3.29.

[51] Cf. Cic. *Acad. Prior.* 2.18; *De Nat. Deor.* 1.79; *De. Orat. passim;* and see H. O. Simon, *Vita Q. Lutatii Catuli* (Berlin, 1874), 307.

[52] Cic. *Pro Mur.* 36; cf. *Pro Rab. Perd.* 26; *Pro Planc.* 12.

[53] On this divorce and remarriage, see Badian, *Studies,* 232, n. 7, against Münzer, *RE,* 26.2073, "Lutatius," n. 7.

[54] Cic. *De Orat.* 3.42.

those two men. Among those who served on Scaevola's staff and testified in his behalf was a certain Hortensius.[55] He may have been the father of the celebrated orator and consul of 69, Q. Hortensius, who was a close friend of L. Crassus, Scaevola's son-in-law, and was himself the son-in-law of Q. Lutatius Catulus.[56]

A similar pattern may be perceived in another prominent family. The Scipionic background of M. Livius Drusus, the tribune of 122 who wrecked the Gracchan program, has already been noted. His allegiances thereafter do not permit secure reconstruction, but his more famous son, the future tribune of 91, was a staunch figure in the Metellan *factio*.[57] That group seems to have been the chief beneficiary of both disenchantment with Gracchan extremism and the breakup of the old Scipionic alliance. Between 123 and 109, Caecilii Metelli alone held no fewer than six consulships, the four sons of Macedonicus and the two sons of Calvus. The *fasti* in these years are also studded with other names that may be linked to the Metellan coalition.

The Scipios themselves are the most dramatic and decisive illustration of the trend. There had been no keener rivalry than that between Scipio Aemilianus and Metellus Macedonicus. But this was a new generation and a new era. P. Scipio Nasica Serapio, the future consul of 111 and son of the Nasica who had assassinated Ti. Gracchus in 133, married the daughter of Metellus Macedonicus.[58] The older Nasica was no longer recognizable in his son. Serapio was docile, pleasant, of a character completely different from his father, and sought to avoid enemies from any quarter; a man beloved even, it was said, by the lower classes.[59] The following generation continued the trend: Serapio's son, praetor in 93, was betrothed to a Licinia, the daughter of L. Licinius Crassus.[60] Obviously the heirs of Scipio did not find consistency a political virtue. Poets, by contrast, could afford greater independence: Aemilianus' friend Lucilius continued to attack the sons of Macedonicus as he had attacked their father.[61]

The Metelli also had a keen eye for men with potential, *novi homines*

---

[55] Lucilius, II.73-74 (*ROL*, 3.24).

[56] Cic. *De Orat.* 3.228.

[57] See below, pp. 206-214.

[58] Münzer, *RE*, 7.1504-1505, "Cornelius," n. 355.

[59] Cic. *De Off*. 1.109: *itemque in sermonibus alium quemque, quamvis praepotens sit efficere, ut unus de multis esse videatur;* cf. Pliny, *NH*, 21.10.

[60] See note 58.

[61] Schol. on Horace, *Sat.* 2.1.67. This may be plausibly connected with three extant lines of Lucilius lampooning the rustic character of "Cecilius," praetor-designate; V.232-234 (*ROL* 3.72): *Cecilius pretor ne rusticus fiat . . . Ne designati rostrum praetoris pedesque spectes.* Cf. Marx, *Luc. Carm. Rel.*,

and *equites*. Two notable examples stand out; they were to emerge as the most powerful personalities of the next three decades: C. Marius and M. Aemilius Scaurus. Tradition had it that Marius was a humble soldier by origin, a rough unhewn warrior, the self-made man who overcame barriers set by the prejudice and narrowmindedness of the nobility. It was an image that Marius himself perhaps found profitable to perpetuate.[62] In fact Marius came from a municipal family of equestrian census. It was a family prominent in Arpinum, but local distinction had little relevance in Rome. The young Marius strengthened his sinews and expanded his contacts on the battlefield. Association with Scipio Aemilianus at Numantia may have whetted a political appetite. An outstanding war record helped him move up the ladder, but slowly. The Scipios were no longer powerful and patronage was needed for Roman magistracies. Marius, it is specifically recorded, reached the tribunate of 119 through the efforts of the Metelli; an earlier quaestorship may also have been under their patronage.[63] He represented, no doubt, a talented and potentially useful supporter in the lower ranks of the senate.

M. Aemilius Scaurus was rather a different case. His was a patrician family, and there had been consulars among his ancestors, but none for three generations. For Scaurus prospects were dim; he was scarcely better off than a *novus homo*.[64] Lack of money did not help matters. His father had been reduced to the occupation of purveying charcoal.[65] Scaurus had to attain prominence through ingenuity and resourcefulness; his example later inspired Cicero.[66] But there may have been some outside assistance as well. By the time Scaurus reached the consulship he was already forty-seven or forty-eight years old.[67] Yet he was immediately named *princeps senatus* by the censors, one of whom was a Metellus. Later ties with the Metelli were close, and Scaurus eventually married a Caecilia Metella.[68] The *factio* had found another eminently gifted protégé.

---

xlvii. Lucilius would have recalled Scipio Aemilianus' remark about Metellus Caprarius: *si quintum pareret mater eius, asinum fuisse parituram;* Cic. *De Orat.* 2.267. Lucilius' lines were penned in 118 or 117; Marx, *Luc. Carm. Rel.,* 87; Cichorius, *Unt. zu Luc.,* 87-88, 278.

[62] Cf. Sallust, *Iug.* 85.

[63] Plut. *Marius,* 4.1; on Marius' early years, see Carney, *A Biog. of Marius,* 8-18; J. Van Ooteghem, *Caius Marius, Mem. Acad. Roy. Belg.* (Brussels, 1964), 56-78.

[64] Asconius, 23, Clark: *Itaque Scauro aeque ac novo homini laborandum fuit.*

[65] *Vir. Ill.* 72; cf. Val. Max. 4.4.11.

[66] Cic. *Pro Mur.* 16; Asconius, 22, Clark; cf. Bloch, *Mélanges D'Histoire Ancienne,* 25 (1909), 4-9; Pais, *Dalle Guerre Puniche,* 147.

[67] Bloch, *Mélanges D'Histoire Ancienne,* 25 (1909), 18-19.

[68] See below, note 82.

It would be wrong, however, to imagine that the Metelli were without rivals in the senate or that they had everything their own way. The client relationship with Marius was rudely shattered in 119 when, having gained the tribunate with Metellan support, he turned on his patrons. Marius had gained premature over-confidence. His equestrian origins and ties to that class help to explain his actions in that year. His advocacy of a voting bill, whose provisions were apparently designed to curb control of elections by senatorial groups, brought him into direct conflict with the consuls Metellus Delmaticus and L. Aurelius Cotta.[69] Passage might have meant an easier access to higher magistracies for *novi homines* and, of course, for himself. Marius' threat to arrest the consuls who were blocking his measure brought about a serious breach with the Metelli. One other act of Marius is recorded for 119: he successfully opposed a *lex frumentaria* providing for further grain distributions.[70] Again he may have acted in the interests of the *equites,* who stood to lose from increased state involvement in the marketplace.[71] Marius had attracted the support of some segments of the business classes, but politically he had over-reached himself. A break with the Metelli made further advancement more difficult.

Consular elections were still hotly contested and, though the Metelli gained the lion's share of successes, their opponents were also to be heard from. The *factio's* candidates, L. Metellus Diadematus and Q. Mucius Scaevola, secured the consulships for 117, the same year in which Metellus Delmaticus and Q. Marcius Rex celebrated triumphs.[72] But in the elections for 116, a candidate for the patrician post suffered a signal defeat, worthy to be recorded in future generations. M. Aemilius Scaurus was defeated by Q. Fabius Maximus Eburnus, whose family had old Scipionic connections.[73]

[69] Plut. *Marius,* 4.2-4; Cic. *De Leg.* 3.38; Taylor, *Roman Voting Assemblies,* 39, 76.

[70] Plut. *Marius,* 4.4. Plutarch's story is probably exaggerated to the greater glory of Marius; A. Passerini, "C. Mario come uomo politico," *Athenaeum,* 12 (1934), 14-15. But it ought not to be doubted altogether.

[71] Plutarch, probably wrongly, regards Marius' activities in 119 as mutually inconsistent. Consistency is seen by Pareti, *Storia di Roma,* III.392-396; Badian, *JRS,* 46 (1956), 93; Carney, *A Biog. of Marius,* 20; contra: Sherwin-White, *JRS,* 46 (1956), 2; Scullard, *From the Gracchi to Nero,* 2nd ed. (New York, 1963), 47. The whole tradition is doubted by Van Ooteghem, "Marius et Metellus," *LEC,* 32 (1964), 151-154; and *Marius,* 79-86.

[72] *MRR,* I.528-529.

[73] For the election, see Cic. *Pro Mur.* 36. Fabius' consular colleague, C. Licinius Geta, was probably an ally. In any event, the two were colleagues again in the censorship of 108, and Geta was expelled from the senate in 115 during a censorial *lustrum* that saw the appointment of M. Aemilius Scaurus as *princeps senatus; MRR,* I.531-532.

The defeat of Scaurus, whose skills were obviously recognized, seems to have been a matter of great importance to enemies of the Metellan clique. Scaurus tried again for 115, in elections that were bitter and fraught with telling consequences. M. Metellus probably had little difficulty in gaining the first place, but Scaurus was faced with the stiff opposition of P. Rutilius Rufus. Election returns showed Scaurus a winner, but his opponents did not yield easily. Rutilius immediately prosecuted his successful rival on a charge of *ambitus*. The trial resulted in Scaurus' acquittal. Scaurus then proceeded to accuse Rutilius on the very same charge.[74] The background of Rutilius is worth investigating and may shed some light on these events.

P. Rutilius Rufus, to judge from his candidature for the consulship of 115, must have been born in the middle 150's. Cicero refers to him as *adulescens* in the year 138.[75] His early associations were all with the Scipionic circle. He was a pupil of Panaetius, a protégé of Laelius, and a friend of Lucilius.[76] Rutilius was among those who had served under Scipio Aemilianus at Numantia in 134, and presumably shared his views regarding the Gracchi.[77] Poseidonius regarded him, along with Q. Aelius Tubero and Q. Mucius Scaevola, as the only practicing Roman Stoics who still obeyed the rigid *lex Fannia sumptuaria* of 161.[78]

That these associations endured into the 110's cannot be proved. Yet there is no evidence to the contrary, and one slight suggestion that Rutilius kept his old friends. As noted earlier, the poet Lucilius continued to train his poetic fire on the Metelli. In the latter part of this decade Lucilius was attacked by members of the senate for having

[74] Cic. *Brutus,* 113: *Erat uterque natura vehemens et acer; itaque cum una consulatum petivissent, non ille solum, qui repulsam tulerat, accusavit ambitus designatum competitorem, sed Scaurus etiam absolutus Rutilium in iudicium vocavit.* Also *De Orat.* 2.280; Tac. *Ann.* 3.66; cf. Badian, *Studies,* 106-108.

[75] Cic. *Brutus,* 85.

[76] For his asociation with Panaetius, see Cic. *Brutus,* 114; *De Off.* 3.10; with Laelius, see Cic. *Brutus,* 86-87; *De Amicit.* 101; with Lucilius, see Cic. *De Fin.* 1.7; Marx, *Luc. Carm. Rel.* 221; Cichorius, *Unt. zu Luc.,* 108-109.

[77] Appian, *Iber.* 88. Rutilius married a Livia, probably the sister of M. Livius Drusus, the tribune who had opposed C. Gracchus in 122; Val. Max. 8.13.6; Pliny, *NH,* 7.158; Münzer, *RE,* 1(2).1271, "Rutilius," n. 34.

[78] Athenaeus, 6.274. Strasburger, *Hermes,* 94 (1966), 60-72, has recently argued that it is only Cicero's naive idealizations that associated Rutilius with a Scipionic circle. But Poseidonius, here quoted by Athenaeus, connects him with Aelius Tubero, nephew of Scipio Aemilianus, and Appian gives his service with Scipio in Spain. The Ciceronian evidence, however idealized, seems consistent with the facts.

allowed his herds to graze on public land.[79] Among those who criticized Lucilius was Ap. Claudius, almost certainly the suffect consul of 130. Concern with public land and limitations on grazing link him to his cousin, the father-in-law of Ti. Gracchus. Conflict here with Lucilius is reminiscent of earlier clashes between Claudii and Scipiones two decades earlier.[80] An attractive conjecture links this anecdote with Rutilius Rufus. A fragment from the memoirs of Rutilius reads *pro Lucio familiari veniebam*. Citation merely of the praenomen Lucius would be quite unusual, especially in view of the use of *familiari* indicating the person had not been mentioned before. Hence perhaps the *Lucio* should be emended to *Lucilio* and be referred to the senatorial debate mentioned by Cicero.[81] This is not, of course, an argument on which to lay much weight, but support for Lucilius by a trusted *amicus* would not be surprising and suggests that Rutilius remained true to earlier associations.

The point at which Aemilius Scaurus was taken under the wing of the Metellan *factio* cannot be specified. His marriage to Caecilia Metella, daughter of Metellus Delmaticus, came near the end of the century.[82] But that may be the fruit of an association not the inception of it. A first wife foreclosed an earlier marriage alliance. Scaurus' victory in 116 against strong opposition and his acquittal in court argue for powerful support. The *novus homo,* already close to fifty, might otherwise have been put off indefinitely.[83] The strength of Scaurus' backing is revealed unmistakably in 115. The censors of that year appointed Scaurus *princeps senatus* during his own consulship.[84] Prior to him there is no other known example of a *princeps senatus* who was not at least a patrician ex-consul.[85]

[79] Cic. *De Orat.* 2.284: *In senatu cum ageretur de agris publicis et de lege Thoria et premeretur Lucilius ab eis qui a pecore eius depasci agros publicos dicerent.*

[80] For the identification of Ap. Claudius, see Münzer, *RE,* 6.2667-2668, "Claudius," n. 11; Cichorius, *Unt. zu Luc.,* 61-62; Niccolini, *Fast, Trib. Pleb.,* 182; Douglas, *AJP,* 77 (1956), 392-395; "Corrigenda," *AJP,* 78 (1957), 89; Badian, *Studies,* 240.

[81] *HRR,* 189, fr. 9. For this conjecture, see Cichorius, *Unt. zu Luc.,* 61-62.

[82] Münzer, *Röm. Adelsp.,* 280-281. His arguments are not met by Badian, *Studies,* 39.

[83] Badian argues that the Metelli supported Rutilius and turned to Scaurus only after their "special favorite" had been defeated; *Studies,* 39. But it is the election of Scaurus that must be accounted for, and this is precisely what Badian's explanation fails to do.

[84] *MRR,* I.533, n. 2.

[85] There may, of course, have been no patrician ex-censors alive at this time, but there were surely some patrician consulars, including Q. Fabius Maximus, consul in 116, and, more significantly, Q. Fabius Maximus Allobrogicus, consul in 121, the nephew of Scipio Aemilianus.

Of the perpetrators of this extraordinary precedent, one was Metellus Diadematus.[86] It cannot have been an easy matter; Metellus may have had to exert considerable pressure on his colleague Cn. Domitius Ahenobarbus, who was probably unsympathetic.[87] Success demonstrates the power of the *factio*.

Many aristocrats, predisposed to be hostile, had, out of principle or expediency, abandoned older allegiances and swelled the ranks of the Metellan group. But this group did not win them all. The events just discussed indicate that the opposition to the Metelli still owed much to the anti-Metellan sentiments nurtured in the Scipionic circle two decades earlier and to individuals who had been brought up in that atmosphere. Men like Lucilius, Q. Fabius Maximus, and Rutilius Rufus sought to stem the tide.

Aemilius Scaurus, like Q. Scaevola, emerged unscathed and more powerful from judicial attack. But Rutilius Rufus was not to get off so lightly in the counter-prosecution by Scaurus. One anecdote is preserved from this trial.[88] Scaurus had ordered the impounding of Rutilius' election accounts, in which there was an entry under the rubric *A.F.P.R.* The prosecution maintained that this should read *actum fide P. Rutili*, and that it indicated a sum promised for the purposes of electoral bribery. The defense retorted that these letters stood for *ante factum, post relatum*, apparently an end-of-the-month tabulation of previous outlays.[89] At this point, a wit, one C. Canius, who was a supporter of Rutilius, offered the suggestion of *Aemilius fecit, plectitur Rutilius;* that is, "Aemilius is guilty, but Rutilius suffers for it." This interpretation need not be taken literally. It was meant as a joke and there is no reason to believe that Rutilius was actually convicted of *ambitus*. But as a commentary on the practical outcome of the clash between these two candidates it is peculiarly apt. Scaurus went on to become *princeps senatus* in the following year and remained the most powerful figure in the senate during the Jugurthine War and the following two decades. Rutilius did not attain the consulship for another ten years, when he was already past fifty. These differences can hardly be coincidental. In this period when the Metelli were dominating the curule offices, Rutilius suffered a dual reverse at the polls and in the courts. But he ultimately learned his lesson. In 109 Rutilius was the legate of Metellus Numidicus in the Jugurthine

[86] *MRR*, I.532, n. 1.
[87] In any case, Scaurus clashed with Domitius' son in 104, and there was much personal rancor; see below, pp. 173-174.
[88] Cic. *De Orat.* 2.280.
[89] Cf. Bloch, *Mélanges D'Histoire Ancienne,* 25 (1909), 25-26.

War, and followed him to Rome when Marius took over the army in 107.[90] In 105, with the support of the Metelli, he finally reached the consulship.[91] Thus, even Rutilius, who maintained a long loyalty to his early upbringing, at last succumbed to the pressures of practical politics.

The year of the reciprocal trials of Scaurus and Rutilius also saw another *ambitus* prosecution, this time of the erstwhile Metellan protégé, C. Marius. Equestrian association and the accumulation of a small fortune had spurred his political ambition.[92] Marius endured a double *repulsa* at the polls in 118 when seeking first the curule and then the plebeian aedileship. But there was still money available for another attempt. Marius was elected to the praetorship for 115 at the bottom of the slate. He was prosecuted almost immediately for electoral bribery.[93] Plutarch tells us that Marius fared badly in the first days of the trial, but that when the votes were counted, the result to everyone's surprise was a draw, tantamount to acquittal.[94] It was a narrow escape and the hand of the Metelli may be discerned, though not, apparently, on the side of Marius. They remembered his activities in 119. The prosecution of Marius was almost certainly instigated by them, or at least had their support. Marius had not only broken with the Metelli; he did not like to be reminded that he had once required the patronage of any house. When C. Herennius declined to testify on the grounds that the defendant was a client of the Herennii, Marius waived the claim and announced that a praetor was a client of no one.[95] The Herennii retained close connections with Marius, but in the future it was he who played the role of patron.[96]

Though Marius was acquitted, the Metelli got some small satisfaction in the following year. Cassius Sabaco, a friend of Marius and suspected of collusion with him in the alleged electoral bribery, was expelled from

[90] Sallust, *Iug.* 50, 52-53, 86.4; Plut. *Marius,* 10.1.

[91] The path from the Scipionic group toward closer ties with the Metelli may have been smoothed for Rutilius by his brother-in-law M. Aurelius Cotta, whose family shows strong Metellan connections.

[92] On Marius' business contacts and enterprises, see Weynand, *RE*, Supp. 6.1371, "Marius," n. 14; Carney, *NC*, 19 (1959), 79-82; *A Biog. of Marius,* 19-24.

[93] Plut. *Marius,* 5.2: ἔσχατος δὲ πάντων ἀναγορευθεὶς δίκην ἔσχε δεκασμοῦ. Val. Max. 6.9.14: *candidatus supremo in loco adhaesit, quem tamen non sine periculo obtinuit; ambitus enim accusatus.*

[94] Plut. *Marius,* 5.5.

[95] Plut. *Marius,* 5.4-5: αὐτὸς ἀντεῖπεν ὁ Μάριος πρὸς τὸν Ἑρέννιον ὡς, ὅτε πρῶτον ἄρχων ἀνηγορεύθη, τὸν πελάτην ἐκβεβηκώς.

[96] Cf. Carney, "Two Notes on Republican Roman Law," *Acta Juridica* (1959), 232-234.

the senate by the censors of 115, one of whom was Metellus Diadematus.[97] Marius had shown considerable strength and influence, and perhaps, after his marriage into the Julii Caesares, the Metelli sought to woo him again when he received a legateship on Metellus Numidicus' staff in Africa.[98] Of course, as events were to show, reconciliation with Marius was impossible.

The closeness of the vote in Marius' trial shows that even he cannot be said to have had the *equites* in his pocket. The case illustrates once more that one cannot regard the equestrian class as a closed bloc, likely to vote as a unit on all issues. Interference with business interests in the provinces could arouse united hostility, but cases of *ambitus* can hardly be said to have affected the *equites* as a class.[99]

These three *ambitus* trials of 116 indicate that a standing court for electoral bribery existed by that date.[100] Evidence on the prosecutions of Rutilius and Scaurus is indecisive, but Plutarch's account of Marius' trial removes all doubt that the issue was heard by *iudices*.[101] There is no hint of extraordinary commissions for the three cases of 116. The *quaestio de ambitu* must have been organized shortly before this date. Some find it surprising that such a court should be established in the immediate post-Gracchan period.[102] But a law on *ambitus* need not have been "anti-senatorial." Electoral bribery would normally be resorted to by candidates who felt insecure about the strength of their *clientelae*. An assault on this practice would have been in the interests of the more powerful senatorial factions.[103] That the jurors who served on this court

[97] Plut. *Marius,* 5.3-4. It is tempting to associate Cassius Sabaco with the Cassii Longini, enemies of the Metelli. The name may suggest a client relationship.

[98] Cf. Badian, *Studies,* 38. Marius may also have been desirable as a recruiting agent for an unpopular war.

[99] Passerini, *Athenaeum,* 12 (1934), 15-16, Valgiglio, *Plutarco, Vita di Mario,* 27-28, and Carney, *A Biog. of Marius,* 22, recognizing this difficulty, seek to skirt the issue by assuming that Marius' guilt must have been flagrant if he received a tie vote by a jury "biased in his favor." This kind of argument clearly begs the question.

[100] Mommsen, *Strafrecht,* 867; Greenidge, *Legal Procedure,* 422; *History of Rome,* 307.

[101] Plut. *Marius,* 5.5: χρώμενος τοῖς δικασταῖς.

[102] Zumpt, *Criminalrecht,* II.1.76-77, finds it incompatible with a "reactionary period" and ascribes it to C. Gracchus himself. W. Rein, *Das Criminalrecht der Römer* (Leipzig, 1844), 709, on similar grounds, assigned it to Marius. No evidence buttresses either conjecture.

[103] *Ambitus* laws had been passed before, on the basis of *senatus consulta;* Livy, 40.19; cf. Livy, *Per.* 47.

were *equites* cannot be demonstrated beyond question, but the elaborate organization of annual jury panels by the *lex Acilia* makes it most likely that these men would naturally have been drawn upon to staff any new courts.[104]

On the surface, this was a period of calm and harmony. No radical reform programs emerged to disrupt the political scene. Foreign wars were minor and few; expansion was relatively quiet but continuous, profitable for colonists and capitalistic enterprise. In southern Gaul, after the wars of the late 120's, in Spain, and in Africa, Italian businessmen, traders, and settlers began to appear in large numbers. The colony of Narbo became a center of trade for both Gaul and Spain; Sardinia was pacified and piracy stemming from the Balearic isles was cleared. Italian desire for enfranchisement shows no overt manifestation; the energies of the *socii* seem to have been siphoned off into other directions. The *equester ordo* thrived in an era of peace; profits from Asia were large and the aristocracy did not interfere with equestrian control of the judiciary. A series of agrarian laws show moderation and compromise. Popular agitation is unattested and the economic crisis that the Gracchi had confronted seems to have received temporary amelioration. But superficial concord can be deceptive. An analysis of criminal trials shows that political rivalries remained intense and senatorial discord continued to plague the forum and *curia*.

M. Aemilius Scaurus had reached the top of the political pyramid. This son of a charcoal peddler had accumulated a substantial fortune and was now *princeps senatus*. But his past was obscure and shady; among his peers he roused resentment and suspicion. He continued to be a target for judicial attack. Cicero reports that Scaurus was accused by his *inimicus* M. Junius Brutus.[105] Two fragments survive of a speech delivered by Scaurus in his own defense *contra M. Brutum de pecuniis repetundis*.[106] Since this was an extortion case, it can be connected with Scaurus' consulship of 115. In that year Scaurus carried on a campaign against some Gallic and Ligurian tribesmen and celebrated a triumph *de Galleis Karneis*.[107] The trial should probably be dated to 114.[108] The enemies of Scaurus, who had failed to convict him in 116, now seized another opportunity. The prosecutor, M. Junius Brutus, who never sought the higher magistracies, is described by Cicero as merely a pro-

[104] Cf. Badian, *Historia,* 11 (1962), 207-208.
[105] Cic. *Pro Font.* 38.
[106] *ORF,* 166.
[107] Degrassi, *Fast. Cap.,* 106; Frontinus, *Strat.* 4.4.13; *Vir. Ill.* 72.
[108] Bloch, *Mélanges D'Histoire Ancienne,* 25 (1909), 26-27.

fessional *accusator,* sharp-tongued and obnoxious.[109] But since Brutus' relative D. Junius Callaicus, as noted earlier, had deserted the Gracchan alliance and had cooperated with Opimius in a leading capacity in 121,[110] it is not impossible that the trial reflects further hostility between the anti-Gracchan extremists of 121 and the Metellan *factio.*[111] The result of the trial is not revealed in our sources, but in view of the fact that Scaurus' career continued uninterrupted, acquittal is a certainty. Scaurus remained too formidable.

Misdeeds, or alleged misdeeds, of provincial governors continued to provoke judicial procedures. As governor of Macedonia in 114, C. Porcius Cato roused hostility and indignation at Rome. A disastrous defeat by the Celtic tribe of the Scordisci was regarded as inexcusable and upon Cato's return he faced charges of *repetundae.*[112] His early career is almost a blank,[113] but his connections important. Cato was the younger son of M. Porcius Cato, who had died when praetor designate in 152, and grandson of Cato the censor. His mother was an Aemilia, the daughter of L. Aemilius Paullus and sister of Scipio Aemilianus. C. Cato was thus the nephew of Scipio.[114] It was doubtless in this Scipionic circle that as a youth he had made the acquaintance of Ti. Gracchus. As noted earlier, Cato was among those members of the younger generation who were dazzled and attracted by the Gracchan movement. His closeness to Tiberius was well known and he joined the tribune in severing ties with the Scipios.[115] His activities in the succeeding two decades are unrecorded,[116] but he survived the judicial prosecutions of 132 and the slaughter of the Gracchani in 121. His consulship of 114 was probably not much later than *suus annus.* Protection by powerful individuals is a reasonable conjecture. The Metellan *factio* seems to have become more and more the haven for former associates of the Scipionic and Gracchan groups alike. As consul in 114, Cato succeeded two men at

[109] Cic. *Brutus,* 130; *Pro Cluent.* 141; *De Off.* 2.50.

[110] See above, p. 98.

[111] On the only other occasion in which Brutus is known to have been involved in a criminal trial, in the 90's, he clashed with the Metellan L. Licinius Crassus; Cic. *Pro Cluent.* 140; *De Orat.* 2.220, 2.223; Quintilian, 6.3.44; *ORF,* 208.

[112] Livy, *Per.* 63; Florus, 1.39.4; Dio, 26, fr. 88; Festus, *Brev.* 9.1; Amm. Marc. 27.4.4.

[113] He does seem to have served as a *triumvir monetalis* in the 140's and 130's; *MRR,* II.445.

[114] Miltner, *RE,* 43.105, "Porcius," n. 5.

[115] Cic. *De Amicit.* 39.

[116] He may have been involved in the embassy to Jugurtha in 116. See below, Chapter V.

the center of the Metellan bloc, M. Aemilius Scaurus and M. Caecilius Metellus.

Romans were not accustomed to military defeats in recent years, especially by tribes of whom they had barely heard. Righteous wrath was expressed and Cato was convicted. But his influential backers were not idle. The conviction was followed by a *litis aestimatio* that assessed a mere 8,000 sesterces, or, if Velleius can be believed, only 4,000! [117] It was a ludicrously small sum. Moreover, there seems to have been little damage to Cato's political career. He did not finally come to grief until the notorious trials of the Mamilian commission in 109.[118] Powerful influence was thus clearly brought to bear on Cato's behalf in 113 and his trial represented at most a Pyrrhic victory for his enemies.

The destruction of Cato's army in Thrace had so terrified the Roman populace that they regarded it as a dreadful portent from the gods.[119] A sophisticated and educated aristocracy too often obscures the fact that superstition remained widespread and potent in late Republican Rome. A frightened and insecure mob was prepared to see dire warnings in unusual events. On top of Cato's disaster the year 114 witnessed a grave and awful omen. The maiden daughter of a Roman knight was struck by lightning, which took her life, rent her garment, and exposed her nakedness. Soothsayers did not hesitate to judge the meaning of this occurrence: the Vestal Virgins had violated their oaths. Terror and religious disquiet among the masses provided the atmosphere, but calculating members of the nobility were prepared to turn it to their own advantage. In December of 114, the most spectacular case of the decade opened. No fewer than three Vestal Virgins of the most distinguished families in Rome and their alleged paramours were accused of *incestum*.[120]

The three Vestals, an Aemilia, a Licinia, and a Marcia, were first tried, as was customary, before the college of pontiffs, with the result that Aemilia alone was condemned, while Marcia and Licinia were absolved. Public outrage increased: the gods would not be appeased by an obvious cover-up. At the beginning of 113, the tribune Sex. Peducaeus

---

[117] Vell. Pat. 2.8.1. For the figure of 8,000, see Cic. *Verr.* 3.184, 4.22. Some manuscripts give 18,000, still a very low figure. The *lex repetundarum*, line 59 (*FIRA*, I.96), provides that a convicted extortionist is liable for double the sum that was unjustly exacted. Juries, of course, could be quite arbitrary in the sums they assessed; cf. Cic. *Pro Cluent.* 41; Mommsen, *Strafrecht*, 725-726.

[118] Cic. *Brutus*, 127-128; *Pro Balbo*, 28.

[119] Florus, 1.39.4: *simile prodigio*.

[120] Orosius, 5.15.20-21; Obseq. 37; Plut. *RQ*, 83. The exact date is provided by Fenestella, cited in Macrobius, *Sat.* 1.10.5.

introduced a measure to censure the *pontifex maximus* and the whole college of priests for faulty judgment. There was to be no mistake made this time. The formidable, stern, and incorruptible L. Cassius Longinus Ravilla was appointed the head of a special tribunal to retry the case. All three Vestals were condemned.[121]

Whatever their origin, no trials involving members of the noblest houses in Rome could remain divorced from politics.[122] The identities of the Vestals provide illumination. Licinia was daughter of a Gaius,[123] almost certainly C. Licinius Crassus, tribune in 145, who had sought to increase the college of pontiffs through popular elections instead of cooptation, a proposal thwarted through the efforts of C. Laelius and the Scipionic faction.[124] Licinia was defended in this case by L. Licinius Crassus, probably her first cousin and now the son-in-law of Q. Mucius Scaevola.[125]

Political hostilities of an earlier day may also elucidate the backgrounds of Aemilia and Marcia. In the same years in which C. Licinius Crassus clashed with Laelius, a Q. Marcius Rex, praetor in 144, and a M. Aemilius Lepidus Porcina, praetor in 143, were cooperating in a public works project that was opposed by the *decemviri sacris faciundis*.[126] Porcina's involvement is especially revealing because his career provides a precious thread linking these generations. Porcina was a political ally of Ap. Claudius Pulcher and an opponent of Scipio Aemilianus. In his consulship of 137, he opposed the measure of L. Cassius Ravilla to extend the ballot to all criminal trials except *perduellio,* a measure that had the endorsement of Scipio.[127] The hostility between Porcina and Cassius Ravilla perpetuated itself. In 125 Porcina was charged with excessive luxury and fined by the censors of that year, one of whom was Cassius.[128] By 113 Porcina was dead, but Cassius Ravilla appears as the relentless inquisitor who reversed pontifical judgment on the three Vestals. A reputation for severity lay behind Cassius' selection. He allowed no nonsense in his court; advocates were swiftly cut off by his proverbial *cui bono.*[129] But politics was not absent from the choice of Cassius as *quaesitor:* his behavior in the Vestals' trial was regarded as unjustifiably

---

[121] Asconius, 45-46, Clark; Cic. *De Nat. Deor.* 3.74; Livy, *Per.* 63; Obseq. 37; Dio, 26, fr. 87; Val. Max. 6.8.1.

[122] This was recognized by Münzer, *Röm. Adelsp.*, 243-244.

[123] Cic. *De Domo,* 136.

[124] Cic. *De Amicit.* 96; Münzer, *RE,* 25.497, "Licinius," n. 181.

[125] Cic. *Brutus,* 160; *ORF,* 242.

[126] Frontinus, *Aqued.* 1.7; Livy, *Oxyr. Per.* 54; Pliny, *NH,* 31.41, 36.121; Münzer, *Röm. Adelsp.,* 244; cf. *MRR,* I.473, n. 1.

[127] Münzer, *Röm. Adelsp.,* 240-241.

[128] Vell. Pat. 2.10.1; Val. Max. 8.1.7.

[129] Cic. *Pro Rosc. Amer.* 84; *Pro Mil.* 32; cf. *Verr.* 1.30, 3.137.

harsh.[130] Personal and political enmities of a previous generation seem to have been replayed here.

The Metellan *factio* suffered. Licinius Crassus had come to the aid of his cousin in vain. And the affair touched more than the three Vestals involved. The *pontifex maximus* was Metellus Delmaticus. Although no formal charges were leveled against him, the reversal of his verdict and the popular resentment aroused against the whole college of pontiffs was a damaging blow. The trials that followed under Cassius' *quaestio extraordinaria* were overtly a repudiation of Metellus' judgment and an attack on his integrity.[131]

Also under attack, presumably as a paramour, was young M. Antonius, a fiery and brilliant speaker, the only orator of the new generation who bore comparison with L. Crassus.[132] Antonius, devoid of consular ancestors, had just reached the quaestorship in 113 and was on his way to Asia when he learned of the charge of *incestum*. He returned voluntarily to defend himself before the court of Cassius Ravilla.[133] A loyal slave endured torture but refused to implicate his master.[134] Antonius' speech in self-defense secured speedy acquittal. There is no evidence for Antonius' political affiliations at this point. But this gifted and promising *novus homo* is precisely the sort of man who would have attracted the attention of the Metelli, as had C. Marius and M. Aemilius Scaurus. His cooperation with the *factio* at a later date can be documented.[135] The trial in 113 may be adjudged as further evidence for the orator's connection with this group.[136]

Another *reus* bears mention in this context. Cicero reports that C. Scribonius Curio defended a Ser. Fulvius on a charge of *incestum*.[137] The speech was puerile and hyperbolic, though much praised.[138] Occasion

---

[130] Asconius, 46, Clark: *nimia etiam, ut existimatio est, asperitate usus damnavit;* cf. Val. Max. 3.7.9.

[131] Asconius, 45-46, Clark: *Sex. Peducaeus tribunus plebis criminatus est L. Metellum pontificem max. totumque collegium pontificum male iudicasse de incesto virginum Vestalium.*

[132] Cf. Cic. *Brutus,* 138-142.

[133] Val. Max. 3.7.9, 6.8.1. That this trial was in connection with the Vestal affair ought no longer be doubted; cf. Gruen, "M. Antonius and the Trial of the Vestal Virgins," *RhM,* 111 (1968), 59-63.

[134] Val. Max. 6.8.1.

[135] See below, Chapter VII.

[136] Antonius also served as defense counsel for Q. Marcius Rex at some time during this decade; Cic. *De Orat.* 2.125. The defendant was probably the consul of 118; Münzer, *Röm. Adelsp.,* 388-389. He may well have been father of Marcia, one of the three condemned Vestals. The political associations seem confirmed.

[137] Cic. *Brutus,* 122; *De Invent.* 1.80; Schol. Bob. 85, Stangl; *ORF,* 173-174.

[138] Cic. *Brutus,* 124.

and outcome are not recorded, but a connection with the Vestals' trials is possible. Fulvius may also have been an alleged paramour. Of Curio we know only that he was an orator, listed as a contemporary of C. Gracchus, Scaurus, and Rutilius Rufus.[139] But the next generation saw a Curio firmly in the Metellan camp.[140] The Fulvii Flacci, of course, had strongly endorsed the Gracchan movement. Latent hostility against this family may have expressed itself against the obscure and otherwise unknown Ser. Fulvius.[141]

One final name emerges in the Vestal's case. A Roman *eques* had corrupted Aemilia, who in turn involved the other two Vestals in her escapade. He then exposed all three through information brought by a slave. The name of this paramour and informer is confused by the sources but not beyond recovery. Orosius identifies him as L. Veturius, and Plutarch as Βουτέτιος βάρβαρος, almost certainly to be emended to βάρρος on the basis of the name given by Porphyrio: *Barrus*.[142] The name calls to mind T. Betutius Barrus, whom Cicero calls the most accomplished of non-Roman orators. This man, one should note, delivered the prosecution's case in a trial of the 90's against Q. Servilius Caepio, who was defended by L. Licinius Crassus, also a defense counsel in the Vestal Virgins' case.[143] Whether the *eques* who brought damaging evidence in the Vestal trial was this Barrus or a relative, political opposition to the Metellan *factio* is suggested in both instances.

The implications of this striking event stirred the emotions and outraged the consciences of the *populus*. Political manipulations do not tell more than a part of the story. Certainly, the notion that these trials represent an effort on the part of the *optimates* to discredit the *equites* is wide of the mark.[144] Some *equites* were involved as paramours but so were several prominent members of the oligarchy. Indeed, the court

[139] Cic. *Brutus,* 110.

[140] See below, p. 217.

[141] Münzer, *RE,* 7.248, "Fulvius," n. 64, identified him with the consul of 135. But that gentleman would have been in his sixties at the time of the Vestals' trials, not the most likely suspect for adultery. If this case is part of the attack on the Vestals and their paramours, Fulvius may be son or even grandson of the consul of 135. For a possible jibe by Lucilius at the Flacci, see Lucilius, 1212 (*ROL,* 3.394): *Andronis flacci teget utria;* cf. Cichorius, *Unt. zu Luc.,* 328-333.

[142] Orosius, 5.15.22; Plut. *RQ,* 83; Porphyrio, *Ad Hor. Sat.* 1.6.30.

[143] Cic. *Brutus,* 169: *omnium autem eloquentissimus extra hanc urbem T. Betutius Barrus Asculanus.*

[144] As Bloch-Carcopino, *Hist. Rom.,* II.295-296, followed by Pareti, *Storia di Roma,* III.408-409, and now Nicolet, *L'Ordre Equestre,* 529.

itself, composed of *iudices,* was probably staffed by the *equites.*[145] The magnitude of the sin struck sensitive chords among the superstitious. Fear of desertion by the gods provoked almost mass hysteria and culminated in dreadful sacrifice of four men and women, Greeks and Gauls.[146] It was to be another sixteen years before human sacrifice was abolished in Rome.[147] Such was the pervading atmosphere of panic and ignorance that made these events possible. But politicians capitalized on the situation to settle old scores and to embarrass prominent members and protégés of the Metellan *factio.*

Examination of these years has shown that the coalition around the Metelli, although preeminent, was not without senatorial opposition. Evidence is scanty but suggests over and over again that opposition leadership included men raised under the tutelage of the Scipionic circle, and extremists who wiped out the Gracchan movement in 121. In the latter category one recalls the name of C. Papirius Carbo. This decade of the 110's was an unfortunate one for the Carbo brothers. C. Carbo blackened the reputation of his family and aroused enmity from all sides when he transferred allegiance from the Gracchi to their opponents at the last moment. Blatant treachery had made him an easy target for L. Crassus in 119. Now, after the trials of the Vestals and their paramours, Carbo's brothers were subject to attack. Others could also take advantage of public superstition and religious disquiet. Cn. Papirius Carbo, as consul in 113, conducted a disgraceful campaign against the Cimbri and suffered a crushing defeat.[148] It heralded a danger from the north more formidable than any Rome had faced since Hannibal. Again terrible portents marked the occasion; in Gaul the sky appeared to glow with fire.[149] Cn. Carbo became a palpable victim for prosecution. The *accusator,* not surprising in this political context, was M. Antonius. The sources do not reveal the circumstances of the case, but the date is almost certainly 112, after the expiration of Carbo's term of office. The result was not very different from the outcome of his brother's trial. Suicide anticipated certain condemnation.[150]

[145] Val. Max. 6.8.1; Zumpt, *Criminalrecht,* II.1.221; Greenidge, *Legal Procedure,* 379.

[146] Plut. *RQ,* 83.

[147] Pliny, *NH,* 30.1.12.

[148] Livy, *Per.* 63; Vell. Pat. 2.12.2; Plut. *Marius,* 16.5; Appian, *Celt.* 13; Strabo, 5.1.8.

[149] Obseq. 38.

[150] Such is doubtless the meaning of Cicero's *sutorio atramento absolutus putatur; Ad. Fam.* 9.21.3; see H. Malcovati, "Ad Cic. *Fam.* 9, 21, 3," *Studi Funaioli* (1955), 216-220. The case is mentioned also by Apuleius, *Apol.* 66.

It was probably not long after Cn. Carbo's case that the third of these brothers, M. Papirius Carbo, was prosecuted and convicted. Only a single notice is preserved of this trial.[151] Cicero describes him as a *fur magnus* and affirms that he was convicted for offenses committed in Sicily. The charge was, therefore, in all probability, *repetundae*. Curule offices are not known for M. Carbo, but an extortion charge implies a governorship of Sicily, probably a pro-praetorship. If the order of names given in Cicero's text is correct, he was the youngest of the three brothers, probably to be identified with the *monetalis* of 137-134.[152] The prosecutor P. Flaccus is otherwise unknown. It would be enlightening to associate him with the Fulvii Flacci, especially if the *incestum* trial of Ser. Fulvius had taken place in the previous year.[153] A picture emerges, dim but consistent. Individuals damaged in the Vestal trials sought retaliation against a family identified with opportunism, reaction, and treachery.

Senatorial struggles, played out in the courts, were obviously a conspicuous feature of these years, too often overlooked. Given the scrappy nature of our evidence, it is probable that there were several more trials with political connotations of which record is not preserved. Inquiry uncovers two final cases that may come at the end of the decade and that repeat a pattern discerned throughout: patient but largely unsuccessful effort to weaken the Metelli and their political allies.

Q. Metellus, later to acquire the *cognomen* Numidicus, was the most prominent of the new generation of Metelli. A military man and a haughty aristocrat who scorned popular movements, he was nonetheless incorruptible, of unblemished reputation, and carried great prestige within the ranks of the nobility.[154] Three citations reveal that Numidicus was tried on a charge of extortion, but his personal character was so far above reproach that the jurors granted an acquittal without even looking at the evidence.[155] Influence and reputation preserved his career

---

[151] Cic. *Ad. Fam.* 9.21.3.

[152] On the governorship, see *MRR*, I.523; the *monetalis*, II.448.

[153] Münzer, *De Gente Valeria* (Berlin, 1891), 40, n. 10, suggests that this may be a P. Valerius Flaccus, otherwise unknown. But the argument that the *praenomen* Publius was never used by the Fulvii Flacci is not conclusive. Indeed, we know of only one P. Valerius Flaccus, the consul of 227. That he had a son of the same name cannot be proved. The *praenomen* certainly does not appear later among the Valerii Flacci.

[154] Cf. Sallust, *Iug.* 43.1, 43.4-5.

[155] Cic. *Ad Att.* 1.16.4: *cum tabulas Metelli Numidici, cum eae ut mos est circumferrentur, nostri iudices aspicere noluerunt; Pro Balbo*, 11; Val. Max. 2.10.1.

here, not oratory.[156] The date of the trial is nowhere given in the sources. A *repetundae* charge, however, would have followed praetorship or consulship. Consulship and proconsulship were spent in the war against Jugurtha. His return from that campaign in 107, Sallust reports, was greeted with great rejoicing by senate and populace alike.[157] Sallust's partiality for Numidicus notwithstanding, it is unlikely that a charge was laid against him at that time.[158] The date of his praetorship is unknown, but in view of the domination of the curule offices by the Metelli in these years, it was probably *suo anno* 112. Cicero states that Numidicus governed a province, possibly during his praetorship.[159] It is reasonable therefore to place the trial in 111. Numidicus' triumphant acquittal is testimony to his prestigious character and the prevalent influence of the Metelli.

With the trial of Metellus may perhaps be associated another, the otherwise obscure case of a certain Piso. The Piso in question here has been identified, doubtless correctly, as L. Calpurnius Piso Caesoninus, the consul of 112.[160] Again the charge was *repetundae* and again the date is unknown. Either 114 or 111 will do, after praetorship or consulship.[161] Whatever the date, it is noteworthy that the Metellan *factio* utilized its best talent in Piso's behalf. The brilliant orator L. Licinius

[156] Numidicus is not even mentioned among the countless orators described by Cicero in the *Brutus*.

[157] Sallust, *Iug*. 88.1: *Metellus interea Romam profectus contra spem suam laetissumis animis accipitur, plebi patribusque, postquam invidia decesserat, iuxta carus*.

[158] Cf. Münzer, *RE*, 5.1218, "Caecilius," n. 97. Contra: Carney, "The Picture of Marius in Valerius Maximus," *RhM*, 105 (1962), 308-309; Badian, *Roman Imperialism*, 52, n. 18. Carney is seriously misleading when he states that the tribune T. Manlius Mancinus prosecuted Numidicus in 107; so also Nicolet, *L'Ordre Equestre*, 531. In fact, Mancinus' attacks took place *apud populum in contione;* Gellius, 7.11.1; Priscian, *GL*, 2.382.6. This reference cannot apply to an extortion trial. Almost certainly the repartee dealt with the justifiability of Metellus' triumph; Gellius, 12.9.4; *ORF*, 211-212. And does not Valerius' statement (2.10.1), *quid plus tribui potuit consuli quam est datum reo Metello,* imply rather that Metellus was *not* of consular rank than that he was?

[159] Cic. *Verr*. 2.3.209.

[160] See Fraccaro, *Opuscula*, 2.139-140; *ORF*, 258. Since L. Licinius Crassus was involved, the identification seems acceptable. No other Piso is known who might have been subject to an extortion charge within the active career of Crassus.

[161] Cic. *De Orat*. 2.265. The prosecution claimed that large sums of money had been turned over to Piso's prefect, a certain Magius: *ille Gallus olim testis in Pisonem, cum innumerabilem Magio praefecto pecuniam dixisset datam.*

Crassus acted as his advocate and the *princeps senatus* M. Aemilius Scaurus appeared as witness for the defense.[162] Political influence won acquittal despite the ruthless character of Piso Caesoninus.[163] If the trial fell in 111 it may be taken in connection with the similarly unsuccessful assault on Metellus Numidicus in the same year. That year concluded a decade of senatorial battles and established without question the ascendancy of the Metellan group. The consul of 111, P. Scipio Nasica, son of Ti. Gracchus' slayer, but now son-in-law of Metellus Macedonicus, symbolized the strength of the coalition. The year was climaxed by the sensational triumphs of two Metelli celebrated on the same day.[164]

It had been a period of outward calm but inner tensions. It had witnessed the gradual consolidation of supremacy within the aristocracy by a single group. The success of the Metelli at the polls, and, more important, in the courts, had attracted more and more families once associated with their opponents. Insofar as it can be traced through certain individuals, the political migration brought into the orbit of the Metelli families like the Mucii Scaevolae, the Licinii Crassi, the Lutatii Catuli, Rutilii Rufi, Calpurnii Pisones, and perhaps Livii Drusi, Scribonii Curiones, and Porcii Catones. Promising men of no prior political influence, like M. Scaurus and M. Antonius, were also taken under the wing of the *factio*. The Gracchan movement had been a watershed in disrupting public positions and political allegiances, and the resourcefulness of the Metelli had turned this fact to their advantage. Of course, consistency and strength of attachment varied, and individuals cannot always be taken to speak for their relatives. Yet it is interesting that of the families noted above, all, with the single exception of the Rutilii Rufi, remain prominent and central in the events of the immediately succeeding generations. By contrast, opponents of the Metelli, die-hard anti-Gracchani, and heirs of the Scipionic circle largely fade from view.

---

162 For Crassus, see Cic. *De Orat.* 2.285; for Scaurus, *De Orat.* 2.265. Of the two hostile witnesses, Silus and Gallus, nothing is known. Badian suggests Aquillius Gallus for the latter; "Review of Broughton, *Supplement to MRR*," *Gnomon*, 33 (1961), 495-496. Silus may be the later quaestor M. Sergius Silus; cf. *MRR*, II.13. The anecdote in Val. Max. 8.1.6 probably does not refer to this trial, despite Syme, "Piso and Veranius in Catullus," *ClMed*, 17 (1956), 133-134.

163 Cf. Cic. *In Pis.* fr. 11: *Caesonini hominis furacissimi.* Acquittal seems probable; Piso continued in Rome and was later to serve in 107 as legate in Gaul, where he was killed; Caes. *BG*, 1.12.7; Appian, *Celt.* 1.3; Orosius, 5.15.24.

164 M. Caecilius Metellus celebrated a triumph for victories in Sardinia, and C. Metellus Caprarius for campaigns in Thrace; Degrassi, *Fast. Cap.*, 106; Vell. Pat. 2.8; Eutrop. 4.25.

Little, if anything, is heard of again from the Popillii Laenates, the Rupilii, the Opimii, and the Manilii. The great house of the Fabii Maximi secured a last censorship in 108, but thereafter does not appear on the *fasti* until a consul suffect of 45. Still others, like the Papirii Carbones, Junii Bruti, and Octavii emerge again only in the hectic days of civil war in the 80's. Coincidence is implausible. The contest for senatorial ascendancy had been settled in the decade of the 110's.

Aristocratic politics, however, do not exhaust the tale. *Nobiles* could become too wrapped up in their own private squabbles. A period of prosperity and quiescence by *equites, socii* and demagogues lulled them into a false sense of security. Moderate agrarian reform and small concessions to Italian ambition sponsored by the oligarchy were only temporary expedients; commercial expansionism was subject to the vagaries of the military situation. Beneath the surface discontent and resentment were submerged but hardly eradicated. The signs of instability have already been noted. Military defeat and concern for the frontiers could give way to religious hysteria and brutal vengeance. War clouds grew more menacing. The situation was deteriorating rapidly in Gaul and Africa, affecting both business interests and popular sensitivities. The Metellan clan had established a kind of *dominatio* within aristocratic circles. It was quite a different matter, however, to handle the wider forces that threatened the oligarchy.

V. THE JUGURTHINE WAR AND
THE MAMILIAN COMMISSION

Foreign wars had long been the occasion for internal restiveness and upheaval. Frustrating conflict in Spain in the 140's and 130's had played a major role in forming the backdrop to the Gracchan revolution. Rome had fortunately been spared confrontation with a formidable foe since that era, and concord without was reflected by relative calm within. But the Roman populace was sensitive and edgy. It was not the nobility alone to whom *dignitas imperii* was a cardinal principle of foreign policy. C. Cato's disgraceful defeat in Thrace in 114 was, to popular imagination, a sign of divine wrath and necessitated judicial condemnation. Cn. Carbo's disaster at the hands of the Cimbri in the following year was also attended by forbidding omens and issued in political prosecution and conviction.[1] If wars abroad were to promote a really serious threat one could expect the political consequences to be grave.

At the same time, the interests of state outside the Italian peninsula were becoming more entangled with the enterprises of businessmen, financiers, and merchants who knew how to utilize profitable opportunities. The excesses of C. Gracchus had produced a détente between aristocracy and *equites,* but within a decade there were signs of a fissure. It was suggested that a colony of Roman citizens be established at Narbo in Gallia Transalpina. The purposes were perhaps manifold: the settlement of veterans or excess population, the exploitation of good agricultural land, the installation of a military stronghold to observe and discourage Gallic migration.[2] And no one would have overlooked the ideal location of the site as a focus for commerce in Gaul and Spain. L. Crassus spoke vigorously for the proposal, and it secured passage, but only in

[1] See above, pp. 126-127, 131.
[2] Cf. Cic. *Pro Font.* 13: *Narbo Martius, colonia nostrorum civium, specula populi Romani ac propugnaculum.*

the teeth of much senatorial opposition.[3] The affair is traditionally dated to 118, but more probably it occurred near the end of that decade.[4] It did not improve relations between the nobility and the business classes.

These developments, growing popular concern over aristocratic mismanagement of foreign policy and warfare, and increased tension between the senatorial and equestrian *ordines* must be borne in mind as background and prelude to the Jugurthine War. For more than half a decade that grueling conflict was to absorb the energies and anxieties of Romans from every class. Sallust selected it as the subject of a monograph not merely because of the formidable character of the military engagement but because of the serious repercussions on the domestic front.[5] It was a wise choice. The inner discontents and tensions that had been concealed or dormant during a decade of relative tranquillity exploded to the surface during Rome's grim struggle with Jugurtha.

The kingdom of Numidia had hitherto rested in the hands of a dynasty loyal to Rome and bound by ties of clientship. Massinissa had performed signal services for Scipio Africanus in the Hannibalic War and had profited handsomely in a lengthy reign that endured for more than half a century thereafter.[6] Links to the Scipios endured and in 148 Scipio Aemilianus, acting on Massinissa's deathbed request, distributed Numidian holdings among Massinissa's heirs.[7] The results were salutary. Micipsa, the oldest and eventually the only surviving son, brought prosperity and culture to his kingdom. North Africa was at peace and Micipsa could demonstrate continued loyalty to Rome by sending valuable contingents for the Spanish Wars.[8] The Numidian capital of Cirta became a magnet for tradesmen, merchants, and bankers from all over the Mediterranean. Not the least of them were the Roman and Italian businessmen who swelled the population of that bustling metropolis.

[3] Cic. *Brutus,* 160; *Pro Cluent.* 140. The context of the latter passage seems to imply that Crassus spoke on behalf of the *equites.* Contra: Brunt, *2nd Int. Conf. Econ. Hist. 1962,* I.131; Meier, *Res Pub.,* 313; Badian, "Notes on *Provincia Gallia* in the Late Republic," *Mélanges Piganiol* (1966), 903-904.

[4] The testimony of Velleius (1.15.5), followed by Eutropius (4.23), for 118 should not be regarded as sacrosanct. The career of Crassus, as outlined by Cicero, *Brutus,* 159-165, suggests a date between 113 and 107. H. B. Mattingly, "The Foundations of Narbo Martius," *Hommages Grenier* (1962), III.1159–1171, employs numismatic evidence to argue a date in 110. See Badian, *Rom. Imp.,* 23-24, 28, n. 32, who puts it ca. 115.

[5] Sallust, *Iug.* 5.1-2.

[6] On Massinissa, see P. G. Walsh, "Massinissa," *JRS,* 55 (1965), 149-160.

[7] Livy, *Per.* 50; Val. Max. 5.2.ext.4; Appian, *Lib.* 105-106; Orosius, 4.22.

[8] Appian, *Iber.* 67; Sallust, *Iug.* 7. On the prosperity of the realm, see Strabo, 17.3.13; Diod. 34.35.

The deathbed dispositions of Micipsa in 118, however, did not prove to be as fortunate as those of his father. Two sons, Adherbal and Hiempsal, had a claim on the kingdom. But there was a third individual to be reckoned with. Jugurtha was the illegitimate offspring of Micipsa's brother and he had a strong recommendation in his behalf, the endorsement of Scipio Aemilianus. Jugurtha had commanded the Numidian cavalry and infantry that served in Scipio's ranks in Spain in 134. The young prince possessed qualities that won the admiration of superiors and the devotion of subordinates. Physical attractiveness and strength, undiluted by idleness or luxury, set him apart from his peers and captured their loyalty.[9] But, more important, Jugurtha was a man of keen intellect who plotted his rise to the top with cool sagacity and capitalized on every opportunity. At Numantia he made certain to impress Scipio Aemilianus with his courage, unstinting obedience, and dedication to duty. It was a calculated effort, Sallust affirms, and a successful one.[10] There were many distinguished men in Scipio's retinue. Jugurtha made numerous contacts that were to prove invaluable in his maneuvers and intrigues. Among those who served in the ranks of Scipio's force and also caught the eye of his general was a young soldier named C. Marius. History does not record a meeting between Jugurtha and the man who ultimately proved to be his conqueror. No one in 134 would have considered Marius worth cultivating. But there were others who offered assistance and advice in Jugurtha's quest for the Numidian throne and Scipio wrote to Micipsa personally, setting forth the qualities of that impressive youth.[11] The word of the Scipios carried much weight in Numidia. On Micipsa's death, Jugurtha was joint ruler of the realm together with his two less gifted cousins.

The succeeding years found Jugurtha's ambition insatiable. Hiempsal was assassinated, and Adherbal, unsuccessful in the field, sought an audience in Rome with hopes of bringing Roman power to bear on the African situation. The senate confronted a complex and difficult decision. The duties of a patron-state are not easily definable; they were not contained in document or treaty. Rome was the arbiter of her own policy. Adherbal was a client of the imperial city, but so was Jugurtha. Appeals from a client were not lightly dismissed, but Rome could disavow obliga-

---

[9] Sallust, *Iug.* 6.1.

[10] Sallust, *Iug.* 7.4: *Nam Iugurtha, ut erat impigro atque aeri ingenio, ubi naturam P. Scipionis . . . et morem hostium cognovit, multo labore multaque cura, praeterea modestissume parendo et saepe obviam eundo periculis in tantam claritudinem brevi pervenerat, ut nostris vehementer carus, Numantinis maxumo terrori esset.*

[11] Sallust, *Iug.* 8.1-9.2.

tion in an internal dispute between dependents. Jugurtha's adherents in the senate spoke up sharply in his defense.[12] The sedulously cultivated contacts were now paying dividends. The *patres* had recourse to a tried and trusted expedient, the senatorial commission. Between 116 and 112 three different groups of envoys, despatched by the senate, visited North Africa and sought to adjudicate the rivalry for the Numidian throne. An apparently reasonable compromise was instituted. Adherbal would possess Cirta and the eastern portion of Numidia, bordering the Roman province of Africa, in touch with peaceful business interests and commercial activity; Jugurtha would control the inland area, the rich agricultural territory, abundant in human resources. Rome had avoided conflict, again and again, but Jugurtha's incursions did not cease. Duly submissive and humble in the presence of Roman ambassadors, he resumed aggression against Adherbal at every convenient opportunity. In 112 Cirta fell to Jugurtha and Adherbal was tortured to death. On this occasion enthusiasm or haste induced the barbarian characteristics of the Numidian to gain the better of his judgment. He ordered the summary execution of all Roman and Italian *negotiatores* in the city who were found to be armed.[13]

Surely it was clear now on which side Roman *fides* lay. The voices of those urging active Roman intervention could no longer be stilled. The massacre of the merchants had put the issue of war beyond argument. Numidia was allotted as a consular province and L. Calpurnius Bestia, accompanied by the *princeps senatus* M. Scaurus, mobilized an army and transported it to Africa in 111. Bestia appeared to possess the requisite qualities: endurance, sharpness of mind, experience, and fortitude.[14] Yet even at this late stage diplomacy was preferred to warfare. Jugurtha had nothing to lose; he was now without a rival in Numidia. Hence, a solemn *deditio* acknowledged the superiority of Rome, and Scaurus and Bestia regarded their mission as accomplished. Jugurtha turned over some elephants and livestock as a token gesture, but there is no mention of any reduction of his army.[15]

Such was the course of events abroad. Under the circumstances one need not be surprised that indignation and anger at home shattered whatever concord Rome had enjoyed in previous years. The war provided a pretext; it exposed the shallowness of Roman political stability. Once again legal proceedings served as the avenue of political attack. Demagogues and opportunists, filled with righteous wrath, could mobilize

[12] Sallust, *Iug.* 15.2.
[13] Sallust, *Iug.* 26.3.
[14] Sallust, *Iug.* 28.5.
[15] Sallust, *Iug.* 29.5-6.

the emotions of the people against leaders who, it appeared, had engaged in deception and who, through cowardice or greed, had allowed the Numidian situation to deteriorate disastrously.

The assault on senatorial corruptibility and incompetence began in earnest with the diatribes of C. Memmius as tribune-elect in 112 and tribune in 111.[16] Memmius' oratory was undistinguished but it was vehement and emotional, filled with partisan spirit.[17] His forbears also seem to have been of *popularis* tendencies.[18] It was either he or a relative who had served as military tribune in Numantia under Scipio Aemilianus in 134 and had been severely rebuked by Scipio.[19] Revenge was long in coming, but when it came it was not directed against only the heirs of the Scipionic group. It would be wrong to see the actions of Memmius simply as a salvo fired in factional dispute. Discontent with senatorial treatment of African affairs was made the excuse for a popular attack upon the nobility as a whole. This much, at least, is made clear by the otherwise suspicious and perhaps tendentious account in Sallust's *Bellum Iugurthinum*. The ranks of the senate were closed temporarily against *popularis* attacks, as they had been briefly closed in 121 and were again to be in 100. This is not to say that there was unanimity with regard to policy to be followed toward Jugurtha. Strategic and, perhaps, personal motives caused some dissension on this score, but there is no evidence linking this with internal factional rivalry. The events of 111-107 represent a revival of Gracchan policy, silenced for the previous decade while factional struggles held the stage. The disappearance of effective opposition to the Metelli and the threat of tribunes acting once more as organs of anti-senatorial opinion combined to close senatorial ranks in the period of the Jugurthine conflict.

C. Memmius has also often been seen as a mouthpiece of the *equites*.[20] That is an anticipatory judgment and it neglects the very significant difference between Memmius' actions in 111 and the later bill of Mamilius

[16] Sallust, *Iug.* 27, 30-34.

[17] Cic. *Brutus,* 136: *Tum etiam C.L. Memmii fuerunt oratores mediocres, accusatores acres atque acerbi;* Sallust, *Iug.* 27.2: *vir acer et infestus potentiae nobilitatis.* Sallust perhaps makes more of him as a speaker than is warranted; cf. *Iug.* 30.4.

[18] Sallust, *Iug.* 31.5: *Certe ego libertatem, quae mihi a parente meo tradita est, experiar.*

[19] Frontinus, *Strat.* 4.1.1: *mihi paulisper tibi et rei publicae nequam eris;* Plut. *Apophth. Scip. Min.* 17. Cichorius, *Unt. zu Luc.,* 284, identifies the military tribune with the tribune of the *plebs* of 111; also Münzer, *RE,* 29.604, "Memmius," n. 5.

[20] Cf., e.g., G. De Sanctis, *Problemi di Storia Antica* (Bari, 1932), 207-210; W. Schur, *Sallust als Historiker* (Stuttgart, 1934), 147-148.

in 109. Memmius sponsored a measure directing the praetor L. Cassius Longinus to bring Jugurtha to Rome under safe conduct. What were the tribune's intentions? It has not been noticed that he seems to have been preparing for a tribunician prosecution of offenders before the people. This is expressly his motive for the summoning of Jugurtha. Jugurtha's testimony was to be used to indict individuals whom Memmius was preparing to prosecute.[21] There is no mention here of *equites*. L. Cassius had a reputation for *fides* respected even by the Numidian king.[22] But a relative, the tribune of 104, could be designated in terms reminiscent of Memmius himself. That man's *popularis* measures were directed against the *potentia nobilitatis*. The evidence for popular agitation is consistent.[23] Jugurtha was brought before the people at a *contio* to produce testimony preliminary to a formal accusation. That this was a purely tribunician proceeding is clear from the fact that it was voided by the *intercessio* of another tribune, C. Baebius.[24] This was no extortion trial before equestrian jurors. Sallust, to be sure, refers to *pecuniae captae*. That was no doubt mentioned and would certainly have been brought up if judicial proceedings were to come to fruition. But the formal charge contemplated was clearly *perduellio*.[25] Memmius had relied on popular indignation, not on equestrian support, but had not reckoned with the senatorial use of the tribunician veto, which could and did nullify this avenue of attack. When the assault was launched again it took on a completely different form.[26]

[21] Sallust, *Iug.* 32.1: *quo facilius indicio regis Scauri et reliquorum, quos pecuniae captae arcessebat, delicta patefierent.*

[22] Sallust, *Iug.* 32.5.

[23] Asconius, 69, Clark. Two tribunes in the following year hoped to capitalize on the atmosphere. Like C. Gracchus they sought reelection; Sallust, *Iug.* 37.1-2.

[24] Sallust, *Iug.* 34.1: *ubi . . . Iugurtha respondere iussus est, C. Baebius tribunus plebis . . . regem tacere iubet.*

[25] This is made clear by Memmius' own contrasting of the offense of extortion with the crime of treachery that he was pressing; Sallust, *Iug.* 31.25: *Non peculatus aerari factus est neque per vim sociis ereptae pecuniae, quae quamquam gravia sunt, tamen consuetudine iam pro nihilo habentur. Hosti accerrumo prodita senatus auctoritas, proditum imperium vostrum est; domi militiaeque res publica venalis fuit.* Cf. 31.9, 31.18.

[26] One might mention in this connection another abortive trial. Jugurtha ordered the murder of a potential rival, the Numidian Massiva, then resident in Rome. The deed was carried out by retainers of Jugurtha's agent Bomilcar. But the assassins were caught in the act and a criminal proceeding developed against Bomilcar. Nothing came of it; Jugurtha surreptitiously smuggled Bomilcar out of Italy; Sallust, *Iug.* 35. The nature of the trial and the *iudicium* is unspecified. A normal proceeding is hardly to be imagined. Since a foreigner was defendant, it is likely that the *praetor peregrinus* was in charge.

The *equites,* for all we know, may have been well content with the treaty formulated by L. Calpurnia Bestia and M. Aemilius Scaurus in 111, involving, as it did, the *deditio* of Jugurtha, and perhaps envisioning peace and stability in Africa.[27] The first serious Roman defeat did not come until early in 109 under the legate A. Postumius Albinus.[28] That was more than anyone could endure: a Roman aristocrat forced to make humiliating terms with the barbarian, a Roman army shamefully passing under the yoke. It demonstrated beyond question the bankruptcy of a cautious policy toward Jugurtha, aroused the fears of the *equites,* and presented the popular tribunes with a convincing argument of senatorial incompetence. It is no accident that the Mamilian commission followed closely on the heels of this disaster.

The tribune C. Mamilius Limetanus accurately diagnosed the situation. His *rogatio Mamilia* secured passage, probably in the early months of 109. The lesson of Memmius' failure in 111 had been learned. A prosecution for *perduellio* before the people was too uncertain; the *severissimi* jurors of the *equester ordo* were more reliable. There was at this time no standing court for *maiestas,* so that recourse was had to the already established precedent of setting up a *quaestio extraordinaria* to investigate charges specially defined for the occasion.[29] The cases were to be heard by *Gracchani iudices.*[30] Cicero's phrase here is significant. It indicates not that *equites* were now deliberately sought out to sit on the courts as enemies of the senate, but that the panels of equestrian jurors as set up for the extortion court by C. Gracchus were naturally employed for any special *quaestio.* This coalition of populace and *equites* was of brief duration but violent and effective. Sallust, often incorrectly accused of following a strict *popularis* line, leaves no doubt that the Mamilian commission was authorized more out of hatred of the nobility

---

[27] Cf. Hill, *Roman Middle Class,* 118. That the *deditio* of Jugurtha was genuine was convincingly argued by K. von Fritz, "Sallust and the Attitude of the Roman Nobility at the Time of the Wars Against Jugurtha (112-105 B.C.)," *TAPA,* 74 (1943), 147-156. But cf. A. La Penna, "L'Interpretazione sallustiana della guerra contro Giugurta", *AnnPisa,* 28 (1959), 68-69.

[28] Sallust, *Iug.* 36-39; Livy, *Per.* 64; Florus, 1.36.9: Eutrop. 4.25.3; Orosius, 5.15.6.

[29] Sallust, *Iug.* 40.1: *C. Mamilius Limetanus tribunus plebis rogationem ad populum promulgat, uti quaereretur . . .* It is interesting to note the parallel with the events of 90. In that year Varius in his capacity as tribune first attacked Scaurus before the people, and when the attack failed resoundingly, Scaurus was prosecuted before an equestrian court.

[30] Cic. *Brutus,* 128.

than of concern for the state.[31] It is to be expected that the victims of this tribunal were regarded as enemies of the people and not as members of one senatorial faction or another.

To what extent the charges leveled under the Mamilian law were justified or even plausible has received much discussion. Mamilius directed his law against those on whose advice Jugurtha had ignored senatorial decrees, those who had been bribed either as *legati* or commanders, those who had been guilty of returning elephants and deserters to Jugurtha, and, in order to close all loopholes, those who had made any terms of peace or war with the enemy.[32] Sallust sniffs corruption and bribery at every stage of the negotiations from 116 on. But Sallustian innuendo is misleading and inconclusive. The obligations of a patron-state to intervene in an internal dispute among clients were not patent, and Rome had good reasons for hesitation. The threat from the north dramatically reared its head with Carbo's crushing defeat in 113 and Roman concern is suggested by the colony at Narbo, at least partially designed as a *propugnaculum*. A lengthy guerrilla war in the deserts of North Africa would prove difficult and costly to Roman legions ill-equipped, ill-trained, and ill-manned for warfare of that nature. Delay, caution, and "peaceful coexistence" can therefore be seen as a consistent and justifiable senatorial policy, for which corruption need not be postulated.[33]

That some money exchanged hands in the course of negotiations need not be doubted, but senatorial policy does not seem to have been diverted into acting against the interests of the state. Jugurtha had connections in Rome of long standing, who could be relied upon without requiring corruption.[34] The actions of Jugurtha's patrons in Rome were simply typical Roman activities on behalf of a favored client prince. Men like

[31] Sallust, *Iug.* 40.3: *magis odio nobilitatis . . . quam cura rei publicae.* For recent criticism of earlier views on Sallust's bias, see D. C. Earl, *The Political Thought of Sallust* (Cambridge, Eng., 1961), 60-81, and R. Syme, *Sallust* (Berkeley and Los Angeles, 1964), 157-177.

[32] Sallust, *Iug.* 40.1: *quaereretur in eos quorum consilio Iugurtha senati decreta neglegisset, quique ab eo in legationibus aut imperiis pecunias accepissent, qui elephantos quique perfugas tradidissent, item qui de pace aut bello cum hostibus pactiones fecissent.*

[33] See, e.g., Bloch, *Mélanges D'Histoire Ancienne,* 25 (1909), 46-51; Greenidge, *History of Rome,* 331-354; De Sanctis, *Problemi,* 187-207; Schur, *Sallust als Historiker,* 141-148; von Fritz, *TAPA,* 74 (1943), 144-165.

[34] Sallust, *Iug.* 7.7: *munificentia animi et ingeni sollertia, quis rebus sibi multos ex Romanis familiari amicitia coniunxerat;* cf. W. Allen, "The Sources of Jugurtha's Influence in the Roman Senate," *CP,* 33 (1938), 90-92, and Badian, *For. Client.,* 193.

Memmius and Mamilius, in the heat of an explosive situation, depicted such actions as *proditio*. But it was not simply Jugurtha's old patrons who were tainted. Popular agitation managed to tar with the same brush many who could not possibly have had earlier relations with Jugurtha.[35] Among the men prosecuted under the Mamilian law were supporters of the Metelli as well as individuals who might once have had Scipionic connections. The criterion was hostility to the people, not membership in any senatorial group.

A dramatic victim of the Mamilian commission was L. Opimius, the consul of 121. The motives for his condemnation are transparent. Alleged bribery by Jugurtha was made a pretext for elimination of the murderer of C. Gracchus. That this was the real motive involved is indicated by Cicero, who regarded this conviction as the most pernicious of those handed down by the tribunal.[36] Velleius adds that the condemnation of Opimius could arouse no sympathy among people who recalled his actions against the Gracchi.[37] The excesses of C. Gracchus had faded from popular concern; what was remembered most vividly was the slaying of a champion of the people. Cicero could diagnose the situation clearly and painfully from his own experience. In the early 50's the execution of the Catilinarian conspirators loomed much larger than the conspiracy itself. But the analysis need not rest on optimate sources, since Sallust himself says that the Mamilian *quaestio* acted *lubidine plebis*.[38] The formal charge against Opimius was, of course, treason. Opimius had headed the original senatorial embassy to Numidia in 116, in which he adjudicated the claims of Jugurtha and Adherbal. The settlement was, from all appearances, reasonable, and it is noteworthy that there was no resentment aroused against it until Opimius' activities became engulfed in the popular hatred of 109. Sallust, as is to be expected, asserts that Opimius was bribed by Jugurtha on that embassy.[39]

[35] Allen, *CP*, 33 (1938), 90-92, wrongly sees the Roman advocates of Jugurtha simply as members of the Scipionic group. Some of Jugurtha's connections had been made at Numantia, to be sure, but not everyone serving under Aemilianus there can be regarded as "Scipionic." One need think only of C. Gracchus, Marius, C. Metellus Caprarius, and Memmius himself! Cf. Earl, *Latomus*, 24 (1965), 532-536.

[36] Cic. *Brutus*, 128: *Nam invidiosa lege Mamilia quaestorium C. Galbam sacerdotem et quattuor consularis L. Bestiam, C. Catonem, Sp. Albinum, civemque praestantissimum L. Opimium, Gracchi interfectorem, a populo absolutum, cum is contra populi studium stetisset, Gracchani iudices sustulerunt.* Further on the trial of Opimius, see Cic. *Pro Planc.* 70; *Pro Sest.* 140.

[37] Vell. Pat. 2.7.3.

[38] Sallust, *Iug.* 40.5; see also Schol. Bob. 141, Stangl.

[39] Sallust, *Iug.* 16.3, 20.1; bribery is vigorously denied by De Sanctis, *Problemi*, 196-212.

But even if the Numidian king was generous, he was only practicing the standard method of rewarding or winning patrons in Rome. The imputation of corruption is tendentious, for, although Opimius protected the interests of the client prince, his settlement was evidently accepted as serving the interests of Rome as well. His downfall in 109 was the consequence of earlier popular resentment that could now seize upon a specious pretext to make itself felt.

L. Calpurnius Bestia, the consul of 111, had marched off to Numidia with a reputation for valor in war but had returned with only a treaty for peace. In 109 he too fell victim to the *quaestio Mamilia*. It is not difficult to understand popular indignation against him. Men remembered that as tribune in 120 Bestia had sponsored the measure to recall Popillius Laenas from exile.[40] The tribunal of Popillius that had hunted down the Gracchani in 132 now had its counterpart on the other side in the Mamilian court, and Bestia was a natural and convenient target. In 111 he had selected M. Scaurus as a legate and both shared responsibility for the treaty, which postponed hostilities further. For Sallust that is but further indictment: Bestia was seeking to shield his misdeeds through the influence of Scaurus.[41] The historian's partisan interpretation does not warrant credence. Bestia's link with Scaurus suggests that the consul of 111, the first of his family to reach that conveted post, was another of those promising aristocrats who had come under the wing of the Metellan *factio*. Scaurus defended Bestia at the trial and at no small risk to himself.[42] The settlement of Numidia made by Bestia and Scaurus in 111 was a reasonable recognition of the *status quo,* culminating in the act of *deditio* on the part of Jugurtha.[43] Again, corruption was far from proved, but popular hostility did not require proof. It is no accident that Cicero speaks of Bestia's conviction in the same context with his bill to recall Popillius Laenas a decade earlier.[44]

The Mamilian commission also secured the political demise of C. Sulpicius Galba, allegedly the first priest to be convicted on a criminal charge. An eloquent oration in his own defense, admired and memorized in a later generation, was to no avail.[45] Cicero's praise of this man and his denunciation of the judicial decision that condemned him indicate that Galba too was attacked as a staunch member of the nobility. This

---

[40] Cic. *Brutus,* 128.

[41] Sallust, *Iug.* 28.4: *quorum auctoritate quae deliquisset munita fore sperabat.*

[42] Cic. *De Orat.* 2.283.

[43] De Sanctis, *Problemi,* 202-207.

[44] Cic. *Brutus,* 128: *L. Bestia bonis initiis orsus tribunatus — nam P. Popilium vi C. Gracchi expulsum sua rogatione restituit — vir et acer et non indisertus, tristis exitus habuit consulatus.*

[45] Cic. *Brutus,* 127.

motive seems odd at first glance. Galba was married to the daughter of
P. Licinius Crassus Mucianus and was, therefore, the brother-in-law of
C. Gracchus himself.[46] But Galba had, in all probability, long since
abandoned those associations. Evidence for turncoat activities may
exist in the Carthaginian inscription discussed earlier, an inscription
recording the names of a Galba, a Carbo, and a Bestia. The commission
there represented operated in the full tide of anti-Gracchan activity.[47]
The participation of Galba in this venture, together with the despised
Carbo, who was condemned in 119, and with Bestia, who at about the
same time was responsible for the recall of Popillius Laenas, may well
form the background for the popular hostility revealed in 109. The
service with Bestia attested by the inscription makes it likely that Galba
also served on his staff in 111, providing the immediate impulse for the
charge leveled against him by the Mamilian tribunal. A renegade from
the Gracchan cause would naturally have been dealt with particularly
harshly.

Similar emotions may have ruined the career of C. Porcius Cato.
Although Sallust does not record his appearance on a diplomatic or
military mission to Numidia, Cato too was convicted by the *Gracchani
iudices* under the Mamilian law.[48] He had been a friend and supporter
of Ti. Gracchus in 133, but an uninterrupted career since that time
suggests that he had abandoned that losing cause before it was too late.[49]
In the atmosphere of 109, however, a hostile prosecutor would have
represented that dissociation as black treachery. And Cato had more to
live down. His crushing defeat at the hands of the Scordisci during a
consulship in 114 was still fresh in men's minds, as was the blatant
political influence employed in his trial of 113, when a conviction for
repetundae issued in a ludicrously small assessment of damages.[50] That
Cato had been despatched at all on an embassy to Jugurtha should not
cause surprise. He was a nephew of Scipio Aemilianus. The Numidian
connection with the house of Scipio was long-standing, and the senate,
anxious to avoid hostilities, would naturally have utilized a member of
that house to appease Jugurtha. Not that Cato is to be regarded as
"Scipionic" in the context of Roman politics. His sympathy for Ti.

---

[46] Cic. *De Orat.* 1.239; *Brutus,* 98, 127.

[47] *ILS,* 28; cf. Earl, *Latomus,* 24 (1965), 535-536.

[48] Cic. *Brutus,* 128; *Pro Balbo,* 28.

[49] Cic. *De Amicit.* 39.

[50] There is no warrant for Mrs. Henderson's amalgamation of the extortion trial with the prosecution before the Mamilian commission; *JRS,* 41 (1951), 85; cf. Sherwin-White, *JRS,* 42 (1952), 44-45.

Gracchus would have severed those earlier ties, but there was no reason for this break to affect the patron relationship with the Numidian dynasty. Gifts received by Cato would have been in the nature of customary tokens of gratitude from a client, only later construed as bribery. A resentful populace was not prepared to draw the distinction.

For the last known victim of the *lex Mamilia,* Sp. Postumius Albinus, there is no direct evidence for previous popular hostility.[51] It is perhaps worth pointing out that Plutarch mentions a Sp. Postumius who was a rival of Ti. Gracchus, a fact which may help to explain resentment against the consul of 110.[52] But previous misdeeds need not be conjectured in this case. It was Sp. Postumius' blunder and the disastrous loss suffered in Numidia by his forces, left under the command of his legate and brother A. Postumius, that provided the immediate spark for the Mamilian commission. His condemnation was natural and necessary.[53]

The precise role of M. Aemilius Scaurus in the events of these years is not easily discerned from the obviously hostile account of Sallust.[54] Certainly Scaurus' alleged complicity in the intrigues of Jugurtha survived in the tradition. Florus and the author of the *De Viris Illustribus* both affirm that Scaurus was bribed by Jugurtha.[55] Rumors to this effect obviously had been circulated. In an atmosphere of suspicion and hostility anyone who had had dealings with Jugurtha was bound to be whispered about. Nor was Scaurus the man to overlook a money-making

---

[51] Cic. *Brutus,* 128.

[52] Plut. *Ti Gracch.* 8.6: Σπόριόν τινα Ποστούμιον . . . ἡλικιώτην τοῦ Τιβερίου καὶ πρὸς δόξαν ἐφάμιλλον αὐτῷ περὶ τὰς συνηγορίας. That this Sp. Postumius is to be identified with the consul of 110 is possible but unlikely; Münzer, *RE,* 43.900-901, "Postumius," n. 23.

[53] That his brother was also prosecuted is taken for granted by Münzer, *RE,* 43.908-909, "Postumius," n. 32, and seems a natural inference. Nonetheless, there is no explicit information and an A. Postumius Albinus later held the consulship in 99; Broughton, *Supplement to the Magistrates of the Roman Republic* (New York, 1960), 50-51. Whether this is the same Albinus must remain in the realm of conjecture.

[54] Sallust's motives for deliberate falsification cannot be ascribed simply to *popularis* prejudice, as von Fritz, *TAPA,* 74 (1943), 134-168; see Schur, *Sallust als Historiker,* 115-126; K. Vretska, "Studien zu Sallusts *Bellum Jugurthinum,*" *SBWien,* 229 (1955), 46-57; Syme, *Sallust,* 157-177. Nor should it be put down to a mere dislike of political trimmers, as A. R. Hands, "Sallust and *Dissimulatio,*" *JRS,* 49 (1959), 56-60. Personal reasons may be involved; it is well to remember that in 54 Scaurus' son was involved in a notorious criminal prosecution in which a great number of Roman *nobiles* took part on one side or the other; Cic. *Pro Scauro, passim.*

[55] *Vir. Ill.* 72.5: *eius pecunia victus;* Florus, 1.36.5.

proposition.[56] Memmius doubtless made the most of the rumors, and may even have threatened a prosecution of Scaurus in 111.[57]

Nonetheless, Sallust himself provides sufficient evidence to cast serious doubt upon his own conclusions. At the outset of the affair, in 117 or 116, when Jugurtha's envoys first began flashing their gold about, Scaurus remained immovable and supported the claims of Adherbal. Sallust's innuendo, *animum a consueta lubidine continuit,* cannot conceal the fact that he himself records.[58] When Scaurus was later despatched at the head of an embassy to Numidia in 112, it was his appearance above all that struck terror in the camp of Jugurtha.[59] That he would then allow himself to be corrupted as legate on Bestia's staff in 111, when suspicions were mounting and Memmius was on the hustings, would argue not greed but stupidity.

The threats of Memmius clearly went unheeded. Scaurus was not prosecuted. Quite the contrary; when the Mamilian commission was set up, Scaurus himself was appointed a *quaesitor.*[60] That is a telling item. It surpasses belief that the people, incensed as they were with partisan bias, would have appointed Scaurus to this post if there were any genuine and widespread belief in his guilt. That his appointment was simply a demonstration of impartiality on the part of the people is hardly possible in an affair where partiality itself was the keynote.[61] But it is equally difficult to believe that the aristocracy managed to get Scaurus on the commission against the wishes of the populace.[62] The results of the trials themselves surely demonstrate the vulnerability and weakness of the *nobilitas* at this juncture. To imagine that they could have enforced their

[56] Cic. *De Orat.* 2.283; Pliny, *NH,* 36.116.

[57] Sallust, *Iug.* 32.1: *Memmius populo persuadet uti L. Cassius . . . ad Iugurtham mitteretur . . . quo facilius indicio regis Scauri et reliquorum . . . delicta patefierent.*

[58] Sallust, *Iug.* 15.2-5; cf. Bloch, *Mélanges D'Histoire Ancienne,* 25 (1909), 42; von Fritz, *TAPA,* 74 (1943), 145-146.

[59] Sallust, *Iug.* 25.10: *Scaurum quem plurimum metuebat.*

[60] Sallust, *Iug.* 40.4. Sallust states that the Mamilian *rogatio* provided for the election of three *quaesitores: ex Mamilia rogatione tres quaesitores rogarentur.* Whether this means that three separate courts were instituted, as Bloch argued, *Mélanges D'Histoire Ancienne,* 25 (1909), 64, or that a single court was set up with three rotating *quaesitores,* the view of Fraccaro, *Opuscula,* 2.129, cannot be decided conclusively on the basis of Sallust's brief notice. Neither has any known precedent. Speculation is pointless.

[61] Sallust, *Iug.* 40.3, 40.5: *quaestio exercita aspere violenterque ex rumore et lubidine plebis.*

[62] For the view that Scaurus was nominated as a sign of impartiality, see Bloch, *Mélanges D'Histoire Ancienne,* 25 (1909), 65; that he was named despite popular desire, Fraccaro, *Opuscula,* 2.129-130.

wishes by placing Scaurus on the tribunal and yet failed to get any acquittals makes nonsense of the whole affair. The only reasonable conclusion is that Scaurus received the appointment to the commission precisely because he was expected to get the job done with vigor and despatch. This must mean that Scaurus was still expounding the harsh views on Jugurtha that he had expressed as early as 117.[63] Scaurus' last mission had, after all, resulted in Jugurtha's *deditio.* He was wrong, obviously, in believing that a show of force would settle the issue, but charges of corruption against him were clearly given no hearing. The tribunal would gain prestige from the presence of the man who was both *princeps senatus* and censor in that very year of 109. It was a job, no doubt, that Scaurus did not relish. But that subtle politician seems to have handled it without alienating his friends. He appeared even in defense of Bestia, who was prosecuted by Memmius himself, and, though he could not get Bestia off, managed to discharge his personal obligations without violating his official duties.[64]

What were the effects of the *lex Mamilia?* Sallust perhaps ascribes more to it than is warranted. He remarks that one of the consequences was the rout of the nobility and the rise of *novi homines.*[65] That is an excessive and exaggerated claim, as the *fasti* clearly show. In fact, the Mamilian commission seems to have provided a purgation for pent-up hostility. The heat of the tribunal burned itself out quickly. Of the consuls elected in 109 one was Ser. Sulpicius Galba, brother of the Galba who had been condemned in that same year.

There is other evidence, interesting but often neglected. Galba's colleague in the consulship was a Hortensius who was convicted on an unknown charge and replaced by M. Aurelius Scaurus.[66] This trial may indicate that factional politics were indeed going on as usual after the Mamilian conflagration had died down. Much speculation about this case is unwarranted, for neither charge nor prosecutor is known. Hortensius perhaps suffered conviction for *ambitus* in 109 before actually taking office.[67] If so, Aurelius Scaurus stood to gain, and may have been

---

[63] Sallust, *Iug.* 15.3-4: *pauci . . . subveniundum Adherbali et Hiempsalis mortem severe vindicandam censebant; sed ex omnibus maxume Aemilius Scaurus.*

[64] Cic. *De Orat.* 2.283. The case must have been pleaded before one of the other two *quaesitores.*

[65] Sallust, *Iug.* 65.6: *Simul ea tempestate plebs, nobilitate fusa per legem Mamiliam, novos extollebat.*

[66] Sources in *MRR,* I.548.

[67] Münzer, *RE,* 16.2465-2466, "Hortensius," n. 2. Broughton's notion that Hortensius was condemned in office fails to confront the problem of consular immunity; *MRR,* I.548.

behind the prosecution. Hortensius remains unidentified. He may be L. Hortensius, father of the orator and consul of 69, or possibly an unknown uncle.[68] It has been suggested earlier that the Hortensii had connections with the Metelli in this period, as the orator Q. Hortensius certainly did in the 70's.[69] It is not unreasonable to conjecture that this prosecution represents an attack on the Metellan group, perhaps taking advantage of disarray in its ranks after the condemnation of men like Bestia, Cato, and Galba by the Mamilian commission.[70] In the same year Aemilius Scaurus resigned his censorship when his colleague succumbed to a fatal illness, but the resignation was reluctant and prodded by the agitation of some tribunes.[71] Senatorial politics proceeded apace, even in the wake of popular attacks on the aristocracy.

Nonetheless, the trials under the *lex Mamilia* were of more than temporary significance. They demonstrated dramatically that the courts could be employed to serve extra-senatorial interests and not simply to adjudicate the claims of rival senatorial groups. The revived conjunction of popular sentiment and equestrian support had proved damaging. That it led directly to the dominance of Roman politics by *novi homines* is not, of course, true.[72] But the emergence of some new names in positions of authority in the next few years is striking. Marius is only the most obvious and notorious example. Cn. Mallius Maximus, the consul of 105, was certainly a *novus homo*. So was C. Flavius Fimbria, who reached the consulship in the following year.[73] Indeed, even P. Rutilius Rufus, the colleague of Mallius in 105, may be regarded as a *novus homo,* although he did not, of course, owe his election to *popularis* sympathies.

Another "new man," C. Coelius Caldus, tribune in 107, seems to have taken advantage of the new-found *popularis* pressure in the courts by settling a score with an old enemy of the people.[74] That year saw the

[68] See Cichorius, *Unt. zu Luc.,* 338-340; Münzer, *RE,* 16.2465-2466, "Hortensius," n. 2; *MRR,* I.541-542, n. 2.

[69] See above, pp. 116-117.

[70] It is worth noting that this M. Aurelius Scaurus served in 105 on the staff of Cn. Mallius Maximus, the bitter opponent of another Metellan supporter, Q. Servilius Caepio; Livy, *Per.* 67; Gran. Licin. 17 B; Orosius, 5.16.2.

[71] Plut. *RQ,* 50; Degrassi, *Fast. Cap.,* 72-73: *Scaurus coact*[us] *abd* [icavit].

[72] This feature has, however, been too much deprecated by Sherwin-White, *JRS,* 46 (1956), 3, followed by Earl, *Political Thought of Sallust,* 77.

[73] For Mallius, see *MRR,* I.555; also Broughton, *Supplement,* 38; for Fimbria, *MRR,* I.558.

[74] He is called a *novus homo* by Cicero, who puts him in a context with Q. Varius; *De Orat.* 1.117. The date of the tribunate is more probably 107 than 106; see Niccolini, *Fast. Trib. Pleb.,* 187.

return from Gaul of the legate C. Popillius Laenas, son of that bitter opponent of the Gracchi, the consul of 132. C. Popillius had made the political error of protecting the survivors of a Roman army by concluding a peace involving surrender.[75] He considered it better to forfeit his baggage than his soldiers.[76] That seemed a reasonable judgment at the time, but popular enthusiasm is not always governed by reason. Coelius seized the opportunity to bring a *perduellio* charge before the people that resulted in Popillius' conviction and exile.[77]

There was more of importance that emerged from this affair. The exercise of the popular will at the expense of aristocratic influence in criminal trials was significantly strengthened in this trial through a bill of Coelius that extended the secret ballot to *perduellio* cases heard by the *comitia*.[78] This measure entailed, of course, a serious weakening of the *nobiles'* control of their *clientelae* in criminal cases.[79] *Popularis* agitation, not always associated with equestrian interests, clearly contrived to make use of the judicial process in the aftermath of the Mamilian prosecutions.[80]

The mismanagement of foreign affairs and warfare, the wrath of the populace, the anxiety of the business classes, the political manipulation of the courts, the emergence of *novi homines* all culminated in the rise of Marius, the symbol and representative of a new era. *Ita Mario cuncta procedere*.[81] The events of these years were not his doing, but Marius was the fortunate beneficiary and he knew how to exploit the opportunity.

[75] Sources in *MRR*, I.552.

[76] *Ad Herenn.* 1.25: *Satius esse duxit amittere inpedimenta quam exercitum;* cf. 4.34.

[77] Popillius was, at some later date, rehabilitated; Cic. *De Domo*, 87.

[78] Cic. *De. Leg.* 3.36: *uno in genera relinqui videbatur vocis suffragium, quod ipse Cassius exceperat perduellionis; dedit huic quoque iudicio C. Coelius tabellam.*

[79] The notion that Popillius escaped conviction here and only succumbed later on a charge of *maiestas* (Last, *CAH,* IX.159; cf. *MRR,* I.551-552) is unsupported. The fate of Popillius became a favorite topic for rhetorical exercises (*Ad Herenn.* 1.25, 4.34; Cic. *De Invent.* 2.72-73) and later authors frequently confused *perduellio* and *maiestas*. There was no court for the latter in 107 and offenses like that of Popillius would have been heard by the people; Cic. *De Leg.* 3.36; Orosius, 5.15.24; cf. Brecht, *MünchBeitr,* 29 (1938), 291-292; Volkmann, *RE,* 43.58-59, "Popillius," n. 19.

[80] In a careful analysis of Coelius' later career, Badian, *Studies,* 90-94, finds a gradual transference to optimate sympathies. Still, it is well to remember that Coelius won his consulship in 94 against the wishes of the *nobiles;* [Q. Cic.], *Comm. Petit.* 11.

[81] Sallust, *Iug.* 65.5.

The Mamilian commission had discharged its venom against the enemies of the people. But there was a war to be won. Not all aristocrats were cowardly or corruptible, even in the eyes of an enraged populace. Q. Metellus Numidicus assumed supreme control of the military effort in 109. He was a Metellus and a *nobilis* to the core; no friend of the people, Numidicus was arrogant and contemptuous of inferiors. But his integrity was unassailable; he was a man of unblemished repute, valor, and energy.[82] Marius had once been a client of the Metelli, a relationship severed by precipitate actions in 119; the career of that *novus homo* had been a rocky and uneven one. But no one could quarrel with his military record and experience. Metellus duly chose him as a legate and Marius carried heavy responsibilities in the war.[83]

Not that there was any genuine reconciliation between the two men. Metellus could brook no superiors and Marius envisioned the Jugurthine campaigns with the eye of a politician as well as a soldier. It was not his concern to enhance the glory of his commanding officer.[84] Marius sedulously cultivated popularity among the troops and subtly utilized contacts among the business elements in Rome and Africa to promote his stature vis-à-vis that of Metellus.[85] Central in this growing rift between *proconsul* and *legatus* was the case of T. Turpilius Silanus.

Although not a political trial held in Rome, but a case subject to magisterial *coercitio,* the affair of Turpilius may have had important political consequences. Turpilius had been commissioned by Metellus Numidicus to take charge of the Roman garrison at Vaga. The results were unfortunate. Kindness to the inhabitants was rewarded by treachery; the entire Roman contingent was led into a trap and slaughtered to a man. Turpilius was the lone survivor, and as such was in an unenviable position. Sallust reserved judgment on his guilt: perhaps he was spared through mercy, perhaps conspiracy, perhaps chance.[86] Turpilius' survival was, in any case, a severe embarrassment to Metellus, his commander and his patron. An investigation had to be undertaken, conducted by the proconsul, with the result that Turpilius was condemned to be

---

[82] Sallust, *Iug.* 43.1: *acri viro et quamquam advorso populi partium, fama tamen aequabili et inviolata;* 64.1: *Cui quamquam virtus, gloria atque alia optanda bonis superabant, tamen inerat contemptor animus et superbia, commune nobilitatis malum.*

[83] Cf. Sallust, *Iug.* 46.7, 50.2, 55.4, 56.3, 58.5, 60.5-8.

[84] Plut. *Marius,* 7.1.

[85] Sallust, *Iug.* 64.5-6, 65.4; Plut. *Marius,* 7.2-4; Passerini, *Athenaeum,* 12 (1934), 22-32; Carney, *A Biog. of Marius,* 26-28.

[86] Sallust, *Iug.* 67.3; cf. Plut. *Marius,* 8.1; for the story of the massacre, see Sallust, *Iug.* 66-67.

scourged and executed.[87] That is as much as we are told by Sallust and Appian. But Plutarch preserves a further tradition: Marius was a member of the *consilium* that tried the case; he recognized the discomfiture of Metellus, pressed vigorously for Turpilius' conviction, and forced the proconsul to extricate himself by passing the death sentence on his own client. For Plutarch, the result was open and irreversible hostility between Marius and Metellus.[88]

The historicity of this story has often been denied. Plutarch is obviously following an anti-Marian source and hardly warrants implicit confidence.[89] But need one throw out the tale altogether? Marius would not be slow to perceive the political capital to be made out of this affair. No one can be sure what happened behind the closed doors of the *consilium*, but the execution itself afforded an ideal opportunity to step up the propaganda campaign against Metellus: the commander had violated the sacred ties that bound patron to client.[90]

The status of Turpilius, subject of a long-standing scholarly debate, remains uncertain. Sallust states that he was subject to the penalty of scourging and execution *nam is civis ex Latio erat*. That should mean "a Roman citizen, previously a Latin".[91] Yet the implication that Roman citizenship was an invitation to violate *provocatio* is difficult to swallow. Hence some interpret the phrase as meaning that Turpilius was a Latin.[92]

---

[87] Sallust, *Iug.* 69; Appian, *Num.* 3.

[88] Plut. *Marius*, 8.1-2.

[89] See Passerini, *Athenaeum*, 12 (1934), 23-25, followed by S. Accame, "Il primo consolato di Mario," *Riv. di Filol.*, 14 (1936), 64-69; cf. Valgiglio, *Plutarco, Vita di Mario*, 37-39.

[90] Badian, *For. Client.*, 196-197; La Penna, *AnnPisa*, 28 (1959), 84-85. There may be other evidence for Marius' propaganda campaign. The coin of Porcius Laeca, dated to ca. 104, embodies the slogan *provoco;* E. A. Sydenham, *Coinage of the Roman Republic* (London, 1952), 571. That might be an indirect reference to Metellus' condemnation of Turpilius without recourse to *provocatio*, as argued by Carney, *NC*, 19 (1959), 88. Marius could later advertise his own gentleness in contrast to Metellus' severity, when he magnanimously acquitted one of his soldiers, Trebonius, during the Cimbric wars, on the grounds of a justifiable homicide; Plut. *Marius*, 14. On this affair, cf. Valgiglio, *Plutarco, Vita di Mario*, 73-74.

[91] Cf. Greenidge, "The *Provocatio Militiae* and Provincial Jurisdiction," *CR*, 10 (1896), 226-227; M. O. B. Caspari, "On the *Rogatio Livia de Latinis*," *CQ*, 5 (1911), 115-118; Badian, *For. Client.*, 196-197; Kunkel, *AbhMünch*, 56 (1962), 90, n. 331. Turpilius was *praefectus fabrum* (Plut. *Marius*, 8.1), a post not normally held by Latins.

[92] Mommsen, *Strafrecht*, 31, n. 3; Strachan-Davidson, *Problems*, I.115-117; J. S. Reid, "On Some Questions of Roman Public Law," *JRS*, 1 (1911), 77-79. That *civis* could later be used to denote a Latin citizen is shown by the *lex Malacitana; ILS*, 6089.

In either case, Sallust's *ex Latio* indicates that Turpilius' Latin status, whether present or past, had a bearing on the affair. Livius Drusus in 122 had proposed a law to exempt Latins from scourging.[93] No source records its passage but the exercise of *provocatio* by Latins was doubtless still an open question in 108. The dubious legality of Metellus' action enabled Marius to make political capital. Metellus, he could argue, had not only forsaken a client; he had overstepped the boundaries of his authority and perhaps of the law.

The Turpilius case made the breach between Marius and Metellus irremediable. The legate felt confident enough to seek the consulship. Metellus sneered: the year of his own son's prospective consulship would be time enough for Marius to think about that office.[94] But the propaganda efforts had been effective. Metellus had been conducting campaigns in Numidia for well over two years with some military successes but few tangible results.[95] It was not the last time that a lengthy and apparently fruitless guerrilla war abroad caused frustration and impatience at home. Marius returned to Rome to add his personal presence to his supporters' assaults on and vilification of Metellus. The latter, he could argue, had been no more successful or competent than his bungling fellow-aristocrats who had been rooted out by the Mamilian commission. The *novus homo* secured his coveted election for 107.[96]

Students of Republican Rome need no reminder of the momentous character of this event.[97] Election was not the end of the story. A senatorial decree allocating Numidia once more to Metellus was set aside

[93] Plut. *C. Gracch.* 9.3.

[94] Sallust, *Iug.* 64.4; Plut. *Marius,* 8.3. Marius would have been in his seventies by then. The story is perhaps apocryphal; cf. Passerini, *Athenaeum,* 12 (1934), 31-32. But it would appropriately reflect the attitude of Metellus Numidicus. That it was actually an offer of continued patronage (Earl, *Political Thought of Sallust,* 73) is incredible.

[95] On the campaigns of Metellus, see in general Greenidge, *History of Rome,* 383-433; also M. Holroyd, "The Jugurthine War: Was Marius or Metellus the Real Victor?" *JRS,* 18 (1928), 1-20, and Van Ooteghem, *Marius,* 111-142.

[96] Sallust, *Iug.* 73, 84.1; Plut. *Marius,* 8.4-9.4. The version of Cic. *De Off.* 3.79, that Marius did not contemplate standing for the consulship until he reached Rome, where he had been sent on some other mission by Metellus, lacks all plausibility, although it has now been defended again by Van Ooteghem, *LEC,* 32 (1964), 157-161; *Marius,* 135-136. This view involves the scrapping of evidence from both Sallust and Plutarch. Marius did not require the city of Rome to suggest a consulship to him; cf. Carney, *A Biog. of Marius,* 27-28.

[97] Cf. Sallust, *Iug.* 73.7: *ita perculsa nobilitate, post multas tempestates novo homini consulatus mandatur.*

by popular vote and Marius was now supreme commander of the Roman effort against Jugurtha.[98] This dramatic exercise of popular sovereignty was of a piece with events of this and the immediately preceding years. Memmius had prepared the ground in 111. Marius' colleague in 107, L. Cassius Longinus, had aided Memmius' schemes in 111 by bringing Jugurtha to Rome to answer charges. Cassius' election was no coincidence. The *lex Mamilia* had allowed the populace to flex its muscles in the judicial sphere. The prosecution of C. Popillius and the *lex tabellaria* of Coelius promised an extension of popular fervor in this area. Election of one *novus homo* excited the ambitions of others, some of whom were to see those ambitions realized in succeeding years.

Q. Metellus yielded his command, but without grace. He had greeted the news of his supersession with tears of grief and rage.[99] He could not look on the face of his successor and commissioned a lieutenant to transfer the army officially to Marius.[100] The military reforms of Marius eventually proved the difference in the war against Jugurtha. Strategy did not change substantially, but Marius opened up the Roman army to men of all ranks and the volunteers proved abundant. A successful guerrilla war against an enemy on his own terrain requires considerable superiority in manpower. That is what Marius now supplied.[101] By the end of 105 the war in Numidia was over and on the first of January in 104 Jugurtha was led in chains to decorate the triumph of Marius.[102]

The war had had a dramatic impact on Roman politics. The forces that C. Gracchus had unleashed in 121 were galvanized again under the shadow of the Jugurthine conflict. A decade of relative peace in the interim had offered the senate a breathing space it unfortunately consumed in factional contests that promoted aristocratic vulnerability. The interim decade only postponed the coming confrontation with popular grievance, with the emergence of new men, and with the growing claims of the business interests. The Numidian war disclosed that a crisis could bring to the surface elements that rocked the established order. But it would be wrong to imagine that these years set in motion a relentless process involving the steady and consistent dissolution of an aristocratic

---

[98] Sallust, *Iug.* 73.7.

[99] Sallust, *Iug.* 82.2: *neque lacrumas tenere neque moderari linguam.*

[100] Sallust, *Iug.* 86.5; Plut. *Marius*, 10.1.

[101] Holroyd, *JRS*, 18 (1928), 1-20; De Sanctis *Problemi*, 347-349; La Penna, *AnnPisa*, 38 (1959), 79-86, 258-264; Carney, *A Biog. of Marius*, 29-30; Syme, *Sallust*, 143-151. On the remainder of the war in general, a subject not pertinent for this inquiry, cf. Greenidge, *History of Rome*, 434-468; Van Ooteghem, *Marius*, 151-175.

[102] *MRR*, I.558.

society. Sallust may have had that impression, but he was writing from the distance of sixty years when the dissolution seemed complete. If there is any pattern to be found it is not that of a steady downward curve, but that of the Gracchan era repeating itself. A political crisis produced intense passions and promoted class hostilities in which the men out of power looked to new leaders, and the aristocracy found that its common interests were weightier than its internal rivalries. But crises by nature are temporary, and though the bitterness lingered, the old system tended to fall back into place. The molding of extra-senatorial elements into a permanent political force seems to have been beyond the vision or the capacity of popular leaders. Men like Memmius, Mamilius, Coelius Caldus, and Marius himself played upon popular and equestrian prejudices, perhaps more in their own interests than for any wider considerations. Nonetheless, the exploitations of these prejudices would continue and would be employed at convenient times against dominant senatorial groups. This pulsating pattern is to be seen again and again. Contests over basic principles sometimes crowded aristocratic squabbles off the historical stage, but usually not for long. And often, behind the dramatic scenes of war and demagogery that attracted the ancient historian, there lay the less conspicuous infighting within the older power structure. It is the alternation and interaction of these two developments, frequently illuminated by a study of the courts and legal processes, that best epitomizes this era of Roman history.

VI. POPULAR POLITICS AND THE *IUDICIA*

The vagaries of Roman politics were difficult to predict and, from this vantage point, are even more difficult to follow. The ire of the populace might be aroused for a time, and some members of the aristocracy would suffer, perhaps see their careers shattered. But once pent-up emotions were ventilated, the people had a way of turning to their traditional leaders once again. This fluctuation was never swifter or more frequent than in the complex years of the Jugurthine War and its sequel.

Marian propaganda and the frustrations of a lengthy war had brought a *novus homo* to the head of government and to the control of its military operations. The election of Marius signaled the desperate desire of Rome for new directions in her Numidian policy, but the populace had not turned its back on older leaders. Q. Metellus had been unable to bring the conflict to a successful conclusion, but when passions had cooled men recognized his merits and his achievements: *plebi patribusque, postquam invidia decesserat, iuxta carus.*[1] A tribune of 107, T. Manlius Mancinus, the same man whose measure had transferred the Numidian command from Metellus to Marius, unleashed vicious verbal attacks on the returning commander, but to no avail. Metellus received the proud *cognomen* Numidicus for his exploits, carrying on the distinguished traditions of his family, which already included a Macedonicus, a Balearicus, and a Delmaticus. The triumph he celebrated in 106 was splendid and memorable.[2]

The Metellan *factio* remained conspicuous and powerful. It was represented in the consulship of 106 by Q. Servilius Caepio. Connections between the Caepiones and the Metelli stretched back for half a century.[3] Caepio, Cicero maintained, was *vir acer et fortis*. That is partisan judgment, but not unwarranted. His praetorship and promagistracy in Spain had demonstrated martial valor and culminated in resplen-

---

[1] Sallust, *Iug.* 88.1.
[2] Vell. Pat. 2.11: *triumphus fuit clarissimus.* See also *Vir. Ill.* 62; Eutrop. 4.27.6; Degrassi, *Fast. Cap.,* 107. For Mancinus' attacks, see *ORF,* 211-213.
[3] See above, pp. 23, 36-37.

dent triumph.[4] The opportunity was at hand for this group to reassert its supremacy within the senate and to take the lead in restoring the aristocracy to the position it had held prior to the Jugurthine War. It is not surprising that the object of attention, as so often, was the judicial process.

Caepio sponsored a judiciary law that (perhaps among other things) altered the composition of the courts.[5] Debate on the matter was keen; the equestrian administration of justice was at stake. C. Memmius seems to have spoken up in opposition to the measure.[6] But Caepio could draw on the eloquent assistance of the orator L. Licinius Crassus, who was also associated with the Metelli. Crassus delivered one of the most celebrated and powerful of his speeches, lambasting the inequities of judicial conduct as practiced by the *equites*. It was a masterly oration, a model of declamatory argument for the succeeding generation.[7] The effect was telling and the law, almost certainly, was passed.[8] It was, however, and under the circumstances would almost have had to be, a compromise measure. The courts were henceforth to be manned by juries drawn from a mixed panel of senators and knights.[9]

[4] Cic. *Brutus,* 135; Val. Max. 9.6.13: *praeturae splendore, triumphi claritate;* Eutrop. 4.27.5; Degrassi, *Fast. Cap.,* 107.

[5] Sources in A. H. J. Greenidge and A. M. Clay, *Sources for Roman History, 133-70 B.C.,* rev. by E. W. Gray (Oxford, 1960), 78; *MRR,* I.553.

[6] Cicero preserves two bitter jokes by Crassus at Memmius' expense, one of which, at least, was delivered *in concione;* Cic. *De Orat.* 2.267; cf. 2.240. It is not unlikely that both belong to an altercation on the subject of Caepio's bill.

[7] Cic. *Brutus,* 164: *mihi quidem a pueritia quasi magistra fuit.* Also *Pro Cluent.* 140; *De Orat.* 1.225; cf. *Brutus,* 161.

[8] This is stated explicitly by Cassiodorus, *Chron.* 106, Tac. *Ann.* 12.60, and Obseq. 41, and clearly implied by Cic. *De Invent.* 1.92 and Val. Max. 6.9.13. Passages sometimes cited for the reverse view (Cic. *Verr.* 1.38; Asconius, 79, Clark) are inexact and general, proving only that Caepio's law was of short duration, not that it failed to pass. For the view that the bill never passed, see, e.g., Hardy, *JP,* 32 (1912), 99-104; cf. G. L. Hendrickson, "The Memoirs of Rutilius Rufus," *CP,* 28 (1933), 156-158.

[9] Cassiodorus, *Chron.* 106; Obseq. 41. Tacitus' phrase, *senatui iudicia rederrent (Ann.* 12.60), is incorporated in a brief and very general survey of judicial laws and makes no pretense of exactitude. The measure in any case was in the senatorial interest, which accounts for the Tacitean statement. See Balsdon, *PBSR,* 14 (1938), 103-105. For the opposite view, only cautiously put forward, see Hill, *Roman Middle Class,* 122, and Pontenay de Fontette, *Leges Repetundarum,* 74; also, more vigorously, Strachan-Davidson, *Problems,* II.80-81. It is often forgotten that the number of jurors enrolled in an annual panel under the Gracchan law was 450; *lex repet.,* line 12 (*FIRA,* I.87-88). With a senate of only 300 members, mixed panels were unavoidable, unless Caepio also altered the number of men impanelled, for which there is no evidence; cf. Jones, *PCPS,* 186 (1960), 40-41.

What was the meaning of this measure? Scholars have professed themselves puzzled that equestrian jurisdiction in the extortion court should have aroused indignation, for there is no evidence of inequities before the trial of Rutilius Rufus in 92.[10] That is to miss the point entirely. Caepio's law was not a *lex repetundarum* but a *lex iudiciaria*.[11] Clearly, then, it included in its scope more than the extortion court. Application to other permanent *quaestiones* would have been part of the purpose, but no large part. Evidence exists for only one other standing court at this time, and even that is uncertain.[12] The import of the bill surely is that the *album* of *iudices,* set up annually, was now to be changed in composition: not only would the two standing courts (if there were two) no longer draw their jurors from the *equites* alone, but no special *quaestio* could do so. The aim of Servilius Caepio immediately becomes clear. It was the *lex Mamilia* that stood in the background of his measure. The law of 106 was designed as a safeguard against the excesses of special *quaestiones* like the Mamilian commission. That court drew its jurors, as would any *quaestio extraordinaria,* from the already available *album* of jurors, that is, the *Gracchani iudices.* The vicious and bitter language employed by Crassus must refer to the iniquitous partisanship of the Mamilian tribunal.[13]

The Metellan *factio* had calculated its attack well. The passage of time had allowed the *quaestio* of Mamilius to be seen in its true light. As a response to that kind of institution Caepio's law may be regarded as justifiable. It was not merely an instrument of factional politics, for senators of all groups had been under attack in 109; but the circle of the Metelli would not have shrunk from claiming credit for an enhancing of senatorial dignity.[14] Struggles for power within the aristocracy were soon resumed. In the following two years, rivals of the dominant *factio*

[10] See, e.g., F. W. Robinson, *Marius, Saturninus, und Glaucia* (Jena, 1912), 41-43; Greenidge, *History of Rome,* 477.

[11] Cic. *De Invent.* 1.92: *Caepionis legem iudiciariam;* cf. Tac. *Ann.* 12.60; Cassiodorus, *Chron.* 106; Obseq. 41. See E. Schönbauer, "Die römische Repetundengesetzgebung und das neue Gesetzes-Fragment aus Tarent," *Anz-Wien,* 93 (1956), 37-38; Badian, *Historia,* 11 (1962), 206-209.

[12] The *quaestio de ambitu* is probably implied by the trials of Scaurus and Rutilius in 116 and that of Marius in the same year.

[13] Cic. *De Orat.* 1.225: *Eripite nos ex miseriis, eripite nos ex faucibus eorum, quorum crudelitas nostro sanguine non potest expleri.* That these words belong to the speech on Caepio's law is not stated explicitly, but may be safely inferred from the description *universum Senatum, cuius tum causam agebas.* Cf. Cic. *Pro Cluent.* 140: *suasione legis Serviliae summis ornat senatum laudibus; Brutus,* 164: *illa in legem Caepionis oratio; in qua et auctoritas ornatur senatus.* Even Rutilius Rufus thought Crassus' language was somewhat excessive; Cic. *De Orat.* 1.227.

[14] Cf. Cic. *Brutus,* 164: *auctoritas ornatur senatus.*

desperately sought an opportunity to diminish Metellan prestige. But when it finally came, the consequences proved unfortunate. It brought about inadvertently the reversal of that very law which had promised such benefit to the senate as a whole.

Caepio himself was to give an opening to his enemies for an attack on the Metellan group. The rapidly deteriorating military situation in the north provided the background. Migrations of Germanic tribes, stirring up the Celts and making Rome's allies in Gaul restive, were causing serious disquiet, and the record of Roman arms in the area had done little to inspire confidence at home. Cn. Carbo's ill-starred venture against the Cimbri in 113 had produced defeat in the field and a successful prosecution in the courts. M. Junius Silanus, the consul of 109, suffered a similar calamity at the hands of the Germans and was later to have his day of scrutiny before the bar. Marius' colleague in 107, L. Cassius Longinus, drew Gaul as his sphere of operations, but the results were the same. The string of ignominious Roman defeats lengthened, and an army was compelled to pass under the yoke. Cassius himself was spared the inevitable judicial condemnation by perishing on the battlefield. But his legate C. Popillius had the misfortune of surviving and succumbed to the fury of the *comitia*.[15] The dreary succession of failures created a pall of gloom, deepened by the continuing crisis in Numidia. Q. Caepio brought to his consulship a reputation for military success and was the logical choice for a Gallic command. His domestic victory, the *lex Servilia iudiciaria,* it was hoped, could now be followed by victory abroad; and, in fact, initial efforts were promising. In the latter months of 106 Caepio met with little resistance in Gaul and the city of Tolosa fell into Roman hands once again.[16] The *imperium* of the commander was prorogued for 105. But the rosy picture changed swiftly, for politics in Rome once again began to affect the situation adversely.

P. Rutilius Rufus secured one of the consulships for 105. It had been a long time in coming, but was well deserved. Rutilius' efforts a decade before had been thwarted by M. Scaurus and his career had languished. But he was not blind to the drift of Roman politics. Rutilius was chosen by Metellus Numidicus as a legate for the Jugurthine War in 109 and seems to have been particularly close to his commander.[17] He was a man of many talents. A philosopher of wide learning, steeped in Greek

---

[15] On Carbo's defeat and prosecution, see above, p. 131; on Silanus, see below, p. 174; on Popillius' condemnation, see above, pp. 150-151; on Cassius' failures, see sources in *MRR*, I.550.

[16] *MRR*, I.553.

[17] Cf. Sallust, *Iug.* 86.5; Plut. *Marius,* 10.1.

letters, he had studied under Panaetius and was considered Rome's most nearly perfect Stoic.[18] Military experience had given him further insights. This scholar with a practical bent was able in 105 to apply the techniques of the gladiatorial schools to the training of legions with salutary results.[19] His successful consular candidature, doubtless sponsored by the friends of Numidicus and Caepio, kept the Metellan *factio* in a position of authority. But the success was not complete. Caepio's own brother-in-law, Q. Lutatius Catulus, went down to defeat for the second consecutive time. The latter's intellectual gifts fully matched those of Rutilius but he had no military laurels to appeal to the populace. What Marius was achieving in Africa perhaps another *novus homo* could duplicate in Gaul. Cn. Mallius Maximus was elected as colleague to Rutilius and it was Mallius who drew Gaul as his province. The Metellan group, of course, had hoped for a consulship of Rutilius and Catulus, and Cicero, who had read the memoirs of both men, reflects their opinion of the *novus homo* Mallius: *non solum ignobilem, verum sine virtute, sine ingenio, vita etiam contempta ac sordida.*[20]

Indignation at an electoral defeat is understandable. But the proud aristocratic group allowed its indignation to spill over onto the battle-field with disastrous results. Mallius was able to secure no cooperation from Caepio, who disdainfully refused to effect a coalition of their armies. As a consequence, the Germans routed each in turn at Arausio in October of 105, claiming among their victims the ex-consul Aurelius Scaurus, two sons of the consul Mallius, and 80,000 soldiers, the worst defeat Rome had suffered in more than a century.[21] Reaction at home was bitter. By vote of the people Caepio's *imperium* was abrogated and he returned to Rome a private citizen.[22] The opportunity was at hand for his enemies in the senate to rub salt into the wounds. L. Cassius Longinus, tribune in 104, passed a measure entailing expulsion from the senate of anyone who had been condemned or who had his *imperium* abrogated by the people.[23] It would be wrong to label this simply a *"popularis"* bill.[24] Asconius suggests that Cassius passed the bill out of factional bias against Caepio.[25] The suggestion is consistent with other

[18] Cf. Cic. *Brutus,* 114: *doctus vir et Graecis litteris eruditus, Paenati auditor, prope perfectus in Stoicis.*
[19] Val. Max. 2.3.2; cf. Frontinus, *Strat.* 4.2.2.
[20] Cic. *Pro Planc.* 12.
[21] Sources in *MRR,* I.555, 557.
[22] Asconius, 78, Clark: *populus, quia male adversus Cimbros rem gesserat, imperium abrogavit;* Livy, *Per.* 67.
[23] Asconius, 78, Clark.
[24] As, e.g., Pareti, *Storia di Roma,* III.464.
[25] Asconius, 78, Clark: *propter simultates cum Q. Servilio.*

evidence. The Cassii Longini had long been rivals of the Metellan group and were now making a habit of capitalizing on popular impatience with diplomatic and military failure. A namesake of the tribune of 104 had cooperated with Memmius' assaults on the nobility in 111 and had secured election as a colleague of Marius in 107.[26]

Caepio's troubles were not over. Judicial machinery was once again set in motion. The fall of Tolosa, engineered by Caepio in 106, had resulted in the seizure of staggering sums of gold and silver from the sacred shrines of that city. Those treasures, for some reason, never found their way to Rome. The story soon spread, that the baggage train was ransacked enroute to Massilia and the money stolen by barbarians,[27] was not a tale that everyone would have found convincing. It was apparently in 104 that the people instituted a judicial investigation into the matter, the *quaestio auri Tolosani,* a special court on the model of the Vestals' tribunal of 113 and the Mamilian commission of 109.[28] The evidence on the hearing is unfortunately fragmentary and confusing. That Caepio was held responsible for the disappearance of the treasure and accused of embezzlement is strongly implied, though not explicitly stated.[29] The formal charge was almost certainly *peculatus,* not, as Strabo indicates, *sacrilegium.* Thefts of funds from non-Roman temples would hardly be regarded as sacrilege in Rome.[30] The backers of Caepio and the *factio* of his friends doubtless mobilized their resources to salvage the career of an ex-consul who had performed nobly in their behalf in 106. It is clear that Caepio escaped conviction and exile by this *quaestio,* a strange result on the face of it.[31] His own *lex iudiciaria,* by altering the composition of the *album* of *iudices,* meant that his case may well have been heard by a jury on which senators controlled a majority of the votes. Hence, acquittal cannot be ruled out. The solution, however, may

[26] See above, pp. 141, 155.

[27] Cic. *De Nat. Deor.* 3.74; Orosius, 5.15.25; *Vir. Ill.* 73.5; Dio, 26, fr. 90; see Greenidge and Clay, *Sources,* 80.

[28] These are all allocated to the same category by Cic. *De Nat. Deor.* 3.74.

[29] Orosius, 5.15.25: *Caepio proconsule . . . centum milia pondo auri et argenti . . . sustulit . . . Unde etiam magna quaestio post Romae acta est.* Cf. *Vir. Ill.* 73.5.

[30] Strabo, 4.1.13; see Mommsen, *Strafrecht,* 763; F. Vonder Mühll, *De L. Appuleio Saturnino Tribuno Plebis* (Basel, 1906), 68-70.

[31] All the evidence on Caepio's eventual condemnation and exile points to a conviction for *perduellio* on the grounds of his responsibility for the defeat at Arausio. It is surely no accident that the sources on the *quaestio auri Tolosani* do not mention a condemnation for Caepio. On this see the very sensible arguments of J. Lengle, "Die Verurteilung der römischen Feldherrn von Arausio," *Hermes,* 66 (1931), 302-316.

simply be that the penalty fixed for this offense was not capital, but financial. Other men did suffer conviction at the hands of the *quaestio auri Tolosani*.[32] Caepio, in any event, was still around to face more serious charges later.

There is no reason to believe that Caepio's enemies in the senate desired to go any further than this. Disgrace resulting from revocation of *imperium* and perhaps conviction for *peculatus* would have served the purposes of rival senatorial groups. But the opportunity was too good a one for popular leaders to miss. The striking analogy with the events of 110 must have been obvious to all. Senatorial incompetence in the field had been demonstrated again. Once more ambitious young tribunes could use this fact as a springboard for an expansion of popular influence in government. The years 105-103 present a remarkable series of gains on the popular front. The Gallic peril, more menacing than ever, seemed to demand the talents of the hero of the Jugurthine War. Marius was elected *in absentia* to the consulship of 104, as the populace summarily waived the practice of a ten-year interval between tenures of the chief magistracy.[33] His colleague was another *novus homo,* C. Flavius Fimbria, a man of relatively humble origins but high spirit and intelligence.[34] It was probably in this year that the notorious *popularis* agitator C. Memmius reached the praetorship and the sinister Saturninus first caught the public eye as quaestor.[35] The tribune L. Cassius, whose measure stripped Caepio of senatorial rank, also sponsored *plures leges ad minuendam nobilitatis potentiam*.[36] The year 104 witnessed, in addition, passage of a measure transferring pontifical elections from the priestly colleges to the tribes, and perhaps in the same year came the proposal of a sweeping and radical agrarian bill.[37] Young men, anxious to accelerate a political career, often curried popular favor. These years proved particularly fruitful for such activities. But it is interesting that the authors of the bills mentioned above, L. Cassius Longinus, Cn. Domitius Ahenobarbus, and L. Marcius Philippus, were all of families at odds with the Metellan *factio*. Senatorial rivalries and popular agitation were becoming ever more intertwined. These men were taking full advantage of the disgrace of Caepio and the discomfiture of the Metelli.

[32] Dio, 26, fr. 90. No names or penalties are reported. That Caepio endured a financial loss as a result of this inquiry is indicated by *Vir. Ill.* 73.5.

[33] Plut. *Marius,* 11.1, 12.1.

[34] Cic. *Pro Planc.* 12: *fuit enim et animi satis magni et consilii;* cf. *Verr.* 2.5.181.

[35] On Memmius, see below, p. 175; for Saturninus, see *MRR,* I.560. The date is not secure and one cannot rule out 105 for Saturninus.

[36] Asconius, 78, Clark.

[37] For the sources on popular legislation in 104, see *MRR,* I.558-560.

In 105 and 104 the *inimici* of Caepio had been satisfied with a revocation of his *imperium* and, perhaps, a prosecution for *peculatus* under the *quaestio auri Tolosani*. But in 103, two vigorous and violent tribunes, L. Appuleius Saturninus and C. Norbanus, pressed for far more serious charges to demonstrate the influence of the people in judicial decisions The difference between the events of 104 and those of 103 may be partially explained by the character and background of the individuals involved. Men like Cassius Longinus, Domitius Ahenobarbus, or Marcius Philippus might engage in *popularis* activities in the early stages of their careers; if these also involved successful forays against senatorial rivals like Caepio and Scaurus, so much the better. But the tribunes of 104 were all of distinguished consular families. They could be expected to play the aristocratic game along traditional lines. Some appeals to popular sentiment in a tribunate would increase vote-getting potential, but they would eventually get their consulships, almost as a matter of course, and would take their places as moderate or conservative senior senators.[38] The active tribunes of 103 were a different breed. Saturninus' ancestors had not gone beyond the praetorship. He himself had been quaestor at Ostia in 104 but an unfortunate rise in grain prices led to vituperation against him and the ignominious transfer of his duties to the *princeps senatus* M. Scaurus.[39] Saturninus was incensed and utilized his demagogic talents to secure election to the tribunate for the following year. He was a remarkably successful orator, Cicero noted, not so much because of his voice or intelligence, but through skillful use of gesture, movement, and dress.[40] Norbanus could not claim even praetorian forbears. He was a *novus homo* whose name suggests non-Roman origins in a previous generation. The senatorial tradition stamped him as *seditiosum et inutilem*.[41]

For these men, moderate or temporary display of popular sentiments was insufficient. More dramatic demonstrations were required to assure future success. Q. Caepio provided an inviting target and an obvious opportunity. He was now hauled before the *comitia* on a charge of *perduellio* for his role in the disaster of Arausio. Caepio's friends and *factio* sought to come to his assistance. Two tribunes, both with Metellan

---

[38] The actions of Philippus may be taken as typical. Demagogic tactics in public speeches won popularity; that was what he desired. He was not really concerned to push through his agrarian measure if he could gain credit for the proposal; Cic. *De Off*. 2.73: *cum legem agrariam ferret, quam tamen antiquari facile passus est et in eo vehementer se moderatum praebuit sed . . . in agendo multa populariter*.

[39] Cic. *Har. Resp*. 45; *Pro Sest*. 39; Diod. 36.12.

[40] Cic. *Brutus*, 223.

[41] Cic. *De Off*. 2.49.

connections, L. Aurelius Cotta and T. Didius, endeavored to interpose their veto against the proceedings.[42] Norbanus, however, had aroused the *comitia* with harangues and violence. The interceding tribunes were driven off by force and in the ensuing mêlée M. Scaurus was even struck on the head by a tile.[43] Factional considerations were completely overridden, as in the Mamilian *quaestio,* by a spectacular demonstration of popular sovereignty. Cn. Mallius Maximus, though a *novus homo* and no friend of Caepio, was also prosecuted and by Saturninus himself. The senate knew the meaning of these prosecutions. To the celebrated orator M. Antonius was delegated the task of defending Mallius, but in vain. Mallius went into exile.[44] The *seditiosi* were getting full mileage out of the Arausio débâcle. It was on this count also that Caepio was finally condemned and lived out his years in exile.[45] The depth of popular feeling against Caepio, who was clearly to be made an example in order to demonstrate popular power, is indicated not only by the tumultuous assembly, but by the fact that even execution seems to have been contemplated. Exile was not offered as an alternative, for Caepio was imprisoned, and released only by the intervention of a friendly tribune, L. Reginus. The unhappy Caepio, naturally, fled Italy immediately and went into exile in Smyrna, accompanied by Reginus, for whom the hostile atmosphere in Rome would have been intolerable.[46]

Once again a struggle for power within the senate was escalating into an assault on the prestige of the aristocracy as a whole. And once again judicial process was the intermediary. The effects can be seen in new legislation with regard to the courts. Two major bills secured passage in the last years of the second century, altering significantly both the legal and the political situation, the *lex Servilia Glauciae* and the *lex Appuleia de maiestate*. The discomfiture and ultimate disgrace of Caepio provided

[42] Cic. *De Orat.* 2.197. On Cotta's connections with the Metelli, cf. Münzer, *Röm. Adelsp.,* 245-258; Badian, *Studies,* 36-39. Didius was later to reach the consulship of 98 with Q. Metellus Nepos when both cooperated on a number of measures, including the law against "tacking" unrelated provisions onto a bill; Cic. *De Domo,* 53; *MRR,* II.4.

[43] Cic. *De Orat.* 2.197. Further sources in *MRR,* I.564.

[44] On Saturninus as the prosecutor, see Gran. Licin. 21, B. On Antonius' defense of Mallius, see Cic. *De Orat.* 2.125. Caepio's case, once the tribunician veto had been ignored, may have been regarded as beyond succor.

[45] Lengle, *Unt. Sull. Verf.,* 25-32; *Hermes,* 66 (1931), 302-316. The evidence is clear in Val. Max. 4.7.3: *Caepionem in carcerem coniectum, quod illius culpa exercitus noster . . . deletus.* See also Gran. Licin. 21, B: *Cn. Mallius ob eandem causam quam et Caepio . . . e civitate . . . eiectus.* Cf. *Ad Herenn.* 1.14.24; Cic. *De Orat.* 2.197, 2.199.

[46] Val. Max. 4.7.3; Cic. *Pro Balbo,* 28. The other story in Val. Max. 6.9.13, that Caepio perished in prison, is obviously an error.

a convenient focal point for attack. His judiciary law became a swift casualty of the political wars.[47] Demagogery was a profitable enterprise in these years and Caepio's misfortune attracted another new figure who sought to make a name and accelerate a career. C. Servilius Glaucia had no illustrious forbears in recent generations, nor a character to endear him to Rome's nobility. *Ex summis et fortunae et vitae sordibus* Cicero could say of him.[48] Others went further: Glaucia was the "excrement of the Senate house." [49] But the time was ripe for such men; if the hostility of the populace could be aroused, so could the resentment of the *equites*. The latter knew Caepio primarily as the author of a bill that had challenged their integrity and removed their control of the judiciary. Glaucia earned their affection and gratitude by a new *lex repetundarum* that restored equestrian monopoly of the jury panels on extortion cases.[50] Caution forbids a reference to this as a "repeal" of Caepio's measure. The earlier bill was a *lex iudiciaria,* Glaucia's simply *a lex repetundarum.*[51] Nevertheless, the change was crucial. To alter the composition of the *quaestio de repetundis* would almost certainly entail that future special *quaestiones* and future standing courts would be recruited from the available panel of equestrian jurors. Caepio's law was now a dead letter and Glaucia had made his political fortune: *plebem tenebat et equestrem ordinem beneficio legis devinxerat.*[52]

The precise date of the *lex Servilia Glauciae* eludes inquiry, though it has provoked countless conjectures.[53] No ancient source dates the law

[47] That its existence was short-lived is suggested by the fact that Cicero could ignore it entirely when it suited his purpose in speaking of equestrian control of the courts; *Verr.* 1.38; Asconius, 79, Clark.

[48] Cic. *Brutus,* 224. But in the same place Cicero also acknowledged his shrewdness and wit: *peracutus et callidus cum primisque ridiculus;* Cf. *Pro Rab. Post.* 14: *homo impurus, sed tamen acutus.*

[49] *Stercus curiae;* Cic. *De Orat.* 3.164.

[50] Cic. *Pro Scauro,* in Asconius, 21, Clark; *Brutus,* 224; cf. *Pro Rab. Perd.* 20; Asconius, 79, Clark.

[51] On Caepio's law, see Cic. *De Invent.* 1.92: *Caepionis legem iudiciariam;* on Glaucia's law, see Asconius, 21, Clark: *repetundarum lege quam tulit Servilius Glaucia.*

[52] Cic. *Brutus,* 224. For the content of Glaucia's law, beyond the jury change, see Cic. *Pro Rab. Post.* 9; *Verr.* 2.1.26; Ps-Asconius, 230, Stangl; *Ad Herenn.* 1.20; a brief capitulation is given in *MRR,* I.571-572. The clause that restricted alien prosecutors by limiting rewards to Latins was probably originally in Caepio's law; Cic. *Pro Balbo,* 54; see G. I. Luzzatto, "Sul nuovo frammento di legge romana rinvenuto a Taranto," *Arch. Stor. Pugliese,* 4 (1951), 35-38; Badian, "*Lex Servilia,*" *CR,* 4 (1954), 101-102; contra: B. M. Levick, "*Acerbissima Lex Servilia,*" *CR,* 17 (1967), 256-258.

[53] It would be tedious and unprofitable to repeat the lengthy scholarly controversy on this question. Theories that make Glaucia's law pre-date that of Caepio violate both the evidence and logic. They have been effectively

and the problem is made more difficult by the obscure chronology of Glaucia's own career. Only his praetorship in 100, the year in which he illegally presented himself for the consulship, is clearly established. Appian, though in a muddled fashion, apparently reveals a tribunate in 101.[54] It does not follow that the *repetundae* law fell in either of those years. Glaucia may have been in a position to pass legislation earlier as well, perhaps as a tribune. C. Gracchus had held the tribunate twice; Glaucia's own fellow-agitator Saturninus was tribune in 103 and again in 100. The man who sought to hold tribunate, praetorship, and consulship in successive years would hardly have worried about constitutional traditions. It was wise to strike while the iron was hot, and the demise of Caepio would make 104 or 103 more fitting years. Whatever the date of the *lex,* however, it is a clear example again of demagogic pressure seizing on the unfortunate failures of senatorial leaders and mobilizing the temporary discontents of extra-senatorial elements.

Another judicial measure can be seen as the direct outcome of the political events of 104 and 103. The prosecution of Caepio and Mallius before the people had resulted in conviction. But it had not been an easy matter. The convictions were secured only through *seditio,* a display of violence and illegal neglect of tribunician *intercessio.* Comitial trials were still a somewhat risky and troublesome business. It would be practical and efficient to set up more permanent machinery dealing with acts that diminished Rome's dignity and increased her peril. Hence came the *lex Appuleia de maiestate,* a measure sponsored by Saturninus in one of his two tribunates, probably in 103.[55] The bill set up a *quaestio perpetua* to

---

put out of court by Balsdon's excellent article, *PBSR,* 14 (1938), 106-108. Balsdon leans toward 104 for Glaucia's bill; so also Robinson, *Mar. Sat. Glauc.,* 43-47; Last, *CAH,* IX.162-163; Scullard, *From Gracchi to Nero,* 55. Others opt for 101 or 100; Passerini, *Athenaeum,* 12 (1934), 130-134; A. Piganiol, "Sur la nouvelle table de bronze de Tarente," *CRAI* (1951), 62; Tibiletti, *Athenaeum,* 31 (1953), 80-86; Badian, *Historia,* 11 (1962), 205.

[54] Appian, *BC,* 1.28. Glaucia presided over the tribunician elections in that year, as praetor, says Appian: στρατηγοῦντα. That is probably an error for *praetor designatus;* Niccolini, *Fast. Trib. Pleb.,* 195; Gabba, "Note Appianee," *Athenaeum,* 33 (1955), 218-225. For sources on the praetorship, see *MRR,* I.575.

[55] Sources in *MRR,* I.563. For the date, see Lengle, *Hermes,* 66 (1931), 303-305, and Passerini, *Athenaeum,* 12 (1934), 110-113. This is not the place to engage in polemical and inconclusive debate on the identification of the fragmentary epigraphical laws with the various bills of the late second century described by the literary evidence. For the more recent literature, inspired anew by the discovery of a fragmentary law from Tarentum, see esp. Tibiletti, *Athenaeum,* 31 (1953), 5-100; Serrao, *Studi De Francisci,* 2 (1956), 473-511; Schönbauer, "Das Gesetzes-Fragment aus Tarent in neuer Schau," *Jura,* 7 (1956), 92-117; *AnzWien,* 93 (1956), 13-40; Yarnold, *AJP,* 78 (1957), 163-172; Nicolet, *L'Ordre Equestre,* 555-558.

hear cases of *maiestas,* that vague and politically useful concept denoting damage to the prestige of the state. A case tried under this *lex* in the 90's reveals that the jurors were drawn from the *equester ordo.*[56] If this, as seems likely, was true from the beginning, it brings the actions of Saturninus and Glaucia into close conjunction. Popular legislators saw profit in combining the grievances of the people with the aspirations of the *equites.* Once more the pattern of 111-109 was repeated. Just as Memmius' unsuccessful tribunician prosecution had led to the organization of the Mamilian tribunal to hear cases of crime against the state, so now the tribunician prosecution of Caepio, which, though successful, was gained at the cost of great disruption, was followed by the institution of a new court manned by *equites.* By making it a standing court, Saturninus could expect to entrench the popular control of judicial processes that had been only briefly secured by the Mamilian *quaestio.* In a word, the *lex Appuleia* made permanent the temporary court of the *lex Mamilia.*

Senatorial efforts to stem the popular tide were still-born. Tribunician veto against one of Saturninus' measures proved ineffectual. So also did violence against another of his bills.[57] Metellus Numidicus, as censor in 102, sought to remove Saturninus and Glaucia from the senate, but was dissuaded by his own colleague and cousin C. Metellus Caprarius out of fear of violence.[58] The analogy with the Jugurthine War can be pressed further. Another foreign monarch was now soliciting the support of Rome for imperialist ambitions. The envoys of Mithridates of Pontus were in Rome in 102 or 101 and Saturninus did not neglect the opportunity to make history repeat itself. The popular leader leaped into the fray, insulted the diplomatic messengers, and alleged that they had come to Rome for the purpose of bribing the senate. Aristocratic supervision of foreign policy was once more under attack, and the enemies of Saturninus arraigned him before the senate for his ὕβρις. It was no

[56] Cic. *De Orat.* 2.199: *equitum Romanorum, apud quos tum iudices causa* [of Norbanus] *agebatur.* Nicolet, *L'Ordre Equestre,* 535, puts the *maiestas* law before the trial of Caepio and argues that its juries were drawn from senators, thus claiming to explain why Caepio was tried by the people and not under the new law. That is surely a peculiar and paradoxical argument. With Caepio's fate under discussion it would be strange in the extreme if his enemy should create a new criminal procedure that was obviously ineffective and had to be bypassed immediately.

[57] *Ad Herenn.* 1.21; *Vir. Ill.* 73.1.

[58] Cic. *Pro Sest.* 101; Appian, *BC,* 1.28. Violence was not avoided, however. It was precipitated, it seems, by Metellus' refusal to enroll the "false Gracchus," L. Equitius, in the *equester ordo.* Sources in Greenidge and Clay, *Sources,* 96-97; *MRR,* I.567.

doubt precisely the platform which that shrewd demagogue desired in order to dramatize oligarchic suppression of a guiltless champion of the *plebs*. Saturninus was triumphantly released when the mob to which he had addressed pitiful appeals stormed the proceedings.[59] He can only have gained in stature by this affair. Men like Saturninus, Glaucia, and Norbanus were welding anew that powerful coalition of *plebs* and *equites,* which could short-circuit the traditional processes of aristocratic government.

It was not lost on these men that the coalition could be made even more powerful by a link with another man who had also successfully challenged the establishment and who was now triumphantly defending Rome's honor abroad. Marius shattered all Roman precedent. A second consulship, awarded *in absentia* for 104, was only the beginning; five successive years, from 104 to 100, saw him as duly elected head of state, and not in the teeth of oligarchic opposition. The military peril in the north was acute and recognized as such by aristocrat and common man alike. Moreover, the disastrous quarrel between Caepio and Mallius in 105 had demonstrated that supreme command on the battlefield must be unambiguous. Marius was not to have any embarrassing consuls to challenge his proconsular authority; he would be consul himself as long as the military situation required it.[60] The aristocracy engaged in no pointless attempts to disrupt the war effort. But Marius' commands also had their effects on the domestic political situation. The general's popularity and following spread rapidly in Rome. And the *capite censi,* the masses of new soldiers he had enrolled for the Jugurthine War, would have been looking for new employment or for rewards after the termination of that conflict. The demagogues recognized the benefit of enlisting the prestige of Marius and the support of his veterans. Saturninus provided legislation in 103 that granted to the discharged soldiers viritane allotments in Africa amounting to 100 *iugera* of land per man. It was an overt and obvious play to win the affection of the *Mariani.*[61] It was also an event of momentous import for the future, however little that

[59] The story is told by Diodorus, 36.15, who apparently puts the affair shortly before Saturninus' election to a second tribunate. The senate could not, of course, sit as a court of law as Diodorus implies. Possibly an attempt was made to set up a *quaestio extraordinaria* staffed by senators in order to avoid certain acquittal by equestrian jurors.

[60] Cf. Sherwin-White, *JRS,* 46 (1956), 4.

[61] *Vir. Ill.* 73.1: *Saturninus, tribunus plebis seditiosus, ut gratiam Marianorum militum pararet, legem tulit, ut veteranis centena agri iugera in Africa dividerentur.* Cf. P. Quoniam, "A propos d'une inscription de Thiburnica, Marius et la romanisation de l'Afrique," *CRAI* (1950), 332-336; Gabba, "Ricerche su alcuni punti di storia Mariana," *Athenaeum,* 29 (1951), 13-18.

may have been foreseen at the time. Subsequent armies, at the conclusion of their service, could cite it as a precedent to argue state responsibility for veterans' benefits. In 103 Saturninus was concerned for immediate gains, the adhesion of men loyal to Marius and the gratitude of their commander. Marius could also find the demagogues useful. In 103 the death of Marius' consular colleague meant that the general himself would have to come to Rome to preside over his own reelection, an awkward and uncomfortable role. Saturninus cooperated nicely, playing out a staged comedy with Marius that culminated in a popular clamor for Marius' third successive consulship.[62]

The coalition was formidable and growing. In 102 and 101 Marius won his great victories over the Cimbri and Teutones, allowing a terrified populace to breathe again at last, and earning for himself unprecedented honors and admiration bordering on worship.[63] *Novi homines* and popular agitators were not the only men to reap the advantages of these turbulent years. Members of old patrician houses, whose families had suffered obscurity in recent generations, saw a better opportunity to revive past glories in the embrace of rising political figures than with the entrenched plebeian aristocracy. The Julii Caesares had linked themselves to Marius in marriage and the Dolabellae, or a branch of them, to Saturninus.[64] One ought not to forget also that the young patrician Sulla first caught the public eye as quaestor to Marius in the Jugurthine War.[65] Even patricians of more prominent families sought to move with the rising tide. The Aemilii Lepidi show a marriage tie with Saturninus, and L. Valerius Flaccus was Marius' colleague and consistent supporter in 100.[66] The net could be cast wider. Italians, as well as Romans, served in Marius' campaigns and many of them returned as new Roman citizens, thanks to the generosity of their general.[67] These men would add potential voting strength in the assemblies and swell the *clientela* of the popular leaders. Constitutional traditions inspired little awe in the members of

[62] Plut. *Marius*, 14.7-8.

[63] Val. Max. 8.15.7: *nemo fuit, qui non illi tanquam diis immortalibus apud sacra mensae suae liberavit;* cf. Plut. *Marius*, 27.5. On the German wars, see Carney, *A Biog. of Marius*, 36-39; Van Ooteghem, *Marius*, 176-231.

[64] For Marius' marriage to Julia, see Plut. *Marius*, 6.2. The Caesares also helped to carry out the colonial and agrarian laws of Saturninus; *MRR*, I.577. A Dolabella was *frater* of Saturninus; Orosius, 5.17.

[65] *MRR*, I.551.

[66] M. Lepidus, future consul of 78, was married to an Appuleia; Pliny, *NH*, 7.122. For Flaccus, see Plut. *Marius*, 28.5. On the composition of the group that supported Marius, see further Badian, *For. Client.*, 200-203.

[67] Cic. *Pro Balbo*, 47-48; Val. Max. 5.2.8; Plut. *Marius*, 28.2.

this coalition. Marius' battlefield enfranchisements were at best extra-legal. His string of consulships was perhaps justifiable in view of the military crises; but it would not promote respect for constitutional precedent. Saturninus held two tribunates, and Glaucia saw no barrier to a tribunate, praetorship, and consulship in successive years. The passage of legislation and the conduct of criminal trials were accompanied by pandering demagogery and overt violence. All this, combined with a revived militancy on the part of the *equites,* who were now in control of the judiciary again, could spell the end of the old order.

Yet, as so often, the picture is more complex than it appears on the surface. The literature, ancient and modern, concentrates its attention for these years on foreign affairs, the Jugurthine and Cimbric Wars, and the rise of Marius, Saturninus, and Glaucia, the popular attack on the establishment. But there is another dimension. Struggles for power within the ranks of the traditional governing class did not cease in the last decade of the second century, nor did family feuds and personal *inimicitiae.* These conflicts, often obscured to our eyes because of paucity of evidence, continued as a kind of counterpoint to the more spectacular and more fully reported events of the period. Indeed, perhaps the most striking, though sadly neglected, aspect of the years 104-100 was the senatorial infighting, simultaneous with and despite the fundamental attacks on the aristocracy as a whole. The Metellan *factio* might have claimed an almost monolithic ascendancy in 111. But the embarrassment of some of its leaders in the course of the Jugurthine and German crises began to alter the picture. Aristocratic enemies found it more tempting to take advantage of Metellan embarrassment than to close senatorial ranks against popular dissension. Once again, an investigation of criminal trials discloses the dim outlines of these contests.

A large number of prosecutions occurred in this brief period, parallel to but unconnected with the great political trials of Caepio and Mallius. Four of them at least fell in or around the year 104.[68] They all seem to have involved senatorial enemies of the Metellan faction. T. Albucius, that Hellenic dandy who had once unsuccessfully prosecuted Q. Scaevola in 119, had suffered for his miscalculation in the interim. While the Metelli and their friends virtually monopolized the curule offices in the succeeding decade, Albucius was left out in the cold. It was not until long after his abortive forensic effort that he got as far as the praetorship. The date is unrecorded but 107 is approximate and would be appropriate. That year witnessed the first consulship of C. Marius, over the

---

[68] For more detailed discussion of these cases, see Gruen, "Politics and the Courts in 104 B.C.," *TAPA,* 95 (1964), 99-110.

objections and to the detriment of Metellus Numidicus, and also the consulship of L. Cassius Longinus, whose family had caused the Metellan group much grief in the previous generation and whose cousin initiated the attack on Q. Caepio in 104.[69] Albucius profited from the anti-Metellan sentiment, but his political sagacity had matured very little in the past decade and a half. His ineffectual propraetorship in Sardinia was punctuated by an undeserved triumph, sponsored by himself since Roman authorities would not hear of it.[70] Even his own subordinates found that to be more than they could stomach. Albucius' quaestor, Cn. Pompeius Strabo, applied for the right to prosecute him, but that privilege was awarded to another young man anxious to place his credentials before the public, C. Julius Caesar Strabo.[71] Caesar Strabo was an orator of unsurpassed wit, later acknowledged as an expert in the use of humor in public oratory.[72] One can imagine what a field day he must have had with Albucius. But he may have been chosen as much for his political connections as for his oratorical skill. Caesar Strabo's step-brother was Q. Lutatius Catulus, the prominent littérateur and scholarly patron of the arts, whose marriage into the Servilii Caepiones and *amicitia* with the Aurelii Cottae demonstrate his association with the Metellan group.[73] Albucius was duly condemned in 105 or 104 for *repetundae* and, as might be expected of that Epicurean, lived out the remainder of his life in Athens.[74] The old political enmities he had aroused had finally served to remove him.

A not dissimilar pattern can be discerned in another case at about this same time. Q. Fabius Maximus Eburnus, the consul of 116, was a strict moralist of the old school. When his son's alleged unchastity was reported to him, Eburnus promptly exercised his *patria potestas* and had the boy executed. Perhaps such behavior seemed outmoded to a modern age. At any rate, Eburnus was to suffer for his act. Pompeius Strabo, thwarted in his effort to prosecute Albucius, was swift to seize this fresh opportunity. The ambitious *novus homo,* father of Pompey the Great,

[69] For L. Cassius Ravilla, the consul of 127, see above, pp. 128-129; on L. Cassius Longinus, the tribune of 104, see above, p. 161; on Albucius' prosecution in 119, see above, pp. 112-116.

[70] Cic. *De Prov. Cons.* 15.

[71] Cic. *Div. in Caec.* 63; *De Off.* 2.50; Suet. *Iul.* 55.2; Apuleius, *Apol.* 66.4; Ps-Asconius, 203, Stangl.

[72] Cic. *Brutus,* 177; *De Orat.* 2.234-289.

[73] For the relationship of Catulus and Caesar Strabo, see Cic. *De Orat.* 2.12; for Catulus' connections with the Metelli, see above, pp. 116-117.

[74] On the conviction, see Cic. *Pro Scauro,* 40; *In Pis.* 92; the exile, *Tusc. Disp.* 5.108. That the charge was *repetundae* is clear from Cic., *Div. in Caec.* 63, and *De Off.* 2.50.

172

brought Eburnus to trial before the people, probably in 104, and secured conviction, thus successfully promoting a political career that grew progressively more ruthless in succeeding years. Eburnus closed out his life in exile at Nuceria.[75] His demise meant the elimination of another man whose family evinced political enmity toward the Metellan *factio*. The Fabii Maximi had been close allies of the Scipiones in the previous generation and Eburnus himself showed no signs of transferring allegiance. He was the nephew of Scipio Aemilianus. Like others who had had Scipionic connections, his career languished in the 120's but he eventually reached the consulship in 116, defeating the protégé of the Metelli, M. Aemilius Scaurus.[76] No proof can be adduced to demonstrate that the Metellan *factio* engineered the convictions of Albucius and Fabius Maximus, but opportunities to redress old grievances would not have been overlooked.

The enemies of that *factio* were not idle. The dissolution of the old Scipionic group, as we have seen, did not leave the Metelli without rivals in the aristocracy. In addition to the Fabii Maximi and the Cassii Longini, one may discern the Domitii Ahenobarbi. They show no links to the Metellan group and an earlier generation had seen cooperation with the Scipios.[77] In the late 120's Roman expansion into Gaul had enlisted the close collaboration of a Domitius Ahenobarbus and a Fabius Maximus.[78] The year 104 saw that family represented in magisterial office by the volatile tribune Cn. Domitius Ahenobarbus, later consul in 96 with, it might be noted, another Cassius Longinus. As tribune, Domitius utilized the judicial process to initiate two criminal trials, against Aemilius Scaurus and M. Junius Silanus. The attack on Scaurus grew out of a personal grievance. Scaurus had refused to coopt young Domitius into the priestly ranks to fill a vacancy left by the death of his father. Domitius retaliated by bringing a charge before the people involving some religious misdemeanors.[79] He further took advantage of

---

[75] Orosius, 5.16.8; Val. Max. 6.1.5; Ps-Quintilian, *Declam. Maiores,* 3.17. For the date, see Orosius, 5.16.8, and further on the trial, Gruen, *TAPA, 95* (1964), 102-106. The arguments of Rowland, "The Date of Pompeius Strabo's Quaestorship," *CP,* 63 (1968), 213-214, reversing the trials of Eburnus and Albucius, are weak and inconclusive. For the exile of Eburnus, see Cic. *Pro Balbo,* 28.

[76] Cic. *Pro Mur.* 36; see Gruen, *TAPA, 95* (1964), 105-106.

[77] Scullard, *Roman Politics,* 116, 123, 208, 212, 227.

[78] *MRR,* I.516, 520, 522; C. H. Benedict, "The Romans in Southern Gaul," *AJP,* 63 (1942), 44-49.

[79] Asconius, 21, Clark; Suet. *Nero,* 2.1; Cic. *Pro Deiot.* 31; Val. Max. 6.5.5; Dio, 27, fr. 92; Plut. *Ex Inim. Util.* 9. For the date, see Niccolini, *Fast. Trib. Pleb.,* 191.

the popular tide in that year to pass a bill allowing *pontifices* to be elected by the tribes, securing his own election in the process.[80] Personal vendetta and popular enthusiasm, however, need not be the only elements involved in this affair. It was not irrelevant that Scaurus, the *princeps senatus,* was perhaps the most prominent leader of the Metellan faction. Factional considerations are certainly implicit in the trial of Silanus. Attaining the consulship in 109, the year of the censorships of Scaurus and M. Livius Drusus, he was a colleague of Metellus Numidicus, with whom he cooperated. It would not be rash to suggest that he benefited from the Metellan successes in those elections.[81] As consul and proconsul Silanus' military activities in Gaul had led to disastrous losses at the hands of the Cimbri and had helped considerably to precipitate the crisis in the north.[82] Others had suffered swiftly for similar misdeeds. Yet Silanus, protected by powerful associates, escaped indictment for four years. In 104, however, in the wake of Caepio's debacle, he was at last called to account. The Metellan group was more vulnerable now. Domitius saw that the moment was ripe to rake up the old charges against Silanus,[83] but he could not make them stick. Both Silanus and Scaurus secured acquittal; the clients of the Metellan *factio* were discreetly dispersed among the thirty-five tribes of the assembly where both cases were heard. But the results were close. Scaurus, we are told, escaped by only a narrow margin.[84] Silanus, with less influence and a more serious offense, would not have won a much handier victory. It would be myopic to ascribe these four trials exclusively to factional politics, involving, as they did, also personal *inimicitiae* and the ambitions of young quaestorians to display their wares before the public. But they reveal that old rivalries within the senate were not engulfed by the rise of the so-called *"populares,"* and that traditional political contests, played out in the courts, continued to be a fact of Roman public life.

Hints survive in the sources of other cases engaging the *princeps senatus* Scaurus that seem to involve a similar combination of personal and political conflicts. Dates are unspecified but Scaurus testified against two men for extortion, C. Memmius, the tribune of 111, and C. Flavius Fimbria, the consul of 104. It was testimony to which upright jurors

[80] *MRR,* I.545.

[81] Cf. esp. Cic. *Brutus,* 135: *Q. Metellus Numidicus et eius collega M. Silanus dicebant de re publica quod esset illis viris et consulari dignitati satis.*

[82] *MRR,* I.545.

[83] Asconius, 80, Clark: *adversus Cimbros rem male gesserat; quam ob causam Domitius eum apud populum accusavit;* Cic. *Div. in Caec.* 67; *Verr.* 2.2.118.

[84] Asconius, 21, 80, Clark. Scaurus' influence among rural voters doubtless proved itself useful here, as so often; Cic. *Ad Att.* 4.16.6.

turned a deaf ear and rendered verdicts of acquittal.[85] It is possible to surmise that both cases fell in this period. Since the trials were for *repetundae,* they would have followed the exercise of either praetorship or consulship. Fimbria's consulship is dated securely to 104, but his praetorship, though it cannot have been later than 107, escapes record. Memmius never reached the consulship, but since he stood for that office in 100 for 99, his praetorship can have been no later than 102.[86] This scanty evidence leaves any number of possibilities open.[87] But since the sources place these two trials in close conjunction, one ought to presume approximate simultaneity. The year 104 witnessed a number of *popularis* types in public office. It was the year of Fimbria's consulship and a perfectly plausible date for the praetorship of C. Memmius, whose popular harangues of 111 would have been remembered. The trials may, therefore, have fallen in 103 or early 102.[88]

Scaurus and Memmius had crossed swords before. At the height of the Jugurthine agitation Memmius had hinted at a prosecution of the *princeps senatus,* and at the trial of Bestia under the Mamilian commission Memmius and Scaurus had clashed overtly.[89] Scaurus was not one to forget aspersions on his integrity and now became a hostile witness in Memmius' trial. Motives here were perhaps largely personal and particular. But it is well to remember that Memmius had opposed the Metellan *factio* in the debate on Caepio's *lex iudiciaria* of 106. The trial of Fimbria may also have possessed political flavor. That *novus homo* had secured his election by defeating Q. Catulus, brother-in-law of

[85] Cic. *Pro Font.* 24: *testimonio neque in C. Fimbriam neque in C. Memmium creditum est; Pro Font.* 26: *equites Romani . . . habuerunt tantum animi, tantum roboris ut L. Crasso, M. Scauro testi non crederent . . . Si inimico testi credi non oportuit inimicior Marcello Crassus aut Fimbriae Scaurus . . . quam huic Galli?* Also Val. Max. 8.5.2: *Scaurus . . . C. Memmium repetundarum reum destricto testimonio insecutus est, item C. Flavium eadem lege accusatum testis proscidit.* These two sources provide our only evidence for the trials, apart from Cicero's added detail that M. Gratidius brought the formal charge against Fimbria; *Brutus,* 168.

[86] For Fimbria's consulship, sources in *MRR,* I.558. On Memmius, *MRR,* I.570, n. 4. The prosecutor of Fimbria, M. Gratidius, served in Cilicia under M. Antonius in 102 and was killed there, thus providing a *terminus ante quem* for that trial; Cic. *Brutus,* 168; *De Leg.* 3.36; *De Orat.* 2.2.

[87] Cf. Niccolini, *Fast. Trib. Pleb.,* 197-198; Gabba. *Athenaeum,* 32 (1954), 72-74.

[88] Jurors who sat on the case of Fimbria are expressly identified as *equites;* Cic. *Pro Font.* 26. If the dating set up in the text (admittedly conjectural) is correct, it lends further support to the theory that Glaucia's *lex repetundarum* had been passed by that time. Cf. Nicolet, *L'Ordre Equestre,* 541, contradicting what he says elsewhere, 533-534.

[89] See above, pp. 140-141, 147-149.

Caepio, and candidate of the Metellan group.[90] The cases fit into the context of internal jockeying for supremacy within the aristocracy. After the disgrace of Caepio the *factio* of Scaurus and Numidicus had much to answer for, and the machinations at the bar suggest the struggle for their political life.

That personal rivalries and family feuds continued to be played out in the courts in this period can be further illustrated. Diodorus relates that L. Licinius Lucullus was sent, probably as pro-praetor in 103, to quell slaves who had revolted in Sicily. Military victory was culminated by ruthless slaughter of the vanquished, to the number of 8,000. Lucullus had inherited the character of his father, the consul of 151, who had shown no respect for treaty or human life in the Spanish wars of that era. But Lucullus did not follow up his victory. Whether out of negligence or corruption he allowed the fugitives to regroup their forces. The senate swiftly sent a successor, the praetor C. Servilius, apparently in 102, to relieve him of his duties. Lucullus did not accept the slight with good grace. He dismissed his troops from service, compounding difficulties for Servilius. As a consequence he was prosecuted upon his return for prolonging the war unnecessarily. Servilius, like Lucullus, proved ineffective, and he too was later charged, convicted, and exiled.[91] More information comes from Plutarch. The biographer, at the opening of his *Life* of the Ciceronian Lucullus, states that his father was convicted of κλοπή, an accusation brought by a certain Servilius the augur, who was himself later prosecuted by the younger Luculli.[92] It is a natural inference to combine this testimony, to identify the two Servilii, and to assume that Servilius returned in 101, convicted Lucullus, and was then prosecuted in turn by his sons.[93] But that is too tidy; careful investigation disen-

[90] Cic. *Pro Planc.* 12. It will not do to adduce the influence of Marius as does Carney, *RhM,* 105 (1962), 314. Fimbria's prosecutor was M. Gratidius, Marius' brother-in-law.

[91] For the despatching of Lucullus to Sicily, see Diod. 36.8.1. For the actions of Lucullus and his prosecution, see Diod. 36.8.5, 36.9.2. For the conviction of Servilius, see Diod. 36.9.1: Γάιος δὲ Σερούιλιος καταπεμφθεὶς στρατηγὸς διάδοχος Λουκούλλου, οὐδ' αὐτός τι ἄξιον μνήμης ἔπραξε. διὸ καὶ ὁμοίως Λουκούλλῳ ὕστερον φυγῇ κατεδικάσθη. This seems to imply that Lucullus also was exiled. The dates have been worked out from the succession of governors of Sicily compiled by J. Klein, *Die Verwaltungsbeamten von Sicilien und Sardinien* (Bonn, 1878), 55-56, and followed by Broughton, *MRR,* I.559, 564, 568. On the consul of 151, see Appian, *Iber.* 51-55.

[92] Plut. *Luc.* 1.1: ὁ μὲν πατήρ, ἑάλω κλοπῆς ... πρῶτον ἔργον ἐποιήσατο τὸν τοῦ πατρὸς κατήγοραν κρῖναι Σερούιλιον αὔγουρα, λαβὼν ἀδικοῦντα δημοσίᾳ ... ἀπέφυγεν ὁ Σερούιλιος. See also Cic. *Verr.* 2.4.147; *Acad. Quaest.* 2.1; *De Off.* 2.50; Quintilian, 12.7.4.

[93] So Münzer, *RE,* 4(2).1762-1763, "Servilius," n. 12; *MRR,* I.568; *ORF,* 308, n. 1.

tangles more than one thread. Whereas the C. Servilius who succeeded Lucullus in Sicily in 102 was himself convicted later, the Servilius who accused Lucullus was acquitted when prosecuted by Lucullus' sons.[94] Amalgamation will not do; at least three trials are suggested by this evidence.

Lucullus was convicted on charges brought by a Servilius called by Plutarch "the augur," presumably in 102. The biographer's κλοπή may be a reference to a charge of *peculatus*. If so, it is important, for it indicates that a standing court on peculation had recently been set up. That there was no such court in 104 is clear from the need to organize a special *quaestio* for the prosecution of Caepio in the affair of the Tolosan gold. It is possible therefore that the popular leaders had established a *peculatus* court in addition to the *quaestio de maiestate*.[95] A stranglehold on the judicial process was clearly a prominent aspect of their program. The quarrel of Lucullus and Servilius, however, was a personal one, and Lucullus' sons felt honor-bound to carry on the feud. The trial of Servilius the augur doubtless fell sometime in the early 90's when the young Luculli came of age.[96] The trial of C. Servilius, the praetor and governor of Sicily in 102, on the other hand, probably followed his return to Rome in 101. The charge here was apparently *repetundae*.[97] Failure to carry out military commands effectively allowed the courts to claim another victim.

It is unfortunate that the *cognomina* of these Servilii have dropped out of the tradition. They may not, however, be beyond recovery. We are told that the feud between the Luculli and the Servilii endured for some time before reconciliation finally came.[98] It is natural, therefore,

[94] Plut. *Luc.* 1.2: οὐ μὴν ἀλλὰ μεγάλης περὶ τὴν ἐκείνην φιλονεικίας γενομένης, ὥστε καὶ τρωθῆναί τινος καὶ πεσεῖν, ἀπέφυγεν ὁ Σερούιλιος. Neither Diodorus nor Plutarch identifies the prosecutor with the governor of Sicily, although it would have been natural for them to do so. They are rightly distinguished by Klein, *Verwaltungsbeamten,* 56. See the sound arguments of Van Ooteghem, *L. Licinius Lucullus* (Brussels, 1959), 14-15.

[95] It may be, of course, that Plutarch is employing loose language. It would not be his first offense of that sort. κλοπῆς may simply be an error for *repetundae.* However, a standing court for *peculatus* almost certainly existed in 86; Plut. *Pomp.* 4; Cic. *Brutus,* 230. And there is no more apt time for its establishment than in the wake of the *lex Appuleia de maiestate.*

[96] Since L. Lucullus the younger became consul in 74, he must have been born ca. 117. Plutarch's ἀδικοῦντα δημοσίᾳ may suggest that the charge was *maiestas,* though further details and context are lacking.

[97] Cicero affirms that Servilius' quaestor, an L. Philo, was rejected as prosecutor in the *divinatio,* in a context that clearly suggests *repetundae; Div. in Caec.* 63.

[98] Cic. *De Prov. Cons.* 22: *Quae fuerunt inimicitiae in civitate graviores quam Lucullorum atque Servilii?*

[99] Sources in *MRR,* II.101.

to think of P. Servilius Vatia, the consul of 79, whose armies in Cilicia eventually, through intrigue and politics, came under the command of L. Lucullus, the consul of 74.[99] Vatia's father was probably the C. Servilius Vatia who was honored in an inscription from Greece and may have held a provincial command there sometime before 100. If so, he can plausibly be identified with the augur Servilius who prosecuted Lucullus in 102.[100] Tenure of an augurate implies a person of prestige and seniority and Vatia would fit that description. The conjecture receives confirmation from an interesting story. Metellus Numidicus, Lucullus' brother-in-law, declined to appear in his defense.[101] Can one say that it was because Lucullus' guilt was obvious? That consideration would hardly have deterred a supporter when a political prosecution was at stake. Numidicus' refusal opened no breach with the Luculli; after Numidicus' exile in 100, the two brothers L. and M. Lucullus were in the forefront of activity for his recall.[102] The puzzle becomes at once clear when it is recalled that C. Servilius Vatia, father of the consul of 79, was also married to a Metella.[103] Numidicus had good reason to decline a defense of Lucullus. He could plead justifiably that he was related to both parties in the prosecution and had no wish to interfere in a purely personal quarrel. That the C. Servilius who succeeded Lucullus in 102 was also of the same family as the augur and was prosecuted in retaliation by friends of the Luculli is an inevitable conjecture. Senatorial *inimicitiae* continued to run their course in the last years of the second century.

We may add still one more case to this complex welter of events. Cicero reports that M. Aurelius Scaurus, quaestor to L. Valerius Flaccus, was denied the right to prosecute him, presumably on an extortion charge. Dating and identification of the personalities has provoked unwarranted conjectures. Cicero clearly associates the trial of Flaccus with two other cases of this period, the trials of T. Albucius and C. Servilius.[104] Flaccus would then be the consul of 100, and the trial

---

[100] *MRR*, II.465. The identification was suggested long ago by Mommsen, *Geschichte des römischen Münzwesens* (Berlin, 1860), 535-536. C. Servilius Vatia cannot be Lucullus' successor in Sicily, since his own province, apparently, was Macedon.

[101] Cic. *Verr.* 2.4.147: *Numidicum . . . illum noluisse sua laudatione iuvare L. Lucullum, sororis virum, quicum optime convenisset.* Similarly, *Vir. Ill.* 62.4; cf. Ps-Asconius, 203, Stangl.

[102] Cic. *Post Red. in Sen.* 37; *Post Red. ad Quir.* 7.

[103] Cic. *Verr.* 2.3.211. He got a better bargain than Lucullus. The latter's wife carried a reputation for loose morals; Plut. *Luc.* 1.1.

[104] Cic. *Div. in Caec.* 63. Ps-Asconius, 203, Stangl, is wrong, however, to state that the three cases are given in chronological order.

doubtless followed his praetorship of ca. 104.[105] M. Aurelius Scaurus, the young quaestor, otherwise unknown, was presumably son of the consul of 108, of the same name. The actual accuser is not recorded. Flaccus' acquittal may be taken for granted in view of his election to the consulship of 100. That election came with the overt support of Marius, who could count on the steadfast loyalty of the new consul. This connection suggests some important implications of the attack on Flaccus.[106] Marius was perhaps being put on notice that the courts could be used for something more than simply aristocratic quarrels or assaults on the *nobilitas*. The allies of the great general were not invulnerable, and the *equites* who controlled the juries were rarely faithful or consistent friends of any political group, as they had proved in the Gracchan era.

All this set the stage for the climactic return of Marius and the pivotal year of 100. The general had covered himself with martial glory, but the war was over. Other spectacular conquerors, like Scipio Africanus and Scipio Aemilianus, had found the going much tougher after their return home, when their military talents were no longer required. Marius, Saturninus, and Glaucia had assembled a formidable coalition that threatened to disrupt the whole traditional pattern of Roman politics. But could this assemblage of diverse individuals and groups, founded essentially during a foreign crisis and welded together largely because of the military incompetence of the ruling class, endure when the crisis had passed and affairs had returned to normal?

The *nobilitas* knew how to exploit the coming of peacetime. The culminating victory over the Germans had come in July of 101, before the elections for the following year. Marius and his compatriots sought to monopolize the principal offices for the succeeding year, but with the war at an end, their success was no longer automotic. The enemies of that coalition were already beginning to make their moves. The trial of Flaccus had probably been the opening salvo in the campaign. Marius found it prudent to share his triumph with Q. Lutatius Catulus. Perhaps he was motivated by generosity, as a favorable tradition reports, perhaps by fear of Catulus' troops, who would not have stood for anything less.[107] Catulus, in any event, wasted no time in claiming sole credit for the crushing of the Germans.[108] The aristocracy could utilize the weapons of propaganda. In the consular elections of 101, a Metellus,

[105] Correctly discerned by Badian, *Studies,* 86-87.

[106] Plut. *Marius,* 28.5; cf. Badian, *Studies,* 86-87.

[107] Plutarch reports both traditions; *Marius,* 27.6; cf. Livy, *Per.* 68; Eutrop. 5.2.2.

[108] Münzer, *RE,* 26.2077, "Lutatius," n. 7.

perhaps Numidicus himself seeking a second consulship, was put up to check the Marian juggernaut. Marius was successful, of course, as was his ally Valerius Flaccus, but the success may not have come easily. Some may affirm that a grateful populace bestowed a sixth consulship on Marius as a reward for his services.[109] But there is other evidence of his need to resort to bribery, and there may be truth in it.[110] Marius was no longer being elected merely as a general. Moreover, Saturninus had difficulties in the tribunician elections. A certain Nonius or Nunnius ran as a strong opposition candidate and only his murder in the midst of tallying the votes prevented his election and assured a place for Saturninus. Nothing is known of that man, although the moralist Valerius Maximus could say of him that the murder of Rome's most virtuous citizen opened the path for her most vicious.[111] The demagogues received their posts, Saturninus his tribunate and Glaucia his praetorship, but the opposition was mounting.

The *popularis* programs of the last few years were pushed further in 100 and in a consistent fashion, designed to appeal to even wider groups of voters. Provisions had been made in Africa for Marius' African veterans in 103; now legislation of Saturninus alloted land in Gaul to veterans of the Cimbric War. Colonies were designated in Sicily, Achaea, Macedon, and perhaps elsewhere, presumably for other demobilized soldiers. The added proviso that Marius could award citizenship to a specified number in each colony clearly presaged a large potential pool of Marian *clientelae.* Italians, eager for the franchise and indebted to Marius, could envision the realization of their hopes.[112] Another bill, framed to deal with piracy in the east and doubtless appealing to business interests in that area and in Rome, may also have been part of this legislation.[113] The demise of the *nobilitas,* it must have appeared, was truly at hand. C. Gracchus had been crushed with sagacity and force.

---

[109] So Vell. Pat. 2.12.6: *sextus consulatus veluti praemium ei meritorum datus.*

[110] Livy, *Per.* 69: *C. Marius . . . sextum consulatum pecunia per tribus sparsa emerat;* so also Plut., *Marius,* 28.5, who gives Metellus as the opponent.

[111] Val. Max. 9.7.3: *caede integerrimi civis facultas apiscendae potestatis taeterrimo daretur.* See also Appian, *BC,* 1.28; Livy, *Per.* 69; Plut. *Marius,* 29.1; Florus, 2.4.1; *Vir. Ill.* 73; Orosius, 5.17.3; and cf. the analysis of Jones, *PCPS,* 186 (1960), 35-39.

[112] For the sources on these measures, see *MRR,* I.575-576; cf. the accounts of Robinson, *Mar. Sat. Glauc.,* 66-75; Passerini, *Athenaeum,* 12 (1934,) 117-129, 278-281; Badian, *For. Client.,* 203-206; Carney, *A Biog. of Marius,* 40-42.

180

But who would venture to utilize force against the veterans of Marius and the following of the demagogues?

Q. Metellus Numidicus, smarting from defeat at the previous consular elections, embittered foe of the popular leaders, was the standard-bearer and symbol of the aristocracy. The attack on Numidicus became the true *cause célèbre* of the year 100. His case combined all the elements discernible in the trials of the preceding years of turmoil: senatorial rivalry, personal vindictiveness, and the politics of the popular movement. Metellus refused to acknowledge the validity of Saturninus' legislation, passed, as it was, with the aid of physical force. The law distributing land in Gaul possessed a built-in safeguard: it contained a clause requiring every senator to swear an oath to uphold it. Of all the members of the senate, Numidicus alone refused compliance; nor was that proud and obstinate aristocrat willing to submit to the attached penalties, a fine and loss of senatorial status.[114] His refusal opened the way for the implementation of old rancor and hostilities. Marius had no more bitter enemy in the senate than the man who had sought to block his original consulship eight years before. As for Saturninus and Glaucia, they had not forgotten that Metellus, in his censorship of 102, had attempted to effect their removal from the ranks of the senatorial order.[115] The elimination of Numidicus would also have its political purposes, of course: a dramatic demonstration of the power of the coalition and the removal of a major obstacle to its program. Saturninus brought capital proceedings against him before the people.[116] Some members of the senatorial order were not unhappy to see the discomfiture of a Metellus. There were professions of sympathy, but no formal actions in the senate on Numidicus' behalf.[117] The head of the Metellan clan withdrew into exile, his departure followed by a decree of *aquae et ignis interdictio* designed to seal his fate.

[113] *FIRA,* I.121-131; cf. Stuart Jones, *JRS,* 16 (1926), 155-173; Passerini, *Athenaeum,* 12 (1934), 121-130, 134-139.

[114] Full citation of sources in *MRR,* I.576. For a more detailed discussion of the case here summarized, see Gruen, "The Exile of Metellus Numidicus," *Latomus,* 24 (1965), 576-580.

[115] The sources, however, writing in retrospect and with aristocratic bias, make too much of Numidicus, even affirming that the alliance of Marius and the demagogues was formed for the specific purpose of eliminating Numidicus; Appian, *BC,* 1.28–29; Plut. *Marius,* 28.4-5.

[116] Cic. *De Leg.* 3.26; Livy. *Per.* 69; Orosius, 5.17.4; see Gruen, *Latomus,* 24 (1965), 578.

[117] Cic. *Post Red. in Sen.* 38: *numquam in hoc ordine de Q. Metello mentio facta est;* cf. *Pro Sest.* 37; *Pro Cluent.* 95.

The moment represents the high-water mark for the popular movement. It was also the crisis of the old order. That it survived at all is, from this vantage point, the most remarkable fact of that tension-filled year. The key to the situation is that Marius himself, in the final analysis, was not interested in the destruction of the old order. The military savior of the state desired to occupy what he could feel was his rightful place at the top of the political pyramid; it was not to his benefit to destroy the pyramid altogether.[118] An alliance with men like Glaucia and Saturninus was useful insofar as it could protect his interests, swell his *clientelae,* and increase his following in areas where he had had no contacts. The demagogues and Marius cooperated fully in the agrarian and colony measures of 100. Nor could the aristocracy, in general, have raised serious objections, since the settlements would not affect Italian land or their own holdings.[119] But, despite collaboration with the demagogues, Marius showed no taste for their extremism or violence. Glaucia's candidature for the consulship in the year of his praetorship was disallowed, apparently by Marius,[120] who also jailed an associate of Saturninus, allegedly an ex-slave, who claimed to be a son of C. Gracchus.[121]

Tension between Marius and his allies was compounded by rifts in their motley coalition, which was no longer held together by the pretext of war-time conditions. The *equester ordo* is a good case in point. It had never liked unrestrained violence, which disrupted the normal affairs of the city. In 102 or 101, a band of *equites* had rescued Metellus Numidicus from an assault by Saturninus' mob.[122] It is noteworthy and revealing that Saturninus in 100 chose to prosecute Numidicus before the people, bypassing the *maiestas* court that he had himself instituted but that was staffed by the *equites.* Hostility developed also between the veterans and the urban *plebs,* who felt that the former had received a lion's share of benefits from the legislative program of 100. Mutual jealousy arose also, or was provoked, between Romans and Italians in the Marian following.[123] There were many areas of dissension that the aristocracy could use to full advantage.

The remainder of the story is well-known. The consular elections of

[118] See the judicious remarks of Sherwin-White, *JRS,* 46 (1956), 3-5; also Badian, *For. Client.,* 209-210.

[119] Passerini, *Athenaeum,* 12 (1934), 278-281. Whatever the truth, if any, in Marius' wavering on the oath for the agrarian law (Appian, *BC,* 1.30; Plut. *Marius,* 29.1-4), it would be foolhardy to deny his interest in a measure that benefited his veterans.

[120] Cic. *Brutus,* 224; *Har. Resp.* 51.

[121] Val. Max. 9.7.1 puts this event in 101, probably wrongly; see Cic. *Pro Rab. Perd.* 20.

[122] Orosius, 5.17.3.

[123] Appian, *BC,* 1.29.

100 brought further riots, which, among other things, encompassed the death of the candidate C. Memmius. That deed of violence, whether premeditated or accidental, would have split further the following of the demagogues. Memmius had been an active and popular figure, his career now on the verge of well-earned high magistracy. The aristocracy had no intention of letting the opportunity slip. Once more, a *senatus consultum ultimum* authorized the consul to gather what forces he needed to eliminate the disruptive elements. C. Marius confronted an awkward and critical dilemma. Unlike P. Scaevola, another consul in an analogous situation thirty-three years before, Marius decided to heed the call of the senate. The unity of the oligarchy at this juncture must have impressed the *novus homo,* who wanted nothing better than to become a fully accepted member and leader of that oligarchy. Aemilius Scaurus was conspicuous in the forefront, hobbled though he was by injury or illness; he always seemed to discern the proper moment to strike. Aligned with him were all the great names of the Roman aristocracy, men from every senatorial faction, combining in the common interest of the *nobilitas.* Members of the *equester ordo* lent their voices and arms in support as well. The ranks included even parts of the populace, friends of Memmius or clients of the aristocracy.[124] The prospect of becoming once more the salvation of the state would also have appealed to Marius. Yet we need not doubt our sources when they report that he set about this task with reluctance.[125] Marius had hoped to have his cake and eat it too: acceptance as leader of the aristocracy and the loyal following of *equites,* popular elements, veterans, and Italians. When the demagogues and their die-hard supporters were trapped in the Capitol, Marius offered a pledge of safety, suggesting that due process of trial might yet restore their position. The general could envision himself in the role of grand peace-maker and reconciler of the factions. It was not to be. Oligarchic enemies of Marius arranged to have the fugitives murdered before they could be rescued. The populace would feel righteous indignation at the violation of Marius' pledge and dismay at his lack of skill or authority to carry it out, while the oligarchy could exult in having outmaneuvered the unhappy consul. The Marian coalition had been dissolved and the aristocratic order had survived in triumph.[126]

[124] For the actions of Scaurus, see Val. Max. 3.2.18; *Vir. Ill.* 72.9; cf. Cic. *Pro Sest.* 101. The list of *nobiles* who took up arms against Glaucia, Saturninus, and their followers is proudly recounted by Cicero, *Pro Rab. Perd.* 21. On the *equites,* see Cic. *Pro Rab. Perd.* 20, 27; Val. Max. 3.2.18; Plut. *Marius,* 30.3; the *plebs:* Cic. *Pro Rab. Perd.* 20; Appian, *BC,* 1.32; Orosius, 5.17.7.

[125] Appian, *BC,* 1.32; cf. Florus, 2.4.16.

[126] Sources on the year 100 are collected in *MRR,* I.574-576; cf. the acute discussion of Passerini, *Athenaeum,* 12 (1934), 269-297.

A summary is in order. Factional politics, family rivalries, popular gains, and struggles over the courts and legal processes: the period between 106 and 100 had witnessed them all and bound them all more closely together. Predominance and effective leadership in the senate by the Metellan group had resulted in 106 in a restoration of senatorial control in the judiciary. But success bred jealousy and deeper enmity. Senatorial rivals toppled Servilius Caepio, but popular leaders capitalized on his fall. The years 104 and 103 saw gains for the *populus* on all fronts, especially in the courts. The equestrian class, once more linked to popular interests when its own advantage dictated, regained a monopoly in the *quaestio de repetundis*. The hated tribunal of Mamilius was revived in a more insidious and permanent form by Saturninus' *maiestas* court. The *quaestio de peculatu* also seems to have been a fruit of this movement. Aristocratic infighting in the courts continued. Metellan ascendancy was challenged further by families like the Domitii Ahenobarbi, Cassii Longini, and Fabii Maximi; but the real gainers were Marius, Saturninus, and Glaucia. Nevertheless, what may legitimately be called the "age of Marius" was brief. Alleged "champions" of the *populus* like Memmius and Mamilius had been either too moderate or too disinterested to effect substantial reform. Saturninus and Glaucia were the reverse, but violence and extremism alienated their backers and wrecked their movement. Marius was caught in the middle. Seeking to achieve senatorial respect while operating through men who undermined it, he failed to resolve the contradiction. The following decade was to see him try a new avenue of approach — factional politics — but never with real success. The exile of Metellus Numidicus was a personal victory for Marius and the *populares,* but the very moment of victory precipitated defeat. The equestrian classes knew where their real interests lay; they were wedded to the existing social order. Metellus' expulsion had followed legislation passed by force and actions dedicated to popular sovereignty. The *senatus consultum ultimum* was inevitable; the senate closed ranks once more. Extremist leaders discredited the popular movement for another decade. After 100, Saturninus and Glaucia were gone: the *quaestiones de repetundis, de ambitu, de maiestate,* and *de peculatu* remained. As in the decade after C. Gracchus' murder, so in the decade after Saturninus' murder popular fervor abated and factional rivalries grew more intense. The judicial legislation of the past few years assured that these rivalries would be more and more settled in the courts.

VII. THE BUILDING OF CRISIS

A political crisis and its aftermath inevitably inspire much re-thinking. Conflicts of loyalty and interest come into sharp focus and individuals are forced into conscious decisions on matters normally taken for granted or suppressed, decisions that can shape or ruin careers. The various interests of family, faction, social group, and economic class rarely converge in a moment of great upheaval. Ti. Gracchus, his actions, and his program had scrambled old political lines and cut across traditional divisions. The demise of the Gracchan *factio* in 121 and its aftermath produced further reassessment and new alignments. Patterns shifted as factions responded to sharp change by adjusting policy or personnel. Nimble maneuvering was often required for individuals and groups to sidestep political disaster and successfully ride the waves of change. As Thucydides had long ago observed, with characteristic acumen, principled idealists seldom survive a period of cruel strife and violent change.[1] This pulsating rhythm, noted again and again, continued to dominate the political history of Rome. The events of 104 to 100 had, in many ways, exerted an even more serious challenge to the established order than had the Gracchan movement. As is to be expected, the fall of Saturninus and Glaucia brought a renewed shake-up in political attitudes and allegiances.

It has been possible to follow to some extent the redrawing of old lines and policies that followed the deaths of Tiberius and Gaius Gracchus. That is not so easy for the decade ushered in by the deaths of the demagogues. Paucity of evidence makes the problem of reconstruction even more acute than before. Yet the relative silence of sources ought not to leave the impression of tranquillity and concord. Enough indications survive to show that the 90's comprised a period of great importance and excitement. That decade began with a wholesale reassessment of political postures and concluded with massive war in the Italian

---

[1] Thuc. 3.82-83.

185

peninsula. Domestic politics touched at almost every point on Rome's
sensitive relations with her allies in Italy. The growing heatedness of
internal struggles brought concomitant strains in the Roman federation,
and these two elements exploded simultaneously in 90 creating the
bellum Italicum. The decade of the 90's obviously warrants close and
careful scrutiny.[2]

The demagogues and their loyal allies had suffered execution, sudden
and violent, under cover of the *senatus consultum ultimum.* But their
actions were not sponged off the records without a trace. The leaders of
the Roman aristocracy were intelligent enough to know that one could
not turn back the clock altogether. In the aftermath of the Gracchan
movement, the oligarchy had made prudent concessions in matters like
land reform and appeals to a wider public including the business classes
and the Latins. The popular agitation of the end of the second century
also had enduring aspects. Some, at least, of the demagogic legislation
remained on the books, first and foremost the new courts, that on *maiestas*
and that (apparently) on *peculatus,* which, together with the earlier
quaestiones, were now staffed by panels drawn from the *equester ordo.*
The courts were to play a central role in the political maneuverings of
the 90's. The veteran problem loomed large after the Marian army
reforms and Saturninus' subsequent legislation. Oligarchic leaders wisely
eschewed stubborn intransigence. The African settlements, apparently,
remained untouched and colonial foundations are attested for Corsica,
Cercina, and Eporedia. Tangible evidence survives in inscriptional form
to show the operation of a commission implementing colonial and agrarian legislation; and even where proposed colonies fell through, the
Marian enfranchisements in connection with them remained, at least
for a time, unchallenged. One may add also the law to check piracy, duly
recorded on stone and doubtless welcomed by business interests.[3] Revo-

---

[2] The reader will be aware that judgments and conclusions in this chapter
are sometimes expressed without detailed argumentation. This is particularly
true of some points of chronology and prosopographical identifications, many
of which are highly controversial. For more thorough documentation and
arguments, out of place here, one may refer to Gruen, "Political Prosecutions in the 90's B.C.," *Historia,* 15 (1966), 32-64, and the citations assembled there. Add also, on the date of Saturninus' death, R. Seager, "The
Date of Saturninus' Murder," *CR,* 17 (1967), 9-10.

[3] Cicero makes it clear that there was no annulment of Saturninus' measures; *De Leg.* 2.14; *Pro Balbo,* 48. On all these matters, see the judicious
analysis of Passerini, *Athenaeum,* 12 (1934), 350-351, and "Epigrafia Mariana," *Athenaeum,* 17 (1939), 54-77. It has been suggested that Eporedia,
founded in 100, was not part of Saturninus' program but an act of the sena-

lutionary upheaval was brought to a halt but social change was a political reality acknowledged by conservatives and *populares* alike.

The turbulent events of 100 shattered the amalgam of groups that had been so meticulously assembled in the previous few years. Some men, out of principle, loyalty, or false hopes, stood by Glaucia and Saturninus to the end and were slain with them. A few names are preserved: Cn. Dolabella, L. Giganius, Q. Labienus, C. Saufeius, and Equitius.[4] It was a motley crew of patricians and *novi homines* who had cast in their lot with what they expected to be the wave of the future. Others had anticipated the change of fortune and drew back in time, lining themselves up conspicuously with the government and partaking in the final slaughter. It was the sordid aftermath of the Gracchan demise repeating itself once more. Scarcity of evidence forbids a detailed reconstruction of factional realignment; but testimony is not altogether lacking. Marius, of course, led the way. His actions were reluctant, but the consequences were inevitable. There was no longer any possibility of patching up relations with the surviving associates of Saturninus. The unscrupulous adventurer M. Aemilius Lepidus conveniently forgot a marriage with Appuleia and drew his sword against the demagogues in 100. Some families were split down the middle in the final scene, the Labieni for certain, and probably the Dolabellae as well.[5] Who can say how many others of those who stood staunchly with the aristocracy in 100 had only recently abandoned former associates? Valerius Flaccus was there in the forum with his friend and colleague Marius; so was Flavius Fimbria, a *novus homo* who had recently reached the consulship by exploiting the popular agitation of previous years. In one case — that of the insidious P. Furius — turncoat activities can be documented in somewhat greater detail.

The son of a freedman, Furius had risen to notoriety and influence through attachment to Saturninus and Glaucia. In 102, the censor Metellus Numidicus, having failed to expunge the names of the latter two from the senatorial rolls, gained a minor victory by removing Furius from the *equester ordo*. That did not stop the ambitious agitator from securing the tribunate of 100 on the coattails of the demagogues. But

---

torial oligarchy; Vell. Pat. 1.15.5; Pliny, *NH*, 3.123; U. Ewins, "The Early Colonization of Cisalpine Gaul," *PBSR*, 20 (1952), 70; Carney, *A Biog. of Marius*, 43. If so, it demonstrates oligarchic recognition of the need for concession and flexibility.

[4] Cic. *Pro Rab. Perd.* 20; Appian, *BC*, 1.32-33; Val. Max. 3.2.18; Orosius, 5.17.8-10.

[5] For Lepidus and the Labieni, see Cic. *Pro Rab. Perd.* 20-22. On the Dolabellae, see Gruen, "The Dolabellae and Sulla," *AJP*, 87 (1966), 385-399.

when the tide began to turn Furius prudently shifted ground. He was not caught in the massacre. To dramatize his new posture he hastened to propose the confiscation of property belonging to the fallen Saturninus and his friends. What Marius could do, Furius could do also. The enmity with Metellus Numidicus still rankled, as it did with Marius. When a proposal was made to recall Numidicus from exile, Furius exercised his tribunician veto, proudly backed by the authority of Marius. The pleas and tears of Numidicus' son, earning him the nickname of Pius, were of no avail. But the actions of Furius roused the disgust and hatred of every group. An outraged citizenry, we may imagine, anxiously awaited the expiration of his tribunate.

By comparison with P. Furius even Saturninus must have appeared a man of integrity, and he still had some friends left. One of them, C. Appuleius Decianus, whose name reveals an adoption by the family of the murdered tribune, prosecuted Furius in 99. Popular sympathies could be played upon once again. Proceedings took place before the *populus,* naturally; it would have been foolhardy to turn to an equestrian tribunal since *equites* had helped to crush the demagogues in the previous year. Decianus, it seems, was not the only speaker, but he was the most effective. He invoked the name of Saturninus, lamented his unhappy fate, and stirred the crowd. Furius had no chance. Formal procedure degenerated into riot and the defendant was torn to pieces by an enraged mob. Few would have mourned. Even the *boni,* especially the friends of Numidicus, welcomed the elimination of an irresponsible and treacherous person. Tradition spares no invective: "he was preeminently worthy of death." [6]

The case of Furius illuminates the kind of reshuffling that the fall of the demagogues had brought about. A son of a freedman with dubious origins and character proved an easy target. Others, less impetuous and more influential, had transferred their allegiance with impunity. The case is revealing also in other ways. *Popularis* sentiment was not dead in 99 and the heirs of Saturninus could still find the atmosphere congenial. They were influential or noisy enough to block for still another year the recall of Metellus Numidicus, whose intransigence had once been the chief obstacle to Saturninus. Not even the consul M. Antonius used his office or his oratory to promote the exile's return.[7] New *popularis* legis-

[6] Dio, fr. 95.3: ἀξιώτατον μέν που ἀπολέσθαι ὄντα; cf. Val. Max. 8.1. damn. 2: *P. Furium inquinatissimae vitae.* Record of these events is preserved also in Cic. *Pro Rab. Perd.* 24-25; Appian, *BC,* 1.33; Orosius, 5.17.10-11. For the chronology, see Gruen, *Historia,* 15 (1966), 32-36.

[7] Cic. *Post Red. ad Quir.* 11: *de Metello . . . ne . . . quidem M. Antonius homo eloquentissimus . . . senatum aut populum est cohortatus.*

lation appeared as well. Sex. Titius, a tribune in 99, openly honored the memory of Saturninus; he possessed a bust of the martyred popular champion. He was active also in the *comitia,* sponsoring, among other things, another agrarian law, perhaps to create more settlements for the Marian veterans. That bust of Saturninus had apparently provided inspiration and inspired imitation.[8] Rome was not yet free of tumultuous demonstrations demanding vengeance for the deaths of Saturninus and Glaucia.[9] Decianus engaged in a second prosecution in 99: the trial of L. Valerius Flaccus, future consul of 86. Whatever the motive behind this affair, it was surely not irrelevant that Flaccus' cousin, as Marius' colleague in 100, had helped to trap the fugitive demagogues.[10]

All these activities, however, proved to be only the dying embers of the *popularis* conflagration. Marius, even if he had so desired, was no longer in a position to lend support. The oligarchy, after prudent appeasement and patience, now girded its loins. Antonius exerted his consular prestige to block the radical measures of Titius in 99, and the following year saw safe men in the magisterial offices. The Metellan *factio,* as so often in the past, reasserted control when men tired of demagogic excesses. A Metellus once more sat in the curule chair in 98 and with him was T. Didius, who had established his credentials in 103 by vigorous, though futile, efforts on behalf of Servilius Caepio. The way was clear at last for the restoration of Metellus Numidicus. That event was more significant for its symbolic effect than for practical consequences. Numidicus had never been a man who could move readily with the times. Aristocratic arrogance and an uncompromising nature had from the beginning marked his career, highlighted by his vain resistance to Marius in 108 and his lone stance on Saturninus' measure in 100. True political leadership was never a virtue of this man, and the years following his return show no further trace of his activity. It may be conjectured that death was not long in coming. But the symbolic value of Numidicus' recall cannot be overstated. None of his titles or triumphs brought more glory than his exile and his return.[11] It marked the real end of the popular agitation of previous years. For the aristocracy it was a return to normalcy. Once more illumination and confirmation come from the

[8] This is further suggested by a law regulating the allotment of quaestorian duties. Titius doubtless remembered that Saturninus had once been summarily dismissed from his post as quaestor in Ostia. For the legislation of Titius, see the references in *MRR,* II.2.

[9] Schol. Bob. 94, Stangl.

[10] Cic. *Pro Rab. Perd.* 20, 27; Plut. *Marius,* 28.5. The younger Flaccus, however, apparently escaped conviction; Cic. *Pro Flacco,* 77.

[11] Vell. Pat. 2.15.4: *Nec triumphis honoribusque quam aut causa exilii aut exilio aut reditu clarior fuit Numidicus.*

criminal processes. The vocal tribunes of the preceding year duly met their fate in the courts. Decianus and Titius both succumbed to political prosecution, apparently for *maiestas*. They could now rue in exile their unfortunate expressions of sympathy for Saturninus. It was a sobering and embittering experience. The family of Decianus, in the succeeding generation, joined the forces of Rome's greatest foreign foe, Mithridates of Pontus.[12] Equestrian *iudices* had once more demonstrated their solidarity with the established order.[13]

And what of C. Marius? There seemed little place for him in the new scheme of things. Though personally a man of moderation, he had risen to power in a time of turmoil and disruption, and under the practical rules of Roman politics his successes could hardly have come in any other way. But those conditions, at least on the surface, were no longer present. Members of the oligarchy felt no further need to cater to the great general. Friends of Saturninus and Glaucia were implacably alienated over what they would have regarded as Marian treachery in 100. Of whatever inconsistencies Marius might be accused, his hostility toward Metellus Numidicus had remained constant and fervent. To no man was the restoration of Numidicus a more bitter blow. Marius could not bear the humiliation of remaining in Rome to witness the return of his *inimicus*. On six occasions he had been consul. There was a time when the prospect of culminating this extraordinary career with the coveted censorship would have been a foregone conclusion. Under normal circumstances Marius would surely have entered the censorial elections of 98, but the situation had changed considerably and political realities dictated otherwise. Marius knew that it was pointless even to submit his *professio* and preferred to withdraw from the city altogether.[14]

Not that Marius was suddenly stripped of all influence and standing. The massive following carefully assembled over the past decade would not have deserted him en masse. When the split came with Saturninus in 100, some of their former allies found their more natural place with Marius. One need cite only the Julii, Valerius Flaccus, Flavius Fimbria, and (perhaps in this category) M. Lepidus. Others, not present or conspicuous in 100, but whose fortunes remained linked with Marius, were men like M'. Aquillius and the Herennii. Numerous ex-Italians owed their Roman franchise to Marius and would regard the ties of *clientela* as sacred and binding. Many other veterans had served him

[12] Cic. *Pro Flacco*, 5, 51, 70-71; Schol. Bob. 94, Stangl.

[13] On all the matters discussed in this paragraph, see further Gruen, *Historia*, 15 (1966), 36-38.

[14] Plut. *Marius*, 30-31, esp. 30.4: τιμητείας παραπεσούσης ἐπίδοξος ὢν οὐ μετῆλθεν, ἀλλ᾽ εἴασεν ἑτέρους ὑποδεεστέρους αἱρεθῆναι δεδιὼς ἀποτυχεῖν.

190

loyally at the front and could justifiably regard Marius as the source of new land allotments or fortunes made in war. But the support was scattered and Marius was no more interested now than before in establishing a *dominatio* by force, even if it had been possible. Absence, he could hope, might make the heart grow fonder. His popularity had been at its peak when he was fighting Rome's wars abroad and his reputation had suffered by comparison when he was induced to play the game of domestic politics. Perhaps it was not too late to add to his military laurels, and it was possible to foresee a potential conflict with the ambitious king of Pontus. With the censorial elections pending and the return of Numidicus imminent Marius found the moment convenient to advertise his religious piety. He would go to Asia to perform sacrifices and fulfill a vow made to the mother of the gods when she had vouchsafed him military victories.[15] No one need doubt that *absentia* was the motive; the rest was pretext.

Trouble was brewing in the east. Saturninus had warned of the aggrandizement and machinations of Mithridates as early as 102. The pirate law was also designed to strengthen Rome's position in the eastern Mediterranean. By 98 Mithridates had his eye on Cappadocia, as did his erstwhile ally Nicomedes of Bithynia. Rome could expect renewed embassies and potential trouble. Plutarch alleges that Marius' chief interest in his eastern voyage, which included trips to Galatia and Cappadocia, was to fish in these troubled waters and to provoke Mithridates to action in the hopes of a further military command for himself. The account betrays anti-Marian bias, but we may be sure that the prospect did not escape the general's attention. In a personal confrontation with Mithridates, Marius delivered a stern warning and rebuke.[16]

Absence, it appears, was of some benefit to the general, struggling to avoid political eclipse. No military command came out of it. Indeed, when the government eventually decided to take some action on the eastern situation an enemy of Marius was despatched to do the job, a decision that would have been unthinkable five years before. But the trip was not altogether in vain. Marius could show concern with business investments and interests in that part of the world. He doubtless did not miss the opportunity to indicate to the *equites* that he was prepared to champion them again if necessary, as he had once done in the Jugurthine

[15] Plut. *Marius*, 31.1; cf. 17.5, 26.2; Diod. 36.13.

[16] Plut. *Marius*, 31.3: ''Η μεῖξον, ὦ βασιλεῦ, πειρῶ δύνασθαι 'Ρωμαίων, ἢ ποίει σιωπῇ τὸ προστασσόμενον.' Cf. Badian, *Studies*, 171; *Rom. Imp.*, 31; Van Ooteghem, *Marius*, 254-257. The doubts of Passerini, *Athenaeum*, 12 (1934), 352-355, are unnecessary. One certainly cannot follow him in the suggestion that the censorship was unappealing to Marius.

War.[17] It was in his absence also that Marius was informed of his election to the augurate. That suggests some continued influence in the tribes, which elected priestly officials.[18] Marius could return to Rome now (probably in 97) in the hopes of repairing some of the damage incurred in 100.

The general had to seek allies and friends. Acceptance by the aristocracy was still his aim, but he would have to play the game by their rules. Demagogery had, for the moment, been discredited, and Roman politics returned to the forms and practices of the pre-Jugurthine War period: senatorial contests and factional struggle in the courts. Marius could at least live like an aristocrat. An expensive town house near the forum was an immediate purchase upon his return and villas in the country followed, perhaps not long after.[19] But it would take more than this to recover a place in the political limelight. Marius needed to attach himself to a senatorial group with influence and power.

Metellus Numidicus was dead, or, at least, shunted into the background. The demonstrations that accompanied his return from exile had fulfilled the purposes of his faction. His heavy-handed leadership would not be missed. Immediate relatives and heirs had no love for Marius, of course; nor would Marius make any headway with Q. Catulus or Rutilius Rufus, both of whose activities in the German wars he had overshadowed and whose embittered memoirs have poisoned the tradition against him. But there were other members of this group less intransigent and prepared to show flexibility when it was politically expedient. Moreover, Marius had more to offer now than when he was first taken under the wing of the Metellan *factio* a quarter of a century earlier. M. Antonius was a valuable man to have on one's side. The distinguished orator had just, in 97, capped a successful career, which included all the higher magistracies and a military triumph, with election to the censorship, the office that Marius had coveted in vain. Marius could appeal to a prior connection with Antonius. A relative of the general, M. Gratidius, had served in Cilicia under M. Antonius, with whom he became intimate, and

---

[17] It is possible that an inscription set up by the *Italici* of Delos to honor a benefactor refers to Marius; *ILLRP*, I.203, no. 343. The interests of the *Italici* were, of course, predominantly commercial; they would have welcomed strong gestures against Mithridates; cf. Passerini, *Athenaeum*, 17 (1939), 73. Since, however, the name of the benefactor is missing in both the Greek and Latin versions of the text, this suggestion remains conjectural.

[18] Cic. *Ad Brut.* 1.5.3. That this was a "bargain" struck in return for Marius' giving up on the censorship (Badian, *Studies*, 48; *For. Client.*, 212) is an unwarranted conjecture. Election to the augurate presupposes an opening in that college. Did someone perish conveniently to seal the bargain?

[19] Plut. *Marius*, 32.1, 34.1-2, 35.5-6; Schol. Bob. 89, Stangl.

had perished there during Antonius' campaigns against the pirates.[20] There is no hint of any earlier cooperation between Marius and the orator, but both may have found association now of mutual benefit. It is precisely in the year 97 that evidence for the association begins. In addition to Antonius there were other men connected with the Metellan group who found more room for maneuvering with the passing of Metellus Numidicus. One such man was L. Crassus, a close personal and political friend of Antonius, and his only peer in the forensic art.[21] He already had behind him a lengthy and full political career that began with his dramatic appearance against C. Carbo in 119 and was highlighted by involvement in the Vestals affair, sponsorship of the Narbo colony, and the powerful speech on behalf of Caepio's judicial bill in 106. It was a career marked, above all, by flexibility and political sagaciousness that had brought him widespread respect and *dignitas*. In 95 Crassus was to reach the consulship together with Q. Mucius Scaevola, his *amicus* and ally, who had shared every office with him but the tribunate.[22] It was about this time that Marius contracted an important marriage alliance: his son was betrothed to the daughter of Crassus.[23] It brought Marius within the orbit of Crassus and the Scaevolae. And perhaps to the list of Marius' new friends we might add the most consummate politician of them all, M. Aemilius Scaurus. No one was more adaptable than he, nor swifter to see in which direction lay political advantage. Evidence survives, obscure but important, that Scaurus and Marius cooperated in some business enterprises, apparently in the 90's.[24] Marius had learned the lessons of 100. Acceptance by the oligarchy required adeptness in the art of factional politics.

There had been marvelous senatorial unanamity in 100 when the demagogic threat had reached its peak. The crisis had seen Metelli shoulder to shoulder with Julii, a Crassus with a Domitius, a Catulus with a Fimbria, a Cassius with a Mucius Scaevola, a Drusus with a Philippus, all the strangest of political bedfellows.[25] Such concert of

---

[20] Cic. *Brutus,* 168; cf. Badian, *Studies,* 47.

[21] Cic. *De Orat.* 1.24: *M. Antonius, homo et consiliorum in republica socius, et summa cum Crasso familiaritate coniunctus.*

[22] Cic. *Brutus,* 161. Crassus had long ago married into the Scaevolae, taking the hand of the daughter of Q. Scaevola, consul in 117; Lucilius, II.86 (*ROL,* 3.28).

[23] Cic. *Pro Balbo,* 49; *De Orat.* 1.66, 3.8; *Ad Att.* 12.49.1, 14.8.1; on the date, see Gruen, *Historia,* 15 (1966), 43.

[24] Pliny, *NH,* 36.116, refers to Scaurus as *Mariani sodalicii rapinarum provincialium sinus;* cf. Gruen, *Historia,* 15 (1966), 58.

[25] For the list of senators engaged in the slaughter of Saturninus and his crew, see Cic. *Pro Rab. Perd.* 21.

purpose had not been witnessed since 121 when, under similar circumstances, the oligarchy had coalesced to massacre the Gracchani. The sequels of these two events were also analagous. When the danger to the establishment had passed, the monolithic unity of the senatorial order naturally evaporated. Aristocrats felt free to resume their traditional squabbles. Evidence is fragmentary, but criminal prosecutions are a useful index and preserve traces of the internal struggles.

It was possible again to settle personal scores. Thus, young C. Scribonius Curio gained some notoriety by a judicial attack on Metellus Nepos, and L. Crassus vented private wrath in a case against M. Marcellus, both some time in the 90's.[26] These were instances of personal animosity, but there were other cases that may have had political implications. M. Antonius' road to the censorship of 97 was not altogether a smooth one. He had first to hurdle an *ambitus* prosecution initiated by a certain M. Duronius, a man of intemperate speech and a champion of libertarianism who opposed government censorship of private morals. It is of interest that Duronius' past, otherwise obscure, shows a clash with P. Crassus, *propinquus* of Crassus the orator and himself now consul in 97.[27] Attacks on Antonius and Crassus suggest a new movement to weaken the *factio* once centered in the Metelli.[28] At about this same time came the trial *repetundarum* of M'. Aquillius. As proconsul of Sicily he had exploited provincials and sated his avarice, for which condemnation, it seems, was warranted. But Aquillius had a distinguished war record and, more important, he had powerful friends. His military service had been performed under Marius in the German wars and the general had placed implicit faith in his lieutenant.[29] At the trial Marius appeared in person, not to speak, but to weep appropriately. There was no need for oratory from him; M. Antonius handled the defense. His participation is interesting, the first fruit perhaps of their association. It was one of Antonius' most celebrated efforts. He played with consummate skill on feelings of pity and patriotism. Aquillius was coached to appear in mourning garb and to present the figure of a man broken by illness

[26] On the Nepos trial, see Asconius, 63-65, Clark; Apuleius, *Apol.* 66; on the prosecution of Marcellus, see Cic. *Pro Font.* 24; Val. Max. 8.5.3; cf. Gruen, *Historia,* 15 (1966), 42, 51.

[27] On the trial, see Cic. *De Orat.* 2.274; cf. 2.257 and Münzer, *RE,* 10.1862-1863, "Duronius," n. 3. For the character of Duronius and the earlier clash, see Val. Max. 2.9.5.

[28] The Metelli themselves provided no significant leaders in the 90's. But the group possessed continuity in men like Scaurus, Scaevola, Crassus, Antonius, and Rutilius.

[29] Aquillius was entrusted with the army in 103 when Marius went home to preside over the elections; Plut. *Marius,* 14.7.

194

and age. Antonius chose the most opportune moment to strip the defendant's tunic and expose to view the painful but glorious scars of battle. As Marius wept, the jurors were overcome with emotion and (we may surmise) overawed by the powerful combination of personalities.[30]

The evidence indicates then that enemies of the Metellan clique were once again utilizing the courts to challenge the ascendancy of that faction. And now Marius, striving to recover old stature with new associations, was among the targets. The rise of a powerful new group is suggested immediately by the consuls of 96, Cn. Domitius Ahenobarbus and C. Cassius Longinus. Both men, or their families, carried a record of hostility to the Metelli.[31] Moreover, the old Metellan alliance was showing signs of weakness. Cracks began to appear in what had once been a solid unity. The flirtation of Antonius, Crassus, and Scaevola with the Mariani would not have been welcome to Q. Catulus, Rutilius Rufus, or Metellus Pius, the son of Numidicus. There were further rifts. The judicial clash between Metellus Nepos and C. Curio had exposed one, and now young Q. Servilius Caepio, son of the ill-fated consul of 106, began to drift away from his father's political associates. He broke with his close friend and brother-in-law M. Livius Drusus over some obscure quarrel that culminated in each man divorcing his wife. The hot-headed Caepio further contracted an *inimicitia* with M. Scaurus, who had once suffered bodily injury in defense of Caepio's father. Motives for these actions evade inquiry; Caepio was impetuous, emotional, and even given to violence.[32] In any event, the Metellan alliance seemed vulnerable and its rivals had no intention of not capitalizing on this weakness. The year 95 demonstrates with striking clarity the political clash, played out in the *iudicia*.[33]

Caepio's recent career, apparently, offered no pretext for an attack; but memories could be jogged to recall his activities as a young quaestor in 103, the year in which Saturninus and Norbanus had brought about the humiliation and exile of his father for the Arausio débâcle. Caepio had retaliated in force. When Saturninus brought his *lex frumentaria* to a vote in the *comitia,* Caepio stormed the proceedings, wrecked the

[30] Sources quoted and cited by Greenidge and Clay, *Sources,* 116. See also Diod. 36.4; Nicolet, *L'Ordre Equestre,* 543. The prosecutor was an otherwise unknown L. Fufius, an orator of inferior ability, for whom this case finally won some repute; Cic. *Brutus,* 222; *De Off.* 2.50.

[31] See above, pp. 161-162, 173-174.

[32] Cf. *Ad Herenn.* 1.21.

[33] The picture sketched in outline here and in the following paragraphs is drawn in fuller detail, with references, in Gruen, *Historia,* 15 (1966), 43-47. Cf. also the stimulating account in Badian, *Studies,* 34-36, 39-44, 49-50.

voting passages, and scattered the ballot boxes.[34] No one took action at the time, but now, eight years later, Caepio faced a charge of *maiestas* for that behavior. Enemies of the Metellan group obviously utilized the occasion to expose the disunity of the *factio*. They made their point. L. Crassus, who had once delivered his most devastating oration on behalf of Caepio the elder's jury bill, appeared again in defense of the younger Caepio, but this time his speech was perfunctory.[35]

The *factio,* however, had some plans of its own. Scrutiny of the events of 103 could prove to be a double-edged sword. For all his excesses, Caepio had, after all, carried the banner of the oligarchy against the demagogues. By attacking him for those actions, it could be argued, his opponents had unwittingly ranged themselves on the side of sedition and revolution. A counter-demonstration was now in order. Saturninus was dead, but Norbanus could still be dredged up and made to stand trial for his policies and activities of 103. The result was another *maiestas* prosecution indulging in all the propaganda of the establishment against its disrupters. It was a brilliant counter-stroke, masterminded, one might conjecture, by the subtle M. Scaurus, who also put in an appearance to testify against Norbanus.[36] The prosecutor was a young protégé of the Metellan group, P. Sulpicius Rufus, sharpening his oratorical powers in conscious imitation of the style of Crassus.[37] Antonius found himself on the other side, though with some reluctance. Norbanus, it happened, had been Antonius' quaestor, perhaps in 99,[38] and the orator was now discharging an obligation of *pietas*. His friends in the *factio* were disconcerted, and this awkward predicament revealed a further strain in the alliance.[39] For the moment, in any case, results were nebulous. Equestrian jurors, showing a cool disdain for aristocratic squabbles, rendered acquittal verdicts for both Caepio and Norbanus.

But the political fencing proceeded. Events in the east had grown steadily more serious and they could be expected to influence the domestic situation, as they had so often in the past. Marius' efforts to accelerate events and bring the situation to a head had borne some fruit, but not for him. New contacts with some members of the nobility had increased his expectations, but a warm and full welcome by the *ordo senatorius*

---

[34] *Ad Herenn.* 1.21: *cum viris bonis impetus facit, pontes disturbat, cistas deiecit, inpedimento est quo setius feratur;* cf. 2.17; Sallust, *Hist.* 1.62, Maur.

[35] Cic. *Brutus,* 162: *non brevis ut laudatio, ut oratio autem brevis.*

[36] Cic. *De Orat.* 2.203; Val. Max. 8.5.2.

[37] Cic. *De Orat.* 2.89.

[38] Gruen, "The Quaestorship of Norbanus," *CP,* 61 (1966), 105-107.

[39] Cic. *De Orat.* 2.198: *vix satis honeste viderer seditiosum civem . . . defendere;* cf. Gruen, "The *Lex Varia,*" *JRS,* 55 (1965), 67-68.

was never to be his. The oligarchy knew better than to entrust Marius again with extensive military authority. Such a move could have been far more dangerous for them than whatever troubles Roman dependencies might be having in the east. Hence when a decision was made to install a pro-Roman monarch in Cappadocia, the man selected to effect the installation was the governor of Cilicia, P. Cornelius Sulla. The decision served to check not only the aggrandizement of Mithridates but also the ambitions of Marius.

Sulla was a man with few initial material advantages, but abundant subtlety and intellect, which he employed in scrupulous fashion to further his career. Ancestors, patrician though they were, had left a legacy of obscurity and Sulla grew up in circumstances that smacked more of poverty than of nobility.[40] A taste for pleasures, combined with generous liberality, may have made matters more difficult, but also produced popularity and a following. The historian Sallust, who certainly felt no kindness for the woeful devastations that Sulla eventually brought to his own and the succeeding generation, nevertheless cannot help expressing admiration for his qualities. Sulla had a penetrating intellect supplemented by deep learning and possessed the capacity to enjoy life while never shifting his gaze from serious business and the goal of personal glory.[41] When Marius' fortunes were on the rise, Sulla wisely inaugurated his career by joining the bandwagon. He served as Marius' quaestor in Africa and continued to work under him in the German wars. Military experience was enhanced by an extraordinary capacity for diplomacy that made Sulla indispensable and spread his reputation. Success bred confidence and he soon showed signs of independence. In the course of the German wars, Sulla transferred his allegiance to Q. Catulus, a less gifted military commander who could offer more room for a subordinate's exploits. The sequel showed that both Catulus and Sulla were prepared to advertise their achievements at the expense of Marius. Sulla ostentatiously carried about a signet ring representing his role in the capture of Jugurtha; and when the African monarch Bocchus presented tokens of esteem to Rome they were in the form of trophies depicting his surrender of Jugurtha to Sulla, much to the dismay and frustration of C. Marius.[42] Enemies of Marius could find Sulla a useful ally and the oligarchy could already see him as another M. Scaurus, with whose talents and background he had much in com-

[40] Plut. *Sulla*, 1.1-4.

[41] Sallust, *Iug.* 95.3: *litteris Graecis et Latinis iuxta atque doctissume eruditus, animo ingenti, cupidus voluptatum sed gloriae cupidior, otio luxurioso esse; tamen ab negotiis numquam voluptas remorata.*

[42] Plut. *Sulla*, 3.4, 6.1; *Marius*, 32.2; cf. *Vir. Ill.* 75.6.

mon. The decision to have Sulla settle affairs in Cappadocia, probably in 96, was a deliberate and obvious demonstration of aristocratic feelings toward the former savior of Rome.[43]

The return of Sulla brought the inevitable *repetundae* prosecution. In the bustling year of 95, it may represent another jab at the Metellan bloc: Sulla was a friend of Catulus and was later to marry into the family of the Metelli themselves. The prosecutor, C. Marcius Censorinus, failed to carry through the case and the charges were dropped.[44] The outcome may have been premeditated. Sufficient evidence to make conviction likely was doubtless lacking, and this maneuver sufficed to plant lingering suspicions, including rumors of bribery by Mithridates. Sulla found his career duly delayed for another seven years. Judicial contests among senatorial factions were the prominent order of the day in 95. Another may be surmised. Q. Hortensius Hortalus, a young man of exceptional promise as a public speaker, thrilled auditors with his maiden public oration in that year. He was a man of indefatigable industry and of great natural gifts, including an unparalleled memory.[45] Within a decade he was to surpass without question all his elders and contemporaries and gain recognition as the leader of the Roman bar. His political connections are clear. He was a protégé of Crassus and the son-in-law of Q. Catulus, both of whom expressed great delight at Hortensius' initial political prosecution, as did Mucius Scaevola.[46] The case was apparently one of extortion involving alleged mistreatment of African provincials. Unfortunately, the defendant is unrecorded, but a hint survives that may point to L. Marcius Philippus, an *inimicus* of Catulus and the man who later in this decade was to assume senatorial leadership in the struggle against the Metelli.[47] Talented men were still attracted to the resourceful Metellan *factio,* but the challenge to its authority in the senate was growing more heated.[48]

[43] On the chronology, see the careful exposition of Badian, *Studies,* 157-178.

[44] Plut. *Sulla,* 5.6: οὐ μὴν ἀπήντησεν ἐπὶ τὴν κρίσιν ἀλλ' ἀπέστη τῆς κατηγορίας; Firm. Mat. *Mathesis,* 1.7.28.

[45] Cic. *Brutus,* 301-302: *Primum memoria tanta quantam in nullo cognovisse me arbitror . . . ardebat autem cupiditate sic ut in nullo umquam flagrantius studium viderim.*

[46] Cic. *De Orat.* 3.228-229; *Brutus,* 229.

[47] Cic. *De Orat.* 2.220; see Gruen, *Historia,* 15 (1966), 49-50.

[48] One further trial deserves a mention here. The *accusator* M. Junius Brutus charged Cn. Plancus under the *lex Servilia* before a jury of *equites.* Since L. Crassus was the defense counsel and engaged in a sharp exchange with Brutus, political considerations may have been involved. But the occasion can be no more accurately dated than some time between 104 and 92. Circumstances and outcome remain unknown. For sources and brief discussion, see Gruen, *Historia,* 15 (1966), 59-60.

Factional struggles do not exhaust the events of these years. It is at this point that we can begin to perceive again with some clarity how selfish political rivalries impinged upon and raised issues of more momentous proportions. Most notably, they opened the festering sore that marked Rome's deteriorating relations with her Italian allies.

The Italian question, so far as the sources indicate, had lain dormant since the death of C. Gracchus. Certainly overt manifestations of hostility were few and insignificant. Italians had made their presence felt, as we have seen, in the 120's. Outraged barons and their dependents, as well perhaps as other Italians, protested loudly over confiscations of property and stalled the agrarian program in 129. The Gracchan *factio* hoped to meet their objections and seduce their loyalties by offers of enfranchisement in 125. But when the measure was shelved there was no stir from the *socii*. A solitary town revolted, Fregellae, a Latin colony filled with ambitious emigrants from the Paeligni and Samnites who had hoped to have their status regularized.[49] It was the exception that proved the rule. The Italians in general, it seems, were not anxious for Roman citizenship. And why should they have been? They had traditions of their own that most were unwilling to engulf in the Roman constitution. Italian states possessed the advantages of association with Rome while retaining treaties that gave at least the illusion of dignity and autonomy. Hence, when C. Gracchus' franchise bill fell through, its author murdered, and his non-Roman supporters expelled from the city, there was no discernible reaction in Italy. If the Italians had any grievances, they were not caused by lack of franchise, but by lack of recourse against the arbitrary actions of Roman magistrates, particularly during military campaigns. This is supported by the fact that the right of *provocatio* was offered more than once in this period as an alternative option to the citizenship.[50] It helped to quiet the malcontents and salvage harmony. For those who did desire the citizenship, notably the Latins, with institutions and culture close to Rome's, there were ways to obtain it. Men who held magistracies in Latin towns became automatically eligible for Roman franchise, a practice instituted perhaps after the Fregellan revolt.[51] And a clause in the Gracchan *lex repetundarum* provided citizenship for non-Romans who proved to be successful prosecutors.[52] Such institutions would have satisfied many of the more in-

---

[49] Cf. Livy, 41.8.

[50] Cf. A. N. Sherwin-White, *The Roman Citizenship* (Oxford, 1939), 126-130.

[51] Asconius, 3, Clark; cf. Tibiletti, "La politica delle colonie e citta Latine nella Guerra Sociale," *RendIstLomb,* 86 (1953), 54-60.

[52] *Lex repet.*, lines 76-85 (*FIRA,* I.101). Here again the alternative of *provocatio* is also offered.

fluential and vocal elements of the Italian populace. For the rest, the prevailing mood was indifference.

Yet these *socii*, who stood by quietly when the Gracchan *factio* was massacred, were, by the late 90's, filled with passion and hostility, and on the brink of all-out war. That the *bellum Marsicum* came as a startling explosion after a lull of thirty years is a proposition to which few reasonable men will subscribe. Tensions, we may be sure, were building under the surface in this period, the details of which escaped the concern of ancient historians who were interested in the manifestations, not the background, of discontent. No solitary element serves to encompass the reasons for the Social War. Historians have too often occupied themselves with the search for a single key to this complex and elusive problem. The very notion of "Italian" is, after all, no more than an abstraction. Italy included a multitude of peoples and communities, as well as its own differentiation of social and economic classes. Among almost all groups the desire for Roman citizenship increased in this period, but one cannot expect their various reasons to be identical. Many landless Latins and Italians had sought to emigrate to Rome from the early second century; in the city there might be employment and opportunity. Rome had more than once resorted to expulsion in order to keep the numbers down.[53] The Gracchan land distributions might have eased the situation for some of them, but by the end of the century, distributable public land in Italy seems to have been virtually exhausted. Saturninus revived their hopes by proposals of foreign assignations and colonies. But, as has been observed, the selfishness of the Roman *plebs,* unwilling to share new advantages, helped to frustrate these efforts and to bring about the fall of the demagogues. For the lower classes of Italy, the Roman franchise must now have appeared more and more indispensable for the purpose of landed benefits.[54] Italian veterans would have felt this discrimination most poignantly. Years of service in the ranks, side-by-side with Romans, had not earned them equality. Marius had made no distinctions on the battlefield; indeed, he could ignore constitutional practice in the din of battle and had enfranchised men for signal bravery on the spot.[55] The

[53] Livy, 39.3.4, 41.8.6, 42.10.3.

[54] Carcopino, "Les lois agraires des Gracques et la Guerre Sociale," *Bull. Ass. Budé,* 22 (1929), 3-23, and Bernardi, *Nuov. Riv. Stor.,* 28-29 (1944-45), 60-99, rightly point to the connection between the land problem and the Italian question. But that issue alone does not explain all. Their accounts tend to simplify or to ignore the gradual aggravation of tensions. On Saturninus and propaganda for the *socii,* see Rowland, "Saturn, Saturninus, and the *socii,*" *CP,* 62 (1967), 185-189, who, however, is wedded to a schematic notion of conflict between the "optimate faction" and the "popular faction."

[55] Cic. *Pro Balbo,* 46; Plut. *Marius,* 28.2; Val. Max. 5.2.8.

relative eclipse of Marius in the 90's would have increased Italian frustrations and anger.

Discharged veterans and landless proletariate are the stuff of revolution, but they cannot effect it alone. There would have been no Italian problem for Rome without leadership at the top. Business and commercial classes in the peninsula had been gradually expanding their influence in overseas ventures, as is abundantly shown by the events of the Jugurthine War and increased Italian presence in places like Spain, Gaul, Delos, and Asia. How far these *negotiatores* cooperated or clashed with Roman *equites* in the provinces is beyond knowing. The *equites,* at least, could protect their activities through control of the extortion court and could exercise some leverage, as we have seen, on Roman foreign policy. Their Italian counterparts doubtless found Roman citizenship increasingly desirable in order to insure guarantees of a similar sort.[56] More important leadership, however, would have come from the more established Italian aristocrats and landowners. The events of the end of the second century had opened the Roman political scene to ambitious *novi homines* and had seen new faces and new families obtain shares in the centers of power. The spectacular example of C. Marius, whose family was only second generation Roman, would not have been lost on Italian magnates. If Marius could make it, why not they? The status afforded by a home-town magistracy still could not compare with the luster of the Roman senate. For such aims Roman citizenship, of course, was a prerequisite. In the eyes of the municipal aristocracy the franchise must have looked increasingly inviting.[57] Finally, one must not discount less calculated and more emotional factors, including even latent ethnic rivalry, especially in the Sabellian areas. Roman exclusiveness made discrimination more manifest and humiliating. The Social War was soon to betray how deep the bitterness ran. Not only was the fighting to be fierce and violent, but in some areas it continued even after concession of the franchise; many were struggling for autonomy, not absorption.[58]

It is useful now to return to the tension-filled year of 95. The crosscurrents of Roman politics and Italian aspirations were swiftly coming

[56] See esp. Gabba, *Athenaeum,* 32 (1954), 41-82; also E. T. Salmon, "The Cause of the Social War," *Phoenix,* 16 (1962), 107-119. Both, however, overstate the case by stressing this single element; cf. Sherwin-White, "Review of Gabba, *Le Origini della Guerra Sociale,*" *JRS,* 45 (1955), 168-170.

[57] See Brunt, "Italian Aims at the Time of the Social War," *JRS,* 55 (1965), 101-106.

[58] Brunt strains his argument unnecessarily in trying to reject this element; *ibid.,* 95-97.

to a head. Influential spokesmen of the Roman oligarchy feared massive enfranchisement no less now than they had in the Gracchan era, and for the same reasons. The prospect of large numbers of new citizens eligible for the assemblies and unconnected by ties of patronage to noble houses remained abhorrent. The two consuls of 95, L. Crassus and Q. Scaevola, were closely linked through background, *adfinitas,* and political principle. They shared most offices together and complemented one another nicely: Crassus, the brilliant orator with a strong interest in the law, Scaevola the learned jurist with a talent for oratory. Cicero was fond of comparing them through neat parallellisms: Crassus was the ablest lawyer among orators, Scaevola the ablest orator among lawyers; Crassus the most frugal of the elegant, Scaevola the most elegant of the frugal; Crassus the sternest of the gentle, Scaevola the gentlest of the stern.[59] In 95 these two turned their attention to the Italian problem. It is evident that many *socii,* despairing of other avenues of enfranchisement, had in past years succeeded in having their names illegally registered on the citizen-rolls. These were not simply rabble looking for hand-outs or land grants but *principes Italicorum populorum,* with influential contacts and friends in Rome.[60] Reaction was stern. The consuls sponsored a *lex Licinia Mucia* that struck from the lists those who had been illegally enrolled and instituted a *quaestio* to investigate further any dubious cases.[61] Behind this measure stood the advice and impetus of the *princeps senatus* M. Scaurus, an aristocrat with nothing but contempt for new citizens.[62] The Metellan *factio* had made clear its stand on the matter of Italian enfranchisement.[63]

The matter, however, became further embroiled in politics. Enemies of the *factio,* men whose interest in checking Italian aims were equally great, could nonetheless embarrass it on this issue. The connection of

[59] Cic. *Brutus,* 145: *eloquentium iuris peritissimus Crassus, iuris peritorum eloquentissimus Scaevola; Brutus,* 148: *Crassus erat elegantium parcissimus, Scaevola parcorum elegantissimus; Crassus in summo comitate habebat etiam severitatis satis, Scaevolae multa in severitate non deerat tamen comitas;* cf. *De Orat.* 1.180.

[60] Asconius, 68, Clark.

[61] Sources in *MRR,* II.11. The law did not involve physical expulsion, but simply the revision of the citizen register; Cic. *De Off.* 3.47; see R. W. Husband, "On the Expulsion of Foreigners from Rome," *CP,* 11 (1916), 321-323; Gabba, "Politica e cultura in Roma agli inizi del I secolo a.C.," *Athenaeum,* 31 (1953), 260-262.

[62] Cic. *De Orat.* 2.257; cf. Fraccaro, *Opuscula,* 2.132-135; Badian, "Review of Taylor, *Voting Districts,*" *JRS,* 52 (1962), 207-208.

[63] Cf. also the restriction of prosecuting privileges to Latins in the *lex Servilia,* apparently that of Caepio; Cic. *Pro Balbo,* 54; Badian, *CR,* 4 (1954), 101-102.

Crassus and Scaevola with Marius was a sore point. The general still had a large Italian following, veterans and *principes* who looked to him as a champion or an example. Here was the setting of the trial of T. Matrinius, a Spoletine enfranchised by Marius under the terms of Saturninus' colony bill of 100. Not only was Matrinius' citizenship challenged, but the case had to be heard by the *quaestio* instituted by Marius' own new *adfines,* Crassus and Scaevola. It was an obvious effort to expose the incongruity of a link between Marius and the oligarchs and to divide further the Metellan *factio.* The alliance, however, held firm, at least for the moment. Marius had no intention of alienating his Italian supporters and spoke up to protect Matrinius. Crassus would not have been happy, but political expediency dictated that he offer his services as well. He might salve his conscience by reflecting that Saturninus' measure was a legal statute and did not encompass the illegal registration with which the *lex Licinia Mucia* was concerned.[64] Matrinius was acquitted and Marius' stature with new and prospective voters remained high. Crassus, though yielding temporarily to political expediency, had not changed his attitude on the matter of alien elements in Rome. As censor in 92 he and his colleague, Cn. Domitius Ahenobarbus, with whom he disagreed on all other matters, published a joint edict expelling Latin rhetors from Rome.[65] The result of this maneuvering by Roman politicians to advertise their "purity" on the issue of "Rome for the Romans" can only have alienated Italians further.[66] Marius was too concerned with attaining aristocratic *dignitas* to use the Italians as a springboard to political power, and the oligarchy, despite inner tension, continued to harden on the matter of exclusiveness. The bitter proceedings of the mid 90's had not only shattered senatorial unity but dangerously exacerbated relations between Rome and her *socii.*

These same years introduced still another major element of friction. The solidarity of purpose that had joined the senatorial and equestrian orders in the years 100-98 was rapidly breaking down. The senate had acquiesced without difficulty in equestrian control of the criminal juries

[64] Cic. *Pro Balbo,* 48-49; see Gruen, *Historia,* 15 (1966), 48-49.

[65] *MRR,* II.17. That the rhetors were expounding doctrines with political implications and associated with Italian cultural nationalism has been suggested; R. Pichon, "L'Affaire des *Rhetores Latini,*" *REA,* 6 (1904), 37-41; Gabba, *Athenaeum,* 31 (1953), 267-272. But the evidence is scanty and inconclusive; cf. M. L. Clarke, *Rhetoric at Rome* (New York, 1963), 12-13; Douglas, "*Clausulae* in the *Rhetorica ad Herennium* as Evidence of its Date," *CQ,* 10 (1960), 77; Gelzer, *Kleine Schriften,* I.212-215.

[66] Cicero later regarded the *lex Licinia Mucia* as perhaps the chief provocation for the *bellum Italicum;* Asconius, 67-68, Clark.

since the passage of the *lex Servilia Glauciae*. There had been close cooperation in the crushing of the demagogues and the conviction of their imitators in the courts. But the *equites,* as we have seen more than once, were not basically men of politics. If the interests of their class were at stake they would coalesce to protect friends, overawe enemies, and exert influence on public policy. Otherwise they showed a distinct preference for tending to their own affairs. The vagaries of senatorial politics interested them not at all and we may imagine that the series of blatantly political prosecutions that filled the docket in the 90's produced impatience and scorn. The striking feature of the cases recorded in this period is that not once since 98, when the remnants of Saturninus' movement were dissipated, had equestrian *iudices* handed down a condemnatory verdict. Antonius, Marcellus, Aquillius, Caepio, Norbanus, Sulla, Philippus (?), and Matrinius had all escaped conviction. Coincidence is unlikely. The *equites* had their ways of demonstrating contempt for senatorial misuse of the judicial process. It is not difficult to surmise aristocratic frustration and a growing desire to reform the courts once more.

The ill-concealed hostility between politicians and the *iudices* burst into full view with the notorious affair of Rutilius Rufus in 92. Events in the east provided the backdrop. If Mithridates were to make headway with the people linked or subject to Rome, it would be largely due to the ire roused among them by Roman businessmen. The province of Asia was the wealthiest of Rome's overseas possessions; investors and profiteers took full advantage. While *equites* controlled the *quaestio repetundarum,* proconsuls of Asia would be very reluctant to interfere with the extortionate practices of the *publicani* and money lenders in their province, and indeed most probably connived in those activities. But if Asia was becoming ripe for revolution and Mithridates was waiting in the wings to capitalize on it, some steps had to be taken. The interests of the senatorial order now, as in the preliminaries to the Jugurthine conflict, were to stabilize the situation, remove the roots of discontent, and avoid a costly war. Among other fears, a major war might produce a new Marius, or revive the old one. In 95 or 94 the new governor of Asia, Q. Scaevola, shouldered the difficult task of reforming the provincial administration and improving Rome's image abroad. A man of integrity and learning, Scaevola was ideal for the job. The importance of the mission is underlined by the fact that Scaevola took with him as legate a man senior to himself, the very symbol of rectitude and Stoicism, Rutilius Rufus, who had held the consulship a decade before. The senate wanted no repetition of the Jugurthine embassies and the Mamilian commission; Scaevola and Rutilius were virtually synonymous with incorruptibility. They were also close friends and politically aligned.[67] The job was duly accomplished: a wholesale reform of administrative practices, a rigid suppression of equestrian abuses, and the creation of a model code that became the envy of later generations.[68] Scaevola returned in nine months; Rutilius remained abroad for some time thereafter, completing the task and setting the new reforms into operation. An oppressive burden had been lifted from the shoulders of the grateful provincials, and the Metellan *factio* could take credit for the defusing of a dangerous situation.

The fury of the *equites,* however, knew no bounds. The upsetting of business operations, even in the national interest, was unforgivable. In 92, after the return of Rutilius and the completion of his task, that proud Stoic was hauled before the extortion court on the ludicrous charge of oppressing the Asian provincials. Equestrian *iudices,* however, were not laughing. The prosecution and conviction that followed were pure acts of vengeance calculated to discourage any further senatorial interference in the affairs of the *publicani.* The case soon became a prime *exemplum* of iniquity, cited in the ancient tradition for centuries thereafter. Rutilius Rufus, perhaps, had known what to expect. The Metellan group was prepared to rally to his aid, but Rutilius declined offers from Crassus and Antonius and permitted only brief speeches by Scaevola and his own nephew, C. Aurelius Cotta. He employed the courtroom as a platform to advertise his rectitude and underline his martyrdom. When Rutilius marched off haughtily into exile among the Asian provincials themselves, he had insured himself an undying reputation as the innocent victim of vengeful injustice.[69]

For the first time in years equestrian *iudices* had produced a *condemnatio.* To some this was a signal for renewed militancy in the courts. The hot-tempered Q. Servilius Caepio, a man of political independence, had been nursing his own vengeance. The unhappy fate of his father a

[67] Cf. esp. Diod. 37.5.1: Κοίντος Σκαιουόλας . . . ἐπιλεξάμενος τὸν ἄριστον τῶν φίλων σύμβουλον Κοίντον Ῥοτίλιον.

[68] Sources in *MRR,* II.7; for the chronology, see Badian, "Quintus Mucius Scaevola and the Province of Asia," *Athenaeum,* 34 (1956), 104-112; contra: Balsdon, "Q. Mucius Scaevola the Pontifex and *Ornatio Provinciae,*" *CR,* 51 (1937), 8-10.

[69] Cf. Vell. Pat. 2.13.2: *P. Rutilium, virum non saeculi sui sed omni aevi optimum, interrogatum lege repetundarum maximo cum gemitu civitatis damnaverant;* see further the discussion and references in Gruen, *Historia,* 15 (1966), 53-55, and, in general, Pais, *Dalle Guerre Puniche,* 37-89. The effort of Nicolet, *L'Ordre Equestre,* 546-549, to dismiss equestrian vengeance and to reduce the trial to a struggle between Rutilius and the *factio* of Marius flies in the face of all our evidence.

205

decade before still rankled. A violent quarrel with Drusus had embittered him further and estranged him from the Metellan *factio*. No one could blame him for righteous indignation at having been made the guinea pig for an attack on the *factio* in 95 and at the luke-warm support he had then received. In 92, inspired by the conviction of Rutilius, Caepio began to lash out. If Rutilius could be condemned, who could feel secure in his own innocence? [70] Caepio brought a prosecution for *ambitus* against L. Marcius Philippus, canvassing in that year for the consulship, a man who (we might conjecture) had probably supported the attack on Caepio in 95. At about the same time or early in 91 Caepio indicted also his *inimicus,* the *princeps senatus* M. Scaurus, for *repetundae*. In that case, the prosecutor could take advantage of Scaurus' recent trip to Asia to spread rumors of bribery by Mithridates, in the hopes of rousing further the ire of the *equites*. The indefatigable Scaurus, however, had another card up his sleeve. He turned the tables and accused Caepio of a criminal offense, apparently also *repetundae*.[71] Reaction of the *iudices* ought to have been predictable. Philippus, Caepio, and Scaurus were all acquitted. The *equites* had protected their friends and their economic interests in the condemnation of Rutilius. That accomplished, they renewed their indifference and disdain for factional and personal contests in the courts.

All these events pointed to a climax in 91. Senatorial struggles had grown more heated; the frustration of the aristocracy at equestrian management of the courts had become intolerable; the humiliation of Italian *socii* and the *provinciales* in general had put them on the verge of explosion. These various strands were now closely intertwined. Action in any one area was bound to affect them all.

From the point of view of the Metellan *factio,* the matter of prime concern was the composition of the courts. The ascendancy of that group had come, above all, through its successes in the judicial process, but equestrian control was now proving to be a bottle-neck for senatorial politics. The chosen instrument of the *factio* for the purposes of reform was a young tribune of 91, M. Livius Drusus. His links to the *factio* were

[70] Asconius, 21, Clark: *cum iudicia penes equestrem ordinem essent et P. Rutilio damnato nemo tam innocens videretur ut non timeret illa.*

[71] For the prosecution of Philippus, see Florus, 2.5.5. For the double trials of Scaurus and Caepio, see Asconius, 21, Clark; Val. Max. 3.7.8; *ORF,* 167; and Gruen, *Historia,* 15 (1966), 55-59. In the trial of Scaurus, Caepio had the assistance of Cn. Cornelius Dolabella, whose father had been slain in 100 when Scaurus led the assault on the demagogues; Asconius, 26, 74, Clark; cf. Orosius, 5.17.10.

close: he was tied in marriage to the Servilii Caepiones and was a nephew of Rutilius Rufus.[72] Drusus also profited from the *exemplum* of his father, the anti-Gracchan tribune of 122. From him he could learn how to manipulate popular legislation and a reform program in the interests of the aristocracy.[73] Sources are virtually unanimous that the younger Drusus' efforts in 91 were designed to enhance the prestige and influence of the senatorial order.[74] Clearly, jury reform was the central purpose, at least at the outset, of Drusus' program. Resentment at the fate of his uncle Rutilius provided sufficient personal motivation. Drusus was capable and impressive, a promising young man and ostensibly an excellent choice to provide leadership in this campaign, but he was not the most stable of individuals. Possessed of a volatile temper, he was greatly enamored of his own importance, and from an early age he displayed precocious ambition and arrogance.[75] He reveled in controversy and enjoyed being conspicuous. Drusus served as his own best press agent: "When will Rome ever see my like again?"[76] The background and character of the tribune were to have their effect on the events of 91.

Legislative change in the jury system would arouse resistance. Hence its promoters would do well to mobilize *clientelae* and woo a neutral populace. Such motives may well be behind Drusus' *lex frumentaria* and an agrarian bill involving both colonial foundations and viritane grants. With the latter he could claim also to be renewing the *beneficia* of his father. Of his own laws, characteristically enough, Drusus was

---

[72] The tie with Caepio was broken by the latter, but Drusus remained with the *factio;* see above, note 33. For the relationship with Rutilius, see Val. Max. 8.13.6; Pliny, *NH,* 7.158.

[73] Cf. Boren, *CJ,* 52 (1956), 27-36.

[74] Cic. *Pro Mil.* 16: *Nobilissimus vir senatus propugnator atque illis quidem temporibus paene patronus; De Orat.* 1.24: *Drusi tribunatus pro senatus auctoritate susceptus;* Diod. 37.10: μόνος ἔδοξεν ἔσεσθαι προστάτης τῆς συγκλήτου; also Vell. Pat. 2.13.2; Livy, *Per.* 70-71; Florus, 2.5.1; [Sallust], *Ad Caes.* 2.6.3; Tac. *Ann.* 3.27.3; Suet. *Tib.* 3. Appian, *BC,* 1.35, alone makes Drusus' chief aim the enfranchisement of Italians. But that is the product of Appian's myopia, focused throughout, as it is, on the Italian question. Cf. Gabba, *Appiano,* 13-25.

[75] Seneca, *De Brev. Vit.* 6.1: *Ausus est enim et pupillus adhuc et praetextatus iudicibus reos commendare et gratiam suam foro interponere tam efficaciter quidem, ut quaedam iudicia constet ab illo rapta; Vir. Ill.* 66.2: *quaestor in Asia nullis insignibus uti voluit, ne quid ipso esset insignius;* cf. Cic. *De Off.* 1.108.

[76] Vell. Pat. 2.14.2: *ecquandone . . . similem mei civem habebit res publica?* Cf. the anecdote in Vell. Pat. 2.14.3.

to be both administrator and promulgator.[77] Judicial reform, however, was the major item on the agenda. The oligarchy in general would benefit, but the Metellan *factio,* as in the case of Caepio's bill fifteen years before, sought to gain credit for the initiative. Its most prominent figures, M. Scaurus and L. Crassus, served as Drusus' counselors, especially in the matter of the *lex iudiciaria.*[78] On more than one occasion in recent years their appearances as prosecutors or hostile witnesses had been stifled by equestrian *iudices.* Reform seemed inevitable.

The nature of Drusus' proposal still provokes scholarly debate.[79] The controversy does not warrant lengthy rehearsal. As so often, contradictions in the sources are more apparent than real. Appian affirms that three hundred *equites* were to be enrolled in the senate and that the enlarged body would then provide *iudices* for criminal hearings. This version is endorsed by the author of the *De Viris Illustribus* and is doubtless accurate. Velleius is simply giving a shorthand version of the same when he states that Drusus proposed to transfer the courts to the senate, and the Livian Epitomator is being only slightly sloppier than usual when he reports the proposal as dividing the *iudicia* between the senatorial and equestrian orders.[80] The format was, apparently, similar to that of Caepio's earlier law in 106, but it was administratively easier to draw jurors from an enlarged senate than to share courts between the two *ordines* as in the *lex Servilia Caepionis.* It was Drusus' solution, not Caepio's, that was eventually to be adopted by Sulla.[81]

It is often repeated that Drusus sought by this concession to mollify the *equites.* That is difficult to accept. The senate, as it stood, simply did not have the manpower to staff the juries, so that some alteration along these lines was necessary. A few *equites,* with ambition and a taste for politics, may have welcomed the proposal. But Drusus could hardly fail to foresee that enrollment of three hundred would only arouse the resentment and hostility of the rest. That, of course, is precisely what did

[77] Cf. *ILS,* 49: *x vir a.d.a. lege sua.* For sources on the legislation, see *MRR,* II.21. A currency measure may have been for the purpose of financing the grain and land bills; Pliny, *NH,* 33.46. The order of the laws is a matter of guesswork. On this one cannot do better than to consult the perceptive analysis of R. Thomsen, "Das Jahr 91 v. Chr. und seine Voraussetzungen," *ClMed,* 5 (1942), 13-47, easily the best modern account of Drusus' tribunate.

[78] Cic. *De Domo,* 50: *M. Drusus . . . M. Scauro et L. Crasso consiliariis;* Asconius, 21, Clark: *Scaurus . . . M. quoque Drusum tribunum plebis cohortatus sit ut iudicia commutaret.*

[79] A brief bibliography is in Gruen, *Historia,* 15 (1966), 61, n. 180.

[80] Appian, *BC,* 1.35; *Vir. Ill.* 66.4, 66.10; Vell. Pat. 2.13.2; Livy, *Per.* 71.

[81] Cf. Gabba, "M. Livio Druso e le riforme di Silla," *AnnPisa,* 33 (1964), 1-15.

happen. The nephew of Rutilius Rufus was not concerned to appease the men who had ruined his uncle. This is clear from another of his judicial measures, an extension of the Gracchan law *ne quis iudicio circumveniretur*. C. Gracchus sponsored the latter, it will be recalled, with the insidious *quaestio* of Popillius Laenas in mind. It forbade collusion and conspiracy designed to condemn innocent men. Under the circumstances of Gracchus' day, it was logical to direct that measure against the *ordo senatorius*.[82] But the hands of the *equites* in the intervening years had not been clean. The Mamilian *quaestio* of 109, it could be argued, had engaged in willful persecution of the innocent; and, although that furor had long since died down, the conviction of Rutilius Rufus had revived all the fears of the oligarchy and exposed the ruthlessness of the business classes when their profits were threatened. Yet the *equites* had remained immune; the law of Gracchus had specified senatorial offenders only and the *Gracchani iudices* could hide comfortably behind that clause. Drusus set about to close the loophole. Henceforth, *equites* too were to be liable on charges of corruption to secure an unjust conviction. A *quaestio* was proposed to investigate such offenses. And that was not all. Drusus intended to extract his pound of flesh; the measure, it appears, was to apply retroactively as well.[83] The *iudices* who had condemned Rutilius preoccupied the mind of the tribune. This measure is generally described as a clause in Drusus' *lex iudiciaria*.[84] But there is no suggestion that he intended to limit its operation to the *equites* enrolled in the senate and Cicero implies just the reverse: *in equestrem ordinem*.[85] Drusus, it seems, like Gracchus before him, was not only thinking of the present but sought to prevent any future *quaestiones extraordinariae* that might be manned by the *equites*. It is not surprising that the *equester ordo* vented their indignation and ire on the tribune.[86]

One need not doubt that judicial reform was welcome to the aristoc-

---

[82] See above, pp. 84-86.

[83] Cic. *Pro Rab. Post*. 16: *M. Druso, novam in equestrem ordinem quaestionem ferenti: "si quis ob rem iudicandam* [codd.: *iudicatam*] *pecuniam accepisset"*; Cic. *Pro Cluent*. 153: *ut ei qui rem iudicassent huisce modi quaestionibus in iudicium vocarentur;* Appian, *BC*, 1.35: εὐθύνας τε ἐπ' αὐτῶν γίγνεσθαι δωροδοκίας προσέγραφεν; contra: Gabba, *App. BC Lib. Prim*., 119; cf. Ewins, *JRS*, 50 (1960), 104-106.

[84] Cf. *MRR*, II.21; Gabba, *App. BC Lib. Prim*., 119.

[85] Cic. *Pro Rab. Post*. 16.

[86] Appian, *BC*, 1.35; Cic. *Pro Rab. Post*. 16; *Pro Cluent*. 153; Florus, 2.5.17. Meier, *Res Pub*., 211-212, regards judicial reform as an instrument to weaken the *equites* and thence to cripple their opposition to Italian enfranchisement. But such opposition is unattested; cf. the acquittal of T. Matrinius. Meier's theory ignores the whole history of the struggle over the courts, into which Drusus' effort evidently fits.

racy as a whole. But, as we have seen on many occasions, a senatorial faction might oppose legislation not on principle but out of reluctance to see credit won by a rival group. Enemies of the Metelli had a rich field for controversy. They could capitalize on the outrage of the *equites,* and on the fact that his other bills had made Drusus vulnerable to the charge of demagoguery. Factional strife, consequently, again supervened to muddy the waters. The loudest voice raised in opposition was, as one might expect, that of Q. Caepio, the ex-brother-in-law of Drusus, eager now to disrupt the plans of his adversary and to discredit the Metellan *factio.*[87] But the real leadership of the opposition fell into the hands of the consul of 91, L. Marcius Philippus. Philippus had come into his own as a political figure of the first importance. He had made *popularis* noises during his tribunate in 104, a not untypical gambit, but had duly dropped his agrarian bill, in accepted senatorial fashion, when he failed to win support in the *curia.*[88] Since that time he had sharpened his political skill and showed himself a staunch aristocrat, carrying out the traditions of a family that traced its ancestry to the kings of Rome. Philippus was in evidence in 100, engaged in the slaughter of Saturninus and his friends. He was a member of all the right clubs and associations. In eloquence Philippus was surpassed only by Crassus and Antonius; he was at his best in a repartee tailor-made for his crackling wit.[89] He enjoyed the luxury of patronizing humble clients and prided himself upon having achieved political success without pandering to vulgar tastes.[90] He could prove a formidable opponent; and his background suggests prior hostility toward the Metellan group. Philippus' father was cooling his heels in exile in Nuceria along with C. Popillius Laenas and Q. Fabius Maximus, all apparently victims of political prosecutions engineered by the Metelli.[91] His tribunate of 104 had coincided with the disgrace of Caepio and enmity between Philippus and Caepio's son continued. *Inimicitia* is attested also with Q. Catulus.[92] Drusus could expect to find no support from the consul. Efforts were

[87] Florus, 2.5.17; *Vir. Ill.* 66.8; cf. Cic. *De Domo,* 120; Pliny, *NH,* 28.148.

[88] See above, p. 164.

[89] Cic. *Brutus,* 166: *summa nobilitate hominem, cognatione, sodalitate, collegio, summa etiam eloquentia;* 173: *duobus igitur summis, Crasso et Antonio, L. Philippus proximus accedebat . . . in altercando cum aliquo aculeo et maledicto facetus;* cf. 186; *De Off.* 1.108; *De Orat.* 3.4.

[90] Cic. *De Off.* 2.59; *gloriari solebat se sine ullo munere adeptum esse omnia, quae haberentur amplissima;* cf. the anecdote in Horace, *Ep.* 1.7. Philippus was also a renowned gourmet; Varro, *De Re Rust.* 3.3.9-10; Columella, *De Re Rust.* 8.16.3. On his character in general, see J. Van Ooteghem, *L. Marcius Philippus et sa Famille* (Brussels, 1961), 157-170.

[91] Cic. *Pro Balbo,* 28; cf. Gruen, *Historia,* 15 (1966), 62-63.

[92] Cic. *De Orat.* 2.220.

now underway to block the reform legislation of 91. Philippus and Caepio found it convenient to ignore their differences and to cooperate in a venture that promised political profit to both. One need not imagine that they had come to love one another, or that they were primarily concerned with the welfare of the *equites*.[93] Resistance to Drusus and his *factio* alone linked the *equites,* Philippus, and Caepio.

The arrogance of the tempestuous tribune was only aggravated by opposition. When the senate summoned him to the *curia,* Drusus shot back: "Let them come to me." [94] When his *inimici* got in his way, Drusus threatened to hurl Caepio from the Tarpeian rock and engaged Philippus in a physical scuffle that drew blood from the consul's nose.[95] Such a man was not to be deterred by persuasion or resistance from carrying through his program; nor would he hesitate to stir up dangerous issues if they might assist in the pursuit of his aims. The Italian question had now reached a boiling point. The *principes Italicorum populorum* were no longer willing to endure humiliation patiently. One of these *principes,* Poppaedius Silo, was a guest of Drusus and used the opportunity to plead the Italian cause.[96] The tribune, whose father had once sponsored a measure to extend the right of *provocatio* to non-Romans, apparently retained credit among the *socii.* Impetuosity and ambition spurred him to further action. Drusus' espousal of Italian enfranchisement promised him a wide and vocal following with which he expected to overawe the opposition, guarantee the success of the rest of his program, and gain his coveted *gloria* by resolving once and for all a burning issue that Rome could no longer ignore with impunity.[97]

On this matter Drusus would not have carried with him the united support of his *factio.* Men like Scaurus, Crassus, and Scaevola had made their stands on Italian franchise clear in recent years. They shared the conservatism of the bulk of the Roman senate at the prospect of a multitude of new and uncontrollable voters in the *comitia.*[98] Drusus, in his

[93] Despite Cic. *Brutus,* 223, and Florus, 2.5.17, still followed by Meier, *Res. Pub.,* 213. Hindsight obscured the picture; cf. Thomsen, *ClMed,* 5 (1942), 26-27.

[94] Val. Max. 9.5.2.

[95] Florus, 2.5.17; *Vir. Ill.* 66.8-9; Val. Max. 9.5.2.

[96] Plut. *Cato Min.* 2.1-2; Val. Max. 3.1.2; *Vir. Ill.* 80.1; cf. Diod. 37.11.

[97] Sources on the Italian agitation and Drusus' measure in *MRR,* II.21-22. That Drusus' stand on the enfranchisement of the *socii* was an afterthought and not part of his original plan is stated explicitly by Velleius, 2.14.1: *Tum conversus Drusi animus, quando bene incepta male cedebant, ad dandam civitatem Italiae.*

[98] Cf. Bernardi, *Nuov. Riv. Stor.,* 28-29 (1944-45), 92-94; Gabba, *Athenaeum,* 31 (1953), 259-267; contra: Carcopino, *Bull. Ass. Budé,* 22 (1929), 3-23; Badian, *Historia,* 11 (1962), 223-225.

anxiety and enthusiasm, had stirred a hornet's nest. Philippus could now press home his opposition on all fronts. The fury of the *equites* could already be relied upon. In the senate Philippus played a different angle; many old-line aristocrats found unacceptable a proposal that would enroll three hundred *novi homines* in their order.[99] The consul could frighten others by denouncing Drusus' demagogery and raising the specter of revolution. For a time, his efforts remained unsuccessful. A majority of the *curia* stayed with Drusus, prompting Philippus to lose his temper and denounce the senate as a body with whom a consul could no longer carry on the business of the state.[100] Those were hasty and regrettable words. L. Crassus used the occasion to deliver one of his most brilliant orations. Illness and infirmity had not dulled his powers; he chastised Philippus for his impudence and defended in rounded periods the *dignitas* of the senatorial order. The result was a vote of censure for the consul, and Drusus' program, for the moment, survived.[101] The specific context of the debate, unfortunately, is unrecorded. That it concerned the Italian question is most unlikely. Crassus was the last man to defend a policy of enfranchisement and it is revealing that his speech, so far as quotations are preserved, dwelled on generalities and stressed Philippus' unforgivable affront to senatorial dignity.[102] The aristocracy had no reason to sanction, as ends in themselves, the agrarian or frumentary laws, still less the proposal for Italian enfranchisement. The favorable vote for Crassus and for Drusus reveals unquestionably how strongly the senate felt on the matter of judicial control. That was the issue which, spoken or unspoken, lay in the background of this heated debate; it was for that issue that Drusus had organized his program initially and on it that the Metellan *factio* gambled its prestige.

[99] Cf. *Vir. Ill.* 66.11: *equites in senatum lecti laetabantur, sed praeteriti querebantur; senatus permissis iudiciis exsultabat, sed societatem cum equitibus aegre ferebat.*

[100] Cic. *De Orat.* 3.2: *videndum sibi aliud esse consilium, illo senatu se rempublicam gerere non posse;* Val. Max. 6.2.2 This is sufficient to dispose of Meier's efforts, *Res Pub.*, 214-215, to reduce the contest to one between the aristocracy on the one hand and a powerful and unconventional personality on the other.

[101] Cic. *De Orat.* 3.3-5.

[102] That Drusus' associates were unhappy with his Italian proposals is suggested also by Cicero's story of a lengthy consultation by the *factio* before Crassus even agreed to deliver a speech on Drusus' behalf. In the course of it, Crassus, Scaevola, and Antonius all expressed displeasure with the situation; Cic. *De Orat.* 1.24-26: *multum inter se usque ad extremum tempus diei collocuti sunt. Quo quidem in sermone multa divinitus a tribus illis consularibus Cotta deplorata et commemorata narrabat;* cf. Bernardi, *Nuov. Riv. Stor.*, 28-29 (1944-45), 92-94.

Whatever his differences with Drusus on the Italian question, Crassus showed, as he had in 95, that his principal loyalty was to the unity of the *factio*. Its political future, like its past, rested with the fate of the *iudicia*.

This victory, however, was Drusus' last. Crassus' mighty effort had strained his failing energies beyond the breaking point and he perished within a week.[103] Without his powerful voice, the *factio* swiftly lost ground to Philippus. Not only was the senate divided and the *equester ordo* alienated, but Philippus could show that even the Italians were split on Drusus' laws. The consul dramatized that fact by bringing into the forum angry Etruscans and Umbrians who found intolerable the agrarian and colonial legislation foreboding renewed confiscation of Italian land.[104] Scipio Aemilianus had employed similar tactics in 129. The remainder of the story is well-known. Philippus' campaign proved successful, the laws of Drusus were all invalidated by the senate, and the tribune, defiant to the end, was slain in the forum. So bitter was the feeling roused against him from all sides that no inquiry into the circumstances of his death was instituted.[105]

The triumphant maneuvers of Philippus settled the factional contest, but they did so at the cost of allowing the *equites* to retain control of the judiciary. And worse, they exasperated the Italians beyond endurance. No longer would the *socii* allow their interests to be subject to the vagaries of Roman politics. The murder of Drusus filled them with a rage that could be expiated only by revolution and war.[106] The year 91 had proved the culmination of all the events traced for the past decade: heated struggles within the oligarchy, growing enmity between the senatorial and equestrian orders, and the increasing alienation of the *socii* from Rome. The aim of Drusus was simple at the outset and it remained the fundamental concern of his *factio:* a reform of the judiciary. But by that time any change in this institution was bound to have repercussions in every sphere of Roman political life. Before the year 91 was over the efforts of one aristocratic group to alter the judicial arrangements had split the senate irrevocably, galvanized the hostility of the capitalist

[103] Cic. *De Orat.* 3.6.
[104] Appian, *BC,* 1.36; cf. Badian, *For. Client.,* 217-222; *Historia,* 11 (1962), 225-226.
[105] Cic. *Pro Mil.* 16: *Nihil de eius morte populus consultus est, nulla quaestio decreta a senatu est.* Other sources on the collapse of Drusus' program and his fate in *MRR,* II.21-22. On the consulship of Philippus, see also Van Ooteghem, *Philippus,* 113-133.
[106] Vell. Pat. 2.15.1: *Mors Drusi iam pridem tumescens bellum excitavit Italicum.*

classes, and turned the Italian peninsula into a battlefield. It was not without reason that later authors saw the struggle over the courts as a prime element in Rome's agony and even as the precipitating cause of the *bellum Italicum.*[107]

[107] Cic. *De Off.* 2.75: *tantum Italicum bellum propter iudiciorum metum excitatum;* cf. Livy, *Per.* 71.

VIII. CIVIL WARS AND THE *CINNAE DOMINATIO*

In a war against her erstwhile allies, Rome faced as serious a challenge as any she had ever encountered before. Confronted by men who were as well trained, equipped, and experienced as Roman legionaries, the state saw its two-hundred-year hegemony over the peninsula in serious jeopardy. Yet politicians in the city were not convinced that unity was necessary or desirable. By 90 the political exploitation of national crises had become standard practice. The *bellum sociale* was no exception. Rome was shocked and unprepared for the conflagration that followed the death of Livius Drusus. A Roman commander with *imperium* was assassinated by Italians at Asculum, and a massacre of all Roman citizens in the town ensued.[1] It is not difficult to imagine the outrage in the capital; the moment was appropriate to conduct a search for scapegoats. The *quaestiones perpetuae* had been busy in the 90's; it was inevitable that they be once again utilized to crystallize public indignation.

Drusus' plan for Italian enfranchisement, it could be argued, had stirred the passions of the *socii,* who might otherwise have continued in their happy and tranquil state of inferiority. Similar claims can be heard today about "outside agitators" for Negro civil rights in the southern part of the United States. In the mouth of L. Philippus and in the circumstances of popular outrage, that argument might seem plausible. Drusus was dead, but Philippus and his *factio* could press charges against the surviving friends of the martyred tribune. If the process of venting patriotic wrath also effected the dissolution of the Metellan group that would not grieve L. Philippus or Q. Caepio.

The Italians were now rebels, faithless traitors, and assassins. Sympathy with Italian aims was naturally described by interested parties as disloyalty and treason. The *quaestio de maiestate* was available. But the enemies of Drusus and his faction were taking no chances on being caught up by the vagueness of the *maiestas* law. Antonius had shown

[1] Sources in *MRR,* II.20.

how it could cut both ways in the trial of Norbanus five years before. Hence a new measure was passed redefining *maiestas* by adopting an explicit clause that exposed the motives of its sponsors. The charge would apply directly to those *quorum ope consiliove socii contra populum Romanum arma sumpsissent*.[2] There were to be no mistakes this time; even the death penalty, it seems, was prescribed.[3] The man who was suborned to propose this new legislation was a tribune of obscure past and Spanish origin, but considerable persuasive talents. Q. Varius Hybrida may have been unkempt and repellent in appearance but even his detractors had to acknowledge his natural gifts.[4] No one could doubt against whom the *lex Varia* was directed. Q. Caepio stood behind Varius,[5] and both he and Philippus were prepared to capitalize on popular feelings in order to have before the bar the men who had been associated with Drusus and the Metellan *factio*. It could be expected also that the *equites* who still sat on the benches would remember Drusus' effort to cancel their judicial influence. War might rage in Italy, but internecine conflicts in the city proceeded unabated.

Passage of the *lex Varia* was no easy matter. Members of the tribunician college of 90 were on the hustings almost daily. The measure faced the veto of several of Varius' colleagues.[6] Four tribunes are known for that year apart from Varius himself.[7] Their allegiances can be conjectured and their identities reveal the sharp split in the state as reflected in the roster of tribunes. C. Papirius Carbo Arvina had good cause for resenting the Metellan *factio*. Three Papirii Carbones had suffered prosecution and conviction between 119 and 112 by men connected with the Metelli.[8] Bitterness continued in the following generation. A pre-

[2] Asconius, 22, Clark; cf. Val. Max. 8.6.4; Appian, *BC*, 1.37. That the measure was a *lex de maiestate* is affirmed by Cicero in Asconius, 79, Clark. On the nature of this law, see Gruen, *JRS,* 55 (1965), 59-60, with references to earlier literature. Seager, *"Lex Varia de Maiestate," Historia,* 16 (1967), 37-43, has now reverted to the older view that the *lex Varia* set up a *quaestio extraordinaria*. But his arguments are quite inadequate; the major objections to that thesis remain unaffected: the trials of Varius and Pompeius Strabo under the *lex Varia*.

[3] Cic. *De Nat. Deor.* 3.81.

[4] Cic. *De Orat.* 1.117: *Quis vestrum aequalem, Q. Varium, vastum hominem atque foedum, non intellegit illa ipsa facultate, quaecumque habet, magnam esse in civitate gratiam consecutum?* Cf. Cic. *Brutus,* 121. On Varius' origins, see Val. Max. 3.7.8, 8.6.4; Asconius, 22, Clark; [Cic.], *Anteq. in exsil. iret,* 27.

[5] Asconius, 22, Clark.

[6] Appian, *BC,* 1.37; Val. Max. 8.6.4. For the forensic activity of that year, see Cic. *Brutus,* 221, 305.

[7] *MRR,* II.26, 30-31, nn. 7-9.

[8] See above, pp. 107-109, 131-132.

served fragment of one of Carbo's tribunician speeches in 90 denounces the rashness of M. Drusus' program and charges it with having violated the sacred precepts of the Republic.[9] Carbo evidently lent his voice to the cause of Varius.[10] Another name may be added. Cn. Pomponius was a vigorous, noisy orator who was constantly at the rostra in that year with bitter, and often unintelligible, speeches. Cicero's descriptive phrase, *acer, acerbus, criminosus,* suggests that Pomponius engaged in prosecutions in 90, doubtless under the *lex Varia de maiestate;* no other courts were in operation.[11] He may be reckoned also as a supporter of the Varian measure. Two other tribunes stood on the opposite side. C. Scribonius Curio, we may be certain, interposed his veto. Varius' measure threatened him directly.[12] Tribunician immunity would protect Curio at least for the duration of the year, but it did not protect his father-in-law L. Memmius, who was convicted later in 90 under the Varian law.[13] Another veto, it can be surmised, was delivered by Q. Metellus Celer in the interests of his family, although his mediocre oratorical gifts may have kept him out of the center of the struggle.[14] More information is unavailable on the tribunician college. But there was an aedile in 90 who did his best to make matters difficult for Varius. C. Julius Caesar Strabo, it will be recalled, had inaugurated his forensic career in 104 with an attack on T. Albucius, an old enemy of the Metellan clique.[15] He was the stepbrother of Q. Catulus and a close friend of P. Sulpicius Rufus, both connected with the *factio.*[16] Strabo, an accomplished speaker and renowned wit, would not have been silent when Varius launched an attack on his group. Valerius Maximus transmits the revealing remark that the murder of Caesar Strabo in 87 was vengeance for the death of Q. Varius.[17] The air must have been filled with denunciations and counter-

[9] Cic. *Orator,* 213; *ORF,* 304: *tu dicere solebas sacram esse rem publicam . . . quicumque eam violavissent ab omnibus esse ei poenas persolutas . . . patris dictum sapiens temeritas fili comprobavit.* On Carbo's identity, see further Niccolini, *Fast. Trib. Pleb.,* 222-223; Münzer, *RE,* 36(2).1020-1021, "Papirius," n. 34; *MRR,* II.30, n. 8.

[10] A personal reconciliation with L. Crassus need not have affected Carbo's feelings toward the *factio* as a whole; Val. Max. 3.7.6; cf. Cic. *Verr.* 3.1.3.

[11] Cic. *Brutus,* 221; cf. 207, 305; *De Orat.* 3.50. For the suspension of other judicial activity, see Cic. *Brutus,* 304.

[12] Asconius, 74, Clark: *ex eis qui illa iudicia metuerant vigens tum maxime C. Curio.*

[13] Sisenna, fr. 44 (*HRR,* 1.283).

[14] Cicero damns him with faint praise: *non ille quidem orator, sed tamen non infans; Brutus,* 305.

[15] See above, p. 172.

[16] Cic. *De Orat.* 2.12, 2.16.

[17] Val. Max. 9.2.2. The epithets *consularis et censorii* are a confusion with C. Caesar Strabo's brother, L. Caesar; Carney, *RhM,* 105 (1962), 316, n. 75.

charges in that first year of the *bellum sociale*. Varius and his backers held the upper hand for the moment; the vetoes were overridden and the bill passed into law.

As expected, the defendants under the *lex Varia* were men who could be associated with Livius Drusus and the *factio* that had for so long been a prime force in the Roman senate. It was factional politics in the traditional sense. The victims in this new round of prosecutions need never have espoused Italian enfranchisement; a connection with Drusus or his group made them fair game for Philippus, Caepio, and Varius. Passions aroused by the war were made to serve political purposes, just as they had been during the Jugurthine conflict. Later writers could reflect on the situation and gauge it accurately: *cum multi Varia lege inique damnarentur, quasi id bellum illis auctoribus conflatum esset*.[18]

Prime target for the prosecutors was M. Aemilius Scaurus, the *princeps senatus*. Q. Caepio, his *vetus inimicus,* induced Varius to denounce him at a *contio* and then himself prosecuted him under the Varian law.[19] Philippus too sought to capitalize. He was conspicuous in the courtroom as witness for the prosecution in at least two trials before the *quaestio Variana,* the cases of Q. Pompeius Rufus and L. Memmius.[20] Pompeius' links with the Metellan group were close. Some would have remembered his espousal of the recall of Metellus Numidicus a decade before. An intimate friendship with Sulpicius Rufus is also on record. But more important, Pompeius was praetor in 91; it is a fair guess that he had helped to promote the schemes of Livius Drusus.[21] L. Memmius certainly did. He had been a *consiliarius* of Drusus in 91, perhaps a fellow-tribune. His son-in-law Curio escaped prosecution only through a tribunate in 90.[22] M. Antonius, the veteran orator, *consularis* and *censorius,* friend of Crassus, Rutilius, and Sulpicius, was another object of the *lex Varia*. Enemies of the dominant *factio* were not put off by the prestige of men like Scaurus and Antonius. The names of two other defendants have survived in the tradition. C. Aurelius Cotta was one, a young man of bright promise, who compensated for the lack of a strong voice by the sincerity, polish, and fluency of his speech. He had learned his oratory well, at the feet of L. Crassus; his talent is attested many times by Cicero. The links of Cotta's family with the Metelli require no further demonstra-

[18] Asconius, 73, Clark; cf. Appian, *BC,* 1.37.

[19] Asconius, 22, Clark; cf. Val. Max. 3.7.8; *Vir. Ill.* 72.11; *ORF,* 296.

[20] Cic. *Brutus,* 304.

[21] On the proposal to recall Numidicus, see Orosius, 5.17.11; the friendship with Sulpicius, Cic. *De Amicit.* 2.

[22] Sisenna, fr. 44 (*HRR,* I.284); cf. Appian, *BC,* 1.37. On Memmius, see T. P. Wiseman, "Lucius Memmius and his Family," *CQ,* 17 (1967), 164-167, not altogether persuasive.

tion. Nephew of Rutilius Rufus, close friend of Drusus and Sulpicius Rufus, Cotta was expected to carry the banner of the group in a tribunate of 90. Unfortunately, he was not elected and rendered himself vulnerable to *accusatio* before the Varian *quaestio*. The other was L. Calpurnius Bestia, a man closely linked with Aemilius Scaurus. It was Bestia or his father who had collaborated with Scaurus in Numidia in 111 and had been defended by the *princeps senatus* before the Mamilian court two years later. Such are the preserved names of the Varian victims, or would-be victims. The evidence is consistent. All show associations with the circle behind Livius Drusus, men who were being made scapegoats for a war they did not desire by a group who used the charged atmosphere for its political advantage.[23]

If Philippus and his friends expected to reap the harvest of equestrian resentment against the *factio* of Drusus, however, they were to suffer disappointment. Solidarity among the *equites* was not to be expected when their pocketbooks were unaffected. Indeed, it was a Roman *eques* who performed signal service for the Varian defendants. L. Aelius Stilo Praeconinus was a man of immense erudition, well trained in Latin and Greek literature and the history of Rome, a predecessor and model for Terentius Varro.[24] His activities confirm the continuity of the Metellan group. Stilo's friendship with Metellus Numidicus extended even to accompanying the latter into exile. His most conspicuous merits lay in the composition of speeches for others. Q. Metellus Celer made use of his talents, as did Q. Servilius Caepio, doubtless when Caepio was still part of the group. Aurelius Cotta and Q. Pompeius Rufus employed orations written by Stilo when they confronted the Varian *quaestio*.[25] The *equites* were not crazed with vengeance. To be sure, there were convictions; Cotta succumbed, as did Memmius and Bestia. But Scaurus was acquitted with little difficulty; and both Antonius and Q. Pompeius escaped unscathed. Equestrian *iudices* had demonstrated their independence before; they refused to be a vehicle for the implementation of politically inspired judicial measures.[26] By the time the year 89 opened

[23] On the trial of M. Antonius, see Cic. *Tusc. Disp.* 2.57; for Cotta's trial, see Appian, *BC,* 1.37; Cic. *Brutus,* 205, 305; *De Orat.* 3.11; [Cic.], *Anteq. in exsil. iret,* 27; on his personality and oratory, cf. esp. Cic. *Brutus,* 202, 317; the trial of Bestia is noted by Appian, *BC,* 1.37. For details on all the cases heard in the Varian court in 90, with further references, cf. Gruen, *JRS, 55* (1965), 62-68.

[24] Cic. *Brutus,* 205.

[25] On the association with Numidicus, see Suet. *De Gramm.* 2; on the ghost-writing, see Cic. *Brutus,* 169, 205-207.

[26] Appian's statement, *BC,* 1.37, that the *lex Varia* was an all-out equestrian attack on the senatorial oligarchy is clearly refuted by the facts.

219

it was clear that the tide had turned. The *lex Julia* had demonstrated Rome's willingness to conciliate Italian opinion and to extend her citizenship, at least to loyal *socii*.[27] Under a changed climate of opinion it was fruitless to attack men on the grounds of sympathy with the Italians. If the *equites* exacted vengeance at all it was against the man who had sought to make them his instruments in a factional contest. In 89 Varius himself was condemned under his own *maiestas* law, perhaps for *seditio* in his overriding of tribunician veto in the previous year.[28] The prosecutor is unknown, but evidence suggests C. Caesar Strabo, who was later associated with the demise of Varius.[29] Friends of the *factio* would have spared no venom in that trial. It was suggested, among other things, that Varius had been responsible for the deaths of Drusus and even Metellus Numidicus. Varius' allies, Philippus and Caepio, some men said, were also involved in the murder of Drusus. It was calumny and rumor, but effective. The *iudices Gracchani* condemned Q. Varius and the erstwhile tribune suffered execution.[30] There is little evidence for partisanship on the part of the *equester ordo* in these affairs.

Wars are expensive and money in Rome was tight. Only the revenues from the *ager Campanus* kept the Roman economy afloat during the Social War.[31] Storm clouds were beginning to gather once again in the east and for the business classes it was critical to protect the proceeds from the wealthy province of Asia. It is pertinent here to contrast the behavior of the *equites* in the political struggle within the senate with their actions on behalf of their own pocketbooks. While sitting as *iudices* under the *lex Varia,* they could afford to be non-partisan and judicious; they could expose political manipulation of the courts for what it was. They were not so circumspect when their own economic interests were at stake. In the midst of the Social War the Roman treasury was in a state of near exhaustion. Even the gods had to suffer, witnessing the sale of sacred property to bolster the *aerarium*. An inflationary readjustment of the coinage followed, a blow to Rome's creditor class.[32] And in

[27] Cic. *Pro Balbo,* 21; Appian, *BC,* 1.49; Vell. Pat. 2.16; Gellius, 4.4.3; cf. Brunt, *JRS,* 55 (1965), 95-96, 107.

[28] Lengle, *Unt. Sull. Verf.,* 35.

[29] Val. Max. 9.2.2: *ut Vario Caesar piaculo caderet.*

[30] Cic. *De Nat. Deor.* 3.81: *summo cruciatu supplicioque Q. Varius, homo importunissimus periit;* cf. *Brutus,* 305; Val. Max. 8.6.4. For rumors about Caepio and Philippus, see Pliny, *NH,* 28.148; *Vir. Ill.* 66.13.

[31] Cic. *De Leg. Agrar.* 2.80: *Italico bello amissis ceteris vectigalibus, quantos agri Campani fructibus exercitus alueritis?*

[32] For the state of the *aerarium,* see Orosius, 5.18.27: *cum penitus exhaustum esset aerarium et ad stipendium frumenti deesset expensa, loca publica . . . cogenti inopia vendita sunt.* On the *lex Plautia* that introduced the semiuncial *as,* see Pliny, *NH,* 33.46.

89, the *praetor urbanus,* A. Sempronius Asellio, cracked down further on the money lenders by reviving obsolete usury laws in the interests of the indebted. The latter class doubtless included many Roman senators, absentee landlords whose rural estates fell victim to the ravages of the *bellum sociale.* The *equites,* however, reacted vigorously and violently. Asellio was slain in cold blood, while in the midst of performing a sacrifice.[33]

Tensions and passions produced by these events had their repercussions on the judicial system. Equestrian control of the *iudicia* had frustrated the Metellan *factio* in the 90's, provoking in part the reform program of Drusus. Now the enemies of the *factio* knew the same frustration. *Equites* had acquitted the more prominent defendants under the *lex Varia.* From the point of view of the Roman aristocracy, the *iudices* had not been too partisan, but rather too impartial. Pressure in the senate for jury reform undoubtedly grew more intense and the murder of Asellio, reflecting discredit on the *equester ordo,* may have provided the plausible pretext for reform. The *lex Plautia* of 89 created a new system for the selection of jurors: fifteen were to be chosen by each tribe annually and the status of the candidates would be irrelevant. Since the senatorial class exercised wide control over voting power in the tribes, it was clear that equestrian influence in the courts would henceforth be minimal.[34] On the proposer, M. Plautius Silvanus, the sources are otherwise silent. But it is noteworthy that he also collaborated in that year with C. Papirius Carbo to pass a measure facilitating the enrollment of certain groups of Italians.[35] Hostility of the Carbones toward the Metellan *factio* has already been noted. The new judicial measure may well have been sponsored by the men who were disappointed in the failure of the *lex Varia* to achieve its political aims.

The Social War was a critical turning point in the history of the late Republic. Its effect on the judicial structure was only a minor part of the consequences. The war and the impact of the military were to alter profoundly and irreversibly the nature of Roman politics. The Marian army reforms of nearly two decades before had begun to fill the ranks with recruits of little or no property, men whose stake in the national enterprise weighed less than loyalty to individual leaders who could bring immediate benefits. Fighting in the Italian war, for which even freedmen were enrolled, brought the development of private armies significantly closer to fruition. The allies' revolt was dangerous and deadly, and the state was compelled to rely more heavily on individual commanders,

[33] Appian, *BC,* 1.54; Livy, *Per.* 74; Val. Max. 9.7.4.
[34] Asconius, 79, Clark.
[35] Cic. *Pro Arch.* 7; Schol. Bob. 175, Stangl; Vell. Pat. 2.17.1.

their personal retainers, and their loyal and avaricious troops. The client army was now in the making.[36]

Three Roman generals stand out in the war against the *socii;* their ventures were all to have political repercussions. C. Marius had not been successful in the intricate game of factional politics in the 90's. But war was another matter. When the *bellum Marsicum* broke out, the old soldier was reactivated. He proved to be Rome's most effective military leader in the campaigns of 90.[37] Many men with previous service and long memories would fight for Marius as for no one else. Not the least of his attractions was his influence among the *socii* themselves. Yet his command extended only to the end of the year 90. Enemies at home were not anxious to see Marius reassemble his clients and revive his political authority. The general also probably had his eye on bigger ventures. It would not do to compromise himself too far with Italians who might look to him again as a champion. And with the eastern situation deteriorating, he could anticipate a new Mithridatic war in which the business classes might find him once more their most reliable standard-bearer.[38]

In 89 the conduct of military operations was largely in the hands of two men, the consul Cn. Pompeius Strabo and the *legatus* L. Cornelius Sulla. Strabo's credentials were obvious and ominous. His services were principally in Picenum, his home territory and an area where he could recruit clients and retainers from his own estates and from those of his friends. He did not hesitate to reward alien soldiers by assigning citizenship under the *lex Julia* and to extend Latin franchise to the Transpadani on his own authority.[39] The government could see the immediate advantages of giving Strabo a free hand in the north to enroll loyal troops, but they did not foresee the consequences. Sulla, fighting with equal success in the south, also molded an army whose future became intimately tied to their *imperator*'s fortune. He knew how to win the attachment of the new breed of Roman soldiers. Lack of discipline went unpunished when the general's leniency might earn the gratitude of the troops.[40] Strabo and Sulla, no friends of one another and operating virtually as independent *imperatores,* were the men chiefly responsible for turning the mili-

[36] Cf. E. Valgiglio, *Silla e la Crisi Repubblicana* (Florence, 1956), 15-19; Badian, *For. Client.*, 228-229, 234.

[37] Sources in *MRR*, I.27, 29; cf. Van Ooteghem, *Marius,* 270-275.

[38] Plut., *Marius,* 33.3, says that Marius resigned his command voluntarily on account of ill health, not the most likely of explanations; cf. Passerini, *Athenaeum,* 12 (1934), 360-361; Valgiglio, *Silla,* 6; Carney, *A Biog. of Marius,* 52.

[39] *ILLRP,* II.28-34, no. 515; Asconius, 3, Clark; Pliny, *NH,* 3.138; see Gelzer, *Kleine Schriften,* II.109-121; Badian, *For. Client.*, 228-229.

[40] Plut. *Sulla,* 6.8-9; cf. Badian, *For. Client.*, 234.

tary tide in Rome's favor. The government earned credit by prudent extension of the franchise, but victory in the field made the reputations of the commanders. Marius, seeking renewed influence and prestige through more traditional channels, was not prepared to utilize military support to effect his aims. Pompeius Strabo and Sulla proved to be less scrupulous.

As has been noted over and again in this study, political and military crises provoke a reassessment of old alignments within the senatorial aristocracy. The Metellan *factio* had survived the attacks of the *lex Varia,* but it had not emerged unscathed. Recent years had witnessed the erosion of its leadership. The death of L. Crassus in 91 removed its most eloquent spokesman, and the death of M. Aemilius Scaurus, probably in 89, eliminated its most astute politician. Rutilius Rufus had been in exile, his public career at an end, since 92. M. Antonius was somewhat compromised through associations with Marius and had no further attested political influence after the Varian trial. What was worse, the bright young hopes of the new generation were in large part cut off. Q. Servilius Caepio had already abandoned the group in the mid 90's. Livius Drusus was slain in 91. C. Aurelius Cotta suffered conviction at the hands of the Varian *quaestio* and fled the country. P. Sulpicius Rufus, sensing the drift of the tide, was preparing to cast his fortune with Marius. The last three, all close friends and raised under the tutelage of L. Crassus, were slated for three consecutive tribunates in 91, 90, and 89.[41] By 88, the first was dead, the second in exile, and the third had abandoned the *factio*.

But the group was resilient and resourceful. It could bend with the winds of change blowing from the Social War. L. Cornelius Sulla emerged from that conflict with a devoted army and a powerful military reputation. It won him the consulship for 88. Ruthless ambition had marked his rise to the top; he had been willing to use the coattails of both C. Marius and Q. Catulus in the past to advance his own career. He had broken with Marius in no uncertain terms when it behooved him to stress his own exploits at the expense of his former commander. Similar motives did not apply to his relations with Catulus, and he seems to have found mutual advantage with some members of the Metellan group in the 90's when he was despatched to Asia, thus curtailing the ambitions of Marius.[42] Loyalty to faction was not a principal ingredient in Sulla's makeup, but there was mutual advantage again in 88. The

[41] Cic. *De Orat.* 1.25: *adolescentes duo, Drusi maxime familiares, et in quibus magnam tum spem maiores natu dignitatis suae collocarant, C. Cotta qui tum tribunatum plebis petebat, et P. Sulpicius, qui deinceps eum magistratum petiturus putabatur.*

[42] See above, pp. 196-198.

factio needed strong and conspicuous leadership to recover its fortunes; Sulla would not turn down access to the inner circles of the nobility. The death of Scaurus left Caecilia Metella an eminently eligible widow. She was married to Sulla in 89 or 88.[43] Sulla might have reminded many men of the deceased *princeps senatus*. They were both of patrician families that had long languished in obscurity, and they were both men who overcame initial economic handicaps by force of personality and immense natural ability. The bargain was sealed when Sulla's colleague in the consulship, Q. Pompeius Rufus, a successful defendant in the Varian trials, gave his son in marriage to the daughter of Sulla.[44] In this alliance, the *factio* of the Metelli demonstrated its astuteness, but also its weakness. Sulla was not a man to be readily absorbed into a group. He would mold his political allies as he had molded his army. The group that had in the past four decades gathered around men like Macedonicus, Numidicus, Scaurus, and Crassus had always been stronger in aggregate than any of its individual leaders. Henceforth, it would become in a very real sense the *factio* of Sulla.

In the year 88 Mithridates of Pontus overran the Roman province of Asia and massacred 80,000 Italians resident in the area.[45] The *publicani* and *negotiatores* had reaped the harvest of hostility aroused by a generation of avaricious Roman entrepreneurs. A major war in the east could no longer be postponed. The sharp political struggle that ensued revolved around the question of leadership in this coming conflict. A successful commander in the Mithridatic war, it could already be envisioned, would be in a position to write his own ticket upon return. Several candidates emerged. Marius was available and eager. To his mind and to others' it was the Jugurthine War all over again. Marius was twenty years older, but he had demonstrated his skill again in the Social War two years before, and the *equester ordo* might look to him once more. The position of the *equites* was vulnerable and growing worse; the *lex Plautia* had deprived them of control of the *quaestio de repetundis* and its effective protection of business interests abroad. The massacre by Mithridates had cut off lucrative revenues from Asia and had caused the collapse of credit in Rome.[46] For the *equites,* a successful war and a vigorous leader were not only desirable, but imperative. Marius, it is not unlikely, had been cultivating his old associations among the business classes during the year or so since the termination of his command in the

[43] Plut. *Sulla,* 6.10.

[44] Livy, *Per.* 77; Appian, *BC,* 1.56; Vell. Pat. 2.18.6; J. Carcopino, *Sylla ou la Monarchie Manquée* (Paris, 1931), 25-29.

[45] Sources in Greenidge and Clay, *Sources,* 168-169.

[46] Cf. Cic. *De Imp. Pomp.* 19.

Social War. There were troops ready to be recruited for a war under Marius, and there were *socii* who remembered his *beneficia* in the past. Even in the ranks of the senate he could find some support. The flirtation with the Metellan *factio* in the 90's had not been entirely in vain. Crassus was dead, Antonius had perhaps drifted away; but Q. Mucius Scaevola the augur, an aged elder statesman by 88, did not fear to express himself on Marius' behalf at a critical moment.[47] More important, Marius in 88 could count on a young and energetic refugee from the Metellan *factio,* the tribune P. Sulpicius Rufus. Sulpicius, as we have seen, had been one of the bright hopes of the new generation for the *factio.* As late as 90 he was still associated with the group and was even threatened by the *lex Varia.*[48] He deserted what may, at the time, have seemed a sinking ship. Optimate sources naturally brand Sulpicius with every kind of infamy and depict him as a greedy instrument in the hands of Marius.[49] The conversion was perhaps not as sudden or shocking as is sometimes portrayed. Marius had, after all, also had connections with Crassus and Antonius, friends and teachers of Sulpicius; and by 91, so Cicero would suggest, Sulpicius and Marius were already intimate and mutual admirers.[50] Sulpicius served as a *legatus* in the Social War, perhaps, one may surmise, with Marius.[51] Continued association with the general would have cost Sulpicius some old friends who could not stomach Marius, like C. Caesar Strabo and Q. Pompeius Rufus. Intimacy with both those men, shattered by 88, is on record.[52] Sulpicius had escaped prosecution under the *lex Varia,* perhaps already a sign of new political allegiances; his close friend C. Aurelius Cotta had not escaped and was now in exile. When Marius aimed for the Mithridatic command, Sulpicius was in his corner.

Sulpicius Rufus was a useful ally: a fluent and persuasive public speaker, well trained by L. Crassus, utilizing to the fullest voice, gesture, and dramatic movement.[53] He also did not scruple to employ armed

[47] Val. Max. 3.8.5: *nunquam tamen efficies ut, propter exiguum senilemque sanguinem meum, Marium, a quo Urbs et Italia conservata est, hostem iudicem.*

[48] Cic. *De Orat.* 3.11; further on Sulpicius' connections, see Münzer, *RE,* 7(2).843-846, "Sulpicius," n. 92; Schur, *Zeit. Marius u. Sulla,* 127-129; Gruen, *JRS,* 55 (1965), 72.

[49] Plut. *Sulla,* 8.1; *Marius,* 35.1; Appian, *BC,* 1.55; Vell. Pat. 2.18.5-6.

[50] Cic. *De Orat.* 1.66: *Ita si de re militari dicendum huic erit Sulpicio, quaeret a C. Mario affini nostro, et, cum acceperit, ita pronuntiabit, ut ipsi C. Mario paene hic melius, quam ipse, illa scire videatur.*

[51] Cic. *Brutus,* 304.

[52] For Strabo, see Cic. *De Orat.* 2.16; *De Amicit.* 2.

[53] Cic. *Brutus,* 203.

bands of men, *equites* it should be noted, as a bodyguard to precipitate or to counter violence in the streets in that chaotic year of 88.[54] Politics need not be the only element inspiring the actions of Sulpicius. He had witnessed the assassination of his friend Livius Drusus, who had attempted to grant long overdue *beneficia* to the Italians. Now, with the Social War over and the *socii* enfranchised, he saw the oligarchy attempting to salvage their control of voting power by restricting the new citizens to a small number of tribes.[55] Opposition to this gerrymandering would also have put Sulpicius on common ground with Marius, who was anxious to solidify his support among the ex-*socii*. It was a formidable coalition of *equites* and new citizens headed by a volatile tribune and the old soldier. A Mithridatic command would add military force and perhaps presage *dominatio*.

The faction on which Sulpicius Rufus had turned his back had now tied its fortunes to the star of L. Sulla. If Mithridatic war there must be, Sulla was the appropriate and logical choice. The senate duly conferred upon him the *provincia* of Asia and leadership in the campaign against the king of Pontus. Not everyone in the old Metellan group would have concurred in that decision. The Social War scrambled loyalties and placed a premium on ambitious adventurers. C. Caesar Strabo had once sat with Sulpicius Rufus at the feet of L. Crassus. But matters had changed. Caesar Strabo (so it seems) had recently put himself in the public spotlight with a successful prosecution of Q. Varius. He had not yet held even the praetorship, but a war with Mithridates required a consul. In 88 Strabo stood for the highest magistracy in opposition to Marius. The event demonstrated how the Social War had introduced violence and chaos into Roman political life. Sulpicius opposed the illegal candidature of his old friend in the interests of Marius, but with the equally illegal tactics of force.[56] As for the Mithridatic command, Sulpicius would secure it in advance by browbeating the assembly into transferring that prize from Sulla to Marius.[57] The sequel is well known and requires no delineation here. While Marius was attempting to reassemble a coalition along the lines of that he had once led in 104-101, Sulla forsook political maneuvering and resorted to force. He had

---

[54] Plut. *Sulla*, 8.2; *Marius*, 35.2; Appian, *BC*, 55-56.

[55] Appian, *BC*, 1.49; Vell. Pat. 2.20; Gran. Licin. 21, Flemisch; cf. Taylor, *Voting Districts*, 101-103.

[56] Diod. 37.2.12; Cic. *De Har. Resp.* 43; *Brutus*, 226; Asconius, 25, Clark; Quintilian, 6.3.75; see Gruen, *JRS*, 55 (1965), 72; cf. R. E. Smith, "The Anatomy of Force in Late Republican Politics," *Ancient Society and Institutions; Studies to Ehrenburg* (Oxford, 1966), 265, 272.

[57] Sources in *MRR*, II.40-41.

absorbed the proper lessons of the *bellum Marsicum;* a devoted soldiery heeded his call to march on the capital and enforced his claims by repealing Sulpicius' legislation at the point of a spear.[58]

The political group that had led the assault on Drusus and his backers in 91 and 90 is not conspicuous in 88. Q. Caepio had been killed in action during the Social War and the trial and execution of Varius was a further blow. L. Philippus was an accomplished politician, but it was clear that this new era required military men and leadership that was not cut from the traditional mold. Such leadership was perhaps available. In north Italy, Cn. Pompeius Strabo held forth with baronial power and a dedicated army of clients and retainers that had not been demobilized, though the fighting had ceased. Extension of franchise and Latin rights widened his following. A hint survives of a connection with Philippus,[59] and a son of Philippus (so it appears) served on the staff of Pompeius Strabo in 89.[60] Certainly Strabo was no friend of the faction that backed Livius Drusus; he may well have found common ground with Philippus in 91.[61] But "party" loyalty was never a prime consideration with Strabo. He had not scrupled to inaugurate his political career by applying for a chance to prosecute his own commander a decade and a half before.[62] He was now acting out an independent role, prepared to bargain but not to yield the source of his power, a loyal army and a base of operations. Sulla, a man of similar instincts, could recognize the danger. He despatched his *adfinis* and colleague Q. Pompeius Rufus to assume command of the forces under Strabo's direction in Picenum. The act was futile and disastrous. If Sulla could march a Roman army on Rome, Strabo could hardly be expected to submit meekly as if the Republic were functioning normally. Pompeius Rufus was slain by Strabo's troops. Strabo could feign innocence and regret; he could also resume unchallenged control of the forces.[63] There was one final effort to deal with the recalcitrant *imperator.* Pompeius Strabo was indicted for *maiestas.* But, under the circumstances, what meaning could judicial procedures have had? That

---

[58] *MRR,* II.40. It is distressing to see the latest scholarly pronouncement on Sulla's march repeating tendentious propaganda: the act of Sulla was "nur eine Polizeiaktion gegen den *seditiosus tribunus* und dessen *factio";* Meier, *Res Pub.,* 224. Meier's analysis of Sulpicius Rufus is singularly unsatisfactory. After having set up *equites* and *socii* as polarized enemies in 91, he must now make them suddenly and inexplicably coalesce in support of Sulpicius; *Res Pub.,* 210, 212, 216-221; cf. 83.

[59] Plut. *Pomp.* 2.2.

[60] *ILLRP,* II.32, no. 515; cf. Cichorius, *Röm. Stud.,* 168-169.

[61] Plut. *Pomp.* 37.4; cf. Gruen, *JRS,* 55 (1965), 70.

[62] See above, p. 172.

[63] Appian, *BC,* 1.63; Livy, *Per.* 77; Val. Max. 9.7.ex.2; Vell. Pat, 2.20.1.

there was formal acquittal is nowhere recorded, but Strabo was once more in full command of his troops in 87.[64]

In a period of revolution and civil war, normal judicial processes are out of place. After Sulla's march on Rome in 88, twelve of his leading enemies were exiled, some of them killed. The names are suggestive; ten are known, and at least five of those are of non-Roman origin. Marius had done his work well with the *socii*. But there were also some aristocratic names in the Marian entourage: besides Sulpicius Rufus, a Junius Brutus, a Cornelius Cethegus, a Laetorius.[65] Sulla had had to act swiftly to dissolve a growing coalition. To assess the action in legal terms would be superfluous and meaningless. Sulpicius was slain, betrayed by a slave; for the rest, precipitate flight forestalled formal trials, if such were contemplated, which is unlikely. Voluntary exile in the course of or prior to a prosecution would normally be hardened into outlawing by the populace: the *aquae et ignis interdictio*. One source suggests that a *lex* did legitimize the proceedings.[66] That is not to be believed; Sulla would hardly have bothered. All the other testimony is unanimous; senatorial action was the sole justification for this expulsion and murder.[67] Men could still harbor the exiles with impunity and later rhetorical exercises dwelled on the questionable validity of Sulpicius' slaying. Q. Scaevola pronounced an unequivocal verdict on the illegality of senatorial proceedings intimidated by force of arms. The most that Sulla had succeeded or troubled to obtain was a *senatus consultum ultimum*. The triumphant *imperator* could dispense with legal formalities.[68]

The march on Rome against men unarmed and unprepared left Sulla master of the city, but at no small cost. The aristocracy could hardly accept such an act with equanimity. All of Sulla's officers, with one exception, deserted him rather than partake in a military occupation of

[64] *MRR*, II.48-49; on the trial see Asconius, 79, Clark; for its date and background, Gruen, *JRS*, 55 (1965), 70-71.

[65] For the names, see Appian, *BC*, 1.60; Cic. *Brutus*, 168; cf. E. Pais, "I dodici romani fatti dichiarare publici nemici da Silla nell' 88 a.c.," *Atti Accad. Napoli*, 4 (1916), 65-72; Gabba, *Athenaeum*, 29 (1951), 258-259; corrected by Badian, *Studies*, 59-60; also Carney, "The Flight and Exile of Marius," *Greece and Rome*, 8 (1961), 101. That most of these individuals represented equestrian interests (Meier, *Res. Pub.*, 218) is not susceptible of proof.

[66] Vell. Pat. 2.19.1: *urbe exturbavit ac lege lata exules fecit.*

[67] Livy, *Per.* 77: *duodecim a senatu hostes . . . iudicati sunt;* Appian, *BC*, 1.60; Cic. *Brutus*, 168; Plut. *Sulla*, 10; Val. Max. 3.8.5; Florus, 2.8. For further sources on these events, see *MRR*, II.40.

[68] For Scaevola's statement, see Val. Max. 3.8.5; the harboring of the exiles, Cic. *Verr.* 2.2.113; *Pro Planc.* 26; the rhetorical exercise, *Ad Herenn.* 1.15.25; cf. Carney, "Cicero's Picture of Marius," *WS*, 73 (1960), 112; *RhM*, 105 (1962), 323, n. 79.

the *res publica*. Sulla was no Aemilius Scaurus; the men who had linked themselves to him began to reconsider that decision. His action, Plutarch says, aroused the private hostility of the senate. That is conjecture, but reasonable conjecture. Sulla stood idly by while his *adfinis* Q. Pompeius Rufus was murdered by the troops of Pompeius Strabo and while the latter secured acquittal on a *maiestas* charge or, perhaps, even ignored the verdict of the court with impunity. Sulla was not even able, or willing, to control the consular elections for 87. One of the successful candidates was L. Cornelius Cinna, who bursts onto the stage of Roman history with no prior warning from our sources. Almost nothing is preserved of his background and previous career; a father in the consulship, perhaps, and service in the Social War form the extent of our information. Of previous association with Sulpicius Rufus or the Marians there is no sign and little likelihood; Cinna had not been named in the *senatus consultum* that authorized a witch-hunt of Sulla's *inimici*. But his election in 88 was doubtless unwelcome to Sulla. It is further evidence of the resentment stirred by that unprecedented march on Rome. The Mithridatic war beckoned, however, and Sulla was not prepared to trouble with domestic nuisances at this point; he could wait for a later time when no one would be in a position to offer challenge.[69]

Cinna was swift to take advantage of that atmosphere of resentment. The inception of his consulship witnessed an immediate recourse to the judiciary. Cinna induced a tribune, M. Vergilius, to indict Sulla before the people.[70] The charge is unrecorded, but conjecture is not difficult. It no doubt concerned the slaying of Sulpicius and the unauthorized hunting down of the Mariani. There was legislation on the books to cover precisely this kind of action: the *lex Sempronia* of 123. The charge against Sulla forms a close parallel to that brought against Popillius Laenas in 123.[71] Under the circumstances, however, the proceedings seem curiously obsolete and archaic. Sulla, we are told, ignored both prosecutor and prosecution and stalked off to the east. That Cinna's

---

[69] For the desertion of Sulla's officers, see Appian, *BC,* 1.57. Plutarch reports the secret distaste of the oligarchy for Sulla's action; *Sulla,* 10.2: ἐφ' οἷς ὁ Σύλλας τὴν μὲν σύγκλητον ἀδήλως ἠνίασεν. On Cinna's service in the Social War, see Cic. *Pro Font.* 43; Livy, *Per.* 76. Sulla, it is said, extracted from him a pledge of good behavior before the consular elections; Plut. *Sulla,* 10.3-4; Dio, fr. 102; Schol. Gronov. 286, Stangl; cf. H. Bennett, *Cinna and His Times* (Menasha, 1923), 3-6; Meier, *Res Pub.,* 226. That, however, is probably later propaganda, designed to brand Cinna as a turncoat; C. Lanzani, *Mario e Silla* (Catania, 1915), 5-6; Carney, *A Biog. of Marius,* 60; cf. Gabba, *App. BC Lib. Prim.,* 181.

[70] Cic. *Brutus,* 179: *M. Vergilius, qui tribunus plebis L. Sullae imperatori diem dixit;* Plut. *Sulla,* 10.4. Plutarch's Οὐεργίνιον is, apparently, an error for *Vergilius.*

[71] So Pareti, *Storia di Roma,* III.564; Carney, *A Biog. of Marius,* 56, 58.

purpose here was to drive Sulla out of Italy is an oft-repeated conjecture.[72] Whatever Cinna's intent, indictment was superfluous. Sulla was going anyway. The eastern war had been uppermost in his mind from the beginning; he would have been there already had it not been for the troubles stirred by Sulpicius and the transfer of command to Marius. Sulla's contemptuous gesture is eloquent testimony to the meaninglessness of standard judicial procedures in a time of violence.

It is not the purpose of this study to recount the grim and brutal events of 87. The deposition of a consul, civil war, and the forceful imposition of a new regime were hardly conducive to moderation or constitutionalism. The relentless ambition of Sulla drove him to the east and to further military glory. Unsettled matters were left behind, over which lesser men could quarrel and destroy themselves. The implementation of Italian enfranchisement was the overriding issue. Around it petty jealousies, greed, and vengeance were played out. Few now seemed to question the legitimacy of force as a means of settling political disputes. There was little room for traditional senatorial politics or the cumbersome techniques of the criminal courts. C. Marius was among the last to abandon the old paths, but his consistent need to be accepted by the establishment finally collapsed when there seemed no longer to be a discernible establishment. Marius and Cinna professed no love for one another; combination, however, promised success and they found common enemies in the men who had hoped to keep Sulla's place warm while he toiled abroad.[73] The two men could muster a mighty following of frustrated *socii,* disgruntled *equites,* and those who had been alienated irrevocably by the actions of Sulla. With him out of the country, there were no military men who could match the talents of Marius and no politician who could gather the backing that Cinna and Marius championed as self-styled martyrs in the cause of republicanism and of a united Italy. Only one man might offer a challenge, but Pompeius Strabo, after intrigues on all sides, a man "hateful to gods and the nobility," was carried off by the plague. Cinna could reclaim the chief magistracy, and Marius, aged and duly bedraggled, at last achieved his seventh consulship, fulfilling that grand destiny long heralded by the gods.[74]

[72] Lanzani, *Mario e Silla,* 7; Bennett, *Cinna,* 6-7; Carney, *Greece and Rome,* 8 (1961), 116.

[73] That the combination of Marius and Cinna was a marriage of convenience is clear from Plut. *Sert.* 5.1-2.

[74] For the events of 87, see Lanzani, *Mario e Silla,* 15-145; Bennett, *Cinna,* 6-37; Van Ooteghem, *Marius,* 303-320. On the role played by Pompeius Strabo, see esp. Gelzer, *Kleine Schriften,* II.121-125. For the flight and exile of Marius, see Valgiglio, *Plutarco, Vita di Mario,* 162-190; Carney, *Greece and Rome,* 8 (1961), 98-121; Van Ooteghem, *Marius,* 288-302.

CIVIL WARS AND THE *CINNAE DOMINATIO*

The victory of Cinna and Marius in late 87 issued, so later writers report, in a bloodbath. Anti-Marian bias, however, is discernible; so also is exaggeration and sensationalism in the sources. "Revisionist" historians take pride in readjusting a proper equilibrium: the "massacres" were not really massacres; "only" fourteen men are known to have been executed in the last days of 87.[75] Does that amount to some twisted form of exculpation? Such revisionism can strain patience. The victims included men of stature, experience, and reputation, men with records of lengthy service to the state. Among them were six consulars, Q. Catulus, M. Antonius, P. Crassus, L. Julius Caesar, Cn. Octavius, and L. Cornelius Merula. That Marius was crazed with drunkenness, obsessed by the spilling of blood, and on the verge of insanity may be sheer romance. But the seventy-year-old general had suffered grievous humiliation, and it was only desperate resourcefulness that had enabled him to escape death. One could hardly expect to talk to Marius of clemency. His career since 100 had often promoted bright hopes but had known only frustration. Harrowing flight and exile bred an intelligible urge for vengeance. Cinna too had *dignitas* to defend and personal outrage to avenge. No Roman consul had ever before been deposed from office, much less seen his franchise stripped away by senatorial fiat. Other returned exiles or unscrupulous profiteers could utilize the occasion as well to settle vendettas and hunt down *inimici* like common criminals.

Responsibility for the murders is difficult to fix and conjecture generally unrewarding. Ancient testimony is hopelessly confused and contradictory on Cinna, Marius, and their subordinates. Excesses like looting, rape, and indiscriminate killing by slaves were checked by Cinna; but several of those victims whose names are sufficiently prominent to have been preserved are identifiable as enemies of the victors. There is no evidence that either Cinna or Marius displayed much moderation.[76] Execution was much to be preferred to exile; the banished might fly to the east and swell the following of Sulla. Cn. Octavius had deposed Cinna; L. Merula had replaced him. Cinna had an obvious personal stake in the elimination of those men. The actual murderer of Octavius was C. Marcius Censorinus, who had appeared once in history before — as the prosecutor of Sulla in 95. Now he proudly bore the severed head of Octavius to Cinna, for public display. Q. Catulus had once shared a

---

[75] See Lanzani, *Mario e Silla,* 120-145; Bennett, *Cinna,* 21-35; Carney, *A Biog. of Marius,* 66.

[76] Reference to the sources in *MRR,* II.46. Bennett, *Cinna,* 30-35, and Lanzani, *Mario e Silla,* 120-135, are doubtless right in not assigning sole responsibility to Cinna or Marius or both. Personal grudges and political *inimicitiae* were alike indulged.

triumph over the barbarians with Marius. Pride and ambition, however, had persuaded him to claim chief responsibility for those victories. In this instance, the sources are unanimous; Marius bears sole responsibility for the execution of Catulus. His death cost Rome a man of literature as well as of politics. Worse still was the loss of M. Antonius, a public career closed after thirty years of conspicuous service in the forum and at the bar. The identity of the man responsible for that deed may not be beyond conjecture. Cn. Papirius Carbo was among the Marian leaders in the 80's. He would have remembered that Antonius had successfully prosecuted his father a quarter of a century before, in a trial that resulted in the defendant's suicide. Carbo, a chance remark informs us, had also been an *inimicus* of another great orator, L. Crassus. Crassus, mercifully, had perished of natural causes in 91. But an *adfinis*, P. Crassus, pursued by assassins, witnessed the death of his son and took his own life in late 87. Two Julii Caesares, brothers, also fell in this slaughter. One, L. Caesar, was the former consul of 90 and author of the statesmanlike enfranchisement measure of that year. The other was C. Caesar Strabo, orator, wit, and mercurial politician. Marius was in no mood to forgive the man who had challenged him for the Mithridatic command in the previous year. A Q. Ancharius came to plead for mercy to Marius personally and was slain in cold blood before his eyes. Remaining victims are only names to us. If more were known, connections and motives for murder might be isolated. C. Flavius Fimbria, for example, was preeminent among the assassins. His father had been consul with Marius in 104 and had clashed in the law courts with M. Scaurus. Who can tell what private grievances and bitter memories drove him to butchery in 87? Many suppressed enmities, indiscernible now, must have found grim outlet in that year.[77]

Two cases seem to afford a contrast with these lawless assassinations. Formal charges apparently were brought against Q. Catulus and L.

---

[77] Sources in *MRR*, II.46. On Censorinus, see above, p. 198; on the trial of the elder Carbo, cf. Lanzani, *Mario e Silla*, 135-136; for Carbo's *inimicitia* with Crassus, see Cic. *De Leg*. 3.42. It has been argued that some of the victims were former friends of Marius who had betrayed him; Badian, *Studies*, 39, 46, 54. But the evidence does not always hold up; cf. C. Bulst, "Cinnanum Tempus," *Historia*, 13 (1964), 313-318. To get behind the sources is here particularly difficult. Appian and Plutarch stress the role of Marius, whereas Cicero regards Cinna as the moving partner throughout; see Carney, *WS*, 73 (1960), 115-118; *A Biog. of Marius*, 66-67. On the breakdown of constitutional practices, cf. Valgiglio, *Silla*, 31-32; *Plutarco, Vita di Mario*, 200-209. A response of the *haruspices* regarding *oratores interfectos* may also be a reference to these turbulent events; Cic. *Har. Resp*. 34; cf. M. van den Bruwaene, "Quelques Eclaircissments sur le *De Haruspicum Responsis*," *AntCl*, 17 (1948), 81-92.

Merula.[78] Some scholars profess to take seriously the procedures described in those instances. Merula was cloaked with priestly office; perhaps his enemies feared divine retribution. Possibly the moderating hand of Cinna is discernible. Some even claim that Octavius would have been spared for judicial hearing, had he not been cut down in the heat of passion at the outset of the massacre.[79] All this ascribes too much to those who were exacting bitter revenge. Merula's being a *flamen* only made his offense all the more grievous in the eyes of his enemies. No such heavenly aura surrounded Catulus, whose case is linked closely with that of Merula. Cinna's "moderation" is nowhere in evidence here. The responsibility for Catulus' death is, in any event, ascribed unanimously to Marius alone, even by Cicero.[80] As for Octavius, when Censorinus brought his head to Cinna he received no reprimand.[81] Another suggestion is probably closer to the mark; the trials of Merula and Catulus resulted from a lack of unanimity on their fate in the council of Marian leaders.[82] Correct forms seem to have been observed. Appian plainly reports the triple *anquisitio* and the *iudicium populi* of a tribunician prosecution before the people. Other evidence serves as confirmation and we know even the name of the prosecutor of Catulus, M. Marius Gratidianus, nephew by birth and adoption of C. Marius. The charge, if formal charge there was, must have been *perduellio*.[83] But it would be rash to make much of this from a legal or constitutional point of view. Condemnation was obviously inevitable. A last-minute appeal to Marius by the friends of Catulus was to no avail. Both Catulus and Merula committed suicide before the delivery of the verdict.[84] The judgment of Appian is cynical and plausible: the trials were a mere screen of sham legality. Other sources regard these cases as no different from those of

[78] Appian, *BC*, 1.74; Diod. 38.4; Schol. Bern on Lucan, 2.173.

[79] Lanzani, *Mario e Silla*, 138-142; Badian, *Studies*, 69, n. 176, 222.

[80] Cic. *Tusc. Disp.* 5.51; *De Nat. Deor.* 3.80; Appian, *BC*, 1.74; Plut. *Marius*, 44.5; Diod. 38.4.

[81] Appian, *BC*, 1.71.

[82] Bennett, *Cinna*, 27-28; see also Carney, *RhM*, 105 (1962), 325-328.

[83] Appian, *BC*, 1.74: τετράκις δὲ ἐχρῆν κηρυττομένους ἐν ὡρισμένοις ὡρῶν διαστήμασιν ἁλῶναι. Cf. also Diod. 38.4. The prosecuting tribune is given by Schol. Bern. on Lucan, 2.173. On the charge and trial, see E. G. Hardy, *Some Problems in Roman History* (Oxford, 1924), 27; Brecht, *MünchBeitr*, 29 (1938), 301.

[84] The fullest account is in Appian, *BC*, 1.74, who maintains that Merula was attacked simply because he had succeeded Cinna in his consulship, and Catulus because he had been ungrateful to Marius. The suicides of both men are mentioned by Florus, 2.9.16; Vell. Pat. 2.22; and Aug. *Civ. Dei*, 3.27. The attack on Catulus and his death are also recorded by Plut. *Marius*, 44.5; Diod. 38.4; Cic. *De Orat.* 3.9; *Tusc. Disp.* 5.56; *De Nat. Deor.* 3.80; and Schol. Bern. on Lucan, 2.173. Merula's suicide is given by Val. Max. 9.12.5.

the men cut down in the streets without trial.[85] So they seemed in retrospect, and there is no need to quarrel with that estimate. Such procedures were hardly a revival of standard juridical process. It was at this time that Sulla was declared an enemy of the state. Also about this time a tribune indicted the Sullan officer Ap. Claudius Pulcher who, it appears, had already departed when Cinna had wooed his army from him earlier in the year. Claudius now had his *imperium* abrogated and was presumably interdicted.[86] That a formal trial took place may be doubted. It is only an incidental reference that informs us of Claudius' *damnatio;* perhaps others among Sulla's officers were similarly banished. These bare vestiges of judicial practice were no more than facades for revolutionary vengeance.[87]

The same fervor, again screened by a thin veneer of legality, appears in the events of early 86. The tribunes of 87 who had shown no sympathy with the Marian cause remained unmolested until their year of office came to a close. After this show of deference to constitutionality, customary legal machinery was foregone. Some antiquarian dredged up the long obsolete practice of hurling offenders from the Tarpeian rock and the tribune P. Popillius Laenas performed the ancient rite. The unhappy victim was a Sex. Lucilius, tribune in the previous year. Others participated in this grim execution; the younger Marius, a strain of cruelty emerging early in his career, may have assisted, and Marius himself seems to have given his blessing, so celebrating the inauguration of his seventh consulship.[88] This form of tribunician *coercitio,* bypassing legal procedure and *provocatio,* was not unprecedented. The early Republic had seen its use, but, apart from a threat in 131, that archaic practice

[85] Appian, *BC,* 1.74: ὑπόκρισιν ἀρχῆς ἐννόμου. This is the implication also of Plutarch, Florus, Velleius, Valerius, and even Cicero; see previous note.

[86] For the outlawry of Sulla, see Appian, *BC,* 1.73, 1.77; *Mithr.* 51; Eutrop. 5.7.3. That the government was willing to negotiate with Sulla later does not obviate this action; cf. Memnon, fr. 24; *FGH,* III B, no. 434. For Ap. Claudius, see Cic. *De Domo,* 83: *patrem tuum . . . qui, cum de eo tribunus plebis promulgasset, adesse propter iniquitatem illius Cinnani temporis noluit, eique imperium est abrogatum.* Claudius, the praetor of 89, had been in charge of a Sullan legion at Nola in 87, only to have it snatched from him by Cinna; Livy, *Per.* 79; cf. Vell. Pat., 2.20.4, and Appian, *BC,* 1.65, neither of whom gives the name. Claudius' whereabouts thereafter are unknown. He would not have remained in Italy.

[87] The author of the *Ad Herennium* hypothesizes a trial of Sulpicius Rufus' slayer; 1.15.25. That this has reference to an actual event is doubtful.

[88] For Popillius, see Vell. Pat. 2.24.2; for the action of the younger Marius, see Dio, fr. 102.12; the acquiescence of Marius appears in Livy, *Per.* 80, and Plut. *Marius,* 45.1. The name Sex. Lucilius is given by Velleius. The Livian Epitomator has Sex. Lucinius, and Plutarch gives Sex. Lucinus. All, of course, refer to the same individual; cf. Niccolini, *Fast. Trib. Pleb.,* 235-236.

had fallen into desuetude with the development of more sophisticated legal mechanisms.[89] Other tribunes and, apparently, two praetors had fled to Sulla and were now interdicted. No hint survives of formal proceedings in those instances.[90] If there was any retention of legal forms, it can only have been a mockery of the traditional institutions.

Marius perished, probably of pneumonia, in January of 86. An incident at his funeral pointed dramatically to the chaotic state of affairs in the courts. C. Flavius Fimbria's hands were already soaked with the blood of L. Caesar and P. Crassus. He now arranged for the murder of the distinguished consul of 95, Q. Mucius Scaevola, jurist, statesman, *pontifex maximus,* and author of the model provincial code of Asia that had brought equestrian vengeance on his friend Rutilius. That Scaevola had hitherto been spared may be ascribed to his *adfinitas* with Marius. That relationship, unlike so many others, had survived civil war and recrimination. The elder Scaevola, consul in 117, had openly defended Marian interests against the Sullani in 88 and 87. It is no coincidence that an attack on the consul of 95 came immediately after the protective hand of Marius was removed.[91] The attempt of Fimbria miscarried. When he learned that Scaevola had sustained only a wound, he undertook a prosecution of that individual before the people. Men inquired what possible charge could be brought against Scaevola. Fimbria had a reply: "He is charged with not having received the weapon full length into his body." [92] The story may be, in part, apocryphal, but Fimbria's reported comment is a neat and eloquent summation of the judicial circumstances. Charges no longer mattered. One did not even require tribunes to bring an action before the assembly. Judicial decisions were at the mercy of the victorious Mariani. The "trial," so far as is known, never came to fruition. Not that Fimbria suddenly developed legal scruples; he simply had more pressing matters — service in the east.[93] So much for the traditions of due process and equity.

[89] For the case in 131, see Livy, *Per.* 59; Pliny, *NH,* 7.143. For the practice in the early Republic, see Mommsen, *Strafrecht,* 931-932; Strachan-Davidson, *Problems,* I.13-14, 41-42.

[90] Vell. Pat. 2.24.2; Dio, fr. 102.12.

[91] Cf. Bennett, *Cinna,* 39; Carney, *WS,* 73 (1960), 116-117. For the actions of Scaevola, consul in 117, see Val. Max. 3.8.5; Plut. *Marius,* 35.6; cf. Carney, *RhM,* 105 (1962), 328-329.

[92] Cic. *Pro Rosc. Amer.* 33; followed by Val. Max. 9.11.2.

[93] Cf. Lanzani, *Mario e Silla,* 168-169. Bennett, *Cinna,* 39-40, suggests that Fimbria was tribune in 86 and could claim constitutional authority by alleging interference with his official prerogatives. But that scholar here goes too far in trying to place a legal veneer on the regime. Fimbria was no tribune; he was despatched as legate to L. Valerius Flaccus in that year; *MRR,* II.56. The sending of a tribune on a military command would indeed have been a constitutional breakdown.

It is noteworthy that amidst the numerous references to tumultuous and irregular trials in 87 and 86, there is not the slightest mention of the *quaestiones*. One might suppose that they were suspended, as in 90. More likely, they were simply bypassed. The people sitting in assembly was to exercise its sovereign authority directly in a period of revolution. The conjecture that Cinna repealed the *lex Plautia* and transferred the courts entirely to the *equites* is without foundation and superfluous. He obviously did not have to take the trouble. Can it be accident that, apart from the case of Pompey in 86, to be discussed below, not a single criminal trial is recorded between the death of Marius and the prosecution of Sex. Roscius in 80? Cicero, who remembered the period well, reports that the three years of Cinna's ascendancy formed an era of peace and tranquillity. But there was a darker side, which he also recalled; the tranquillity was reinforced by the fact that the former leaders of the bar were either dead or in exile.[94] Cicero mentions just six orators of whose activities he knows anything for the mid 80's. Of these, three were involved in the trial of Pompey. Evidently, there were not many other cases of significance in those years. This striking absence of criminal trials, unparalleled since the pre-Gracchan era, indicates that political prosecutions were at a minimum after the death of Marius. But it is well not to obscure the other side of that coin. Lack of activity at the bar, long the heart of Roman politics, should arouse suspicion that tranquillity did not come easily. It was presumably an enforced policy of the regime.[95]

The composition and attitude of that regime and of its enemies warrant scrutiny. Sulla's march on Rome in 88, followed by the brutal civil war of 87, had severely shaken political allegiances and had made most of the old alignments obsolete. Many in the aristocracy had found a proconsul's march against the city intolerable. Only one officer had remained with Sulla; others gave him a chilly reception in Rome. When Sulla took his forces to Asia, each man had to make his own decision. The Metellan alliance was split irrevocably; many brothers and cousins found themselves on opposite sides. To serve with Sulla was to make a political decision; it was to legitimize his actions and to endorse his position. Nonetheless Sulla could claim some illustrious names on his staff in Asia. Patrician families were represented there, as might be expected in the service of a Cornelius, even if it involved condoning revolu-

---

[94] Cic. *Brutus,* 308: *Triennium fere fuit urbs sine armis, sed oratorum aut interitu aut discessu aut fuga.*

[95] The absence of prosecutions in these years is also affirmed by Cicero elsewhere; *Pro Rosc. Amer.* 11: *Longo intervallo indicium inter sicarios hos primum committitur; Pro Rosc. Amer.* 28: *quod iudicia tam diu facta non essent, condemnari eum oportere qui primus in iudicium adductus esset.*

tion. Patricians of the late Republic were not noted for conventionality or conservatism; witness Sulla, Cinna, Lepidus, Caesar, Catilina, Clodius. With Sulla in the Mithridatic war were a Sulpicius Galba, a Cornelius Dolabella, and a Manlius, probably a Manlius Torquatus.[96] We may add perhaps Ap. Claudius Pulcher, whom Sulla had entrusted with forces at Nola in 88, but who must have abandoned Italy when those troops deserted to Cinna.[97] Abrogation of his *imperium* and an *interdictio* strongly suggest that Claudius sought refuge with Sulla. The Cinnan regime did not take such actions against neutrals.[98] Some refugees from the old Metellan *factio* can also be discerned in Sulla's following. First and foremost was L. Lucullus, son of a Metella and the nephew of Metellus Numidicus; he had worked assiduously for his uncle's recall in the days of an ardent youth. Now he was a devoted officer of Sulla, under whom he had served in the Social War and whom he followed loyally in the 80's. One officer only had stayed with Sulla when he marched on the city; that may well have been Lucullus. Sulla found him a kindred spirit, a man of cultured tastes and a "liberal education," to whom he later dedicated his memoirs and whom he appointed as guardian of his son.[99] Victims of the Varian commission also found refuge with Sulla. C. Scribonius Curio escaped a prosecution only through tribunician immunity; he next turns up fighting for Sulla in Greece and then in Asia Minor.[100] His high-spirited friend C. Cotta had succumbed to the tribunal and marched off into exile. No informant reports that he was with Sulla in the mid-80's, but he is linked with Curio for those years and both men returned to Rome upon Sulla's triumph in the civil war. The dictator evidently rescinded Cotta's banishment.[101] L. Hortensius was in the Sullan ranks as well; the Metellan connection may also help to explain

[96] *MRR,* II.56, 61, 65.

[97] See above, note 86.

[98] Still another patrician, Mam. Aemilius Lepidus, fought for Sulla in the Italian war in 82; Appian, *BC,* 1.94. That of itself, however, cannot prove service earlier in the east; cf. Badian, *Studies,* 217. On this man, see G. V. Sumner, "Manius or Mamercus?" *JRS,* 54 (1964), 41-48.

[99] On Lucullus' relations with Sulla, see Plut. *Luc.* 1.3-4, 3.3. For the advocacy of Numidicus' recall, see Cic. *Post. Red. in Sen.* 37; *Post Red. ad Quir.* 7. On service with Sulla in the Social War see Plut. *Luc.* 2.1; later: *MRR,* II.47, 55-56, 58. For the conjecture that Lucullus accompanied the march on Rome, see Badian, *Studies,* 220. In general, see Van Ooteghem, *Lucullus,* 18-38.

[100] The threat of the Varian commission is recorded by Asconius, 74, Clark. References to his service in the east in *MRR,* II.56, 59.

[101] Cic. *Brutus,* 227: *Cotta aberat et Curio;* Cic. *Brutus,* 311: *reditus Cottae Curionis Crassi Lentulorum Pompei, leges et iudicia constituta, recuperata res publica.*

his decision.[102] A certain Servilius lost his army to the Mariani in 87 and, it may be conjectured, is the same man who served as legate to Sulla in the civil war of 82. It is reasonable to suppose that he was in the east in the interim. This man is, almost certainly, P. Servilius Vatia. He had been Sulla's unsuccessful candidate for the consulship in 87. In 79 when Sulla was in a better position to dictate the results, Servilius reached that office. His mother, one might note, was also a Metella.[103] Sulla's association with the Metelli was still serving him well in some quarters. Finally, the slain orator M. Antonius had at least one son who accompanied Sulla to the east. C. Antonius was no credit to his martyred father, using his military authority and a force of cavalry to ruin the hapless Greeks. Yet he returned later in splendor, conspicuous in Sulla's triumphal parade.[104] Association with the Metellan clan was not, however, a prerequisite to attract men of noble birth. Sulla relied heavily on the energy and military gifts of L. Licinius Murena, who was given the post of honor at the battle of Chaeronea and left in charge of Asia when Sulla withdrew. Murena was only of praetorian family, but among his loyal subordinates were Roman *nobiles* with consular ancestors like M. Junius Silanus and A. Terentius Varro.[105] It is evident that many aristocrats swallowed pride and principle in calculating the future. Sulla's staff was not limited to nonentities and desperate adventurers. He was building his own faction.

Some men possessed more principle. Q. Metellus Pius, the son of Numidicus, was related to Sulla in marriage, and had other *adfines* in Sulla's camp. But Pius, the leader of that renowned family, inherited

---

[102] *MRR*, II.56.

[103] For Servilius in 87, see Gran. Licin. 27, B; in 82, Plut. *Sulla*, 28.8; Vell. Pat. 2.28.1; cf. *MRR*, II.53, n. 11. For his candidacy in 88, see Plut. *Sulla*, 10.3; the Σερουηίον is doubtless a bungled reference to Servilius; cf. Münzer, *RE*, 4(2).1812, "Servilius," n. 93. The relationship to Metella is given by Cic. *Verr.* 2.3.211.

[104] Asconius, 84, 88, 92, Clark. Badian, *Studies*, 216, is at pains to argue that M. Antonius Creticus, eldest son of the orator, was in Rome in the mid 80's. There is no evidence either way. Unfortunately, he omits C. Antonius altogether.

[105] Sources on Murena in *MRR*, II.56, 61, 64; on Silanus, II.60; on Varro, II.72. Badian's fine article, *Studies*, 206-234, on the 80's rightly stresses the number of *nobiles* who refrained from joining Sulla and waited upon events. But the reaction against Last, *CAH*, IX.264-269, can go too far. In the process Badian unduly denigrates the following of Sulla. Cf. Meier, *Res Pub.*, 229-230, n. 143. There was some substance to the remark of Vell. Pat. 2.23.3: *Dominante in Italia Cinna maior pars nobilitatis ad Sullam in Achaiam ac deinde post in Asiam perfugit;* cf. Plut. *Sulla*, 22.1; Orosius, 5.20.1; Eutrop. 5.7. None of these, of course, is to be taken literally.

his father's independence and, perhaps, his self-righteousness. In 87 he possessed an army, still waging the remnants of the Social War against the Samnites. But he had his differences with Octavius and his negotiations with Cinna also broke down. Pius withdrew to Africa, refusing cooperation with the Cinnan regime, but at the same time studiously snubbing Sulla.[106] Similarly, young M. Crassus, the future triumvir, whose father and brother were cut down by the Mariani in 87, found the atmosphere in Rome uncongenial. He spent the mid 80's in Spain; hereditary connections would eventually enable him to round up an army there. But he showed no interest in joining Sulla.[107] We have definite evidence of independence from both camps for only these two men, but there may well have been more. Some of the promising young orators shunned Rome during the *Cinnae dominatio;* the Lentuli, Cn. Lentulus Clodianus and P. Lentulus Sura, are mentioned specifically, men whose dignity of bearing and speech concealed their mediocre talents. They may have joined the other patricians who fought for Sulla or, perhaps more likely, sat out these years abroad.[108]

Cinna's task was no easy one. Aristocratic sources, some relying on the memoirs of Sulla, have blackened the reputation of the *Cinnae dominatio.*[109] Cinna has been variously described as a *popularis,* a democrat, an autocrat, a revolutionary, a man who placed interests of party above welfare of the *res publica* — familiar phraseology.[110] Recent modern scholarship has properly supplied a corrective. Rome in the mid 80's was calm and stable. Cinna has enjoyed rehabilitation.[111] But, as so often, the reaction to orthodoxy can be over-enthusiastic. One reads now even that "all of Cinna's career shows him to be a moderate, a respecter of the constitution, and a compromiser." [112] This statement courts unnecessary paradox. It is difficult to imagine that the man who authorized the execution of six *consulares* and other *nobiles* in late 87 had suddenly become a gentle and generous soul in 86. Scholars have pointed to

---

[106] Sources in *MRR,* II-48, 54. For friction between Pius and Sulla, resolved only during their joint consulship in 80, see Plut. *Sulla,* 6.5.

[107] Plut. *Crassus,* 4-6. On Crassus' earlier career, see A. Garzetti, "M. Licinio Crasso," *Athenaeum,* 19 (1941), 6-20.

[108] On their absence, see Cic. *Brutus,* 308, 311; their characteristics, Cic. *Brutus,* 234-235.

[109] Cf. Livy, *Per.* 79-83. For the phrase *Cinnae dominatio,* see Cic. *Ad Att.* 8.3.6; Asconius, 23, Clark; Val. Max. 6.9.6; Tac. *Ann.* 1.1; cf. Cic. *Phil.* 1.34, 2.108; *Vir. Ill.* 67.6.

[110] Cf. the account of Valgiglio, *Silla,* 33-46.

[111] Bennett, *Cinna, passim;* Badian, *Studies,* 206-234; Bulst, *Historia,* 13 (1964), 307-337.

[112] Carney, *A Biog. of Marius,* 66.

Cicero's remark about the Cinnan era: *triennium fere fuit urbs sine armis.*[113] And so indeed it was. But it will not do to ignore another remark of the orator in the same work: *inter profectionem reditumque L. Sullae sine iure fuit et sine ulla dignitate res publica.*[114] *Dignitas* may be ambiguous but Cicero knew what he meant by *ius;* the courts were relatively idle and oratory languished. Cinna might practice conciliation, but he did not encourage dissent. Judicial activity, the heart of Roman political life for many decades, was carefully reduced and controlled. The cessation of murders after the death of C. Marius in early 86 was the better part of prudence. Cinna was not benign; he was practical. If he was to bring order and stability and build a following to rival that of Sulla, divisiveness must be eschewed. The new regime ignored traditional animosities; it could embrace all the old factions in the interests of unity and legitimacy. Like Sulla, Cinna recognized that the factional rivalries of the 90's and before had been rendered obsolete by the shock of civil war. The proconsul of Asia could conduct his campaigns abroad; Cinna was forging a consensus at home.

His policy is revealed by an examination of the men who cooperated and participated in the Cinnan government. With Marius dead, the Mariani naturally gravitated toward Cinna. M. Marius Gratidianus was a nephew of the fallen general. In 87 he had launched the prosecution against Marius' *inimicus* Q. Catulus; in the Cinnan years he owned the distinction of serving two praetorships and gained wide reputation as a protector of sound currency. His activity was part of the new image of stability.[115] Another nephew of Marius (by marriage), the future dictator C. Julius Caesar, was taking his first political steps in these years. An appointment as *flamen dialis* was a signal honor for the young man. His marriage to one of Cinna's daughters removes any doubt of his affiliation.[116] Even loftier honors were reserved for the Valerii Flacci. L. Valerius Flaccus, once Marius' consular colleague and devoted ally in 100, received the coveted appointment as *princeps senatus* in 86. His *adfinis* and namesake became *consul suffectus* in the same year, upon the death of Marius; to him also fell the command against Mithridates, left vacant by Marius' demise. Before his departure, Flaccus acted to relieve the indebted class by inducing creditors to settle for one quarter

[113] Cic. *Brutus,* 308.

[114] Cic. *Brutus,* 227.

[115] On the dual praetorship, perhaps 85 and 84, see Asconius, 84, Clark. Sources on the currency measure in *MRR*, II.57; cf. II.60. Gratidianus' career is summed up in Münzer, *RE*, 28.1825-1827, "Marius," n. 42.

[116] For the marriage, see Suet. *Iul.* 1; Plut. *Caes.* 1.1. Suetonius puts the appointment as *flamen dialis* in 84; Vell. Pat. 2.43.1 puts it in 86.

of what was due. Sound money mollified the creditors, debt reduction relieved the oppressed. Cinna could be a friend to all.[117] One more Flaccus, C. Flaccus, brother of the consul of 86, loyally held the province of Spain and may indeed have controlled Transalpine Gaul as well, in the interests of the government of Rome.[118] Of the censors of 86 one was M. Perperna, whose Etruscan origins and connections may also suggest a link with Marius.[119] It is abundantly clear that the ex-Mariani were at the very center of power in the mid 80's.

But Cinna cast his net wider. The group associated with L. Marcius Philippus, the enemies of the Metellan *factio* in the 90's, had played a large role in the previous decade. They could be seduced by a regime that offered them renewed and increased *dignitas*. Philippus himself was awarded the censorship of 86, a coveted honor that had eluded him in 89.[120] That eloquent speaker and influential politician would add luster to any government. The censorship of Philippus and Perperna is at once anomalous and revealing. Philippus had been no friend of the Mariani. The proud aristocrat had suffered a bitter setback in his first candidacy for the consulship in 94, defeated by the staunch Marian M. Herennius. That Philippus tried again in 93 is not unlikely but failure came again; one of the victorious candidates was M. Perperna. Philippus did not succeed until 92 for 91. But in 86 Philippus and Perperna cooperated happily as censors. The combination discloses Cinna's policy of forging a grand alliance by erasing old factional lines. The two censors effected the appointment of L. Valerius Flaccus as *princeps senatus*. And more significant, Philippus acknowledged overtly the new situation in the *lectio senatus,* pointedly ignoring his uncle Ap. Claudius Pulcher, who was under sentence of banishment and probably in the camp of Sulla.[121] Linked with Philippus in hatred of the Metelli and even closer to the Cinnan regime was Cn. Papirius Carbo. Carbo's father had perished as the result of a prosecution by M. Antonius in the previous generation and he himself had clashed in the 90's with L. Crassus. In 86, during the censorship of Philippus, Carbo was named Cinna's colleague as

[117] On L. Flaccus, the *princeps senatus,* see Livy, *Per.* 83. On the consul of 86, see sources in *MRR,* II.53. Cf. on the financial legislation of the 80's T. Frank, "On Some Financial Legislation of the Sullan Period," *AJP,* 54 (1933), 54-58; Bulst, *Historia,* 13 (1964), 330-337; Nicolet, *L'Ordre Equestre,* 381-383.

[118] Cf. Badian, *Studies,* 88-96.

[119] Badian, *Studies,* 55. The 80's probably also saw an increased number of *novi homines* reach office, at least among the lower magistracies; cf. Meier, *Res. Pub.,* 219.

[120] Cf. Cic. *De Domo,* 84.

[121] On Philippus' unsuccessful candidature in 94, see Cic. *Brutus,* 166; for

consul for 85, the first of his three years at that post. Carbo's *adfinis* C. Carbo Arvina had joined Philippus and Varius in denouncing Drusus' program as tribune in 90. Arvina profited also, reaching the praetorship sometime in the Cinnan years.[122]

Other men belong in this company. The Domitii Ahenobarbi, it will be recalled, had been prominent in the senatorial opposition to the Metelli in the previous twenty years. Cn. Domitius, the consul of 96, was notorious as a fierce *inimicus* of M. Scaurus and L. Crassus. He was dead by the early 80's, but his son (or nephew) Cn. Domitius was available. That fact did not escape the eye of Cinna, into whose plans Domitius could fit nicely; Domitius promptly married a daughter of Cinna,[123] and became a loyal defender of the government to the end. Mention might be made also of the Pomponii. Cn. Pomponius had been a prosecutor of the *nobilitas* in 90 when the *lex Varia* was in force. Nothing more is heard of him, but a relative, M. Pomponius, secured the aedileship in 82.[124] Even the lesser families who had cooperated with Philippus and Varius found the Cinnan government congenial.

In this assemblage, Cinna would not have forgotten the friends and supporters of Cn. Pompeius Strabo. Only fate and untimely death prevented what would have surely been a *Pompeii dominatio*. Strabo had been an enemy of the Metelli, had successfully defied Sulla and had cooperated with Philippus. His *amici* turn up again and again in the mid 80's. The army of Strabo naturally turned its allegiance to his son Pompeius Magnus, who remained in Italy and cooperated with the government until after the death of Cinna. Pompey's father-in-law, P. Antistius, saw his forensic career suddenly blossom in these years. Antistius had made his initial mark as tribune in 88 when he had joined with Sulpicius Rufus in checking the illegal consular candidacy of C. Caesar Strabo and had eclipsed even Sulpicius in the force of his arguments. Under the Cinnan regime his oratory was much admired, his skills much in demand.[125] A precious inscription records the *consilium* and officers of Pompeius Strabo in 89.[126] Several of the names reappear as active or passive collaborators with Cinna in the 80's. Pompey himself, of course, was in his father's entourage in the Social War. So also was a son of Philippus, and lest it be forgotten, a budding young orator named M.

the censorship of 86, see *MRR,* II.54, and esp. Cic. *De Domo,* 84.

[122] He was *praetorius* by 82; Vell. Pat. 2.26.2.

[123] Orosius, 5.24.16.

[124] *MRR,* II.68.

[125] Cic. *Brutus,* 226-227: *Itaque post tribunatum primo multae ad eum causae, deinde omnes maximae quaecumque erant deferebantur . . . Hic temporibus floruit eis, quibus inter profectionem reditumque L. Sullae.*

[126] *ILLRP,* II.28-34, no. 515.

Tullius Cicero, who pursued his rhetorical training and gained his first public exposure during the *Cinnae dominatio*. L. Junius Brutus Damasippus was among the first listed on Strabo's staff in 89, probably as a legate. He was, evidently, in Rome in the succeeding years and reached the praetorship in 82 when he carried out the brutal dirty work of the regime in order to stiffen its resolve against the imminent return of Sulla. The Junii Bruti were firm in their opposition to the Sullani. One M. Brutus had fled the city in 88 when Sulla commenced his first march; another secured the tribunate in 83. Immediately after L. Brutus on the list of Strabo's officers stands Q. Minucius Thermus, possibly as quaestor. He turns up next as loyal legate to L. Flaccus in his Asian campaign of 86. Other subordinates of Strabo played less active roles in the 80's but certainly remained safe and secure under the Cinnan government, transferring allegiance to Sulla only when military expediency dictated their choice. In this group fall M. Lepidus, Cn. Dolabella, and the notorious temporizer L. Sergius Catilina, all of whom show Marian connections as well as service with Pompeius Strabo.[127]

The picture begins to take on real shape. Cinna was able to assimilate diverse elements and form wide backing for a consensus to challenge the backing of Sulla. Most striking is the fact that some members of the old Metellan *factio* found the Cinnan regime acceptable and comfortable. Q. Mucius Scaevola, the consul of 95, stands out as the preeminent example. *Pontifex maximus* and a senior statesman, he had suffered insult and humiliation in early 86 when Flavius Fimbria brought a meaningless charge against him, mocking legality and due process. But the affair collapsed and Fimbria went off as legate to Asia. Scaevola did not allow the event to alienate him from those who remained in Rome. He attended the senate and let his feelings be known; fate might prove unkind, but he preferred to face it in Rome rather than march on his *patria* in arms.[128] Also conspicuous in the city in these years was the celebrated orator Q. Hortensius. In the 90's his young career had been promoted by the Metellan group, by his father-in-law, Catulus, and by L. Crassus. A relative, L. Hortensius, was at that moment serving with

---

[127] The brilliant analysis of the inscription by Cichorius, *Röm. Stud.*, 130-185, is indispensable for any study of this period. Each of the men noted here receives fuller discussion in this connection by Cichorius: the younger Philippus, 168-169; Cicero, 181-184; Pompey, 164; L. Brutus, 141-142; Thermus, 143; Lepidus, 147; Dolabella, 147-148; and Catiline, 172-174. On the activities of Thermus and Brutus in the 80's see *MRR*, II.56, 67. For more on Lepidus, Dolabella, and Catilina, cf. Gruen, *AJP*, 87 (1966), 389-399.

[128] Cic. *Ad Att.* 8.3.6: *qui tamen ita dicere solebat, se id fore videre quod factum est sed malle quam armatum ad patriae moenia accedere.*

Sulla in the east; but the orator not only remained in Rome, he reached the top of his profession in the mid 80's, displaying his prodigious memory, his meticulous training, and his sonorous tones. Hortensius was the acknowledged leader of the bar.[129] One more name can perhaps be added, Hortensius' brother-in-law Q. Catulus, the future consul of 78. Catulus' father had been slain in 87 by the Mariani after a sham trial. But sins of the father do not seem to have been visited upon the son. Catulus is not recorded among the legates of Sulla either in the Mithridatic or in the civil wars. Positive evidence is lacking, but what his brother-in-law could do Catulus could do also.[130] Cinna's arms were open wide.

Enforced tranquillity is perhaps the most accurate description of the Cinnan years. The government aimed at conciliating all factions and creating a new unity. It was not a unity, however, that would readily tolerate dissent. Romans knew who was in charge; Cinna held three consecutive consulships and Carbo was his colleague in the latter two. The courts, long the focus for discontent or political strife, were controlled and subdued. The consensus did not allow for internal divisions. One trial only stands on record for the mid 80's. It bears out perfectly what has been argued in the preceding pages. The trial of Cn. Pompeius Magnus, on the one hand, exemplifies the atmosphere of conciliation; on the other, it indicates how carefully judicial procedures were "managed."

Pompeius Strabo, it was alleged, had embezzled the booty accruing from the capture of Asculum in 89. His son now suffered the consequences of that report; Pompey was prosecuted for *peculatus* in 86. There is no suggestion here of a special *quaestio,* a fact which implies that a permanent *peculatus* court did exist in the pre-Sullan period.[131] No prosecutor is recorded. Perhaps it did not much matter. The leading pillars of the Cinnan establishment converged in defense of Pompey. L. Philippus spoke up for him with unctuous flattery, comparing Pompey

[129] Cic. *Brutus,* 308: *primas in causis agebat Hortensius.* For his qualities as an orator, see *Brutus,* 301-303; *De Orat.* 3.230; Seneca, *Controv.* 1.pr.19; Quintilian, 10.6.4, 11.2.24.

[130] See Badian, *Studies,* 217-218; contra: J. P. V. D. Balsdon, "Review of Badian, *Studies in Greek and Roman History*," *JRS,* 55 (1965), 231-232.

[131] So Lengle, *Unt. Sull. Verf.,* 40-42. Malcovati, *ORF,* 268, describes Pompey's trial as a *repetundae* case, but Plutarch's language strongly implies *peculatus; Pomp.* 4: δίκην κλοπῆς ἔσχεν ὑπὲρ αὐτοῦ δημοσίων χρημάτων ὁ Πομπήιος; cf. Val. Max. 5.3.5, 6.2.8. For a suggestion on the origin of the *peculatus* court, see above, p. 177. The date of the trial is nowhere given, but since Plutarch places it shortly after the death of Strabo, it presumably occurred some time in 86.

favorably with Alexander the Great. Connection with Pompeius Strabo would have helped to motivate Philippus. Cinna's closest collaborator, Cn. Papirius Carbo, also appeared in Pompey's defense, an act for which the latter was to show little gratitude four years later. To this motley gathering Q. Hortensius added his stentorian voice, thus pointedly demonstrating his endorsement of the regime.[132] Cinna's policy of conciliation evidently bore fruit. Pompey, of course, was acquitted, and it is difficult to avoid the conclusion that the acquittal was deliberately planned and contrived from the outset. The presiding officer, Antistius, had no doubts. He displayed conspicuous favor to the defendant throughout the hearing, and even made a private arrangement for his betrothal. Shortly after Antistius announced the favorable verdict, he gave his daughter to Pompey in marriage.[133] This was hardly a political prosecution in the old sense. In all probability it was part and parcel of the Cinnan effort to place the state on a sound financial basis. The *bellum sociale,* followed by Mithridates' "Asiatic vespers" and the ravages of civil war had ruined the treasury and played havoc with public and private credit. The murder of Asellio, who had tried to check usury in 89, shows how bitter feelings were. Cinna's efforts to remedy the situation and restore financial confidence seem genuine: hence, the measure of Flaccus to cancel three quarters of the outstanding debts, and the bill of Marius Gratidianus to recall inflated coins and guarantee sound money. The trial of Pompey belongs in this context. It was not so much an attack on the defendant as a vehicle to recover funds for the treasury. The blame for embezzlement could easily be transferred, as it was, to a luckless freedman of Strabo named Alexander. Pompey emerged from the case with renewed and enhanced reputation. A dummy accuser was chopped to bits by Pompeian repartee, the state's leading politicians and orators waxed eloquent on Pompey's *dignitas,* and the presiding magistrate smiled on the fortunes of his prospective son-in-law. No better

[132] On Philippus' appearance, see Plut. *Pomp.* 2.2; for Hortensius', Cic. *Brutus,* 230; for Carbo, Val. Max. 5.3.5, 6.2.8. That the connections were inherited from Pompeius Strabo is suggested by Gelzer, *Kleine Schriften,* II.125-126, and *Pompeius* (Munich, 1949), 34, though there is no evidence for this in the case of Hortensius.

[133] The affair is described in full by Plut. *Pomp.* 4-5. Antistius is almost certainly the P. Antistius who was tribune in 88 and later murdered in 82; Klebs, *RE,* 2.2547, "Antistius," n. 18. The latter is called an *aedilicius* at his death by Vell. Pat. 2.26. This led Lengle, *Unt. Sull. Verf.,* 40-42, to dissociate him from the "praetor" who, according to Plutarch, sat on Pompey's case. But Plutarch's στρατηγοῦντα is probably anachronistic. Praetors regularly sat on *quaestiones* in the post-Sullan period, but this was not a fixed practice prior to 81; Klebs, *RE,* 2.2547, "Antistius," n. 18.

example can be imagined to illustrate the careful stage-management of judicial procedures by the Cinnan government.[134]

The policy of Cinna seems clear and consistent: control of the springs of power, suppression of internal strife, and cultivation of unity among all factions and classes.[135] Compromise and conciliation, for a time, appear to have been successful. Cinna had been able to fashion a government that included not only his own dedicated supporters, but ex-Mariani, the faction of Philippus, friends of Pompeius Strabo, and even men previously associated with the Metellan group. Cooperation was evoked from both patrician noble and *novus homo;* L. Scipio Asiagenus and C. Norbanus held a joint consulship in 83 and neither yielded to the blandishments or threats of Sulla. The consensus went beyond a reconciliation of old factional enmities. The *equester ordo* stood by Cinna. Drastic reduction of private indebtedness may have alienated some of the *faeneratores,* but business classes on the whole appreciated the policy of restoring financial confidence and sound currency.[136] The Italian problem was handled with caution and circumspection. Cinna had ridden to power as champion of Italian aims and he could not afford to lose that image. At the same time he did not intend to alienate his new political allies by swamping the assemblies with masses of new voters. The process would be gradual. A censorship in 86 (only three years after the previous censorship) was a gesture of good faith. The censors enrolled a number of Italians, but not too many; census figures increased by a factor of only 17 percent over the number recorded for 115 B.C. Distribution of new voters into all thirty-five tribes does not seem to have taken place until 84.[137] Compromise is here again the guiding principle.

[134] The dire straits of the treasury are noted by Orosius, 5.18.26. The connection of the financial measures of Flaccus and Gratidianus with the trial of Pompey was suggested by Bennett, *Cinna,* 40-43. For the shifting of blame to the freedman Alexander, see Plut. *Pomp.* 4.1. Further on the trial, see Lanzani, *Mario e Silla,* 189-193; Gelzer, *Kleine Schriften,* II.125-126; J. Van Ooteghem, *Pompeé le Grand* (Brussels, 1954), 51-52.

[135] It is gratifying to note substantial agreement with this analysis of Cinna in Meier's new work, *Res Pub.,* 225-237. But Meier does not shake off altogether the outworn dualistic notion: Cinna, the *equites,* and new citizens on one side, Sulla and the oligarchy on the other; see esp. 218-219, 228, 230, 235-236, 262-266; cf. 84.

[136] Asconius, 89, Clark: *Equester ordo pro Cinnanis partibus contra Sullam steterat;* Cic. *Pro Rosc. Amer.* 140; cf. Bulst, *Historia,* 13 (1964), 334-337; Meier, *Res. Pub.,* 219.

[137] Even the powerful Samnites seem to have been satisfied and tranquil; cf. E. T. Salmon, *"Sulla Redux,"* *Athenaeum,* 42 (1964), 69-74. For the census of 115, see Livy, *Per.* 63; for 85, Jerome, *Chron.* 151, H. Distribution into thirty-five tribes is put in 84 by Livy, *Per.* 84; cf. Badian, *For. Client.,*

Cinna's endeavor was a noble experiment. The Social War, followed by unprecedented domestic violence, had wiped away most of the traditional bases for political differentiation. Old factional lines dissolved and tame contests in the senate and the courts had become curiously archaic. The contrast between the 90's and the 80's could not have been more severe. Cinna hoped to take advantage of the new situation by offering peace, stability, and a coalescence of political groups. The combination would be wide enough to embrace Sulla also, or perhaps powerful enough to overawe him. But it was not to be. Sulla had his own following, not compiled through compromise or desire for tranquillity, but based on fear and greed, and hardened by war. Sulla did not intend to settle for a comfortable place within Cinna's scheme. He controlled legions of experienced veterans who hungered for reward and *gloria*. One more bloody civil war was required to complete the brutal cycle begun by the *bellum sociale*.

241-242; contra; Taylor, *Voting Districts,* 105-106; Meier, *Res Pub.,* 230. For an extreme view, denying even that any regular census took place in 86, see J. Carcopino, "Sur un passage de la Chronique de saint Jerome," *Mélanges en Hommage à la Mémoire de Fr. Martroye* (1940), 73-79.

IX. THE SULLAN RESTORATION

L. Cornelius Sulla fought the battles of Rome against her most persistent enemy, Mithridates of Pontus. Whether he was acting as a duly constituted governor of Asia or as a rebel and private adventurer depended entirely upon one's point of view. The government in Rome would not have given the same answer to that question as the officers of Sulla. Modern debate on the subject consequently seems peculiarly pointless.[1] The Cinnani also desired the demise of Mithridates, but naturally they hoped that *gloria* would not redound exclusively to the reputation of Sulla. If an army of men loyal to the Cinnan regime could overwhelm Mithridates independently of Sulla or in concert with him, *concordia* could be preserved and civil war averted.

In 86 L. Valerius Flaccus succeeded Marius in the consulship and secured the Mithridatic command that would have been Marius' had he lived. Sulla cannot be expected to have been happy about the prospect of a new army despatched to steal or share his laurels. The sources have been duly infected by Sulla's memoirs and by pro-Sullan apologists. Propaganda emerges most clearly in the analysis of Plutarch: Flaccus was sent out ostensibly to wage war against Mithridates, but in reality to attack Sulla himself. Unfortunately, that version remains standard orthodoxy in modern discussions.[2] It would have been foolhardy indeed for Flaccus to challenge Sulla openly while Mithridates was loose and thus to shatter the image that the Cinnan regime was seeking to promote. The truth emerges in an account not polluted by Sullan apologia: Flac-

---

[1] For the most recent contributions to the controversy, see Badian, *Studies,* 206-234, an article most admirable, except for its invective, and Balsdon's review of Badian, in *JRS,* 55 (1965), 230-232.

[2] Plut. *Sulla,* 20: λόγῳ μὲν ἐπὶ Μιθριδάτην, ἔργῳ δὲ ἐπ' ἐκεῖνον αὐτόν; cf. Appian, *BC,* 1.75; *Mithr.* 51; followed by Lanzani, *Mario e Silla,* 176-181; Bennett, *Cinna,* 45-46; Valgiglio, *Silla,* 34-35. It has been vigorously and persuasively challenged by Badian, *Studies,* 223-224, to which the account here is evidently much in debt. See also Meier, *Res Pub.,* 233-234.

cus' instructions were to summon Sulla to a joint enterprise against Mithridates; if Sulla refused, Flaccus was to engage Mithridates himself.[3] That analysis is borne out by the facts. Flaccus made no effort to challenge the army of Sulla, and, indeed, when his successor Fimbria later sought Sulla's cooperation in bottling up Mithridates, it was Sulla, through his lieutenant Lucullus, who refused.[4]

The course of the Mithridatic war is beyond our scope here. As is well known, Sulla concluded his own peace with the Pontic king, and the army of Fimbria, who had treacherously slain Flaccus, deserted to the victorious commander. The government in Rome was prepared to negotiate in the interests of harmony. Fear may have been the principal motive, but the action was consistent with the policy pursued in the past few years. Sulla's message expressed a willingness to come to terms but he offered nothing but terror and vengeance to those who had opposed him in Rome. The *princeps senatus* L. Flaccus pronounced the regime's policy of *concordia* in a speech to the senate, and emissaries were sent. But Cinna and Carbo continued frantic recruitment; they knew the man with whom they were dealing. Sulla's reply allowed of no misinterpretation; he would not return to an undistinguished and quiet post in the Cinnan system; he demanded all the honors and privileges to which his previous services entitled him. As the ancient commentator rightly reported, his conditions were tantamount to a demand for supreme power.[5]

Men in Italy and elsewhere made their calculations accordingly. Cinna was murdered by his own mutinous troops in 84. Carbo found opposition even in the tribunician college to his status as sole consul for the remainder of the year. Neutrals and waverers suddenly found Sulla's credentials impeccable and his appeal irresistible. Young Pompey conveniently forgot a hereditary quarrel and brought his loyal Picentine troops over to the side of Sulla. So also did M. Crassus, bringing forces that he had recruited in Spain. Metellus Pius, who had maintained inde-

---

[3] Memnon, f.24 (*FGH*, III B, no. 434): ἡ δὲ σύγκλητος Φλάκκον Οὐαλέριον καὶ Φιμβρίαν πέμπει πολεμεῖν Μιθριδάτη, ἐπιτρέψασα καὶ Σύλλᾳ συλλαμβάνειν τοῦ πολέμου, ὅμοια φρονοῦντι τῇ συγκλήτῳ· εἰ δὲ μή, τὴν πρὸς αὐτὸν πρότερον συνάψαι μάχην.

[4] Sources in *MRR*, II.53, 59; cf. Badian, *Studies*, 224-225.

[5] Appian, *BC*, 1.79: ᾧ δὴ καὶ μάλιστα δῆλος ἐγένετο ἐνὶ ῥήματι τῷδε, οὐ διαλύσων τὸν στρατόν, ἀλλὰ τὴν τυραννίδα ἤδη διανοούμενος. For the earlier message of Sulla, see Appian, *BC*, 1.77; the speech of Flaccus, Livy, *Per.* 83. On these negotiations, cf. Valgiglio, *Silla*, 42-51. The despair of the senate, faced with Sulla's intransigence, may be suggested by Cic. *Ad Fam.* 2.16.1: *recordor enim desperationes eorum, qui senes erant adulescente me;* also *Pro Font.* 6; pointed out by Meier, *Res Pub.*, 243-245.

pendence in Africa during the Cinnan years, was now swift to join the swelling Sullan ranks. Sulla was not one to bear a grudge when a Roman *nobilis* deserted to his camp. Indeed, many of the turncoats were to reap the largest benefits from Sulla's victory. L. Philippus himself, never a man to allow principle to interfere with political advantage, was soon to be found fighting on Sulla's behalf, as a legate. The Valerii Flacci profited also from a last-minute switch; L. Valerius Flaccus, once an intimate ally of Marius, secured Sulla's appointment as dictator in 82 and became his master of the horse; C. Flaccus returned from Gaul in 81 to celebrate a triumph. M. Lepidus and Cn. Dolabella shed their backgrounds easily and showed themselves good Sullani; both received praetorships in 81. There was even a Papirius Carbo in Sulla's camp in 80. If evidence were fuller, many other names would doubtless appear. Lesser men as well as leaders deserted to Sulla: L. Catilina, C. Verres, M. Pupius Piso, Q. Lucretius Ofella, P. Cornelius Cethegus.

The pattern is clear. Sulla could be remorseless toward implacable enemies, but only implacable enemies. The new order needed respectability and the luster that only noble *nomina* could offer. Sulla welcomed allies, last-minute or not, especially patricians and *nobiles*. They could expect to benefit, through magistracy or material gain. For Sulla and his new friends there were mutual advantages. A final string of murders in Rome, ordered by the son of Marius and executed by the praetor L. Brutus Damasippus in 82, was doubtless for the purpose of setting an example and preventing further defections to Sulla. The slain men included P. Antistius, father-in-law of Pompey, who was already in Sulla's camp, and C. Carbo Arvina, who also had a relative serving with Sulla. Similar motives may have inspired the slaying of L. Domitius and the *pontifex maximus* Q. Scaevola, whose distinguished career now came to a grievous close. All was in vain. The diversified collection of groups that Cinna had painstakingly assembled had not had the time to coalesce. When the crisis came it fell apart. Prudence dictated the choice of many, and Sulla had the bigger battalions. Cinna had been a shrewd politician and might have become a genuine statesman; but Sulla operated by the lessons of the Social War and the events of 88. Military force held the balance, and the new "friends" of Sulla, as well as his hardened veterans, recognized that grim fact.[6]

---

[6] See esp. Livy, *Per.* 85: *Cn. Pompeius . . . ad Sullam venerat, ad quem se nobilitas omnis conferebat, ita ut deserta urbe ad castra veniretur.* Most of the sources on these events can be found in *MRR*, II.60-74. For Pompey, see 64, 70; for Crassus, 71; Metellus Pius, 63, 68; L. Flaccus, 67-68; C. Flaccus, 77-78; C. Carbo, 81; Ofella, 72. On Cethegus, see Appian, *BC*, 1.80; Philippus, Livy, *Per.* 86; on Pupius Piso, see Cic. *Verr.* 2.1.37; Vell. Pat. 2.41.2.

The motives and aims of Sulla the dictator remain elusive. To pierce the psychology of that complex personage is hardly feasible, given the present state of our information. Modern scholarship has offered two avenues of approach. It is possible to analyze Sulla as a champion of orthodoxy and oligarchy. On this interpretation, Sulla stands in the tradition of Scipio Aemilianus, L. Opimius, and M. Scaurus, a consistent opponent of "democrats" and "radicals," an upholder of the antique constitution. Violence and military force were necessary only as means to a salutary end. Hence, the reforms of his dictatorship aimed at the reconstituting of aristocratic government and the entrenchment of stability by muzzling the instruments of popular discontent. Sulla's retirement to private life was the natural culmination of a career devoted to the interests of the oligarchy. The cultivated patrician, linked to the Metelli and to senatorial conservatives, addicted to the genteel traditions and the privileges of his class, had restored the control of the *nobilitas* and could then withdraw to the sidelines, as he had long planned, in order to survey his handiwork. Rome could feel safe and secure in the hands of the *ordo senatorius*. On the other hand, one so inclined can find a very different picture of Sulla in the sources. The patrician family from which the dictator sprang had for many generations been shunted into the background. Consequently, he felt no loyalty to the establishment. He might use a valuable marriage alliance with the nobility to his own ends, but he was hardly a dedicated agent of the senatorial class. Sulla's previous career had been almost exclusively a military one. If there was consistent loyalty it was loyalty to himself. The beneficiaries of his favors were legionaries who could install him in power and whose devotion would keep him there. Constitutional readjustment did not aim at the supremacy of the senate; its purpose was to assure that no adventurer would imitate the Sullan example and challenge the dictator himself. Sulla exercised the powers of a monarch in fact, if not in name. Retirement came only when he felt it no longer possible to exercise those powers, rather than as a calculated act planned from the outset.[7]

On Lepidus, Dolabella, Verres, and Catilina, see the discussion in Gruen, *AJP,* 87 (1966), 385-399. For the murders in 82, see *MRR,* II.67, and the analysis of Badian, *Studies,* 231. In general on the civil war, see Lanzani, *Mario e Silla,* 233-371; Gabba, *App. BC Lib. Prim.,* 208-262.

[7] The first view has been expounded often and in many forms. One may consult the work of Valgiglio, *Silla, passim;* esp. 201-207, 225-233; see 204: "Per comprendere Silla bisogna vedere in lui quello che realmente fu, uno schietto e ardente repubblicano, al servizio dell' oligarchia senatoria." The brilliant, if misguided, analysis of Sulla as a would-be monarch with a vision of a unified empire is largely the contribution of Carcopina, *Sylla, passim;*

That there should be conflicting interpretations among modern historians is not surprising. The ancients themselves were puzzled about the enigmatic Sulla. The problem lies in the fact that his early career shows only ruthless ambition while the acts of his dictatorship appear directed toward stability and order. Sulla had first attached himself to the fortunes of Marius and then pursued his own *gloria* at the expense of his former commander. He had not scrupled to offend and shock the aristocracy by turning his own troops on the city of Rome when his *dignitas* was threatened in 88. His negotiations with the Cinnan government were conducted with a conscious air of superiority; his terms were harsh and he preferred to enforce them by once again bringing civil war on his *patria*. He welcomed defections but he crushed enemies, adding confiscation, proscription, and execution to the devastations of war. Yet when the dust had settled, enlightened constitutional reform, promoted by the dictator, aimed at perpetuating peace and strengthening civil institutions at the expense of ambitious individuals and of the military. Hence modern scholars argue about which is the "true" Sulla. Depending on their bent, they explain the earlier career in terms of the later, or the later in terms of the earlier. In either case, reconciliation seems artificial and forced. Perhaps reconciliation is precisely what one should avoid. The assumption of a static personality underlies most reconstructions. But the ancient testimony, unmanipulated, suggests change, and that, surely, is what common sense would dictate. The Sulla of 81 is not the man of 88. By 81 he was fifty-six years old, his victories behind him, his enemies hamstrung, and his fame assured. Security would then have been more appealing than further conquest or tyrannical power. Sulla, for all his intense drive and fierce pride, had always enjoyed the physical and intellectual pleasures that only leisure could bring. The time was ripe now to reap those fruits from his labors.[8] He could best accomplish this aim by installing a stable regime manned by competent and experienced *nobiles,* and fenced about by strong institutions that would be

---

see 241: "l'oeuvre qu' il avait entreprise ne marquait pas une régression vers le passé; elle tendait à l'adaption de Rome, par la monarchie universelle, à l'immensité de ses territoires et à la diversité de ses masses populaires." The most recent analysis, that of Meier, *Res Pub.*, 222-228, 235, 237-266, tends to see Sulla once again as a senatorial standard bearer from the outset. But Sulla was a complex character; Meier acknowledges the intense personal motivation and the ruthlessness in twisting institutions to his own ends that make Sulla a genuine forebear of Caesar. The picture that emerges from his account is not entirely clear.

[8] Cf. Plut. *Sulla*, 2.2: ἐπεὶ δὲ κύριος ἁπάντων κατέστη, συναγαγόντα τῶν ἀπὸ σκηνῆς καὶ θεάτρου τοὺς ἰταμωτάτους ὁσημέραι πίνειν καὶ διαπληκτίζεσθαι τοῖς σκώμμασι, τοῦ γε γήρως ἀωρότερα πράττειν δοκοῦντα καὶ πρὸς τῷ καταισχύνειν τὸ ἀξίωμα τῆς ἀρχῆς πολλὰ τῶν δεομένων ἐπιμελείας προιέμενον.

self-perpetuating. Dictatorial powers were justified if order was to be brought out of the chaos of civil war and there is no evidence that those powers were ever meant to be permanent. As Cicero knew full well, the acts of a dictator could be perfectly consistent with the reestablishment of a constitutional system.[9]

The alleged megalomania of Sulla dissolves upon analysis. He was not the man to desire a divine monarchy modelled on decadent Hellenistic kings. Great pride and supreme confidence allowed him to believe that he was a favorite of the gods. But it is precisely for this reason that he could display many superstitious traits while at the same time conveniently ignoring omens that appeared to others to be unfavorable. For Sulla, *virtus* and *felicitas* were complementary, not mutually exclusive. The man who was smiled upon by divinity did not have to institutionalize his position.[10] Sulla's purpose was to reconstitute the *res publica*. In the circumstances of 82, after almost a decade of internal bloodletting, this required drastic steps. The dictator's enemies could not expect to get off lightly. Sulla was a passionate man and those who had opposed him to the end received no mercy. Executions, exiles, and the sequestering of property plagued Italy for months. Worse, the sins of these fathers were visited upon the sons; the descendants of Sulla's victims found their civil rights rigidly curtailed, a bitter legacy for the succeeding generation. If anyone cared to honor the memory of Marius, the dictator had an answer for that also; the remains of his fallen foe were disinterred and ruthlessly scattered.[11] Memories of the proscriptions lingered long and left a dark cloud over the Ciceronian age. But Sulla's hands had not been entirely free. Victorious troops and clamoring supporters demanded *beneficia*. The process initiated by Marius and Saturninus and accelerated by the Social War now came to full fruition. The grisly aspect of Sulla's dictatorship was not so much the product of the man as of the times.[12] And the proscriptions came to an end in 81. Sulla could turn his attention to genuine reconstruction.

[9] Cic. *Har. Resp.* 54: *iterum Sulla superavit; tum sine dubio habuit regalem potestatem, quamquam rem publicam receiperarat.* Cf. Livy, *Per.* 89: *Sulla dictator factus . . . Legibus novis rei publicae statum confirmavit.*

[10] For the notion of Sulla as a divine monarch, see Carcopino, *Sylla,* 79-119; cf. J. Gagé, "Sylla, Pompeé et la théologie de la victoire," *RHist,* 171 (1933), 1-5. Few would endorse it today; see the trenchant comments of Balsdon, "Sulla Felix," *JRS,* 41 (1951), 1-10. On Sulla's willingness to twist unfavorable omens to his own ends, see Plut. *Sulla,* 12.3-5; cf. Valgiglio, *Silla,* 155-197.

[11] Cic. *De Leg.* 2.56. For sources on the proscriptions, see *MRR*, II.69.

[12] Cic. *De Leg. Agrar.* 3.5: *Est invidiosa lex* [which instituted the dictatorship], *sicuti dixi, verum tamen habet excusationem; non enim videtur hominis lex esse, sed temporis.*

With enemies duly punished and veterans installed on farms and in colonies, Sulla fashioned a *res publica*. The government would be a conspicuous coalition of men who had been loyal Sullani and those who had seen the light in 83. L. Valerius Flaccus, once an admirer of Marius and a pillar of the Cinnan regime, remained as *princeps senatus* and became Sulla's *magister equitum*. His cousin C. Flaccus received a triumph for victories in Gaul and Celtiberia. The consulship of 81 was shared by a Sullan lieutenant and a *novus homo;* two of the praetors, at least, M. Lepidus and Cn. Dolabella, had come over to Sulla only at the last minute, and both received provincial appointments. Sulla himself held the consulship in 80, together with Metellus Pius, who had endorsed him only as late as 83. Young Pompey, having demolished Sulla's enemies in Sicily and Africa, returned also to a triumph. Men like M. Crassus, Lepidus, and Catilina were among the greatest profiteers in the proscriptions. In a very real sense, Sulla was implementing the schemes of Cinna. The old aristocratic infighting would be made obsolete; former opponents would be honored and absorbed. The *factio* of Sulla would coincide with the *res publica. Equites* could fit into the scheme as well. Peace was always appreciated by the business classes and profits would begin to flow once more from the province of Asia now that the Mithridatic war was settled. Equestrians anxious for a political career found a place in Sulla's new, expanded senate.[13] Nor were the Italians ignored. Even in 82, in the midst of civil war, Sulla had recognized the advantage of mollifying the ex-*socii;* he announced his acknowledgment of their distribution into all thirty-five tribes. Of course, those Italians who joined his foes suffered after their defeat and suffered grievously: confiscations of land, implanting of Sullan colonies, and disenfranchisement. Samnites were the most notorious and conspicuous victims. Such violent persecution may have been deliberate policy. By turning his fire especially on the Samnites, Sulla could cloak the civil war in part as a Roman crusade against the old, intransigent foes of the state. But the Italians who joined Sulla's forces or preserved neutrality found the dictator a generous master. Many were enrolled directly in the senate. Italian names henceforth play an increasingly larger role in the Roman governing class. The Sullan years mark a real acceleration in the gradual Italianization of

[13] The notion of Sulla's enmity to the *equester ordo* has been effectively dispelled by Gabba, "Il ceto equestre e il senato di Silla," *Athenaeum,* 34 (1956), 125-128; Brunt, "Sulla and the Asian Publicans," *Latomus,* 15 (1956), 17-25; and Nicolet, *L'Ordre Equestre,* 573-581. Some *equites* fell in the proscriptions, as indeed did many senators; those men had fought against Sulla to the end. But that fact does not amount to Sullan hostility to the *equites* as a class.

Roman politics.[14] Sulla's plans, however, went beyond those of the *Cinnae dominatio*. Reconciliation of factions and *concordia* among classes were to be buttressed by institutional reform and a more solid governmental structure. Sulla was not a sweeping innovator; his "constitution" was an amalgam: a resurrection of some old forms, a confirmation of recent developments, and the introduction of some new elements, all in the interests of a stable order and of a self-perpetuating mechanism.[15]

Our main focus here must be upon Sulla's reforms in the judicial sphere, but these may be taken as illustrative of the temper of his program as a whole. As is well known, the dictator restored full control of the courts to the senate. A responsible body in charge of legal processes would best suit his concern for continued stability. The fluctuation of jury personnel, reflecting shifts in political power, that had plagued Rome in previous decades could now, he hoped, cease, and perhaps the courts could be removed altogether from the realm of politics. The ancient evidence suggests that the *iudicia* were simply transferred from the *equites* to the senate. Yet the last known law on the books was the *lex Plautia iudiciaria* of 89, which provided for the selection of fifteen men from each tribe as potential jurors, with all classes eligible. Hence, some have postulated another law in the interim, passed under the Cinnan regime, and restoring a monopoly to the *equites*. That is a rash and needless assumption. The sources on Sulla's law make no pretense at exactitude and ought not to be read in a literal fashion. There is no evidence for any intervening measure since the *lex Plautia,* nor would it be consonant with the purposes of Cinna to favor the *equites* excessively

[14] See Gabba, *Athenaeum*, 32 (1954), 102-108. On Sulla's promise to the Italians in 82, see Livy, *Per.* 86: *Sulla cum Italicis populis, ne timeretur ab his velut erepturus civitatem et suffragii ius nuper datum, foedus percussit;* cf. Appian, *BC,* 1.77; Cic. *Phil.* 12.27; Badian, *For. Client.,* 244, 246-248; Taylor, *Voting Districts,* 118-119. On Italian sufferings, see esp. Appian, *BC,* 1.96; cf. Cic. *De Domo,* 79; Sallust, *Hist.* 1.55.12, Maur. The attractive suggestion that Sulla deliberately excluded Samnites from his favors for propaganda purposes was recently made by Salmon, *Athenaeum,* 42 (1964), 74-79.

[15] It is now generally recognized that the novelty and the rigidity of the Sullan settlement ought not to be exaggerated. E.g., the old Mommsenian notion that Sulla provided a rigid scheme to keep magistrates at home and pro-magistrates in the provinces must now be given up; see A. E. R. Boak, "The Extraordinary Commands from 80 to 48 B.C.: A Study in the Origins of the Principate," *AHR,* 24 (1918-19), 1-25; Balsdon, "Consular Provinces under the Late Republic," *JRS,* 29 (1939), 58-65. The flexibility of Sulla's constitution needs further stressing. For sources on the legislation, see *MRR,* II.74-75; cf. the analysis of Valgiglio, *Silla,* 76-154. See also U. Laffi, "Il mito di Silla," *Athenaeum,* 45 (1967), 177-213.

at the expense of other classes. The *lex Plautia,* drawing, at least in theory, on all classes, suited perfectly the interests of his regime. The comparative lack of judicial activity in the mid 80's made a new Cinnan law not only undesirable, but unnecessary. Sulla's bill, we may be reasonably certain, superseded the *lex Plautia.*[16]

A transfer of judicial duties to the senate naturally required a substantial increase in senatorial membership. Civil wars and proscriptions had reduced the personnel of that body considerably. But a gap in the numbers was not Sulla's only motive for the addition of new members. The normal number of pre-Sullan senators seems to have been three hundred whereas the Ciceronian senate numbered six hundred.[17] Sulla therefore did not simply fill up the senate's depleted ranks; he substantially increased its normal personnel. One can perhaps commend the dictator's vision here; an enlarged government would be a more genuine representative of all Italy and could best reflect the incorporation of new citizens into the Roman body politic. There can be little doubt, however, that the immediate problem of the judiciary would in any case have demanded a considerably larger number of *patres.* The senate as it had stood previously simply did not have the membership to handle the expanded criminal court system that the dictator planned.

It is possible that Sulla already had expansion in mind in 88. Under that year Appian reports that he proposed a measure to enroll three hundred new members into the senate. The plan, of course, bears a striking resemblance to the program of Livius Drusus in 91; a transfer of the courts to the senate, combined with an increase in its number drawn from the "best men" who were still outside its ranks.[18] It is pertinent to recall the situation at that time. With the Italian menace largely eliminated and the passions of the *lex Varia* cooled down, the Metellan judicial proposals may well have been brought up again, this time by the consul Sulla, only recently linked in marriage to the Metellan group. As we have seen, equestrian jurors had, on the whole, acted moderately under the *lex Varia* in 90, and a measure that offered something like a reconciliation of the orders may have seemed reasonable in 88. *Equites* stood to gain from a bill that superseded the *lex Plautia.*

[16] So, rightly, Zumpt, *Criminalrecht,* II.1.264-265; Hill, *Roman Middle Class,* 138. Sources on Sulla's law: Cic. *Verr.* 1.37-38, 1.47-49, 2.2.77; *Pro Cluent.* 55; Vell. Pat. 2.32; Tac. *Ann.* 11.22; Ps-Asconius, 189, 219, 222, Stangl; Schol. Gronov. 326, Stangl; *Digest,* 1.2.2.32.

[17] See P. Willems, *Le senat de la république romaine. Sa composition et ses attributions* (Louvain and Paris, 1878-1883), I.30, 404-406.

[18] Appian, *BC,* 1.59: κατέλεξαν ἐς τὸ βουλευτήριον . . . ἀθρόους ἐκ τῶν ἀρίστων ἀνδρῶν τριακοσίους; cf. Gabba, *Athenaeum,* 34 (1956), 124-133; *Ann-Pisa,* 33 (1964), 7-8.

For his own purposes, Sulla would certainly have sought to strengthen the senate by adding men who would be loyal to him while he fought Rome's wars in the east. Whether the bill was actually put into effect in 88 as Appian suggests remains dubious.[19] Real reform along these lines, in any case, would have to await Sulla's return.

In 81, the plan was implemented in full; three hundred more members were added to the senate. Whence came these men? The flower of the equestrian order was recruited, say Appian and the Epitomator of Livy; common soldiers and "any old person," report Sallust and Dionysius.[20] The sources evidently offer their analysis in accordance with their view of Sulla. Modern historians, in accordance with *their* view, have adopted one tradition or the other or a combination. One can imagine a senate packed with men loyal to Sulla, drawn from even the lowest social rungs. Conversely, a case can be made out for the *equites equo publico,* men who were a part of and indistinguishable from the most oligarchical elements of Roman society. These conjectures do not exhaust the possibilities. Some have argued that the business classes formed the backbone of the new senate, but that Sullan soldiers, loyal and with distinguished military records, perhaps enriched by the proscriptions, were also added to it. Others see the incorporation of the Italian aristocracy, many of whom had been Sullan supporters, whether early or late, in the civil wars.[21] The point is that Sulla sought to put firm control of the judiciary in the hands of the *nobilitas* without alienating those groups on whom continued stability in the state depended. Certainly the fact that there was some judicial corruption in the 70's does not imply that Sulla filled the *curia* with greedy men of the *nouveaux riches.*[22] The senate, seriously

[19] On Sulla's purposes, see Syme, "Caesar, the Senate, and Italy," *PBSR,* 14 (1938), 22-25. Doubt on the implementation of the measure is expressed by Hardy, "The Number of the Sullan Senate," *JRS,* 6 (1916), 59-62. Others have rejected Appian's evidence altogether; Schur, *Zeit. Marius u. Sulla,* 134. Conclusive demonstration is impossible.

[20] Appian, *BC,* 1.100: ἐκ τῶν ἀρίστων ἱππέων; Livy, *Per.* 89: *ex equestri ordine;* Sallust, *Cat.* 37: *ex gregariis militibus;* Dion. Hal. 5.77: ἐκ τῶν ἐπιτυχόντων ἀνθρώπων.

[21] That Sulla cynically enriched his supporters, even the rankers, and enrolled them into the senate is the view of Carcopino, *Sylla,* 65. That the new senators were *equites equo publico* has been argued by Hill, "Sulla's New Senators in 81 B.C.," *CQ,* 26 (1932), 170-177. On Sulla's incorporation of the business classes and his own soldiers, see Gabba, *Athenaeum,* 34 (1956), 124-133; *App. BC Lib. Prim.,* 343-345; Valgiglio, *Silla,* 94-99. For the view that he installed many from the Italian aristocracy, see Schur, *"Homo Novus,"* *BonnJbb,* 134 (1929), 54-66; Syme, *PBSR,* 14 (1938), 22-25; Meier, *Res Pub.,* 256-258.

[22] J. R. Hawthorn, "The Senate after Sulla," *Greece and Rome,* 9 (1962), 53-60, too readily identifies corruptible jurors with men of lower-class back-

depleted in the 80's and now expected to provide jurors for at least seven permanent *quaestiones,* had to be increased substantially. Loyal Sullani, young aristocrats, politically-minded members of the business classes, and distinguished Italians were all probably recruited for the purpose. Sulla put the best possible face on the reform: the new senators were not to be appointees, but were to be elected by the tribes. It is possible even that he arranged approximate equality in tribal representation. The *lex Plautia* had also provided for tribal election of jury panels, another small hint that that measure was still on the books when Sulla instituted his reform. Whatever the democratic appearance of this *lex Cornelia,* however, the dictator was taking no chances. Sulla made certain to handpick the candidates presented to the tribes.[23] The plan of Livius Drusus, proposed a decade earlier for somewhat different purposes, was now at last implemented.

It is time now to examine the system of *quaestiones* as reorganized by Sulla. To what degree the Sullan courts represent novel institutions and to what degree a legacy from earlier legal evolution is a question not easily answered. It would be pointless to assert that any conclusion on this matter can be definitive. But considerable light may be shed by a setting forth and an analysis of the ancient evidence for each of the courts.

The *quaestio de repetundis,* of course, had a long history prior to the Sullan constitution. The last extortion law for which any evidence exists, the *lex Servilia* of Glaucia of ca. 104, was presumably still in effect in 81. Almost certainly there was a Sullan law on the matter that superseded the *lex Servilia.* In his speech for Rabirius Postumus under the *lex Iulia de repetundis,* Cicero refers to a clause of that law, *quo ea pecunia pervenerit,* which, he affirms, occurred also in the *lex Cornelia* and in the *lex Servilia* before that. This passage ought to mean that there was a Sullan extortion law, though the lack of any further reference to it indicates that it made few, if any, changes in the earlier legislation on *repetundae.*[24] Other testimony from Ciceronian speeches may provide

---

ground. Judicial corruption in the 70's may be somewhat exaggerated anyway. Cicero, it should be remembered, has axes to grind in the *Verrines* and the *Pro Cluentio;* cf. L. P. Hoy, "Political Influence in Roman Prosecutions, 78-60 B.C." (unpub. diss., Bryn Mawr College, 1952), 25-29. See the careful and sober analysis of Nicolet, *L'Ordre Equestre,* 581-591, who argues plausibly that Sulla included many of the *equites* who had served as *iudices,* thus providing some continuity in the judiciary.

[23] Appian, *BC,* 1.100: αὐτῇ δὲ τῇ βουλῇ . . . προσκατελέξεν ἀμφὶ τοὺς τρια- κοσίους ἐκ τῶν ἀρίστων ἱππέων, ταῖς φυλαῖς ἀναδοὺς ψῆφον περὶ ἑκάστου; cf. Gabba, *App. BC Lib. Prim.,* 345. For the suggestion that Sulla sought equal tribal representation, see Taylor, *Voting Districts,* 292-293. The depletion of the senate in the 80's is rightly stressed by Meier, *Res Pub.,* 243-244.

some information on the provisions of the Sullan law, but that any of these were novel provisions is not subject to demonstration.[25] The penalty has been much discussed. The *lex Acilia* had assessed pecuniary damages as twice what had been extorted; in the Ciceronian era the penalty was up to two and a half times the amount. That may have been Sulla's doing, a minor readjustment at best.[26] The nature of the criminal penalty for the offender remains an open question. Romans rarely inflicted capital punishment but that in itself need not be a clue to what was written in the law. It has been argued that Sulla abandoned the capital penalty and substituted a formal pronouncement of *interdictio,* now a legal punishment rather than an administrative decree recognizing the physical fact of exile. There is some evidence that the crime of *res repetundae* carried less than the death penalty. The bulk of the testimony, however, indicates that an offender on this charge put his *caput* in jeopardy.[27] Sulla consequently may have introduced no novelty in this area either.

The evidence is clear for a *maiestas* court that predated the Sullan reforms. Set up in somewhat ambiguous terms by Saturninus in 103, its scope was expanded slightly by Varius in 90. But the question of which

[24] Cic. *Pro Rab. Post.* 8. Elsewhere Cicero speaks of a post-Sullan extortion trial, mentioning a law *de pecuniis repetundis,* but gives no author; *Pro Cluent.* 104. Zumpt, *Criminalrecht,* II.1.357-376, points to the flimsy nature of our evidence on a Sullan extortion law. But his conclusion that the clause *quo ea pecunia pervenerit* was incorporated by Sulla into his *maiestas* or his *ambitus* law does not persuade. Since the *leges Iulia* and *Servilia,* mentioned in the same sentence by Cicero, were both *repetundae* laws, it would be very odd indeed if the *lex Cornelia* were a law on *maiestas.*

[25] Cf., e.g., Cic. *Verr.* 2.2.142, 2.2.146, 2.3.169.

[26] On damages under the Gracchan law, see *lex repet.,* line 59 (*FIRA,* I.96); on the post-Sullan assessment, see Cic. *Div. in Caec.* 19; *Verr.* 1.56, 2.1.27. The mysterious *quadruplatores,* mentioned by Ps-Asconius, 110, Stangl, may suggest a four-fold restitution, but his evidence carries little weight; see Zumpt, *Criminalrecht,* II.1.360-362. Mommsen, *Strafrecht,* 727-732, conjectured that Sulla restored the simple restitution, once provided for in the *lex Calpurnia.* That is sufficiently refuted by Cic. *De Off.* 2.75: *tot leges et proximae quaeque duriores;* cf. also *Pro Rab. Post.* 8.

[27] Cic. *Div. in Caec.* 71: *de capite et fortunis suis; Pro Caec.* 100: *Exsilium enim non supplicium est, sed perfugium portusque supplici;* cf. *Pro Font.* 3. Alleged evidence to the contrary is not so weighty: Cic. *Pro Cluent.* 115-116; Asconius, 78, Clark. Mommsen, *Strafrecht,* 965-980, believed that Sulla wrote *interdictio* into his statutes as a legal penalty; so also Greenidge, *Legal Procedure,* 512-513. Strachan-Davidson, *Problems,* II.10, 16, inclined to the view that the stiff pecuniary penalties of the Sullan law induced exile to avoid bankruptcy, an argument accepted in a modified form by Sherwin-White, *PBSR,* 17 (1949), 8-12; *JRS,* 42 (1952), 43-55. That the penalty for *repetundae* was capital before and after Sulla has been maintained by E. Levy, "Die römische Kapitalstrafe," *SBHeid,* 21 (1930-31), 14-39; Siber, *AbhLeipz,* 43 (1936), 55-67, and Henderson, *JRS,* 41 (1951), 71-75.

crimes did or did not fall within its purview remained unclear to contemporaries, as it does now. The line between *maiestas* and *perduellio*
was evidently still fuzzy, and the existence of a *quaestio perpetua* did
not preclude *perduellio* trials heard by the *comitia*. There were a number
of such trials in the early 90's and early 80's.[28] In this respect, Sulla's
lex de maiestate, unlike his extortion law, made a significant and permanent change. Sulla had directly limited the tribunes' powers of legislation and *intercessio.* He could now indirectly limit their judicial prerogatives also, by eliminating the need for tribunician prosecutions before the
people. This would most easily be effected by a vast extension of the
maiestas law, incorporating within it a large number of hitherto ill-defined
offenses. The evidence indicates that this is precisely what was done.
After 81 there are no recorded *perduellio* prosecutions before the *comitia,*
with the solitary exception of the trial of Rabirius in 63. That prosecution, of course, is eloquent testimony that the procedure had fallen into
meaningless obscurity. The rusty and antiquated machinery resurrected
to try Rabirius converted the case into a farce.[29] Sulla had done his work
well. Of the provisions of his law only a few are known, but they are
sufficient to demonstrate its detailed and precise nature, which brought
within its scope all possible offenses committed by Roman officials in
the course of their duty both outside and inside Rome.[30] Not all ambiguity, however, was removed. The *maiestas* and *repetundae* laws continued to overlap to a certain extent and so perhaps the murder law as
well. But popular trials under tribunician presidency do appear to have
been largely dispensed with.[31] From the Sullan point of view, the removal
of popular trials was a decisive step in the direction of sound and stable
government.

The existence of a pre-Sullan *quaestio de ambitu* should no longer
be called into question. Trials for *ambitus* had not been infrequent in

[28] On these trials, see above, Chapters VII and VIII; on Saturninus' law,
see above, pp. 167-168; on the *lex Varia,* see above, pp. 215-216.

[29] For an examination of the trial of Rabirius, see Strachan-Davidson,
Problems, I.188-204. That Sulla deliberately sought to undermine comitial
trials conducted by tribunes was effectively argued by Lengle, *Unt. Sull.
Verf.,* 45-55.

[30] See, e.g., Cic. *In Pis.* 50: *mitto exire de provincia, educere exercitum,
bellum sua sponte gerere, in regnum iniussu populi Romani aut senatus
accedere, quae cum plurimae leges veteres, tum lex Cornelia maiestatis . . .
vetat.* Other evidence for the law in Cic. *Pro Cluent.* 97, 99; *Verr.* 2.1.12,
2.4.88, 2.5.50; *Ad Fam.* 3.11.2; cf. *Ad Fam.* 1.9.25, 3.6.3; *In Vat.* 12; and
see the thorough treatment of Zumpt, *Criminalrecht,* II.1.376-392.

[31] On the overlapping of the *maiestas* and extortion laws, see Cic. *Verr.*
2.1.12; on overlapping with the murder law, see Cic. *Pro Cluent.* 114. For a
list of the few recorded or alleged tribunician prosecutions in the Ciceronian
period, see Greenidge, *Legal Procedure,* 353.

previous decades and yet no hint survives of any ad hoc *quaestiones* on the matter. Marius had been tried for this offense in 116, Rutilius and Scaurus in the same year, Hortensius in 109, Antonius in 97, Philippus in 92, and P. Sextius in 90.[32] Sulla, it is abundantly clear, did not institute the *ambitus* procedure. He does, however, seem to have sponsored a law on the subject, whose only known clause prescribed a penalty of ten years' prohibition from canvassing for office.[33] Apart from that, ancient testimony fails us. A hardening of the penalty is all that can be ascribed to Sulla in the area of electoral bribery.

Evidence on the murder court is ambiguous and difficult. It is useful to summarize it. The *elogium* of C. Claudius Pulcher, consul in 92, among other things, boasts of the office of *iudex quaestionis veneficis*. That reference establishes at least the existence of a court to try poisoning cases prior to Sulla.[34] For the *quaestio de sicariis* we are not blessed with similar information. L. Hostilius Tubulus sat on such a court as long ago as 142, but since that is the only recorded occasion prior to Sulla, it is likely that Tubulus presided over a *quaestio extraordinaria*. Certainly a murder investigation in 138 against some *publicani* and slaves was handled on an ad hoc basis by the consuls on instructions from the senate. L. Cassius Ravilla, consul in 127 and a judge of notorious severity, has often been cited in this connection. He sat as a *quaesitor,* so it is reported, in many murder trials. But the term *quaesitor* can mislead. It need not imply and, on the face of it, would seem to deny that there was a standing court for homicide in the late second century. The trial, such as it was, of the Numidian Bomilcar in 111 was certainly an extraordinary proceeding.[35] Documentation is fuller on specific cases of parricide. In the pre-Sullan period, the charge seems to have involved a separate procedure. Q. Fabius Maximus Eburnus was convicted of parricide in 104; the case, it appears, came before the assembly. In 101,

[32] On these trials, see above, pp. 120-125, 149, 194, 206, and also Appendix D.

[33] Schol. Bob. 78, Stangl: *Superioribus temporibus damnati lege Cornelia hoc genus poenae ferebant, ut magistratuum petitione per decem annos abstinerent.* Zumpt, *Criminalrecht,* II.1.373-376, assigns this provision to Sulla's legislation on the revival of the *lex annalis.* That ignores the fact that the Bobbiensian scholiast is here commenting on an *ambitus* case, for which the *lex Cornelia* is cited as a precedent.

[34] *ILS,* 45. Zumpt, *Criminalrecht,* II.2.140-141, as might be expected, denies this also. His arguments are successfully refuted by Lengle, *Unt. Sull. Verf.,* 36-40.

[35] The testimony on Tubulus is in Cic. *De Fin.* 2.54. That he sat on a *quaestio perpetua* is conjectured, without evidence, by Mommsen, *Strafrecht,* 612-616, and Lengle, *Unt. Sull. Verf.,* 36-40. On the homicide investigation of 138, see Cic. *Brutus,* 85; on Cassius Ravilla, Asconius, 45, Clark; on Bomilcar, Sallust, *Iug.* 35.

the matricide Publicius Malleolus received the grisly penalty of the sack; his jurors are not specified, though, very likely, they were also the *populus*. By 80, however, Cicero could speak of a parricide case, *non multis annis,* which was decided by *iudices.*[36] To summarize the scattered bits of information: the procedures *de veneficiis, de sicariis,* and *de parricidiis* were all independent prior to Sulla; a *quaestio de veneficiis* was in existence by the 90's, a *quaestio* to hear parricide charges was instituted sometime between 101 and the mid 80's, and the crime *inter sicarios* had frequently been tried by *quaestiones extraordinariae* since 142. In 81 Sulla sponsored a *lex de sicariis et veneficiis.* The measure did more than combine those two offenses under a single law; it obviously also incorporated parricide, since Roscius Amerinus was tried under it in 80. Judicial bribery to procure the unlawful condemnation of a defendant was also attached to this law.[37] Consolidation of procedure for all analagous crimes, not innovation, was the keynote here. Sulla reorganized and stabilized previously existing procedures, placing them all under a single piece of detailed legislation. Poisoning, parricide, assassination, and judicial murder were wrapped in the same package.

It has sometimes been assumed that Sulla also passed a law on *peculatus.* A *quaestio peculatus* certainly functioned in the Ciceronian period,[38] but no record survives of a *lex Cornelia de peculatu.* Nothing

[36] On the trial of Fabius Eburnus, see above, pp. 172-173. That the case was heard by the assembly is indicated by Orosius' *die dicta;* 5.16.8. On the trial of Malleolus, see Orosius, 6.16.23; Livy, *Per.* 68; cf. *Ad Herenn.* 1.33. For Cicero's reference to a parricide case before *iudices,* see *Pro Rosc. Amer.* 64-65; cf. 11, 28, 90; *Ad Herenn.* 4.53. The independence of the *parricidium* charge prior to Sulla is suggested also by Cic. *De Invent.* 2.58. Kunkel, *AbhMünch,* 56 (1962), 45-48, argues that the popular assembly never heard cases of murder or other common crimes, but limited its jurisdiction to political offenses. Proof on this matter is impossible. The sources record few instances of common crimes and Kunkel makes perhaps too much of the scanty testimony on the *tresviri capitales,* to whom he ascribes responsibility for the handling of common crimes. Whatever the normal procedure in the early and middle Republic, it is clear, as Kunkel rightly emphasizes, that special murder *quaestiones* had become frequent before a permanent court was established.

[37] For Sulla's *lex de sicariis et veneficiis,* see Cic. *Pro Cluent.* 148; *Digest,* 48.8. Though a single law now covered the subject, the *quaestiones* that heard charges under the two headings seem to have remained separate; Cic. *Pro Cluent.* 147; *Digest,* 1.2.2.32; cf. Cic. *Pro Cluent.* 148, 151, 157. On the Sullan murder law generally, see Zumpt, *Criminalrecht,* II.2.1-38, and, more briefly, Kunkel, *RE,* 47.741-742, "quaestio."

[38] Cic. *Pro Cluent.* 147; *Pro Mur.* 42; *De Nat. Deor.* 3.74; cf. *Verr.* 1.39, 2.1.11, 2.3.83. The suggestion of a Sullan law was made long ago by Lange, *Röm. Alt.* 3.166.

bars the assumption that a standing court on the theft of public funds existed before the Sullan rogations. The trial of Pompey in 86 very likely took place before such a standing *quaestio*. On the other hand, the *peculatus* case of Q. Caepio in 104 had required a *quaestio extraordinaria*. The inception of a permanent court remains undated. But if, as was suggested earlier, the trial of L. Lucullus in 102 was on a *peculatus* charge, that would fix the chronology rather neatly. The demagogues of 104 and 103 are the logical initiators of such a court.[39] In any case, Sulla, it appears, made no changes here.

A *lex Cornelia de iniuriis* is cited by imperial jurists. That this measure actually established a criminal *quaestio* is, however, subject to dispute. Prior to Sulla, actions for *iniuria* had usually been heard as civil cases by *recuperatores*. Did Sulla replace this procedure by creating a formal criminal court? One telling piece of evidence points to this conclusion. Cicero in 69 contrasts the *iniuria* procedure with the civil law and asserts that conviction involves not restitution but legal satisfaction through *poena* and *iudicium*.[40] How extensive the new legislation was is beyond conjecture. Some include libel under its jurisdiction. But a proliferation of hypotheses is fruitless. No libel cases are recorded in the late Republic and the one extant piece of information suggests a loose connection with *maiestas*.[41] The most that may be said is that Sulla was responsible for a *quaestio de iniuriis* that brought the formerly civil action into the scheme of his criminal *quaestiones*.[42]

It is a relief to know that one standing court may without hesitation

[39] On the trial of Pompey, see above, pp. 244-246; of Caepio, pp. 162-163; of Lucullus, pp. 176-178. On the *peculatus* charge generally, see Mommsen, *Strafrecht,* 759-773.

[40] Cic. *Pro Caec.* 35: *actio enim iniuriam non ius possessionis adsequitur sed dolorem imminutae libertatis iudicio poenaque mitigat.* References to the Sullan law in *Instit.* 4.4.8; *Digest,* 47.10.5, 48.2.12.4, 48.5.23.3. For the pre-Sullan civil procedure, see Cic. *De Invent.* 2.60; Gellius, 20.1.13. Lange, *Röm. Alt.,* 3.166, argued that the Sullan law simply regulated the earlier *actio iniuriarum.* For Mommsen, *Strafrecht,* 784-808, it set up a regular court and brought the *iniuria* procedure closer to criminal procedure, though its features remained essentially those of the civil law.

[41] Cic. *Ad Fam.* 3.11.2: *Verum tamen est maiestas, etsi Sulla voluit, ne in quemvis impune declamari liceret.* On this, see R. J. M. Lindsay, "Defamation and the Law under Sulla," *CP,* 44 (1949), 240-243. That libel was covered by the Sullan *iniuria* law was conjectured by Mommsen and accepted, though with caution, by L. Robinson, *Freedom of Speech in the Roman Republic* (Baltimore, 1940), 51-54.

[42] So Lengle, *Unt. Sull. Verf.,* 42-43; contra: Zumpt, *Criminalrecht,* II.2.50-52, and Kunkel, *RE,* 47.743, "quaestio," who reduce legislation on *iniuria* to a clause within Sulla's *lex de sicariis.*

be ascribed to Sulla as an innovation. Sulla receives specific credit for the *quaestio de falsis,* also known as *testamentaria* or *nummaria.*[43] Even for it, however, there was a precedent of sorts. In 85, as noted earlier, the praetor Marius Gratidianus had issued an edict establishing a sort of "Bureau of Standards" to judge debased and counterfeit coins. Sulla now made the production of false currency a criminal offense. In typical fashion he incorporated this offense into an omnibus bill involving forgery of wills and documents as well as counterfeiting of coins.[44] In this respect, the approach belongs in the same category with that of the *leges Corneliae* on *maiestas* and on homicide.

No other *quaestiones* established or revised by Sulla are known. A few possibilities suggest themselves but offer only questions, no answers. In 73, C. Rabirius was prosecuted before *iudices* by C. Licinius Macer for violating certain sacred groves and places. Did Sulla establish a court to hear religious offenses? In the absence of other evidence, its existence must remain doubtful. The offense could have fallen under the jurisdiction of some other court. Evidence exists for a *lex Fabia* on kidnapping. The year 63 is a *terminus ante quem* for the measure, but there is no specific information to link it with the Sullan legislation. The dictator liked to have his own name on his measures. The passage of the *lex Lutatia de vi* in 78 or 77 is enough to show that Sulla had made no provisions for that particular crime. There were Sullan laws on luxury and adultery, but it is most unlikely that these instituted criminal *quaestiones.*[45] Further speculation is precluded by the absence of testimony.

In general, novelty was not a hallmark of Sulla's judicial reforms. In this sphere he was essentially an organizer and a systematizer rather than an innovator. Older criminal charges were defined more precisely

[43] Cic. *Verr.* 2.1.108: *Cornelia testamentaria, nummaria . . . sancitur, ut, quod semper malum facinus fuerit, eius quaestio ad populum pertineat ex certo tempore;* cf. *De Nat. Deor.* 3.74; Suet. *Aug.* 33; *Instit.* 4.18.7; *Digest* 48.10.33; Kunkel, *RE,* 47.742, "*quaestio.*"

[44] On this crime generally, see Zumpt, *Criminalrecht,* II.2.62-78; Mommsen, *Strafrecht,* 667-681.

[45] On the trial of Rabirius in 73, see Cic. *Pro Rab. Perd.* 7; cf. Lengle, *Unt. Sull. Verf.,* 45. For the *lex Fabia,* see Cic. *Pro Rab. Perd.* 8; Apuleius, *Metam.* 8.24; cf. Zumpt, *Criminalrecht,* II.2.33-37; Lange, *Röm. Alt.,* 2.663; Mommsen, *Strafrecht,* 780-783; Niccolini, *Fast. Trib. Pleb.,* 437. The *lex Lutatia* is noted by Cic. *Pro Cael.* 70. Mention is made there also of a *lex Plautia de vi* of uncertain date, but probably not earlier than the *lex Lutatia;* Niccolini, *Fast. Trib. Pleb.,* 252-253; *MRR,* II.128; J. N. Hough, "The *Lex Lutatia* and the *Lex Plautia de Vi,*" *AJP,* 51 (1930), 135-147. On the crime of *vis,* see Mommsen, *Strafrecht,* 651-666. For the Sullan sumptuary and adultery laws, see Gellius, 2.24.11; Macrobius, *Sat.* 3.17.11; Plut. *Sulla,* 35; *Comp. Lys. et Sulla,* 3; Cic. *Ad Att.* 12.36.1.

and in greater detail and analogous offenses were deftly combined in more comprehensive measures. In so far as new *quaestiones* emerged, they seem to have involved largely a transference of what had been civil judisdiction to the realm of criminal law.[46] That is not to deny for a moment the significance of these institutions. Sulla's shadow hung heavily over future developments in the Roman legal structure. To all intents and purposes, the *comitia* as a court of final jurisdiction disappeared from the scene. The system of standing *quaestiones* that had developed piecemeal, subject to the vagaries of politics, for well over half a century now received official sanction and, more important, reorganization as a totality.

The form was set. But what of the substance? Were criminal procedures truly to be free from politics? Were the courts truly to be arbitrated by responsible and impartial juries with a concern for justice and the security of the community? The Cinnan years, whatever their virtues, had left little room for free judicial expression. The regime had been anxious lest the courts become a vehicle for dissent. Was it likely that the far more autocratic power of Sulla would be less restrictive and would tolerate a free judiciary? For the Roman aristocracy, as well as for budding young orators, this question loomed large. It had been a long time since a criminal case of any sort had been heard in Rome. When the first one came, we may be sure, men followed its development with intense interest, anticipation, and anxiety. The importance of the trial of Sex. Roscius Amerinus in 80 cannot be gainsaid.[47]

The facts of the case are well known. Much of it revolved around an avaricious freedman of Sulla, L. Cornelius Chrysogonus. Evidently he had made a fortune by unscrupulously cashing in on his position during the proscriptions. His character, it should be remembered, is reported only by Cicero, hardly the most objective of authorities on this matter. Chrysogonus, however obnoxious a figure he may have cut in curled and perfumed locks, at least showed some good taste in the objects of

[46] As in the cases of *iniuria* and *de falsis;* cf. Lengle, *Unt. Sull. Verf.*, 45. Kunkel's view, *AbhMünch,* 56 (1962), 51-70, that the Sullan *quaestiones* dealt only with what were already criminal offenses, ignores these two.

[47] For the date, see Gellius, 15.28.5; Quintilian, 12.6.4. Carcopino, *Sylla,* 155-160, put it in 79, followed, more recently, by Pareti, *Storia di Roma,* III.638-643. His arguments have been often refuted; see Gelzer, "Review of Carcopino, *Sylla,*" *Gnomon,* 8 (1932), 607; Van Ooteghem, *Pompeé,* 79-87; Badian, *For. Client.,* 297; T. E. Kinsey, "The Dates of the *Pro Roscio Amerino* and *Pro Quinctio,*" *Mnemosyne,* 20 (1967), 61-67. That the trial of Roscius was the first in a very long time is stated explicitly by Cic. *Pro Rosc. Amer.* 28: *Ita loqui homines: quod iudicia tam diu facta non essent, condemnari cum oportere qui primus in iudicium adductus esset;* also *ibid.* 11.

his plunder: paintings, statues, music, and gourmet cooks.[48] But he was greedy for more. In 80, Chrysogonus suborned a certain C. Erucius to bring charges of parricide against Sex. Roscius of Ameria. The defendant's father had been murdered and his property then purchased by Chrysogonus, who now, Cicero alleges, sought to secure his holdings by imputing the murder to the younger Roscius.[49] The political implications of the prosecution, however, went far beyond the relatively obscure individuals directly involved. Sex. Roscius the elder had traveled in the very best of Roman circles. His son consequently, though Cicero is at pains to portray him as a humble rustic, could claim connections and friendship with the Servilii, the Metelli, and the Scipiones.[50] These were families with a long history of pride in their role as patrons of the Italian aristocracy. The heads of these houses played no active role in the trial of Roscius, but younger members did appear for the defense. Reference is made to a P. Scipio and to a Metellus as advocates in Roscius' behalf. The Scipio is very likely the son of P. Scipio Nasica, praetor in 93. He was himself later to be adopted by the Metelli and to reach the consulship in 52 with the somewhat pretentious but most impressive name of Q. Caecilius Metellus Pius Scipio Nasica. The Metellus apparently was either Q. Metellus Celer, consul in 60, or Q. Metellus Nepos, consul in 57. Still another young member of the nobility, Valerius Messala, prepared and managed the case for the defense. Modesty and youth prevented Valerius from speaking up himself, Cicero reports; more likely it was prudence. This young man was presumably M. Valerius Messala Rufus, future consul of 53, or perhaps M. Valerius Messala Niger, consul in 61.[51] The Metellan family's protection of Roscius was demonstrated in conspicuous fashion. He had sought and received refuge and lodging at the home of Caecilia Metella, daughter of Metellus Balearicus, consul of 123, and sister of Metellus Nepos, consul in 98. Related as she was to both consuls-elect in 80, Ap. Claudius Pulcher and P. Servilius Vatia, Metella was clearly at the very center of the establishment.[52] The pillars of the Roman aristocracy were behind Sex. Roscius in his plight.

[48] Cf. Cic. *Pro Rosc. Amer.* 133-135.

[49] Cic. *Pro Rosc. Amer. passim;* Plut. *Cic.* 3; Schol. Gronov. 301, Stangl. Cf. Kinsey, "A Dilemma in the *Pro Roscio Amerino,*" *Mnemosyne,* 19 (1966), 270-271.

[50] Cic. *Pro Rosc. Amer.* 15.

[51] For Scipio and Metellus, see Cic. *Pro Rosc. Amer.* 27; for Messala, 149. On the prosopographical identifications, see Carcopino, *Sylla,* 161-166.

[52] Cic. *Pro Rosc. Amer.* 27: *Ea Sex. Roscium inopem . . . recepit domum hospitique oppresso iam desperatoque ab omnibus opitulata est.* The remark here that she was the daughter of Nepos must be a slip; see 147; cf. Carcopino, *Sylla,* 177-178. Nor was she the wife of Ap. Claudius, as Münzer

It does not follow, however, that no risks were attached to the defense of Roscius against Sulla's freedman. Quite the contrary. Sulla, to be sure, had shown some displeasure with excessive profiteering, and Chrysogonus himself, so Cicero asserts, was aware that he could not count entirely on the dictator's support.[53] But constitutionalism on the part of the man who had marched Roman troops on Rome, instituted brutal proscriptions, and established military colonies in Italy could hardly be relied upon, even by men who had supported him from the beginning, much less by those who had remained in Rome in the mid 80's. The situation was delicate. An attack on Chrysogonus could easily be regarded as an attack on Sulla himself. Men of influence and authority shirked the task; their actions might be too readily misconstrued.[54] The accusers were supremely confident; there was good reason to believe that the defense of Roscius would be, at best, perfunctory.[55] Uncertainty and trepidation help to explain why leaders of the aristocratic class remained in the background. Only younger cadets of the noble houses put in an appearance for Roscius.

The principal *oratio* for the defendant was delivered by a young Arpinate of a family hardly more illustrious than that of Roscius himself. M. Cicero was only twenty-six years old, with no magisterial ancestors and an Italian equestrian background. He had, however, equipped himself admirably. An eager auditor of Crassus and Antonius as a boy, he had studied philosophy with Diodotus, rhetoric with Molo, and jurisprudence with Q. Scaevola. His oratorical talents were beginning to blossom and his reputation to grow, but his appearances before the bar had hitherto been in civil cases only. Brief service is recorded with Pompeius Strabo and with Sulla himself in the Social War. Since that time his political attachments had been cautious and prudent. Cicero was in Rome in the 80's and, like many others in more responsible positions, had hoped for reconciliation and an avoidance of civil war. Also like many others, however, when it came he made certain to be on

---

believes, *RE*, 5.1235, "Caecilia," n. 135. Were that the case Cicero would surely have referred to the house of Appius, not of Metella. She was doubtles Appius' sister-in-law. The relationship to Servilius Vatia was through her cousin, another Caecilia Metella, Vatia's wife; Carcopino, *Sylla*, 180-182.

[53] Cic. *Pro Rosc. Amer.* 25: *Chrysogonus et ipse ad eos accedit et homines nobilis adlegat qui paterent ne ad Sullam adirent;* cf. 109-110. On Sulla's attitude, cf. Plut. *Crass.* 6.8.

[54] Cic. *Pro Rosc. Amer.* 1-5. See esp. 2: *si qui istorum dixisset quos videtis adesse, in quibus summa auctoritas est atque amplitudo, si verbum de re publica fecisset, id quod in hac fieri necesse est, multo plura dixisse quam dixisset putaretur.*

[55] Cic. *Pro Rosc. Amer.* 5, 28, 60-61, 91.

the right side. He labored to ensure the success of the conqueror.[56] Cicero was a safe choice as defense counsel. His presence would not offend the dictator. His oratory might prove effective.

Cicero's task was no easy one. Chrysogonus had to be attacked, but Sulla had to be spared, indeed, more than spared. Whenever Sulla is touched on in the speech it is always *honoris causa*. Cicero is careful throughout his speech to dissociate the activities of Chrysogonus from his great patron who, the orator affirms, could not have condoned those deeds had he known about them.[57] Praise for the dictator is lofty, perhaps excessively so. It is possible to trace bitter irony in Cicero's words; Sulla overlooked the misdeeds of his freedman, for he was too busy governing the whole of the empire, perusing Rome's past and determining her future. After all, Jupiter himself is omnipotent but not omniscient; in fits of absent-mindedness, he has ruined crops, maimed men, and destroyed cities. Can one be surprised that L. Sulla who rules the terrestrial world should have let some wickedness slip by unnoticed? That is fierce sarcasm; an intent audience could not have mistaken its meaning. That Cicero would have uttered such words in 80 is unlikely in the extreme. It was always possible, and usually desirable, to rework speeches for publication. After the death of Sulla, Cicero would have been interested in suggesting that he had shown more courage and forthrightness than was in fact possible at the time.[58] In 80, the irony would have been soft-pedalled, the praise proper and flattering.

Cicero's *Pro Roscio Amerino* was neither fawning servility nor piercing sarcasm. Its purposes were constructive and important. The argument may be summarized. The aims of the Sullan regime are admirable,

---

[56] Cic. *Pro Rosc. Amer.* 136: *postea quam id quod maxime volui fieri non potuit, ut componeretur, id maxime defendisse, ut ei vincerent qui vicerunt;* 137: *meque in eo studio partium fuisse confiteor;* also 142. For Cicero's part in the Social War, see Cic. *Phil.* 12.27; *De Div.* 1.72, 2.65; Plut. *Cic.* 3; cf. Cichorius, *Röm. Stud.*, 181-184. On his early career generally, see his own account in *Brutus*, 296, 304-312.

[57] Cic. *Pro Rosc. Amer.* 6, 21-22, 25, 91, 109-110, 127, 130-131, 136.

[58] Cic. *Pro Rosc. Amer.* 22: *Neque enim mirum, cum eodem tempore et ea quae praeterita sunt reparet et ea quae videntur instare praeparet . . . cum omnes in unum spectent, unus omnia gubernet . . . si aliquid non animadvertat;* 131: *Etenim si Iuppiter Optimus Maximus . . . hominibus nocuit, urbis delevit, fruges perdidit, quorum nihil pernicii causa divino consilio sed vi ipsa et magnitudine rerum factum putamus . . . quid miramur, iudices, L. Sullam, cum solus rem publicam regeret orbemque terrarum gubernaret . . . aliqua animadvertere non potuisse?* Rightly pointed out by Gabba, *AnnPisa*, 33 (1964), 10-11. That the speech was polished for publication is argued by J. Humbert, *Les plaidoyers écrits et les plaidoiries réelles de Ciceron* (Paris, 1925), 100-111.

the forms of the Sullan constitution appropriate: restoration of harmony, stability, and the rule of an enlightened aristocracy. But it is precisely because the dictator's reforms were so attractive that it was necessary to expose abuses in the system and to ensure that it would function properly. The issue was nothing less than whether the dictator was as sincere in implementing his program as he was clever in conceiving it. If the nobility was truly to resume its governing function, it could not be shorn of its old privileges and responsibilities in advance. Its traditional role as patron of a grateful clientèle could not be usurped by ruthless profiteers who owed their status to a period of anarchy and civil war. Nothing could be more galling to the *nobilitas* than to hear that prominent Italians who should have ties to the Roman aristocracy were putting themselves *in fidem et clientelam* of a freedman! [59] It was for the restoration of "Tory democracy" that the civil war had been fought; if the nobility could not protect its hereditary clients against an unscrupulous prosecutor, what had been the point of it all? [60] Such is Cicero's argument. But he has more to say on another important matter. Fratricidal strife and then proscriptions had perhaps been necessary in a good cause, but they also produce a breed of lawless ruffians who simply indulge their criminal appetites under the umbrella of martial law. Sulla, of course, was not to blame, so Cicero affirms, but the months in which the proscriptions were in effect witnessed the emergence of immoral profiteers who exploited the sufferings of their fellow-citizens. [61] What is worse, such men continue to terrorize the populace. They benefit from the perpetuation of martial conditions and have transformed Rome into a haven for cruelty and fear in which pity and humanity are virtually banished. [62] Courts have been set up to deal with offenders of every

[59] Cic. *Pro Rosc. Amer.* 106: *Nam cum multos veteres a maioribus Roscii patrones hospitesque haberent, omnis eos colere atque observare destiterunt ac se in Chrysogoni fidem et clientelam contulerunt.*

[60] See esp. Cic. *Pro Rosc. Amer.* 149: *haec acta res est ut ei nobiles restituerentur in civitatem qui hoc facerent . . . qui quantum possent in salute alterius quam in exitio mallent ostendere.* This aspect and import of the Ciceronian speech is admirably pointed out by Badian, *For. Client.,* 249-251.

[61] See esp. Cic. *Pro Rosc. Amer.* 80-81, 89-91; cf. Gabba, *AnnPisa,* 33 (1964), 11-14. That Cicero was directing his fire more specifically at M. Crassus, however, as suggested by T. A. Dorey, "A Note on the *Pro Roscio Amerino,*" *Ciceroniana,* 2 (1960), 147-148, is not indicated in the evidence.

[62] Cic. *Pro Rosc. Amer.* 150: *sin ea crudelitas quae hoc tempore in re publica versata est vestros quoque animos . . . duriores acerbioresque reddit, actum est, iudices inter feras satius est aetatem degere quam in hac tanta immanitate versari;* 154: *quae non modo id habet in se mali quod tot civis atrocissime sustulit verum etiam hominibus lenissimis ademit misericordiam consuetudine incommodorum;* cf. 14: *rei publicae calamitatem.*

variety. But will they really be allowed to do the job? Can a genuine judicial system tolerate manipulation by men who wield and abuse great power, capitalizing on their privileged position in the entourage of the dictator? The freedom of the judiciary is Cicero's principal concern, the theme that underlies the whole of his speech.[63]

What was the attitude of Sulla on the Roscius case? No direct testimony exists, but the indirect evidence is decisive.[64] With the families on whom Sex. Roscius relied for refuge and support Sulla had close ties. His marriage to Caecilia Metella had recently been dissolved, but on strictly religious grounds. The priests had insisted that her fatal illness not be allowed to pollute the dictator's home. It clearly did not involve a break with the Metelli, the head of whose house, Metellus Pius, shared the consulship with Sulla in the year of Roscius' trial. Even more revealing, Sulla now married a certain Valeria, a half sister of Q. Hortensius and sister of that very M. Valerius Messala who was a staunch defender of Roscius. It has already been noted that Roscius' hostess and patroness Caecilia Metella was related to the consuls of 79, both evidently elected with Sulla's blessing.[65] All this is more than sufficient to demolish the thesis that Roscius' trial was an attack by the *nobilitas* upon Sulla.[66] The Metelli had made bold before to question the value of prolonged anarchy; a C. Metellus had asked the dictator for a terminal date for the proscriptions. By the time that Roscius was prosecuted, the proscriptions were formally at an end and the dictator had already re-

---

[63] Cic. *Pro Rosc. Amer.* 9: *libertati tempora sunt impedimento;* 91: *a quibus miror ne quod iudiciorum esset vestigium non subsellia quoque esse combusta; nam et accusatores et iudices sustulerunt;* 137: *Sin autem . . . id non modo re prohibere non licet sed ne verbis quidem vituperare, tum vero in isto bello non recreatus neque restitutus sed subactus oppressusque populus Romanus est;* cf. 7, 11, 28, 140; and see Meier, *Res Pub.,* 249-251.

[64] Plutarch's story, *Cic.* 3.3-4, that Cicero had to flee Sulla's wrath after the trial of Roscius is manifestly false. Cicero was still in Rome in the following year; Cic. *Pro Caec.* 97. When he did eventually leave for the east it was for reasons of health and further study; Cic. *Brutus,* 314.

[65] For the death of Metella and Sulla's new marriage, see Plut. *Sulla,* 35.1-3. On Metellus Pius, cf. Cic. *Pro Planc.* 69, and the comments of A. R. Burn, "A Metellus in Two Passages of Dio," *CR,* 63 (1949), 52-53. On the consuls of 79, cf. Schur, *Zeit. Marius u. Sulla,* 206-208. It might be added that Sulla's closest asociate, L. Lucullus, soon to be executor of his will, possessed Caeciliae Metellae as both mother and mother-in-law.

[66] Carcopino's elaborate and ingenious hypothesis, *Sylla,* 147-197, accepted by Pareti, *Storia di Roma,* III.638-643, has been too often refuted to require rehearsal here; cf. Gelzer, *Gnomon,* 8 (1932), 607, and see, especially on the trial of Roscius, the sound arguments of A. Afzelius, "Zwei Episoden aus dem Leben Ciceros," *ClMed,* 5 (1942), 209-217.

buked the excessive profiteering of men like M. Crassus.[67] One need no longer wonder that Chrysogonus had sought to keep his transactions for Roscius' property unknown to Sulla. It does not require much imagination to ascertain the dictator's attitude on this trial. The outcome itself is enough indication; Sulla did not lift a finger to assist his freedman and Roscius was acquitted.[68]

Cicero later took great pride in his maiden political oration. It has been the fashion more recently to deprecate his boastfulness on this score: Chrysogonus was a nonentity, exaggerated out of all proportion by Cicero, and the orator was backed by big names in the nobility and by relatives of Sulla himself.[69] All this is irrefutably true. But none of those big names ventured to come forth himself to challenge Chrysogonus. However large or small the risks, Cicero could rightly look back on the case as a turning point. The defense of Roscius was a defense of legal process. In pleading a case for law and order, Cicero was advocating the claims not only of the *nobilitas* but of his own class, the *equites,* with whom his association was close throughout his career. Sulla was given the opportunity to wash his hands of Chrysogonus with honor and he took it. Roscius' acquittal was an assertion that Sulla's new judicial system could not be exploited by profiteers who relied on the continuation of anarchy and martial conditions. The outcome of the trial set the seal on a new era: *leges et iudicia constituta, recuperata res publica.*[70]

The courts had been restored. To Sulla this restoration might imply legitimacy, system, order; to Cicero it would mean the reopening of an avenue to reputation. To the Roman aristocracy *iudicia* meant politics. The *nobilitas* was in the saddle once more; the claims of pedigree were again acknowledged; thanks to the Roscius affair, the hereditary privileges of patronage were, so it seemed, secure. Furthermore, the courts were in the hands of the *ordo senatorius* for the first time in over forty

---

[67] On C. Metellus' pointed question, see Plut. *Sulla,* 31.1-2. On Sulla's rebuke to Crassus, see Plut. *Crass.* 6.6-7; cf. Garzetti, *Athenaeum,* 19 (1941), 17.

[68] Plut. *Cic.* 3.4; Schol. Gronov. 301, Stangl.

[69] For Cicero's pride in the *Pro Roscio Amerino,* see *De Off.* 3.51: *adulescentes contra L. Sullae dominantis opes pro Sex. Roscio Amerino, fecimus;* cf. *Brutus,* 312; *Orator,* 107; Plut. *Cic.* 3.4; Quintilian, 12.6.4. Skepticism on the risk that he ran in Afzelius, *ClMed,* 5 (1942), 209-217; Gabba, *Ann. Pisa,* 33 (1964), 12-15. Earlier historians were more generous (perhaps too much so) to Cicero on this score: R. Heinze, "Ciceros politische Anfänge," *AbhLeipz,* 27 (1909), 947-966; E. Ciaceri, "L'atteggiamento politico di M. Tullio Cicerone di fronte a L. Cornelio Silla," *AttiVen,* 79 (1919-20), 541-562; C. Lanzani, *L. Cornelio Silla Dittatore* (Milan, 1936), 220-232.

[70] Cic. *Brutus,* 311.

years. Many *illustres* had learned nothing, it appears, from Italian revolt, civil wars, and economic upheaval. For them it was just another turn of the wheel: it was 121 and 100 all over again. By 79 Sulla had resigned his dictatorship.[71] What more logical now than a resumption of factional politics? A single trial is recorded for the year 79. It suggests that ingrained habits of the Roman *nobilitas* did not die easily.

For that trial, some background is in order. The great family of the Metelli had fallen on difficult times in the 80's; but, as always, it was resilient. A marriage alliance with Sulla had been twisted to that general's own purposes. Some reacted with revulsion. But the Metelli were never ones to struggle long against the tides of history. When Sulla's victory seemed likely, Metellus Pius had joined his cause, to his profit and to that of the clan. In 80 the dictator honored Pius by sharing a consulship with him. Sulla had anticipated some difficulties from the strong-willed son of Numidicus, but Pius proved accommodating and obliging in all matters.[72] It was a beneficial relationship: Pius received appointment to the important Spanish command against Sertorius; two of his relatives by marriage secured the consulship for 79; and the Metelli had received satisfaction and success from the trial of Sex. Roscius.[73] But that family was ever alert for promising new alliances. At one time or another they had promoted the fortunes of C. Marius, M. Scaurus, and L. Sulla. They could look to the future now as well. The dictator was fifty-seven years old; in the event that his example be followed by strong men in succeeding years, it would be useful to entice such potential leaders into the Metellan fold by traditional devices. The family had its eye on Cn. Pompeius Magnus.

No one was oblivious to the meteoric rise of young Pompey, his talents, and his resources. He had brought his army of personal retainers and clients over to the Sullan side in 83 and performed signal service in Italy, Sicily, and Africa, demonstrating in the process unlimited energy and also ruthlessness.[74] Sulla had recognized his qualities swiftly. The youth was hailed *imperator* by his general in 83. In the following

[71] Plut. *Sulla*, 34; *Pomp.* 15; Appian, *BC*, 1.103; Orosius, 5.22.1. The precise date is uncertain and disputed. Most scholars opt for the end of the year 80; e.g., Lanzani, *Silla Dittatore*, 318-323; Pareti, *Storia di Roma*, III.636-637; Gabba, *App. BC Lib. Prim.*, 282-283; Syme, *Sallust*, 180; Meier, *Res Pub.*, 260. Badian suggests the end of 81; *Historia*, 11 (1962), 230; cf. Cic. *Pro Rosc. Amer.* 139. A summary of the evidence may be conveniently found in Valgiglio, *Silla*, 199-207.

[72] Plut. *Sulla*, 6.5: πολλὰ γὰρ αὐτῷ πράγματα παρέξειν ἐπίδοξον ὄντα πρῳότατον ἐν τῇ κοινωνίᾳ γενέσθαι τῆς ἀρχῆς.

[73] On the Spanish command of Metellus Pius in 79, see *MRR*, II.83.

[74] Sources in *MRR*, II.64, 70.

year Sulla induced him to divorce his first wife Antistia and to marry Aemilia, the daughter of Scaurus and stepdaughter of Sulla himself, pregnant though she was with another man's child. Sulla clearly wanted close bonds with the young man and he wanted them fast.[75] On the other hand, the dictator was not anxious to see Pompey's career move with undue speed or eclipse his own victories and prestige. Despite Pompey's brilliant campaigns in Sicily and Africa, which crushed and scattered the last embers of resistance to the new regime in that part of the world, Sulla despatched a missive to his lieutenant, requesting him to dismiss his forces and return to Rome to the status befitting his tender years. That would mean, of course, no triumph. In Sulla's *res publica restituta,* Pompey, whatever his astonishing exploits, was too young for such an honor. But Pompey had learned his lessons well from his father. The troops were loyal to their commander first, the *res publica* second. They would acknowledge discharge only when they were satisfied that Pompey had been given his due. The *imperator,* like his father in 88, put up a good show of constitutionalism. He pleaded with his army not to force the issue, even begged and wept; if they persisted, he vowed to do away with himself rather than to insult his superiors. They persisted, of course; Pompey made no move toward suicide. Dropping subtlety, he reminded Sulla that more men worship the rising than the setting sun. Sulla recognized the fire of Pompeius Strabo in Strabo's son. In secret, the dictator nursed his resentment: he cut Pompey out of his will. Perhaps if he could not check the young man's ambitions at the present, he could do so posthumously. In public, however, he yielded gracefully and graciously. He eclipsed Pompey's warmest supporters in the ardor of his welcome, officially dubbing him *Magnus,* the appellation that Pompey's own troops and admirers had accorded him. The conqueror of Sicily and Africa duly received his triumph.[76] Here was a man well worth winning. The Metelli were vigilant

[75] For the esteem in which Sulla held Pompey, see Plut. *Pomp.* 8.2-3, 9.1; *Crass.* 6.4; for Pompey's divorce and hasty remarriage, Plut. *Sulla,* 33.3; *Pomp.* 9.2-3; cf. W. Drumann, *Geschichte Roms,* 2nd ed. by P. Groebe (Berlin, 1899-1929), IV.560.

[76] On the jockeying between Sulla and Pompey, see the (somewhat embellished) account of Plutarch, *Pomp.* 13-14. On Sulla's will, *Pomp.* 15.2-3; *Sulla,* 38.1. On the whole matter, see the discussions of Lanzani, "Silla e Pompeo. La Spedizione di Sicilia e d'Africa," *Historia,* 7 (1933), 343-362; Gelzer, *Kleine Schriften,* II.130-138; and Badian, *For. Client.* 273-275. The date of Pompey's triumph is variously reported by the sources: Livy, *Per.* 89; Gran. Licin. 38-39, B; *Vir. Ill.* 77.2. Most scholars have preferred 79; Gelzer, *Kleine Schriften,* II.127-128; Schur, *Zeit. Marius u. Sulla,* 208-211; Pareti, *Storia di Roma,* III.638-639; Broughton, *MRR,* II.84, modified in *Supple-*

and astute as always. Pompey's marriage to Aemilia had proved calamitous. The unhappy woman, pregnant on her wedding day, perished in childbirth. Magnus swiftly found a new mate, probably in 80: Mucia, the daughter of Q. Scaevola, consul in 95, and the half sister of Metellus Celer and Metellus Nepos.[77]

In the year 79, Celer and Nepos, both in their twenties, carried the banner of their family in a prosecution of M. Aemilius Lepidus. The latter had recently returned from a pro-praetorian governorship of Sicily, an unhappy tenure for the provincials involved. Illegal exactions from the province perhaps helped to finance Lepidus' home, whose beauty was unrivaled by any other dwelling in Rome. The charge against him evidently was *res repetundae*. Lepidus' past was devious; his career and allegiances would not have recommended him to the Metelli. The name of his wife happens to be preserved, a certain Appuleia, doubtless a relative and possibly even the daughter of L. Appuleius Saturninus. Tradition reports him as an adherent of the Mariani; epigraphy reveals him on the staff of Pompeius Strabo in 89. It is a safe assumption that Lepidus, like others with similar backgrounds, remained in Rome in the mid 80's. One of his sons, it is recorded, was adopted by a Cornelius Scipio, no doubt that L. Scipio Asiagenus who fought against Sulla in 83 and remained an unrepentant opponent, preferring exile to collaboration. The allegiance of Lepidus would seem clear, but consistency was not his preeminent virtue. In 100, when the tide had turned decisively against the demagogues, Lepidus had been conspicuous in the streetfighting against the allies of his *adfinis* Saturninus. Though apparently a passive supporter of the Cinnan regime, he was among those who transferred his attachments to Sulla in 83 when the occasion seemed propitious. It was a well-timed maneuver. Lepidus not only earned a praetorship for 81 and a provincial governorship; he reaped handsome profits from the Sullan proscriptions.[78] He was the type of unscrupulous profiteer

---

ment, 47. Others have opted for 81; Lanzani, *Historia*, 7 (1933), 343-362; *Silla*, 45-46; Badian, "The Date of Pompey's First Triumph," *Hermes*, 83 (1955), 107-118; "Servilius and Pompey's First Triumph," *Hermes*, 89 (1961), 254-256. Arguments of the latter have successfully disposed of 79. But a triumph in 81 postulates an extraordinarily brief campaign in Sicily and Africa. March of 80 may well be the correct date; cf. R. E. Smith, "Pompey's Conduct in 80 and 77 B.C.," *Phoenix*, 14 (1960), 10-12.

[77] Drumann-Groebe, *Geschichte Roms*, IV.560-561. For the relationship of Mucia to the Metelli, see Cic. *Ad Fam.* 5.2.6: *sorore vestra Mucia.* Carcopino, *Sylla*, 188-190, conjectures, but without evidence, that the marriage did not take place until 79.

[78] For Lepidus' marriage to Appuleia, see Pliny, *NH*, 7.122; cf. J. E. Neunheuser, *M. Aemilius Lepidus* (Münzter, 1902), 18-20; his connections

whom Cicero, with the blessing of the Metelli, had excoriated in the *Pro Roscio Amerino*. The courts were available once more for their old purposes. The prosecution of Lepidus, it may be assumed, was the opening shot fired in the renewed campaigns of senatorial politics.

Evidence on the case is tantalizingly slender. Defendant and prosecutors are recorded, and one other item: the *accusatores,* after mounting their case, dropped the charges.[79] The reason allegedly was Lepidus' reputation among the *populus*. That is doubtless erroneous conjecture. The "popularity" of Lepidus, stemming from his advocacy of the dispossessed and the victims of Sulla in 78 and 77, is misplaced and predated. Senatorial *iudices* sat on the courts; the prosecutors of Lepidus would not have concerned themselves with the attitude of the *populus*. The Metelli could well have expected that Sulla, in view of the moderation that he had shown in the Roscius trial, would support their case against Lepidus, or at least maintain a discreet neutrality. They did not, however, reckon with the attitude of their powerful new ally. Pompeius Magnus recalled, it seems, an old connection with Lepidus. The two had served in the same military *consilium* during the Social War, both under Pompey's father. Later in the year 79 Pompey was to espouse Lepidus' candidature for the consulship; his personal influence and popularity helped bring the candidate to the top of the poll.[80] To imagine that Pompey also acted in Lepidus' interests at the time of his trial would not be rash and would explain the dropping of the charges. When Pompey applied pressure, the Metelli had no intention of pursuing the matter. It is fitting and appropriate that when Metellus Celer and Metellus Nepos turn up again in history it is as legates of Pompey in the mid 60's.[81] The first attempt to revive factional politics in the courts since

with the Mariani, Orosius, 5.22.16: *Lepidus, Marianae partis adsertor;* cf. Appian, *BC,* 1.105. For his service with Strabo, see *ILLRP,* II.30, no. 515, with Cichorius, *Röm. Stud.,* 147, and Taylor, *Voting Districts,* 187. The adoption of a Lepidus by the Scipiones is indicated by Orosius, 5.22.17; the conjecture of Scipio Asiagenus was persuasively argued by Münzer, *Röm. Adelsp.,* 308-310; for Asiagenus' role in the civil war, see *MRR,* II.62-63. On Lepidus' actions in 100, see Cic. *Pro Rab. Perd.* 21; in the proscriptions, Sallust, *Hist.* 1.55.18, Maur.; on his *domus,* Pliny, *NH,* 36.109; cf. 36.49. That he was in Rome in the mid 80's is more than likely; cf. Badian, *Studies,* 217-218; Gruen, *AJP,* 87 (1966), 391-393; on Lepidus' character, see also Syme, *Sallust,* 183-184, 199, 220.

[79] Ps-Asconius, 259, Stangl: *M. Lepidi praetoris, qui accusari coeperat a duobus Metellis, Celere et Nepote; qui cum legibus interrogassent, victi eius apud populum gratia destiterunt.* The trial is mentioned also in Ps-Asconius, 187, Stangl, and Cic. *Verr.* 2.3.212.

[80] Plut. *Sulla,* 34.4-5; *Pomp.* 15.1-2.

[81] Appian, *Mithr.* 95; Florus, 1.41.9; Dio, 36.54.2-4.

the reforms of Sulla had proved abortive. But it was a significant herald of developments for the next generation.

Far more extravagant claims, however, have been made for this trial. Lepidus, it has been alleged, was under attack as a creature of Sulla, in a position little different from that of Chrysogonus. Confronted with the formidable Metelli, Lepidus preferred collusion to resistance. A secret agreement followed, the accusers dropped their case, Pompey and the Metelli backed Lepidus for the consulship on an anti-Sullan platform. Successful election, over the objections of Sulla, was an unmistakable sign of shifts in the balance of political power. Pompey, Lepidus, and the Metelli were arrayed in intractable opposition to the regime. Sulla reluctantly, but resignedly, acknowledged the fait accompli and retired altogether from public life.[82] It should by now be evident that the facts, properly analyzed, demolish any such reconstruction. A Metellan coalition against Sulla is unattested and unlikely. Moreover, it would have been the height of foolhardiness, a characteristic not normally associated with that clan. Sulla's marriage to Valeria Messalla, whose family cooperated closely with the Metelli in the trial of Roscius, divulges the political lines. The Metelli hitched themselves to the setting as well as to the rising sun. Plutarch, to be sure, claims that Pompey's espousal of Lepidus in 79 met with Sulla's disapproval. And Sallust puts into the mouth of Lepidus a violent and ranting attack on the Sullan "tyranny." These analyses, however, comprise deliberate or bumbling anachronism.[83] The cautious and devious Lepidus would not have evinced overt hostility to the Sullan system in the lifetime of its architect. For Lepidus' oration to have any historical validity, it must be placed in 78 after the death of the former dictator. The advice and warning of Sulla to Pompey implies an insight into events that no man could have predicted in 79. To imagine that Pompey used Lepidus as an advance guard in his premeditated plan to destroy the Sullan constitution is to ignore the facts and the characters of both Lepidus and Pompey. After Sulla's death in 78, Pompey made his position clear immediately: he felt no enduring loyalty to Lepidus; when the consul sought to deprive Sulla of a proper funeral, Pompey

---

[82] Such, in essence, is the hypothesis of Carcopino, *Sylla,* 197-209; if not persuasive, it is always imaginative and provocative.

[83] Plut. *Sulla,* 34.4-5; *Pomp.* 15.1-2; Sallust, *Hist.* 1.55, Maur., *passim;* see, e.g., 1.55.1: *Clementia et probitas vestra, Quirites . . . plurumum timoris mihi faciunt advorsum tyrannidem L. Sullae.* See the acute analysis of Syme, *Sallust,* 184-186. Van Ooteghem, *Pompée,* 79-89, who takes issue with Carcopino on almost every other point, nonetheless asserts, without evidence, that Lepidus' election was due to the support of the Metelli, as well as of Pompey. In all probability, the Metelli, who had no love for Lepidus, refrained from intervening, one way or the other, in the electoral campaign.

rescued the body for an honorable, indeed a spectacular, cremation. And when Lepidus fomented insurrection, it was Pompey himself who defended the Sullan regime.[84]

The retreat of Sulla from office and the public gaze was not an "enforced" one. The ancient evidence refutes any conjecture of an influential coalition against him. Sulla's retirement was calculated and voluntary. It does not follow that he had planned it from the beginning, dutifully laying aside his powers when he had fulfilled the task that the republic had imposed upon him.[85] Sulla's psychology remains impenetrable. Modern conjectures have proliferated, but none has yet improved on the hesitant guess of Appian: Sulla was weary of war, of power, of the city. The remaining days that Fortune vouchsafed him could best be spent indulging his appetites for hunting, fishing, and the pleasures of rural life.[86]

Judicial procedures had suffered during the 80's. The use of force was the dominant feature of that decade. What semblance of legality did exist was no better than a screen. Neither Marian nor Sullan can be absolved from responsibility. Under Cinna violence was temporarily abated, but only at the expense of stifling activity in the courts. Sulla's triumphal march at the end of the decade was on a blood-stained path. But Sulla was, in the final analysis, a friend of reconstruction and stability. Personal security and the claims of his supporters were the first considerations, but lawlessness was checked and order restored. The test case of Roscius Amerinus showed that the dictator would stand by his institutions. Detached and thoughtful enactments affixed the Sullan seal of approval to the *quaestio* system. The old *iudicium populi* was virtually eliminated from the political scene. The long evolution of the permanent criminal court from the time of the *lex Calpurnia* in 149 reached its full realization in the hands of Sulla the dictator. Livius Drusus' once abortive plans also saw fruition. The senate was expanded and the courts restored to the aristocracy. For the traditional leaders

---

[84] On the funeral, Plut. *Sulla,* 38; *Pomp.* 15.3; on the insurrection, sources in *MRR,* II.85, 89-90. The view of Neunheuser, *Lepidus,* 21-24, that Lepidus was simply Pompey's creature is no more defensible than Carcopino's thesis that he was a tool of the Metellan coalition. For Pompey's traditionalist attitude, cf. the astute remarks of Sherwin-White, *JRS,* 46 (1956), 5-8.

[85] Cf. *Vir. Ill.* 75.11: *Repub. ordinata dictaturam deposuit.* For this view of Sulla, see Lanzani, *Silla Dittatore,* 318-323; Pareti, *Storia di Roma,* III.636; Valgiglio, *Silla,* 199-207. Carney, "The Death of Sulla," *Acta Classica,* 4 (1961), 64-79, argues that Sulla had contracted venereal disease and, in full knowledge thereof, speeded his retirement.

[86] Appian, *BC,* 1.104: ἀλλά μοι δοκεῖ κόρον τε πολέμων καὶ κόρον ἀρχῆς καὶ κόρον ἄστεος λαβὼν ἐπὶ τέλει καὶ ἀγροικίας ἐρασθῆναι.

of the *nobilitas* it was the signal for a resumption of the old political games. But to believe that nothing had changed was naive. The years of disruption and turmoil had left their mark. The trial of Lepidus had all the earmarks of traditional factional politics, but the shadow of a new, powerful adventurer hung heavily over it. Pompeius Magnus had read the signs correctly. Recent years had demonstrated not only his military prowess, but his political astuteness. He would defend the Sullan constitution after its author's demise, but he would also manipulate it. The events of 79 presaged the future. Sulla's example was to prove more potent than his institutions.

CONCLUSION

Certain major themes run throughout this study, illuminating and giving meaning to the dizzying shifts and breathless progression of events. To gather up again the threads that have steadily unraveled for nine chapters will be salutary.

Factional politics play a predominant role. The Roman senate was a divided entity; that should no longer be subject to doubt. But the divisions lay not in matters of policy, principle, or philosophy. *Dignitas* and *potentia* were generally the objects of concern. Groups formed about energetic individuals or pedigreed families, expanded through cooperation with *amici* and *clientelae*. Factions were fuzzy around their edges. Individual loyalties were ambiguous, sometimes manifold, and changing patterns were characteristic of the era. But patterns there were. Close examination reveals continuity in the flux. In the 140's and 130's certain prevailing voices are discernible in the aristocracy. The group that gathered around Scipio Aemilianus could capitalize on the military exploits and illustrious contacts of its leader. Others resented his *gloria* and undermined his *potentia*. A powerful faction emerged from collaboration among the families of the Claudii, Fulvii, Lepidi, and Crassi; another was based upon the Metelli, Servilii, and Cottae. The jockeying for position focused on familiar vehicles: military commands, elections, legislation, and, to an increasing extent, criminal trials.

The Gracchan movement grew out of a factional context. But social reform, coupled with radical constitutional change, shook the power structure and unsettled the previous categories. The Claudian group was split, the Scipionic faction became fragmented, defensive, and reactionary. The Gracchi fashioned their own political alliance. It was their strength, but also their weakness. Resistance was able to solidify in 133 and again in 121. The legacy of the Gracchi endured, but the *factio* was sponged off the political scene. The sequel was significant. Certain families vanish from Roman history; the Claudian group dissolved, the Scipionic faction lost its leaders through death or discredit. Chief beneficiary of this upheaval was the aggregation centered upon the Metelli, now swelling in personnel and power. As revolutionary threat to the established order receded, the aristocracy went about its customary business of internal wrestling. Evidence from electoral contests and political prosecutions is consistent: the decade of the 110's witnessed consolidation of authority within senatorial ranks by the Metelli and their *amici*. But how long could the *dominatio* of a single group endure in the matrix of Roman politics? The pattern of the previous generation revealed itself again, at a faster pace, in the last decade of the second century: foreign war roused impatience and exacerbated rivalries within the ruling class; factional struggles were soon engulfed in the rise of new leaders and the feverish activity of popular demagogues. Once more petty feuding had weakened traditional leadership and placed the power structure in jeopardy.

The coalition fashioned by Marius, Saturninus, and Glaucia was more formidable than that of the Gracchi. It not only played on popular and equestrian discontents, but capitalized on the widespread desire to restore Rome's prestige abroad. But it too proved unable to deliver a death blow. The Marian alliance had all the earmarks of a crisis combination; it contained too many disparate elements to endure when foreign danger evaporated and popular agitation became tiresome. Subsequent events betray the familiar pattern. With the demagogues crushed and Marius chastened, the oligarchy regathered its *clientelae* and resumed control of affairs. The 90's proved, in many ways, to be a replay of the themes of the 110's. While external threats faded into the background, internal squabbles occupied the center of the stage. The Roman aristocracy was slow indeed to break old habits. Men like Scaurus, Crassus, Scaevola, and Rutilius were still potent voices in the Metellan *factio* and within the senate. But opposition to that group was mounting. Marius' efforts to scramble back into the political arena through more conventional means confused matters. Enemies of the Metelli received strong leadership from Philippus, Caepio, the Domitii, and the Cassii. Shrewd operators abounded, but men of true foresight were nowhere in evidence. Livius Drusus was perhaps an exception, but his ignominious failure points up all the more sharply the failure of the aristocracy.

The consequences ought to have been predictable. While Rome's leaders consumed themselves in factious strife, the whole structure of orderly government was crumbling. Once again the undulating pattern emerges and once again the pace is even faster. The years 90 to 87 witnessed Social War, civil war, and foreign war supervening one upon the other with brutal swiftness; demagogery became more violent, military figures more prominent. The resiliency of the aristocracy had

280

enabled it to survive the schemes of the Gracchi and the disruptions of Saturninus and Glaucia. But now it was confronted with a whole new body politic and with the ominous specter of private armies. In the mid 80's Cinna, with a modicum of prescience not usually credited to him, sought to adjust to the new situation. His aim, so it would appear, was to gather the old factional groupings under an encompassing umbrella, discard traditional rivalries, and forge a viable consensus. The ex-Mariani joined his government; so did the faction of Philippus and the followers of Pompeius Strabo; even men once associated with the Metelli were included in the assemblage. It was a worthy attempt, but too late. Events had outstripped such efforts. Sulla had a mighty military establishment with him. When he returned to Italy in arms, Cinna's coalition fell apart like a house of cards. The oligarchy enjoyed restoration, but it was a restoration at the cost of massive purges, dictatorship, and constitutional revamping. Sulla had begun in the ranks of Marius, had risen to prominence as a protégé of the Metelli, but ended by forging his own political faction. He now collected remnants of all those groups that had been shattered over the past few decades and instituted a tightened regimen that would have been totally unrecognizable seventy years earlier. When the dictator retired, some optimistic aristocrats hoped to resume traditional politics. It was not to be. A young adventurer had stepped out of Sulla's shadow and emulated his example. Pompey the Great was to guarantee that the position of a forceful leader had made the old aristocratic games obsolete.

Throughout this period the political base was progressively broadened. Maneuverings and intrigues in the early part of the period were principally confined to small but powerful cliques within the establishment. Dependents and *clientelae* went along passively, and cooperated with varying degrees of indifference. The Gracchan movement, however, raised issues of wider dimensions and exposed a larger audience to the contests of the *curia*. Men of wealth outside the senatorial order perceived that they too could benefit from greater involvement in politics. By cooperating on occasion with one faction or another or by mobilizing as a unity they brought influence to bear on the course of events. Through Gracchan legislation they exercised authority in the judiciary. Growing self-awareness was evident also among the *plebs*. The Gracchani had made it clear that the interests of the less affluent members of Roman society were not always bound up with their hereditary patrons in the oligarchy. Matters like land reform, grain distribution, and more equitable treatment of men on military service were becoming items of public discussion and not just private deals between *patroni* and *clientelae*. The issue of an Italian share in Roman franchise also appeared for the first

281

time in the Gracchan era, presaging broadened participation on an unprecedented scale.

The effects were not yet discernible in all their magnitude. The murder of the Gracchani brought no revolution in its wake. The *equites* were more concerned with stability and with their own enterprises, the *plebs* retained ties to old benefactors, and enfranchisement was not yet an overriding concern for the Italians. Hence, the surface calm of the 110's followed. But the example of the Gracchi was stronger than their *factio*. The elder Drusus and Fannius had undermined them only by outbidding them. Land distribution continued to be implemented, *equites* still sat on the courts, colonial foundations appealed to ex-servicemen and to the surplus population. Under the pressure of events, the oligarchy had broadened its interests. But for many the pace was not fast enough. When the ruling class sank back into internal quarrels and demonstrated incompetence in defending the realm, upheavals multiplied. More *novi homines* shouldered their way into prominence; the popular demagogue became a conspicuous figure; *equites* and *plebs* found grounds again for cooperation against an exclusivist establishment. Such was the tumultuous "age of Marius" in the last decade of the second century.

The oligarchy closed ranks as usual under external threat and the Marian coalition disintegrated. But once again the legacy was more potent than the temporary alliance. Most notably is this true of a rising military establishment. Junior officers were being drawn from a broader circle; the lower ranks were coming to expect tangible rewards through loyalty to benefactors, on the model of Marius and Saturninus. Senatorial factions proceeded with myopic feuding in the 90's, but the pressures for widened participation on all levels were building beneath the surface to an explosive climax. Friction between *equites* and senate over the judiciary and over the status of provincial organization embittered feelings; the question of agrarian reform again divided landowners and the *plebs rustica;* and, above all, the *socii* would no longer tolerate inequity and mistreatment. The grisly conflicts of the Social and civil wars speeded considerably the processes that had been developing for over a generation. Tight little senatorial squabbles were a thing of the past. Roman franchise extended throughout the peninsula. Provincial maladministration brought on foreign war. Men of violence unleashed their passions in the city as well as abroad. Loyalties shifted away from institutions and traditional patrons to the strong man who could promise a larger share for those previously outside the power structure. Sulla, it is said, put the senate back in control. But it was a senate of very different dimensions. A decade of bloodletting had decimated the ruling classes. Yet Sulla's senate was expanded, not contracted. Its numbers were swelled by *equites,* ex-officers, and Italians. No better symbol exists for the change that Roman society had undergone in the previous seventy years.

The impact of foreign wars on the domestic scene is also a recurrent theme. Sharp political and constitutional changes in this period were, in almost every instance, precipitated or accompanied by crises abroad. The long series of Spanish wars from 154 to 133 formed the backdrop for senatorial contests of the Scipionic era. The perilous and largely unproductive character of those engagements led to repercussions at home against commanders who returned empty-handed. Frantic efforts to outdo one's predecessor or to discredit his achievements led to implacable enmities and divided the aristocracy as it had rarely been divided before. The Spanish wars split families and alliances. Worse, they served to mold the conflict between Scipio Aemilianus and Ti. Gracchus. The scrapping of Tiberius' Spanish treaty at the behest of Scipio and his *amici* poisoned their conflict beyond conciliation. The violence of reaction to the Gracchan program and its grim aftermath are explicable only in terms of the mounting distrust and bitterness provoked by the wars in Spain. External peace brought a concomitant measure of stability at home after the elimination of the Gracchan *factio.* But not for long. Defeats abroad created fear of divine wrath. Consequent religious hysteria helps to explain the growing number of criminal proceedings in this period, including the spectacular trials of the Vestals. Worse was to come. New hostilities in Africa and in Gaul smashed whatever inner harmony Rome had enjoyed for a short time. The incompetence of military commanders and profound suspicion of treachery produced domestic upheavals of a new order of magnitude. The Mamilian trials, the shuttling of jury control, the rise of Marius, and the implementation of radical popular measures are all closely associated with the Jugurthine and Cimbric Wars. Once more, however, when foreign crises were defused, the internal situation settled into ostensible calm for a decade. The salvation of the aristocracy in 100 was possible only because Roman arms had at last been successful abroad. But the new series of bouts that began in 90 produced irreparable damage. The Social War tore Italy apart. The civil war wrecked the political and legal structure. And the Mithridatic War set the stage for dictatorship and the installation of a new order. As so often, a rhythmic pattern is discerned throughout, and the connection between wars and politics is indissoluble.

The struggle over the courts forms still another recurrent theme. The *lex Calpurnia* of 149 was designed at least in part, and probably in large part, to restore full oligarchic control of foreign affairs. The *quaestio* system was thus born in politics. Association with political developments remained intimate thereafter. For a time no challenge was offered to senatorial staffing of the juries that heard *repetundae* cases. Perhaps it was argued that this was simply an institutionalizing of previous practice: the senate sitting in judgment on complaints from *socii* and *peregrini*. But the *quaestio de rebus repetundis* could also be utilized for political purposes. Provincials were not consistently able to gain redress for grievances. From the early 130's senatorial factions preferred to use the court to embarrass or even to eliminate political rivals. Moreover, it could be an instrument for aristocratic supervision of provincial revenues and business activities abroad. C. Gracchus in 123 recognized the full political implications in transferring control of the *quaestio* to the *equites*. The business classes now possessed a vehicle whereby to express their solidarity when necessary and to protect their foreign enterprises. Equestrian support for the oligarchy in crushing the Gracchani insured their retention of judicial control, and the path was smooth for a decade. *Equites* manned the jury panels and were naturally called upon as new courts like the *de ambitu* were established or as special *quaestiones* were required.

When politics became heated again, however, the issue of the courts was in the very center of the struggle. Frustrating war with Jugurtha roused the fury of the *equites* and the Mamilian tribunal became a device for political vengeance. Rapid turnabouts toward the close of the second century saw equestrian monopoly of the juries removed and then restored, as popular leaders bid for support by making the *iudicia* a political football. With new courts being created, reaching into further areas of political life, control over them had become a vital matter. The events of 100 proved to be a repeat of 133 and 121: *equites* combined with the nobility to crush the demagogues and restore "law and order." In 99 and 98 the judiciary served as a means to wipe out the last vestiges of the popular movement. Consequences were also analagous to those earlier situations. The aristocracy was content to tolerate equestrian management of the courts, but only for a time. With their vital interests no longer involved, the Gracchani *iudices* could affect cold disdain for aristocratic rivalries. They exposed the chain of political prosecutions in the 90's for what they were — a ludicrous game — by handing down a consistent series of acquittals. Senatorial patience gradually wore thin. When the *iudices* finally delivered a condemnatory verdict and exiled Rutilius for interfering with business activities in Asia, agitation for judicial reform was inevitable. This time the struggle over the courts touched off a series of conflicts that engulfed Rome in war.

When the smoke had cleared, reform ensued along new lines: representation on the juries would be determined by election, a system that

might squeeze out the *equester ordo*. Astute politicians knew how significant and how damaging the *iudicia* could be. Cinna required quiescence in
order to effect his aims. Courtroom activity, therefore, was deliberately
reduced to a minimum and criminal cases carefully supervised. When
Sulla installed a new order the question of the judiciary was a key item
in the program. His solution was evidently based on full awareness of
the chaotic history of intermittent struggles for control: the Roman
senate would henceforth monopolize the jury panels, but it would be a
senate enlarged by those very groups who had formerly contested the
aristocracy's right to adjudicate. The contest would evaporate when the
contestants were united. Livius Drusus had tried the same tactic in 91,
unsuccessfully. But a decade of civil war had intervened. In 81 acceptance was guaranteed.

The burgeoning significance of criminal trials is, of course, evident
throughout. Their effect was manifold. As a means to settle factional
disputes, their prominence increased steadily through this period. The
first clear evidence along these lines exists for cases early in the 130's.
The extortion court and the popular hearing became arenas for factional
contests between the Scipionic group and rival alliances. Utilization of
the judiciary for this purpose became more and more frequent in subsequent years. Followers of the Gracchi were attacked in the courts; so
also, on the other side, were the slayers of the Gracchi. Later, the
Metellan *factio* solidified its senatorial supremacy by consistent success
in the *iudicia;* M. Scaurus was many times in the docket, but never
convicted. Numerous instances can be cited of factional rivalries staged
as criminal prosecutions, like the cluster of trials around 104 and again
around 95. Foreign crises might provide the pretext for mobilizing the
judiciary for political vengeance, as exemplified by the *quaestio Mamilia,*
the assaults on Caepio and Mallius, or the *lex Varia.* Well-timed prosecutions might also be a means of self-protection for the oligarchy, as
with the tribunal of Popillius Laenas or the trials that followed the fall
of Saturninus. But there were other uses, readily distinguishable. Personal or family feuds, without broader political connotations, increasingly
found in the courts a satisfactory outlet. Such, for example, may be
reckoned the clash of the Luculli and the Servilii, the contest between
Crassus and Marcellus, or that between Metellus Nepos and Scribonius
Curio. Further, the criminal prosecution was used as a springboard to
launch a young orator's forensic career, for instance, Caesar Strabo's
accusation of Albucius or Hortensius' initial appearance before the bar.

These various elements are by no means mutually exclusive. In any
individual case, all may be operative. The evidence is clear for stepped-up
judicial activity on every level during the three decades before the

Cinnae dominatio. Even more significant is the fact that criminal hearings in this era raised and sometimes settled critical constitutional, legal, or political issues. The trial of Scipio Nasica effectively outlawed the kind of lynch procedure employed against Ti. Gracchus; the exile of Popillius Laenas abolished senatorial commissions without popular sanction; and the acquittal of Opimius legitimized the *senatus consultum ultimum.* Other cases whose outcomes possessed telling consequences can be catalogued: the fiasco of Galba's escape inspired the institution of Rome's first permanent *quaestio* in 149; the exile of Numidicus turned the tide decisively against the popular movement in 100; the conviction of Rutilius Rufus threw politics into the turmoil that precipitated the Social War; and, finally, the acquittal of Roscius Amerinus asserted the sincerity and stability of Sulla's new judicial order. The crucial impact of criminal trials permeates the events of the entire period.

Finally, the era witnessed the development of a system of criminal courts. The *lex Calpurnia* of 149 marked the first step toward effecting some kind of order within the chaos of Roman criminal law. Its purpose, however, was largely political, not legal or administrative. Hence, the value of extending fixed procedures and specified jury panels into areas other than that of *res repetundae* did not immediately impress itself upon the Roman establishment. Ad hoc proceedings and the cumbersome mechanism of trial before the assembly continued to exist in succeeding years. Since control of the *quaestio de repetundis* became such a fierce bone of contention, it is perhaps not surprising to ascertain a reluctance to institute further *quaestiones perpetuae.* When extension of the system came, it very likely came, in each instance, within a political context. This relation can be documented for the *quaestio de maiestate,* organized by the demagogues in 104, with equestrian participation, in order to maintain constant pressure on the aristocracy. The *quaestio de peculatu* probably fits into this context as well. Other specific occasions escaped the attention of the sources. But permanent courts on electoral bribery and murder were installed sometime within the two generations that separate the *lex Calpurnia* and Sulla. Politics may have been the motive and manipulation the consequence. Nonetheless, increasing definition of procedures and the multiplication of permanent *quaestiones* effected the gradual systematization of the criminal law. Sulla, whose principal concern was stability and order, recognized the virtues of that development. By creating new courts and reorganizing the old into a more coherent structure, the dictator performed a signal service. One might hesitate to conclude that justice was being served in an era when proceedings before the bar were completely enmeshed in politics. Yet it remains true that this same era witnessed the emergence of the criminal law from a chaotic and haphazard enterprise to an organized component of the Roman legal and administrative system.

It can readily be discerned even from this summary of conclusions that the six strands here outlined are isolable only in the abstract. In practice, all were tightly interwoven to produce the progress of events that form the history of this period. Factional contests, the broadening of the political base, the impact of foreign wars, struggle over the courts, the role of criminal trials, and the evolution of criminal law: all these elements interacted with one another at practically every significant turn. Understood in combination, they suggest that the period, with all its mercurial shifts and its incessant upheavals, possesses a coherence and meaning of its own.

APPENDICES   BIBLIOGRAPHY   INDEX

Appendix A. The Immunity of the Agrarian Commissioners

Were members of the agrarian commission under the Gracchan law immune from prosecution? It has recently been argued by H. Chantraine that these officials were no different from ordinary magistrates in this respect; they did possess immunity.[1] Chantraine asserts that the bronze *lex repetundarum* lists agrarian triumvirs among those officials exempt from prosecution. The assertion is misleading and dubious. Triumvirs *a[greis] d[andis] a[dsignandeis]* are indeed mentioned in the inscription, but only as officials who, like holders of other magistracies normally monopolized by the senatorial class, were excluded from judicial functions under this law.[2] In the crucial clause on immunity, however, the *III vir a.d.a.* is a restoration.[3]

Other arguments are *ex silentio* and fall far short of conviction. Chantraine points to the fact that C. Carbo was not prosecuted after his tribunate of 131. That hardly proves that he could not have been. Not every active tribune provoked judicial attack upon expiry of his office. It is true that there were no prosecutions following the death of Scipio Aemilianus in 129, but this is doubtless because Scipio's death was generally recognized to have been due to natural causes.[4]

What evidence exists on the matter suggests strongly that the triumviral commissioners possessed no immunity. Q. Pompeius in 133 threatened Ti. Gracchus with a criminal charge, to take effect on the conclusion of his magistracy.[5] Both Orosius and Plutarch place this move after the implementation of the agrarian measure. Yet Pompeius felt that he need only await the end of the tribunate. Moreover, Appian

[1] *Untersuchungen zur römischen Geschichte am Ende des 2 Jahrhunderts vor Chr.* (Kallmünz, 1959), 22-26.

[2] *Lex repet.*, lines 2, 13, 16, 22 (*FIRA*, I.85-86, 88-90).

[3] *Lex repet.*, line 8 (*FIRA*, I.87), It should be added that even if the *triumviri* were included among the immune in the *lex repetundarum* this is evidence only for the commission as revived by C. Gracchus and proves nothing for the *lex agraria* of Tiberius.

[4] See above, pp. 70-71.

[5] Orosius, 5.8.4: *etiam Pompeius spopondit se Gracchum, cum primum magistratu abisset, accusaturum;* cf. Plut. *Ti. Gracch.* 14.2.

clearly implies that Gracchus, despite his role as agrarian commissioner, sought a second tribunate specifically in order to avoid prosecution.[6] The clincher comes in the fact that C. Gracchus, himself a triumvir, was actually prosecuted in 124.[7] Chantraine conjectures that the accusation was intended to injure Gaius' candidature for the tribunate of 123. That may be granted. But whatever the motive of the *accusatores,* no prosecution ought to have been set in motion against an official with immunity. The answer to that awkward puzzle, according to Chantraine, is that Gaius voluntarily waived his immunity and stood trial to clear his name: an ingenious but desperate solution. There is not a hint of this in Plutarch's account, although it is surely an item not likely to be passed over by that biographer. The conclusion seems clear: appointment to the agrarian commission did not entail freedom from prosecution.

[6] Appian, *BC*, 1.13: οἱ δ' ἡσσημένοι δυσφοροῦντες ἔτι παρέμενον καὶ ἐλογοποίουν οὐ χαιρήσειν Γράκχον, αὐτίκα ὅτε γένοιτο ἰδιώτης. 1.14: ὁ δ' ἐγγὺς τοῦ κακοῦ γιγνομένου δείσας, εἰ μὴ καὶ ἐς τὸ μέλλον ἔσοιτο δήμαρχος.

[7] Plut. *C. Gracch.* 3; *ORF*, 183.

Appendix B. The *Lex Junia* and the *Lex Acilia*

The epigraphic *lex repetundarum* lists two previous measures as precedents: the *lex Calpurnia* and the *lex Junia*.[1] The former, of course, is the measure that instituted the original *quaestio de repetundis*. The latter remains elusive and obscure. No other source, literary or epigraphic, reports a *lex Junia*. A. H. M. Jones, undaunted by lack of evidence, developed a novel and ingenious theory.[2] The inscription instructs the praetor to enroll a panel of 450 *iudices* annually, an instruction that Jones assumes was taken over from a previous bill, namely the *lex Junia*. The latter is in turn identified with the law described by Plutarch and the Livian Epitomator, and assigned to C. Gracchus.[3] For Jones, this measure, an opening shot by Gaius and moved by Junius, set up mixed juries to be drawn from a panel of 300 *equites* and 150 senators. But this conclusion can only be reached through a tortuous twisting of the evidence. The Epitomator does say that Gaius gave the *equites* a two to one majority in the senate, but his figures are 600 and 300. Plutarch gives a figure of 300 *equites,* but his total is 600 on the juries. To select what is suitable from each source and reject what does not fit is risky procedure, quite apart from the fact that neither even mentions a *lex Junia*. It is unlikely that those two accounts, which conflict with the rest of our sources and with one another, preserve any valid proposals.

That the author of the *lex Junia* was M. Junius Silanus, the future consul of 109, has been suggested.[4] If so, the bill would, of course, be dated very close to that of C. Gracchus. One may rule out M. Junius Pennus, tribune in 126, who passed a bill for expulsion of aliens from

[1] *Lex repet.,* lines 23, 74 (*FIRA,* I.90, 100).

[2] *PCPS,* 186 (1960), 39-42.

[3] Plut. *C. Gracch.* 5; *Compar.* 2; Livy, *Per.* 60. Jones's argument that the epigraphic law repeated clauses from earlier legislation is irrefutable. But it in no way shows that the *lex Junia* is to be identified with the measure depicted by Plutarch and the Epitomator.

[4] Drumann-Groebe, *Geschichte Roms,* IV.51; Münzer, *RE,* 19.1094, "Junius," n. 169; Niccolini, *Fast. Trib. Pleb.,* 413-414; *MRR,* I.513.

Rome. His father was a Marcus,[5] whereas the proposer of the *lex Junia* was M. Junius D.f.[6] Since the *lex Junia* has left no mark on the literary tradition its provisions are unlikely to have had political content. It should be noted that Silanus' father had been charged with extortion,[7] a fact that may explain the son's interest in a *repetundae* measure. Further speculation would be unwarranted and unfruitful.

One would think that generations of extensive scholarship had exhausted the subject of the *lex Acilia.* Yet the quest for novelty continues. Recently, A. R. Hands has shown that it is still possible to inject a new hypothesis.[8] Hands performs this miracle, unfortunately, at the cost of adopting our worst and latest source as the touchstone of his argument. The Epitomator of Livy delivers the accurate estimate of C. Gracchus' measure: it is an effort to swamp the senate and turn over all judicial functions to a body dominated by his supporters. This Hands identifies as the *lex Sempronia,* unmoved by the fact that no source mentions a *lex Sempronia.* Hands then amalgamates the *lex Acilia* with the epigraphic *lex repetundarum,* calling it not a Gracchan law at all, but an anti-Gracchan maneuver. Acilius took the wind out of Gaius' sails by appeasing the *equites,* but limited his range to the extortion court so as to keep the senate happy. The conjecture is imaginative but misguided. The bulk of the evidence is unanimous that C. Gracchus turned over the *quaestio de repetundis* to the *equites.* Hands' embarrassed and awkward reply: Acilius passed his extortion law under the pressure of Gracchus' more extreme measure; hence the sources assign responsibility to the latter, despite the fact that his bill was repealed almost as soon as it secured passage. Such cavalier treatment of ancient testimony on behalf of hypothesis does not advance scholarship.

Rather more interesting, though equally speculative, is the recent contribution to this subject of P. A. Brunt.[9] For him, the inscription preserves the Gracchan extortion law, but that is only part of C. Gracchus' judiciary legislation. When the sources speak of *iudicia,* they mean *iudicia:* Gracchus removed senatorial control over a variety of judicial functions. The argument rests on a statement of Polybius: the senate provides judges for most public and private cases in which significant issues are at stake.[10] Reference to public proceedings is doubtless to *quaestiones extraordinariae,* already common by Polybius' day. Gracchus, therefore, concerned himself with more than the *quaestio de repetundis.* Then the accounts of Plutarch and the Livian Epitomator

[5] Cic. *Brutus,* 109.

[6] *Lex repet.,* line 74 (*FIRA,* I.100).

[7] See above, pp. 32-33.

[8] *Latomus,* 24 (1965), 225-237.

[9] *2nd Int. Conf. Econ. Hist., 1962,* I.141-148, endorsed by Meier, *Res Pub.,* 70-71.

[10] Polyb. 6.17.7: ἐκ ταύτης ἀποδίδονται κριταὶ τῶν πλείστων καὶ τῶν δημοσίων καὶ τῶν ἰδιωτικῶν συναλλαγμάτων, ὅσα μέγεθος ἔχει τῶν ἐγκλημάτων.

come in. Although the extortion court was reserved for *equites* alone, remaining judicial functions, both civil and criminal, were to be handled by men drawn from a mixed panel of senators and knights. Such is the hypothesis. But Polybius does not say that senators possessed a monopoly of jurisdiction. It is unclear what purpose C. Gracchus could have had in sponsoring a new law that still allowed for senatorial participation in the jury panels. Moreover, it would have been anomalous indeed for the tribune to specify an all-equestrian jury album for the *repetundae* court while drawing up a separate and independent list for other judicial business. One can only reiterate still again that no source speaks of or implies more than a single Gracchan law on jury reform. To exploit the jumbled evidence of Plutarch and the *Periocha* is an exercise in futility.

The most recent effort, that of C. Nicolet, is also the most ingenious of the lot.[11] The *lex repetundarum* belongs to C. Gracchus, but enemies of the Gracchani are responsible for the proposal that *equites* be enrolled in the senate. It is thus a countermove to split the Gracchan following. The construction put upon these maneuvers by Nicolet is therefore precisely the reverse of that offered by Hands, working independently and almost simultaneously, a fact as distressing as it is amusing. Nicolet urges moreover that the proposal to expand the senate was indeed implemented at some point not much later than 123. The reasoning is based on a statement of Sallust that the Gracchi were abandoned by *equites Romanos quos spes societatis a plebe dimoverat*. Nicolet goes for confirmation to Appian's remark that the senate consisted of more than three hundred members before 91. Finally the reform is connected with the celebrated measure requiring senators to yield the *equus publicus*.[12] The argument is attractive but fragile. Cicero puts the proposal *reddendorum equorum* in 129, a date that had previously gone unquestioned. But even if Nicolet is right that the bill postdates the *lex repetundarum* of 123, there is no reason for it to be associated with an enlargement of the senate. The Ciceronian passage places it simply in the context of voting arrangements in the centuriate assembly. It is risky also to press the desire for *societas* that Sallust ascribes to the *equites*. The meaning there is almost certainly that there was expectation of political cooperation with the senate, not actual enrollment into senatorial lists.[13] As for Appian's assertion, it is unsupported anywhere,

[11] *L'Ordre Equestre*, 109-111, 482-485.
[12] Sallust's remark in *Iug*. 42.1; the Appian passage is *BC*, 1.35; cf. 1.59, 1.100; for the *plebiscitum reddendorum equorum*, see Cic. *De Rep*. 4.2.
[13] It is true that the author of the *De Viris Illustribus*, in speaking of the reforms of Livius Drusus in 91, says *senatus permissis iudiciis exsultabat, sed societatem cum equitibus aegre ferebat* (66). But his language proves nothing for the usage of Sallust. Moreover, if he is right, his statement indicates that the *societas* occurred only in 91. It would also be strange indeed if Drusus' father had made a similar proposal in 122 only to have it drop out of the tradition altogether.

contradicts all our other evidence, and has been otherwise unanimously rejected.[14] Although Plutarch and the Livian Epitomator report a measure passed into law by C. Gracchus, Nicolet's conjecture, allegedly utilizing their evidence, requires not a law, but a proposal, and one made not by Gracchus but by his opponent Livius Drusus. Clearly, the information from those sources is too confused to be at all useful for reconstruction.

[14] See Gabba, *App. BC Lib. Prim.*, 119, 343-345. Appian is in any case confused. Senatorial numbers were certainly not sharply reduced by στάσεις in the years immediately preceding 91.

Appendix C. The Cases in Appian, *BC*, 1.22

In justifying his reform of the extortion court, C. Gracchus cited three cases in which senatorial jurors had acquitted obviously guilty extortionists. These were the trials of Aquillius, Aurelius Cotta, and a Salinator.[1] Aquillius' trial, of course, is that of the proconsul of Asia in 124.[2] For Cotta, one thinks naturally of the famous *repetundae* prosecution of 138.[3] Yet C. Cichorius argued that Appian refers not to that case, but to another trial, presumably of the younger Cotta, consul in 119, sometime in the late 120's, a conjecture left open by E. Badian.[4] But C. Gracchus need not have cited only cases that occurred shortly before his proposed reform. The trial of Cotta was obviously a notorious one.[5] There is no evidence for a prosecution of the younger Cotta. The decisive refutation of Cichorius' view is the fact that the same coupling of the trials of M'. Aquillius and L. Cotta that we find in Appian is made twice in Cicero and the reference is clearly to Cotta's prosecution in 138.[6] C. Gracchus would naturally have ransacked the list of extortion trials to find the most outrageous acquittals. It is very unlikely that three would have dropped in his lap in the year of his tribunate, which Cichorius' argument presupposes.

Of Salinator's case not a thing is known but this solitary reference. Cichorius points out that the Salinator was probably a Livius Salinator.[7] The case may have taken place at any time between 149 and 123. Further conjecture is fruitless.

[1] Appian, *BC*, 1.22.
[2] See above, pp. 77-78.
[3] See above, pp. 37-38.
[4] Cichorius, *Röm. Stud.*, 77-79; Badian, *Studies*, 110, n. 4.
[5] Cf. Tac. *Ann.* 3.66.
[6] Cic. *Div. in Caec.* 69: *tum cum P. Lentulus . . . accusabat M'. Aquilium . . . aut cum P. Africanus . . . L. Cottam in iudicium vocabat.* Also *Pro Font.* 38. Appian, *BC*, 1.22, in fact, suggests that the trial of Aquillius came at a later date than the others: Κόττας καὶ Σαλινάτωρ καὶ τρίτος ἐπὶ τούτοις Μάνιος Ἀκύλιος. His statement that provincial envoys in all three cases were still in Rome and complaining in 123 is patently exaggerated.
[7] *Röm. Stud.*, 256.

Appendix D. Alleged Trials in the 80's

Cicero affirms that there was a dearth of criminal trials in the 80's.[1] That would accord well with the character of the Cinnan regime as depicted in the text.[2] Since, however, scattered evidence exists for a number of minor trials that various scholars for various reasons have dated to that decade, it is useful to reexamine the testimony.

One instance can be dismissed swiftly. Appian reports an obscure event in 84 involving a clash between the tribunician college and the consul Cn. Papirius Carbo. Some have taken this as a threatened tribunician prosecution.[3] The date is secure, but the circumstances suggest that the affair amounts to nothing like a trial. After the murder of Cinna in 84, according to Appian, Carbo refused to heed the summons of the tribunes to return to Rome and hold new elections. The outraged magistrates thereupon "threatened to reduce him to the status of a private citizen." [4] The phraseology is peculiar and very probably non-technical. That tribunes had any such authority is most dubious. Q. Caepio's *imperium* had been abrogated in 105 by vote of the people,[5] but he was proconsul in that year. In 84 Carbo was consul in office and certainly could not have undergone prosecution in that capacity. Deposition from office was not entirely unknown. The tribune Octavius had been stripped of his authority in 133; Cinna himself was removed from office in 87; and in 63 the Catilinarian P. Lentulus Sura lost this praetorship and suffered summary execution.[6] In none of these instances, however, was deposition followed by a formal criminal proceeding. One might imagine that the tribunes of 84 threatened an accusation to take place in the following year; but that, of course, would be a year in which they themselves would no longer be in office. Nothing, in any case, came of the matter. Carbo did return to Rome, ostensibly to hold new elections. But

[1] Cic. *Pro Rosc. Amer.* 11, 28; cf. *Brutus,* 308.

[2] See above, Chapter VIII.

[3] Appian, *BC,* 1.78; Zumpt, *Criminalrecht,* I.2.355; Greenidge, *Legal Procedure,* 352-353.

[4] Appian, *BC,* 1.78: ἀπειλησάντων δὲ ἰδιώτην ἀποφανεῖν.

[5] See above, p. 161.

[6] On Sura, see the sources in *MRR,* II.166.

the convenient appearance of unfavorable omens entailed postponement and Carbo served out the year as sole consul.[7]

C. Julius Caesar Strabo was killed in 87 on the orders of Marius and Cinna. The unhappy victim had been betrayed to his enemies by a certain Sextilius. Valerius Maximus adds the detail that Strabo had once defended Sextilius successfully on a capital charge.[8] This Sextilius is otherwise unknown. A recent conjecture identifies him with P. Sextilius, governor of Africa in 88, who refused to allow the fugitive Marius to enter the province in that year.[9] On that hypothesis, Sextilius would have sought, after the victory of the Mariani, to atone for his action in Africa by betraying his former *patronus* to the avengers. But Valerius Maximus states that the Sextilius who turned over Strabo to the Mariani was in Etruria at the time. The governor of Africa who had acted so cautiously when the fugitive Marius was in his area the previous year would hardly have raced back to Italy to grovel at his feet and renounce a former benefactor. There is no reason, in fact, to believe that P. Sextilius left Africa before the arrival of Q. Metellus Pius, probably in 86.[10] Moreover, if Cicero is right that the man who betrayed Strabo was an Etruscan, it is unlikely that he would have been a governor of Africa in 88.[11] The identification collapses. Disposing of that conjecture, however, does not get us any closer to the date of Sextilius' trial. Obviously, it preceded the death of Caesar Strabo in 87. Perhaps it came in 88 when the latter must have been seeking widespread support for his illegal consular candidature.[12] More probably, however, it falls somewhat earlier. It is extremely unlikely that Sextilius' betrayal of Strabo came within a year after Strabo had saved him from a capital penalty.

A single notice preserves the record of a prosecution for *ambitus* involving the praetor-designate P. Sextius and his successful accuser T. Junius L. f.[13] Junius was a man of acknowledged oratorical talents. He was *tribunicius* at the time and is not heard of again, a fact explained by Cicero as due to ill health. One may infer consequently that only a short interval elapsed between tribunate and trial. No specific date is indicated. Cicero's *Brutus,* whence derives our only piece of evidence, is arranged in a roughly chronological fashion, but its scheme cannot be relied upon for detailed precision. Junius is mentioned immediately after two tribunes of 87, but before a series of tribunes who stood for or

[7] Appian, *BC,* 1.78.

[8] Val. Max. 5.3.3: *C. Caesarem, a quo cum studiose tum etiam feliciter gravissimi criminis reus defensus fuerat.* For further sources on the death of Caesar Strabo, see Drumann-Groebe, *Geschichte Roms,* III.123.

[9] Plut. *Marius,* 40; Appian, *BC,* 1.62; see Carney, *A Biog. of Marius,* 59, n. 261; *RhM,* 105 (1962), 324.

[10] Badian, *Studies,* 71-72; Broughton, *Supplement,* 60.

[11] Cic. *De Orat.* 3.10.

[12] See above, p. 226.

[13] Cic. *Brutus,* 180.

held office from 91 to 88.[14] Cicero's use of the particular appellation *tribunicius,* rather than *tribunus,* may indicate a tribunate shortly before 90, but certainty is impossible.[15] An identity for P. Sextius can be recovered: perhaps the quaestor of 111 who served in Africa under L. Calpurnius Bestia.[16] In that troubled year he may be presumed to have been hand picked by Bestia and a member of his *factio.* It is tempting, therefore, to see his prosecutor as a Junius Brutus. The Junii Bruti were no friends of the Metellan group with which Bestia appears to have been associated. M. Junius Brutus, the renowned *accusator,* is known to have appeared against both Scaurus and L. Crassus in criminal prosecutions.[17] Two other M. Junii Bruti were enemies of Sulla in the 80's, the praetor of 88, and the tribune of 83 who later fought with Lepidus against the Sullan system in 77. Still another member of that family, L. Brutus Damasippus was a hatchet man for Carbo and the younger Marius in 82.[18] Titus is not a common *praenomen* among the Iunii; but it is attested once before: a Junius Brutus, aedile in 491.[19] Lucius, of course, is common in the family, and this T. Iunius L.f. may well be a brother of L. Brutus Damasippus, the praetor of 82. Again the date of the trial remains elusive. Possibly Sextius was accused in 90, on the heels of the successful prosecution of Calpurnius Bestia.[20] But conjecture is all that can be offered on this matter. The case, in any event, does not appear to have fallen in the 80's.

Valerius Maximus is our sole source of information on the prosecution of a certain Cn. Sergius Silus by Metellus Celer before the *populus.* Silus, it seems, had attempted to seduce a Roman matron with an offer of cash. The act was never consummated, but on the grounds of intention alone Silus was condemned.[21] Circumstances are unknown and the case, obviously, of little general importance, but it has sometimes been dated to 88. The reasoning may be swiftly reviewed. A prosecution of this kind ought to be within the province of an aedile.[22] Since Q. Metellus

[14] Cic. *Brutus,* 179, 182. On Cicero's method of arrangement in the *Brutus,* see Douglas, *AJP,* 87 (1966), 290-306.

[15] Cf. Münzer, *RE,* 19.965-966, "Junius," n. 32; Niccolini, *Fast. Trib. Pleb.,* 422.

[16] Sallust, *Iug.* 29.4; *MRR,* I.541, 543, n. 4.

[17] On Bestia's connections, see above, pp. 145-146; on Brutus' clash with Scaurus, see above, pp. 125-126; for the interchange with Crassus, see Gruen, *Historia,* 15 (1966), 59-60.

[18] On the praetor of 88, see *MRR,* II.40; the tribune of 83, II.63, 91; on Damasippus, II.67.

[19] *MRR,* I.17.

[20] See above, p. 219.

[21] Val. Max. 6.1.8: *plusque voluisse peccare nocuit quam non peccasse profuit.*

[22] Mommsen, *Strafrecht,* 97, n. 5.

Celer appears to have been tribune in 90, his aedileship would fall ca. 88; hence the date for the trial.[23] The argument obviously is weak. Moreover, the only known Cn. Sergius was a *decumanus* in Sicily in 72. If he was the defendant, his prosecutor is much more likely to have been Q. Metellus Celer, the consul of 60, than his father. The trial is best dated in the late 70's or 60's.[24] Cicero, to be sure, remarked that the younger Celer and his brother Nepos *nihil in causis versati*. That, however, is inexact, or, at most, refers to civil suits, for both men engaged in the prosecution of Lepidus in 79.[25] The trial of Sergius Silus was probably not of political consequence. Yet it is worth noting that a Silus appeared in a case ca. 111 against the defendant L. Piso Caesoninus, who was being supported by the Metellan *factio*.[26] Perhaps some old memories still lingered.

At some unspecified time, two Latin *accusatores*, T. Coponius and L. Cossinius, received Roman citizenship as the consequence of successful prosecutions. Once more a single reference supplies the whole of the extant information.[27] The defendants, C. Papirius Maso and T. Coelius respectively, are as unknown as the prosecutors. It can be argued that the trials are combined because of subject matter rather than chronology. They need not be contemporaneous. Cicero indeed lists them among a series of Roman acts of generosity toward the Latins; the immediately preceding instance is the treaty of Sp. Cassius! T. Coponius is described as grandfather of two Coponii contemporary with Cicero, whereas L. Cossinius is father of a contemporary *eques*. Some, therefore, would date the trials in the Gracchan and Sullan periods respectively.[28] That is a hasty and erroneous assumption. The Gracchan period can be ruled out. Cicero clearly implies that rewards granted to the prosecutors fell under the *lex Servilia*.[29] Whether this means the *lex Servilia Caepionis* of 106 or the *lex Servilia Glauciae* of ca. 104 is uncertain. The trials, in either

---

[23] *MRR*, II.26, 30, n. 7, 41, 45, n. 5.

[24] Münzer, *RE*, 4(2).1691, "Sergius," n. 9; 1719, "Sergius," n. 38; *ORF*, 380.

[25] Cic. *Brutus*, 247; on the trial of Lepidus, see Ps-Asconius, 187, 259, Stangl.

[26] On this trial, see above, pp. 133-134.

[27] Cic. *Pro Balbo*, 53: *Quo modo igitur L. Cossinius Tiburs, pater huius equitis Romani, optimi atque ornatissimi viri, damnato T. Caelio, quo modo ex eadem civitate T. Coponius, civis item summa virtute et dignitate — nepotes T. et C. Coponios nostis — damnato C. Masone civis Romanus est factus?*

[28] Münzer, *RE*, 36(2).1063, "Papirius," n. 59; *RE*, 8.1671, "Cossinius," n. 1.

[29] Cic. *Pro Balbo*, 54: *Quod si acerbissima lege Servilia principes viri ac gravissimi et sapientissimi cives hanc Latinis, id est foederatis, viam ad civitatem populi iussu patere passi sunt.*

case, must postdate 106.[30] Since T. Coponius was the grandfather of
two Ciceronian contemporaries, his prosecution of Maso presumably
came in the immediate wake of the *lex Servilia*. As for L. Cossinius, a
man of that name can be found as praetor in 73.[31] But the family of
Coelius' prosecutor remained equestrian; identification would be rash.
The latter's son is described by Cicero in 56 as *ornatissimus:* presumably,
therefore, not a young man. That the trial of Coelius came in the 80's is
most unlikely, since the question of citizenship for Latins ceased to be
an issue after the Social War. In all probability, the elder Cossinius
seized the opportunity presented by the *lex Servilia* as a young man and,
like Coponius, undertook his prosecution toward the end of the second
century.

One last trial has, on occasion, been dated to the 80's. Valerius
Maximus, a mine of information on obscure trials and pleasant anec-
dotes, tells the story. A certain Valerius Valentinus brought charges,
apparently of extortion, against C. Cosconius under the *lex Servilia*.
Guilt of the defendant was clear. But Valentinus happened to be a poet
and a copy of his verses fell into the hands of Cosconius, who read them
aloud at the trial. They revealed a seamy side of Valentinus. He had
boasted of seducing virgins from noble families, both male and female.
The *iudices* were shocked and the defendant was acquitted. It was more
a condemnation of Valentinus than an absolution of Cosconius.[32] When
did the trial take place? A C. Cosconius appears as a legate and possibly
a praetor in 89 when he served in the Social War. Consequently, the
prosecution has been put in 88 or 87.[33] It is possible that this same man
was later proconsul in Illyricum from 78 to 76; thus, perhaps a trial in
75 or later.[34] Neither of these dates, however, will do. Valerius Maximus
states specifically that the prosecution fell under the *lex Servilia*. This
fact rules out any point after 81 when the *lex Servilia* had been superseded
by the Sullan law on extortion. A trial in 88 or 87 is most doubtful. A
legate who served in the Social War in Apulia would probably not have
carried on activities likely to provoke a charge of *res repetundae*. There
is other evidence. A poet Valerius Valentinus occurs as the sponsor of
a *lex Tappula* ridiculed by the circle of L. Opimius and mentioned by
Lucilius. If he is the prosecutor of Cosconius the trial must be much

[30] The view of H. E. Russell, "Advancement in Rank under the Roman
Republic as a Reward for the Soldier and the Public Prosecutor," (unpub.
diss., Bryn Mawr College, 1950), 70-71, that citizenship was bestowed in
both cases in accordance with the *praemia legis* of the *lex Calpurnia* in 67,
is without foundation.

[31] Sallust, *Hist.* 3.94, Maur.; Plut. *Crass.* 9.

[32] Val. Max. 8.1.8: *Magis vero Valerius in Cosconii absolutione damnatus
quam Cosconius in causa sua liberatus est.*

[33] Münzer, *RE,* 8.1667-1668, "Cosconius," n. 3; Nicolet, *L'Ordre Equestre,* 542-543.

[34] Implied by Broughton, *MRR,* II.86-87, 88, n. 4.

earlier than the Sullan era.[35] The defendant C. Cosconius is presumably a father of the proconsul of 78.

[35] Lucilius, 1239 (*ROL,* 3.404). Correctly pointed out by A. von Premerstein, *"Lex Tappula," Hermes,* 39 (1904), 336-342, and Cichorius, *Unt. zu Luc.,* 341-345. The latter, following Mommsen, misdates the *lex Servilia* to ca. 111, but his placing of the trial toward the end of the second century is doubtless accurate.

Appendix E. A Summary of the Trials

The trials discussed in the text and notes are here arranged in chronological order. Information given, where known, includes defendant, prosecutor, charge, court, sentence, and result. Since much is uncertain, a question mark(?) is inserted after each disputable item. Where the question mark appears at the beginning of an entry it indicates that the date of the trial is not clear in the ancient evidence but has been argued in the text. This list is followed by a list of trials for which only approximate dates can be given.

149
Ser. Sulpicius Galba indicted by L. Scribonius Libo for *repetundae* (?). Trial did not take place.

145
C. Plautius prosecuted for *perduellio* before the people (?). Conviction and exile.

141
L. Hostilius Tubulus prosecuted by P. Mucius Scaevola for judicial corruption before a *quaestio extraordinaria*. Conviction and exile. Eventual arrest and suicide.

140
P. Cornelius Scipio Aemilianus prosecuted by Ti. Claudius Asellus for offenses in censorship, before the people. Acquittal (?).
D. Junius Silanus indicted for *repetundae*. Condemned by father T. Manlius Torquatus at home. Suicide.

139
(?) Q. Pompeius prosecuted by Cn. Servilius Caepio, Q. Servilius Caepio, L. Caecilius Metellus Calvus, and Q. Caecilius Metellus Macedonicus for *repetundae*. Acquittal.

138
L. Aurelius Cotta prosecuted by P. Cornelius Scipio Aemilianus for *repetundae*. Acquittal.

304

Publicani prosecuted for murder before a *quaestio extraordinaria.* Acquittal.

C. Matienus and others prosecuted for desertion under magisterial *coercitio* (?). Conviction, scourging, and sale into slavery.

136

M. Aemilius Lepidus Porcina prosecuted for conducting war without permission, before the people. Conviction and fine.

133

T. Annius Luscus indicted by Ti. Sempronius Gracchus before the people. Charge dropped.

132

C. Blossius prosecuted before tribunal of P. Popillius Laenas and P. Rupilius. Conviction (?) and exile.

(?) Vettius prosecuted before tribunal of P. Popillius Laenas and P. Rupilius (?). Acquittal (?).

C. Villius prosecuted for *parricidium* (?). Conviction and execution.

P. Cornelius Scipio Nasica prosecuted by M. Fulvius Flaccus for murder (?) before a *quaestio extraordinaria* (?). Trial not completed.

131

L. Valerius Flaccus fined by P. Licinius Crassus Mucianus for religious offense. Fine remitted by the people.

124

C. Sempronius Gracchus prosecuted for *perduellio* (?) before the people (?). Acquittal.

(?) M'. Aquillius prosecuted by P. Cornelius Lentulus for *repetundae.* Acquittal.

123

P. Popillius Laenas prosecuted by C. Sempronius Gracchus for condemning citizens without trial, before the people (?). Conviction and exile.

120

L. Opimius prosecuted by P. Decius for executing citizens without trial, before the people. Acquittal.

P. Cornelius Lentulus indicted for executing citizens without trial (?). Trial did not take place.

119

C. Papirius Carbo prosecuted by L. Licinius Crassus for *repetundae* (?). Conviction and suicide.

P. Decius prosecuted for judicial conspiracy (?) before the people (?). Acquittal (?).

Q. Mucius Scaevola prosecuted by T. Albucius for *repetundae.* Acquittal (?).

116

M. Aemilius Scaurus prosecuted by P. Rutilius Rufus for *ambitus*. Acquittal.

P. Rutilius Rufus prosecuted by M. Aemilius Scaurus for *ambitus*. Acquittal.

C. Marius prosecuted for *ambitus*. Acquittal.

114

(?) M. Aemilius Scaurus prosecuted by M. Junius Brutus for *repetundae*. Acquittal (?).

Vestal Virgins Aemilia, Licinia, and Marcia prosecuted for *incestum* before L. Caecilius Metellus Delmaticus, the *pontifex maximus*. Aemilia convicted. Licinia and Marcia acquitted.

113

C. Porcius Cato prosecuted for *repetundae*. Conviction and a small *litis aestimatio*.

Vestal Virgins Aemilia, Licinia, and Marcia prosecuted by Sex. Peducaeus for *incestum* before a *quaestio extraordinaria*. Conviction and execution (?).

M. Antonius prosecuted for *incestum* before a *quaestio extraordinaria*. Acquittal.

(?) Ser. Fulvius prosecuted for *incestum*.

112

(?) Cn. Papirius Carbo prosecuted by M. Antonius for *repetundae* (?). Conviction and suicide.

111

(?) Q. Caecilius Metellus Numidicus prosecuted for *repetundae*. Acquittal.

(?) L. Calpurnius Piso Caesoninus prosecuted for *repetundae* (?). Acquittal (?).

Bomilcar prosecuted for murder before *praetor peregrinus* (?). Trial not completed.

109

C. Sulpicius Galba prosecuted for treason before a *quaestio extraordinaria* under Mamilian law. Conviction and exile (?).

Sp. Postumius Albinus prosecuted for treason before a *quaestio extraordinaria* under Mamilian law. Conviction and exile (?).

C. Porcius Cato prosecuted for treason before a *quaestio extraordinaria* under Mamilian law. Conviction and exile.

L. Opimius prosecuted for treason before a *quaestio extraordinaria* under Mamilian law. Conviction and exile.

L. Calpurnius Bestia prosecuted by C. Memmius for treason before a *quaestio extraordinaria* under Mamilian law. Conviction and exile (?).

Hortensius prosecuted for *ambitus* (?). Conviction.

T. Turpilius Silanus subjected to magisterial *coercitio* for treason before Q. Caecilius Metellus Numidicus as commander in field. Conviction and execution.

107

C. Popillius Laenas prosecuted by C. Coelius Caldus for *perduellio* before the people. Conviction and exile.

104

(?) Q. Servilius Caepio prosecuted for *peculatus* before a *quaestio extraordinaria*. Acquittal (?).

(?) Others prosecuted for *peculatus* before a *quaestio extraordinaria*. Conviction.

M. Junius Silanus prosecuted by Cn. Domitius Ahenobarbus for *perduellio* (?) before the people. Acquittal.

M. Aemilius Scaurus prosecuted by Cn. Domitius Ahenobarbus for religious offense, before the people. Acquittal.

(?) T. Albucius prosecuted by C. Julius Caesar Strabo for *repetundae* (?). Conviction and exile.

(?) Q. Fabius Maximus Eburnus prosecuted by Cn. Pompeius for murder (?), before the people (?). Conviction and exile.

103

Q. Servilius Caepio prosecuted by C. Norbanus (?) for *perduellio*. Conviction and imprisonment. Later released by a tribune, he went into exile.

Cn. Mallius Maximus prosecuted by L. Appuleius Saturninus for *perduellio*. Conviction and exile.

(?) C. Memmius prosecuted by M. Aemilius Scaurus for *repetundae*. Acquittal.

(?) C. Flavius Fimbria prosecuted by M. Gratidius for *repetundae*. Acquittal.

(?) L. Valerius Flaccus prosecuted for *repetundae* (?). Acquittal (?).

102

(?) L. Licinius Lucullus prosecuted by Servilius for *peculatus* (?). Conviction and exile.

101

(?) L. Appuleius Saturninus indicted before a *quaestio extraordinaria* (?). Trial did not take place.

(?) C. Servilius prosecuted for *repetundae* (?). Conviction and exile.

Publicius Malleolus prosecuted for *parricidium*. Conviction and execution.

100

Q. Caecilius Metellus Numidicus prosecuted by L. Appuleius Saturninus for *perduellio* (?). Conviction and exile.

99

(?) P. Furius prosecuted by C. Canuleius (?) and C. Appuleius Decianus before the people. Torn to pieces by mob.

(?) L. Valerius Flaccus prosecuted by C. Appuleius Decianus before the people. Acquittal.

98

(?) C. Appuleius Decianus prosecuted for *maiestas* (?). Conviction and exile.

Sex. Titius prosecuted by M. Antonius for *maiestas* (?). Conviction and exile.

(?) M. Antonius prosecuted by M. Duronius for *ambitus*. Acquittal.

97

(?) M'. Aquillius prosecuted by L. Fufius for *repetundae*. Acquittal.

(?) Q. Metellus Nepos prosecuted by C. Scribonius Curio.

95

Q. Servilius Caepio prosecuted by T. Betutius Barrus (?) for *maiestas*. Acquittal (?).

(?) C. Norbanus prosecuted by P. Sulpicius Rufus for *maiestas*. Acquittal.

(?) T. Matrinius prosecuted by L. Antistius for illegal citizenship before a *quaestio extraordinaria* under the *lex Licinia Mucia*. Acquittal.

(?) L. Marcius Philippus (?) prosecuted by Q. Hortensius (?) for *repetundae* (?). Acquittal (?).

(?) L. Cornelius Sulla indicted by C. Marcius Censorinus for *repetundae*. Charges dropped.

92

P. Rutilius Rufus prosecuted by Apicius for *repetundae*. Conviction and exile.

L. Marcius Philippus prosecuted by Q. Servilius Caepio for *ambitus*. Acquittal.

91

(?) Q. Servilius Caepio prosecuted by M. Aemilius Scaurus for *repetundae* (?). Acquittal (?).

(?) M. Aemilius Scaurus prosecuted by Q. Servilius Caepio for *repetundae*. Acquittal (?).

90

M. Aemilius Scaurus prosecuted (?) by Q. Servilius Caepio for *maiestas* under the *lex Varia*. Acquittal (?).

C. Aurelius Cotta prosecuted for *maiestas* under the *lex Varia*. Conviction and exile.

L. Calpurnius Bestia prosecuted for *maiestas* under the *lex Varia*. Conviction and exile.

L. Memmius prosecuted by L. Marcius Philippus for *maiestas* under the *lex Varia*. Conviction (?) and exile (?).

Q. Pompeius Rufus prosecuted by L. Marcius Philippus for *maiestas* under the *lex Varia*. Acquittal (?).

M. Antonius prosecuted for *maiestas* under the *lex Varia*. Acquittal (?).

89

Q. Varius prosecuted for *maiestas* under the *lex Varia*. Conviction and execution (?).

88

Cn. Pompeius Strabo indicted for *maiestas* under the *lex Varia*.

87

L. Cornelius Sulla prosecuted by M. Vergilius for condemning citizens without trial (?), before the people. Prosecution ignored.

L. Cornelius Merula prosecuted for *perduellio* (?) before the people. Suicide.

Q. Lutatius Catulus prosecuted by M. Marius Gratidianus for *perduellio* (?) before the people. Suicide.

Ap. Claudius Pulcher indicted. Conviction (?) and exile (?).

86

Sex. Lucilius (?) thrown from the Tarpeian rock by P. Popillius Laenas.

Tribunes and two praetors indicted by P. Popillius Laenas before the people. Conviction (?) and exile.

Q. Mucius Scaevola indicted by C. Flavius Fimbria before the people. The trial did not take place.

(?) Cn. Pompeius Magnus prosecuted for *peculatus*. Acquittal.

80

Sex. Roscius Amerinus prosecuted by C. Erucius for murder. Acquittal.

79

M. Aemilius Lepidus prosecuted by Q. Caecilius Metellus Celer and Q. Caecilius Metellus Nepos for *repetundae*. Acquittal.

TRIALS WITH APPROXIMATE DATES

Between 149 and 123
Salinator prosecuted for *repetundae*. Acquittal.

In 140's or 130's
C. Laelius prosecuted (?) before the people. Acquittal (?).

Ca. 119
Valerius Messala prosecuted by Q. Caecilius Metellus Numidicus for *repetundae*. Conviction.

Ca. 117
Q. Marcius Rex prosecuted for *repetundae* (?). Acquittal (?).

Ca. 112

M. Papirius Carbo prosecuted by P. Flaccus for *repetundae* (?). Conviction.

Between 105 and 100

T. Coelius prosecuted by L. Cossinius for *repetundae*. Conviction.

C. Papirius Maso prosecuted by T. Coponius for *repetundae*. Conviction.

C. Cosconius prosecuted by Valerius Valentinus for *repetundae*. Acquittal.

Between 104 and 92

Cn. Plancus prosecuted by M. Junius Brutus before *equites*. Acquittal.

Early 90's

Servilius prosecuted by L. Licinius Lucullus and M. Licinius Lucullus for *maiestas*. Acquittal.

C. Curtius prosecuted for *peculatus*. Acquittal.

M. Claudius Marcellus prosecuted by L. Licinius Crassus. Acquittal.

Late 90's

Sextilius prosecuted on capital charge (?). Acquittal.

Ca. 90

P. Sextius prosecuted by T. Junius L.f. for *ambitus*. Conviction.

Late 70's or 60's

Cn. Sergius Silus prosecuted by Q. Caecilius Metellus Celer for a moral offense. Conviction.

Accame, S. "Il primo consolato di Mario," *Riv. di Filol.,* 14 (1936), 64-69.

Africa, T. "Aristonicus, Blossius, and the City of the Sun," *Int. Rev. Soc. Hist.,* 6 (1961), 110-124.

Afzelius, A. "Zwei Episoden aus dem Leben Ciceros," *ClMed,* 5 (1942), 209-217.

Allen, W. "The Sources of Jugurtha's Influence in the Roman Senate," *CP,* 33 (1938), 90-92.

Astin, A. E. "Scipio Aemilianus and Cato Censorinus," *Latomus,* 15 (1956), 159-180.

———— "Diodorus and the Date of the Embassy to the East of Scipio Aemilianus," *CP,* 54 (1959), 221-227.

———— *"Dicta Scipionis* of 131 B.C.," *CQ,* 10 (1960), 135-139.

———— *"Leges Aelia et Fufia,"* Latomus, 23 (1964), 421-445.

———— *Scipio Aemilianus.* Oxford, 1967.

Badian, E. *"Lex Acilia Repetundarum,"* AJP, 75 (1954), 374-384.

———— *"Lex Servilia,"* CR, 4 (1954), 101-102.

———— "The Date of Pompey's First Triumph," *Hermes,* 83 (1955), 107-118.

———— "P. Decius P.f. Subulo," *JRS,* 46 (1956), 91-96.

———— "Quintus Mucius Scaevola and the Province of Asia," *Athenaeum,* 34 (1956), 104-123.

———— *Foreign Clientelae, 264-70 B.C.* Oxford, 1958.

———— "Review of Broughton, *Supplement to MRR,"* Gnomon, 33 (1961), 492-498.

———— "Servilius and Pompey's First Triumph," *Hermes,* 89 (1961), 254-256.

———— "From the Gracchi to Sulla (1940-1959)," *Historia,* 11 (1962), 197-245.

———— "Review of Taylor, *Voting Districts,"* JRS, 52 (1962), 200-210.

———— "Notes on Roman Senators of the Republic," *Historia,* 12 (1963), 129-143.

———— *Studies in Greek and Roman History.* New York, 1964.

311

———— "Notes on *Provincia Gallia* in the Late Republic," *Mélanges Piganiol* (1966), 901-918.

———— *Roman Imperialism in the Late Republic*. Pretoria, 1967.

Balsdon, J. P. V. D. "Q. Mucius Scaevola the Pontifex and *Ornatio Provinciae*," *CR*, 51 (1937), 8-10.

———— "History of the Extortion Court at Rome, 123-70 B.C.," *PBSR*, 14 (1938), 98-114.

———— "Consular Provinces under the Late Republic," *JRS*, 29 (1939), 57-73.

———— "Sulla Felix," *JRS*, 41 (1951), 1-10.

———— "Review of Badian, *Studies in Greek and Roman History*," *JRS*, 55 (1965), 229-232.

———— "Review of Gelzer, *Kleine Schriften*," *Gnomon*, 37 (1965), 578-587.

Barr, W. "Lucilius and Accius," *RhM*, 108 (1965), 101-103.

Benedict, C. H. "The Romans in Southern Gaul," *AJP*, 63 (1942), 38-50.

Bennett, H. *Cinna and His Times*. Menasha, Wis., 1923.

Berger, A. "A Note on Gellius, *N.A.* I.6," *AJP*, 67 (1946), 320-328.

Bernardi, A. "La Guerra Sociale e le lotte dei partiti in Roma," *Nuov. Riv. Stor.*, 28-29 (1944-45), 60-99.

Biedl, A. "De Memmianorum Familia," *WS*, 48 (1930), 98-107.

———— "Nochmals zur Familiengeschichte der Memmier," *WS*, 49 (1931), 107-114.

Bilz, K. *Die Politik des P. Cornelius Scipio Aemilianus*. Stuttgart, 1935.

Bloch, G. "M. Aemilius Scaurus," *Mélanges D'Histoire Ancienne*, 25 (1909), 1-81.

———— and J. Carcopino, *Histoire Romaine*, Vol. II. Paris, 1940.

Blum, E. "L'Origine des *Leges Repetundarum*," *Rev. Gen. Droit*, 46 (1922), 119-135, 197-206.

Boak, A. E. R. "The Extraordinary Commands from 80 to 48 B.C.: A Study in the Origins of the Principate," *AHR*, 24 (1918-19), 1-25.

Boren H. C. "Livius Drusus, T.P. 122, and his Anti-Gracchan Program," *CJ*, 52 (1956), 27-36.

———— "The Urban Side of the Gracchan Economic Crisis," *AHR*, 63 (1958), 890-902.

———— "Numismatic Light on the Gracchan Crisis," *AJP*, 79 (1958), 140-155.

———— "Tiberius Gracchus: The Opposition View," *AJP*, 82 (1961), 358-369.

Bourne, F. "The Roman Republican Census and Census Statistics," *CW*, 45 (1952), 129-135.

Bracco, V. "L'*Elogium* di Polla," *RendNap*, 29 (1954), 5-38.

———— "Ancora sull' *elogium* di Polla," *RendNap*, 35 (1960), 149-163.

Brecht, C. H. "*Perduellio*," *MünchBeitr*, 29 (1938), 1-317.

312

Broughton, T. R. S. *The Magistrates of the Roman Republic.* 2 vols. New York, 1951-1952.

————— *Supplement to the Magistrates of the Roman Republic.* New York, 1960.

Brown, T. S. "Greek Influence on Tiberius Gracchus," *CJ,* 42 (1947), 471-474.

Brunt, P. A. "Sulla and the Asian Publicans," *Latomus,* 15 (1956), 17-25.

————— *"Amicitia* in the Late Roman Republic," *PCPS,* 191 (1965), 1-20.

————— "The *Equites* in the Late Republic," in *2nd Int. Conf. of Econ. Hist. 1962* (Paris, 1965), I.117-137.

————— "Italian Aims at the Time of the Social War," *JRS,* 55 (1965), 90-109.

Bruwaene, M. van den. "Quelques Eclaircissments sur le *De Haruspicum Responsis,*" *AntCl,* 17 (1948), 81-92.

————— "L'Opposition à Scipion Emilien après la mort de Tiberius Gracchus," *Phoibos,* 5 (1950-51), 229-238.

Buckland, W. W. "Civil Proceedings Against ex-Magistrates in the Republic," *JRS,* 27 (1937), 37-47.

Bulst, C. *"Cinnanum Tempus,"* *Historia,* 13 (1964), 307-337.

Burn, A. R. "A Metellus in Two Passages of Dio," *CR,* 63 (1949), 52-53.

Calvert, R. L. "M. Claudius Marcellus, cos. II, 155 B.C.," *Athenaeum,* 39 (1961), 11-23.

Cambridge Ancient History, The, ed. S. A. Cook, F. E. Adcock, and M. P. Charlesworth. Vols. VIII-IX. Cambridge, 1930-1932.

Carcopino, J. *Autour des Gracques.* Paris, 1928.

————— "Les lois agraires des Gracques et la Guerre Sociale," *Bull. Ass. Budé,* 22 (1929), 3-23.

————— *Sylla ou la Monarchie Manquée.* Paris, 1931.

————— "Sur un passage de la Chronique de saint Jerome," *Mélanges en Hommage à la Mémoire de Fr. Martroye* (1940), 73-79.

Carney, T. F. "Marius' Choice of Battlefield in the Campaign of 100," *Athenaeum,* 6 (1958), 229-237.

————— "Was Rutilius' Exile Voluntary or Compulsory?" *Acta Juridica* (1958), 243-245.

————— "Coins Bearing on the Age and Career of Marius," *NC,* 19 (1959), 79-88.

————— "Two Notes on Republican Roman Law," *Acta Juridica* (1959), 229-234.

————— "Cicero's Picture of Marius," *WS,* 73 (1960), 83-122.

————— "Rome in the Gracchan Age," *Theoria* (1960), 38-42.

————— *A Biography of Marius. Proc. Afr. Class. Ass.,* Supp. No. 1. Assen, Netherlands, 1961.

————— "The Death of Sulla," *Acta Classica,* 4 (1961), 64-79.

———— "The Flight and Exile of Marius," *Greece and Rome,* 8 (1961), 98-121.

———— "The Picture of Marius in Valerius Maximus," *RhM,* 105 (1962), 289-337.

Caspari, M. O. B. "On the *Rogatio Livia de Latinis,*" *CQ,* 5 (1911), 115-118.

Chantraine, H. *Undersuchungen zur römischen Geschichte am Ende des 2 Jahrhunderts vor Chr.* Kallmünz, 1959.

Ciaceri, E. "L'atteggiamento politico di M. Tullio Cicerone di fronte a L. Cornelio Silla," *AttiVen,* 79 (1919-20), 541-562.

Cichorius, C. *Untersuchungen zu Lucilius.* Berlin, 1908.

———— *Römische Studien.* Leipzig-Berlin, 1922.

Clarke, M. L. *Rhetoric at Rome.* New York, 1963.

Corpus Inscriptionum Latinarum. Berlin, 1863————

Crifò, G. *Ricerche sull' Exilium nel periodo Repubblicano.* Milan, 1961.

D'Arms, E. "The Date and Nature of the *Lex Thoria,*" *AJP,* 56 (1935), 232-245.

Daube, D. "The Peregrine Praetor," *JRS,* 41 (1951), 66-70.

Degrassi, A. *Fasti Capitolini.* Turin, 1954.

———— "Un nuovo miliario calabro della Via Popillia," *Philologus,* 99 (1955), 259-265.

———— *Inscriptiones Latinae Liberae Rei Publicae.* Florence, 1965.

De Sanctis, G. *Problemi di Storia Antica.* Bari, 1932.

Dessau, H. *Inscriptiones Latinae Selectae.* 3 vols. in 5. Berlin, 1892-1916.

Dorey, T. A. "A Note on the *Pro Roscio Amerino,*" *Ciceroniana,* 2 (1960), 147-148.

Douglas, A. E. "The Legislation of Spurius Thorius," *AJP,* 77 (1956), 376-395.

———— "Corrigenda," *AJP,* 78 (1957), 89.

———— "Clausulae in the *Rhetorica ad Herennium* as Evidence of its Date," *CQ,* 10 (1960), 65-78.

———— *M. Tulli Ciceronis Brutus.* Oxford, 1966.

———— *"Oratorum Aetates,"* *AJP,* 87 (1966), 290-306.

Drumann, W. *Geschichte Roms,* 2nd ed. by P. Groebe. Vols. I-VI. Berlin, 1899-1929.

Dudley, D. R. "Blossius of Cumae," *JRS,* 31 (1941), 94-99.

Earl, D. C. "Calpurnii Pisones in the 2nd Century B.C.," *Athenaeum,* 38 (1960), 283-298.

———— "M. Octavius, trib. pleb. 133 B.C., and his Successor," *Latomus,* 19 (1960), 657-669.

———— *The Political Thought of Sallust.* Cambridge, Eng., 1961.

———— "Terence and Roman Politics," *Historia,* 11 (1962), 469-485.

———— *Tiberius Gracchus: A Study in Politics.* Brussels, 1963.

———— "Sallust and the Senate's Numidian Policy," *Latomus,* 24 (1965), 532-536.

———— "Tiberius Gracchus' Last Assembly," *Athenaeum*, 43 (1965), 95-105.

Ewins, U. "The Early Colonization of Cisalpine Gaul," *PBSR*, 20 (1952), 54-71.

———— *"Ne Quis Iudicio Circumveniatur,"* JRS, 50 (1960), 94-107.

Ferguson, W. S. "The *Lex Calpurnia* of 149 B.C.," *JRS*, 11 (1921), 86-100.

Fraccaro, P. "Studi nell' età Graccana," *Studi Storici*, 5 (1912), 317-448; *Studi Storici*, 6 (1913), 42-136.

———— *Studi sull' età dei Gracchi*. Vol. 1. Citta di Castello, 1914.

———— 'Ricerche su Gaio Graccho," *Athenaeum*, 3 (1925), 76-97, 156-157.

———— "Review of Carcopino, *Autour des Gracques*," *Athenaeum*, 9 (1931), 302-320.

———— "Un episodio delle agitazioni agrarie dei Gracchi," *Studies Presented to D. M. Robinson*, 2 (1953), 884-892.

———— *Opuscula*, Vol. II. Pavia, 1957.

Frank, E. "Marius and the Roman Nobility," *CJ*, 50 (1955), 149-152.

Frank, T. *An Economic Survey of Ancient Rome*. Vol. 1. Baltimore, 1933.

———— "On Some Financial Legislation of the Sullan Period," *AJP*, 54 (1933), 54-58.

Fritz, K. von. "Sallust and the Attitude of the Roman Nobility at the Time of the Wars Against Jugurtha (112-105 B.C.)," *TAPA*, 74 (1943), 134-168.

Gabba, E. "Ricerche su alcuni punti di storia Mariana," *Athenaeum*, 29 (1951), 12-24.

———— "Ancora sulle cifre dei censimenti," *Athenaeum*, 30 (1952), 161-173.

———— "Politica e cultura in Roma agli inizi del I secolo a.C.," *Athenaeum*, 31 (1953), 259-272.

———— "Le origini della guerra sociale e la vita politica romana dopo 1'89 a.C.," *Athenaeum*, 32 (1954), 41-114, 293-345.

———— "Note Appianee," *Athenaeum*, 33 (1955), 218-230.

———— *Appiano e la storia delle guerre civili*. Florence, 1956.

———— "Il ceto equestre e il Senato di Silla," *Athenaeum*, 34 (1956), 124-138.

———— "Osservazioni sulla legge guidiziaria di M. Livio Druso (91 a.C.)," *Par. Pass.*, 11 (1956), 363-372.

———— *Appiani, Bellorum Civilium Liber Primus*. Florence, 1958.

———— "M. Livio Druso e le riforme di Silla," *AnnPisa*, 33 (1964), 1-15.

Gagé, J. "Sylla, Pompeé et la théologie de la victoire," *RHist*, 171 (1933), 35-43.

Garzetti, A. "M. Licinio Crasso," *Athenaeum*, 19 (1941), 3-37.

Geer, R. M. "M. Aemilius Scaurus (Suetonius, *Nero*, 2, 1 and Asconius on Cicero, *Pro Scauro,* 1)," *CP,* 24 (1929), 292-294.

———— "Notes on the Land Law of Tiberius Gracchus," *TAPA,* 70 (1939), 30-36.

Gelzer, M. *Die Nobilität der römischen Republik.* Leipzig-Berlin, 1912.

———— "Review of Carcopino, *Autour des Gracques,*" *Gnomon,* 5 (1929), 648-660.

———— "Review of Carcopino, *Sylla,*" *Gnomon,* 8 (1932), 605-607.

———— *Pompeius.* Munich, 1949.

———— "Review of Hill, *Roman Middle Class,*" *Gnomon,* 25 (1953), 319-323.

———— *Kleine Schriften.* Vols. I-II. Wiesbaden, 1962.

Greenidge, A. H. J. "The *Provocatio Militiae* and Provincial Jurisdiction," *CR,* 10 (1896), 225-233.

———— *Legal Procedure of Cicero's Time.* Oxford, 1901.

———— *A History of Rome During the Later Republic and Early Principate.* Vol. I. London, 1904.

———— and A. M. Clay, *Sources for Roman History, 133-70 B.C.,* rev. by E. W. Gray. Oxford, 1960.

Gruen, E. S. "Politics and the Courts in 104 B.C.," *TAPA,* 95 (1964), 99-110.

———— "The Exile of Metellus Numidicus," *Latomus,* 24 (1965), 576-580.

———— "The *Lex Varia,*" *JRS,* 55 (1965), 59-73.

———— "The Political Allegiance of P. Mucius Scaevola," *Athenaeum,* 43 (1965), 321-332.

———— "The Dolabellae and Sulla," *AJP,* 87 (1966), 385-399.

———— "Political Prosecutions in the 90's B.C.," *Historia,* 15 (1966), 32-64.

———— "The Quaestorship of Norbanus," *CP,* 61 (1966), 105-107.

———— "M. Antonius and the Trial of the Vestal Virgins," *RhM,* 111 (1968), 59-63.

Hands, A. R. "Sallust and *Dissimulatio,*" *JRS,* 49 (1959), 56-60.

———— "The Political Background of the *lex Acilia de Repetundis,*" *Latomus,* 24 (1965), 225-237.

Hardy, E. G. "Were the *Lex Thoria* of 118 B.C. and the *Lex Agraria* of 111 B.C. Reactionary Laws?" *JP,* 31 (1910), 268-286.

———— "The Judiciary Law of Livius Drusus," *CR,* 26 (1912), 218-220.

———— "Notes on the *Lex Iudiciaria* of C. Gracchus, the *Lex Servilia* of Caepio, and the *Lex Thoria,*" *JP,* 32 (1912), 96-106.

———— "Three Questions as to Livius Drusus," *CR,* 27 (1913), 261-263.

———— "The Number of the Sullan Senate," *JRS,* 6 (1916), 59-62.

———— *Some Problems in Roman History.* Oxford, 1924.

Haug, I. "Der römische Bundesgenossenkrieg 91-88 v. Chr. bei Titus Livius," *WürzJbb,* 2 (1947), 100-139, 201-258.

Hawthorn, J. R. "The Senate after Sulla," *Greece and Rome,* 9 (1962), 53-60.

Heinze, R. "Ciceros politische Anfänge," *AbhLeipz,* 27 (1909), 945-1010.

Henderson, M. I. "The Process *De Repetundis,*" *JRS,* 41 (1951), 71-88.

——— "Review of Scullard, *Roman Politics,*" *JRS,* 42 (1952), 114-116.

——— "The Establishment of the *Equester Ordo,*" *JRS,* 53 (1963), 61-72.

Hendrickson, G. L. "The Memoirs of Rutilius Rufus," *CP,* 28 (1933), 153-175.

Heurgon, J. "Le préteur P. Decius et l'*imperium* de Marius," *REL,* 16 (1938), 161-168.

Heuss, A. "Review of Scullard, *Roman Politics,*" *HZ,* 182 (1956), 593-597.

Hill, H. "Sulla's New Senators in 81 B.C.," *CQ,* 26 (1932), 170-177.

——— "The So-called *Lex Aufeia,*" *CR,* 62 (1948), 112-113.

——— *The Roman Middle Class in the Republican Period.* Oxford, 1952.

Hinrichs, F. T. "Die *lex agraria* des Jahres 111 v. Chr.," *ZSav,* 83 (1966), 252-307.

——— "Der römische Strassenbau zur Zeit der Gracchen," *Historia,* 16 (1967), 162-176.

Hoffman, W. "Die römische Politik des 2. Jahrhunderts und das Ende Karthagos," *Historia,* 9 (1960), 309-344.

Holroyd, M. "The Jugurthine War: Was Marius or Metellus the Real Victor?" *JRS,* 18 (1928), 1-20.

Hough, J. N. "The *Lex Lutatia* and the *Lex Plautia de Vi,*" *AJP,* 51 (1930), 135-147.

Hoy, L. P. "Political Influence in Roman Prosecutions, 78 to 60 B.C.," unpub diss. Bryn Mawr College, 1952.

Humbert, J. *Les plaidoyers écrits et les plaidoiries réelles de Ciceron.* Paris, 1925.

Husband, R. W. "On the Expulsion of Foreigners from Rome," *CP,* 11 (1916), 315-333.

Jacoby, F. *Die Fragmente der Griechischen Historiker.* Berlin, 1923———.

Jones, A. H. M. "De Tribunis Plebis Reficiendis," *PCPS,* 186 (1960), 35-38.

——— "De Legibus Junia et Acilia Repetundarum," *PCPS,* 186 (1960), 39-42.

Katz, S. "The Gracchi: An Essay in Interpretation," *CJ,* 38 (1942), 65-82.

Kinsey, T. E. "A Dilemma in the *Pro Roscio Amerino,*" *Mnemosyne,* 19 (1966), 270-271.

———— "The Dates of the *Pro Roscio Amerino* and *Pro Quinctio*," *Mnemosyne,* 20 (1967), 61-67.

Klein, J. *Die Verwaltungsbeamten von Sicilien und Sardinien.* Bonn, 1878.

Kunkel, W. "Untersuchungen zur Entwicklung des römischen Kriminalverfahrens in vorsullanischer Zeit," *AbhMünch,* 56 (1962), 1-149.

———— "Das Konsilium im Hausgericht," *ZSav,* 83 (1966), 219-251.

Kurfess, A. "Zu Sallust, *Jug.,* 16, 3," *WürzJbb,* 2 (1947), 371.

Laffi, U. "Il mito di Silla," *Athenaeum,* 55 (1967), 177-213.

Lange, L. *Römische Alterthümer.* Vol. III. Berlin, 1876.

Lanzani, C. *Mario e Silla.* Catania, 1915.

———— "Silla e Pompeo. La Spedizione di Sicilia e d'Africa," *Historia,* 7 (1933), 343-362.

———— *L. Cornelio Silla Dittatore.* Milan, 1936.

La Penna, A. "L'Interpretazione sallustiana della guerra contro Giugurta," *AnnPisa,* 28 (1959), 45-86.

La Ville de Mirmont, H. de. "C. Popillius Laenas," *Melanges Boissier* (1903), 319-324.

Lengle, J. *Untersuchungen über die Sullanische Verfassung.* Freiburg, 1899.

———— "Die Verurteilung der römischen Feldherrn von Arausio," *Hermes,* 66 (1931), 302-316.

Lepointe, G. *Q. Mucius Scaevola.* Paris, 1926.

Levick, B. M. *"Acerbissima Lex Servilia,"* *CR,* 17 (1967), 256-258.

Levy, E. "Die römische Kapitalstrafe," *SBHeid,* 21 (1930-31), 1-76.

Lincke, E. *P. Cornelius Scipio Aemilianus.* Dresden, 1898.

Lindsay, R. J. M. "Defamation and the Law under Sulla," *CP,* 44 (1949), 240-243.

Luzzatto, G. I. "Sul nuovo frammento di legge romana rinvenuto a Taranto," *Arch. Stor. Pugliese,* 4 (1951), 28-41.

Malcovati, H. "Ad Cic. *Fam.* 9, 21, 3," *Studi Funaioli* (1955), 216-220.

———— *Oratorum Romanorum Fragmenta Liberae Rei Publicae,* 2nd ed. Turin, 1955.

Marsh, F. B. *History of the Roman World, 146-30 B.C.,* 3rd ed. rev. by H. H. Scullard. London, 1963.

Marx, F. "Animadversiones Criticae in Scipionis Aemiliani Historiam et C. Gracchi Orationem adversus Scipionem," *RhM,* 39 (1884), 65-72.

———— *Lucilii Carminum Reliquiae.* Leipzig, 1904.

Mattingly, H. B. "The Foundations of Narbo Martius," *Hommages Grenier* (1962), III.1159-1171.

Meier, C. "Review of Badian, *Foreign Clientelae,*" *BonnJbb,* 161 (1961), 503-514.

———— "Review of Carney, *A Biography of C. Marius,*" *Gnomon,* 36 (1964), 64-70.

318

———— *Res Publica Amissa*. Wiesbaden, 1966.

———— "Review of A. Lippold, *Consules,*" *AnzAlt,* 19 (1966), 127-131.

Miners, N. J. "The *Lex Sempronia Ne Quis Iudicio Circumveniatur,*" *CQ,* 8 (1958), 241-243.

Mommsen, T. *Geschichte des römischen Münzwesens*. Berlin, 1860.

———— *Römisches Strafrecht*. Leipzig, 1899.

———— *Römische Geschichte*. Berlin, 1903-1904.

———— *Gesammelte Schriften*. Berlin, 1904-1913.

Münzer, F. *De Gente Valeria*. Berlin, 1891.

———— "Anmerkungen zur neuen Livius-Epitome," *Klio,* 5 (1905), 135-139.

———— "Die Fanniusfrage," *Hermes,* 55 (1920), 427-442.

———— *Römische Adelsparteien und Adelsfamilien*. Stuttgart, 1920.

———— "Norbanus," *Hermes,* 67 (1932), 220-236.

Neunheuser, J. E. *M. Aemilius Lepidus*. Münzter, 1902.

Niccolini, G. "Sp. Thorius *Tribunus Plebis* e la *Lex Agraria* del 111 a. Chr.," *RendLinc,* 28 (1919), 189-194.

———— *I Fasti dei Tribuni della Plebe*. Milan, 1934.

Nicolet, C. "L'inspiration de Tiberius Gracchus," *REA,* 67 (1965), 142-159.

———— *L'Ordre Equestre a l'Epoque Republicaine, 312-43 av. J.C.* Paris, 1966.

Ooteghem, J. Van. *Pompeé le Grand*. Brussels, 1954.

———— *L. Licinius Lucullus*. Brussels, 1959.

———— *L. Marcius Philippus et sa Famille. Mem. Acad. Roy. Belg.* Brussels, 1961.

———— *Caius Marius. Mem. Acad. Roy. Belg.* Brussels, 1964.

———— "Marius et Metellus," *LEC,* 32 (1964), 147-161.

Pais, E. "I dodici romani fatti dichiarare publici nemici da Silla nell' 88 a.C.," *Atti Accad. Napoli,* 4 (1916), 65-72.

———— *Dalle Guerre Puniche a Cesare Augusto*. Vols. I-II. Rome, 1918.

Pareti, L. *Storia di Roma*. Vol. III. Turin, 1953.

Passerini, A. "C. Mario come uomo politico," *Athenaeum,* 12 (1934), 10-44, 109-143, 257-297, 348-380.

———— "Epigrafia Mariana," *Athenaeum,* 17 (1939), 54-77.

Peter, H. *Historicorum Romanorum Reliquiae*. Vols. I-II. Leipzig, 1906-1914.

Pichon, R. "L'Affaire des *Rhetores Latini,*" *REA,* 6 (1904), 37-41.

Piganiol, A. "Sur la nouvelle table de bronze de Tarente," *CRAI* (1951), 58-63.

Plaumann, G. "Das sogenannte *Senatus Consultum Ultimum,* die Quasi-diktatur der späteren römischen Republik," *Klio,* 13 (1913), 321-386.

Pontenay de Fontette, F. *Leges Repetundarum*. Paris, 1954.

Premerstein, A. von. *"Lex Tappula," Hermes,* 39 (1904), 327-347.

Quoniam, P. "A propos d'une inscription de Thiburnica, Marius et la romanisation de l'Afrique," *CRAI* (1950), 332-336.

Real-Encyclopädie der Classischen Altertumswissenschaft, ed. A. Pauly, G. Wissowa, et al. Stuttgart, 1894——.

Reid, J. S. "On Some Questions of Roman Public Law," *JRS,* 1 (1911), 66-99.

Rein, W. *Das Criminalrecht der Römer.* Leipzig, 1844.

Renard, M. "L'Assassinat de Scipion Emilien," *Rev. Univ. Brux.,* 37 (1932), 483-498.

Riccobono, S. *Fontes iuris Romani anteiustiniani.* Florence, 1940.

Robinson, F. W. *Marius, Saturninus, und Glaucia.* Jena, 1912.

Robinson, L. *Freedom of Speech in the Roman Republic.* Baltimore, 1940.

Rowland, R. J. "C. Gracchus and the *Equites,*" *TAPA,* 96 (1965), 361-373.

——— "Saturn, Saturninus, and the *socii,*" *CP,* 62 (1967), 185-189.

——— "The Date of Pompeius Strabo's Quaestorship," *CP,* 63 (1968), 213-214.

Rühl, F. "Mummius Achaicus und die *Lex Varia,*" *RhM,* 56 (1901), 634-635.

Russell, H. E. "Advancement in Rank under the Roman Republic as a Reward for the Soldier and the Public Prosecutor," unpub. diss. Bryn Mawr College, 1950.

Salmon, E. T. "The Cause of the Social War," *Phoenix,* 16 (1962), 107-119.

——— "Sulla Redux," *Athenaeum,* 42 (1964), 60-79.

Schäfer, A. "Miscellen," *Jahrb. Class. Phil.,* 107 (1873), 70-72.

Schönbauer, E. "Das Problem der beiden Inschriften von Bantia," *Rev. Int. Droit. Ant.,* 2 (1955), 311-363.

——— "Das Gesetzes-Fragment aus Tarent in neuer Schau," *Jura,* 7 (1956), 92-117.

——— "Die römische Repetundengesetzgebung und das neue Gesetzes-Fragment aus Tarent," *AnzWien,* 93 (1956), 13-40.

Schur, W. *"Homo Novus,"* *BonnJbb,* 134 (1929), 54-66.

——— *Sallust als Historiker.* Stuttgart, 1934.

——— "Das sechste Konsulat des Marius," *Klio,* 31 (1938), 313-322.

——— *Das Zeitalter des Marius und Sulla, Klio Beiheft.* Leipzig, 1942.

Scullard, H. H. *Roman Politics, 220-150 B.C.* Oxford, 1950.

——— "Scipio Aemilianus and Roman Politics," *JRS,* 50 (1960), 59-74.

——— *From the Gracchi to Nero,* 2nd ed. New York, 1963.

Seager, R. "Cicero, *Brutus,* 136," *CR,* 17 (1967), 12-13.

——— *"Lex Varia de Maiestate,"* *Historia,* 16 (1967), 37-43.

——— "The Date of Saturninus' Murder," *CR,* 17 (1967), 9-10.

Serrao, F. "Appunti sui patroni e sulla legittimazione all' accusa nei processi repetundarum," *Studi De Francisci,* 2 (1956), 471-511.

Seymour, P. A. "The Policy of Livius Drusus the Younger," *EHR*, 29 (1914), 417-425.

Shackleton Bailey, D. R. *Cicero's Letters to Atticus.* Vol. V. Cambridge, Eng., 1966.

Sherk, R. K. "The Text of the *Senatus Consultum De Agro Pergameno*," *GRBS*, 7 (1966), 361-369.

Sherwin-White, A. N. *The Roman Citizenship.* Oxford, 1939.

———— "*Poena Legis Repetundarum*," *PBSR*, 17 (1949), 5-25.

———— "The Extortion Procedure Again," *JRS*, 42 (1952), 43-55.

———— "Review of Gabba, *Le Origini della Guerra Sociale*," *JRS*, 45 (1955), 168-170.

———— "Violence in Roman Politics," *JRS*, 46 (1956), 1-9.

Siber, H. "Analogie, Amtsrecht, und Rückwirkung im Strafrechte des römische Freistaates," *AbhLeipz*, 43 (1936), 1-77.

———— "*Provocatio*," *ZSav*, 75 (1942), 376-391.

Simon, H. *Roms Kriege in Spanien.* Frankfurt, 1962.

Simon, H. O. *Vita Q. Lutatii Catuli.* Berlin, 1874.

Smith, R. E. "Pompey's conduct in 80 and 77 B.C.," *Phoenix*, 14 (1960), 1-13.

———— "The Anatomy of Force in Late Republican Politics," in *Ancient Society and Institutions: Studies to Ehrenburg* (Oxford, 1966), 257-273.

Smuts, F. "Stoic Influences on Tiberius Gracchus," *Acta Classica*, 1 (1958), 106-116.

Stevenson, G. H. "Cn. Pompeius Strabo and the Franchise Question," *JRS*, 9 (1919), 95-101.

Strachan-Davidson, J. L. *Problems of the Roman Criminal Law.* Vols. I-II. Oxford, 1912.

Strasburger, H. "Der 'Scipionenkreis,'" *Hermes*, 94 (1966), 60-72.

Stuart Jones, H. "A Roman Law Concerning Piracy," *JRS*, 16 (1926), 155-173.

Sumner, G. V. "*Lex Aelia, Lex Fufia*," *AJP*, 84 (1963), 337-358.

———— "Manius or Mamercus?" *JRS*, 54 (1964), 41-48.

Sydenham, E. A. *Coinage of the Roman Republic.* London, 1952.

Syme, R. "Caesar, the Senate, and Italy," *PBSR*, 14 (1938), 1-31.

———— *The Roman Revolution.* Oxford, 1939.

———— "Review of Schur, *Zeitalter des Marius und Sulla*," *JRS*, 34 (1944), 103-109.

———— "Missing Senators," *Historia*, 4 (1955), 52-71.

———— "Review of Broughton, *MRR*," *CP*, 50 (1955), 127-138.

———— "Piso and Veranius in Catullus," *ClMed*, 17 (1956), 129-134.

———— *Sallust.* Berkeley and Los Angeles, 1964.

Taylor, L. R. *Party Politics in the Age of Caesar.* Berkeley and Los Angeles, 1949.

———— *The Voting Districts of the Roman Republic.* Rome, 1960.

———— "Forerunners of the Gracchi," *JRS*, 52 (1962), 19-27.

————— "Was Tiberius Gracchus' Last Assembly Electoral or Legislative?" *Athenaeum,* 41 (1963), 51-69.

————— "Appian and Plutarch on Tiberius Gracchus' Last Assembly," *Athenaeum,* 44 (1966), 238-250.

————— *Roman Voting Assemblies from the Hannibalic War to the Dictatorship of Caesar.* Ann Arbor, 1966.

Thompson, L. A. "The Relationship between Provincial Quaestors and their Commanders in Chief," *Historia,* 11 (1962), 339-355.

Thomsen, R. "Das Jahr 91 v. Chr. und seine Voraussetzungen," *ClMed,* 5 (1942), 13-47.

————— "Erliess Tiberius Gracchus ein *Iustitium?*" *ClMed,* 6 (1944), 60-71.

Tibiletti, G. "Il possesso dell' *ager publicus* e le norme *de modo agrorum* sino ai Gracchi," *Athenaeum,* 26 (1948), 173-236; *Athenaeum,* 27 (1949), 3-42.

————— "Ricerche di storia agraria romana," *Athenaeum,* 28 (1950), 183-266.

————— "La politica delle colonie e citta latine nella Guerra Sociale," *RendIstLomb,* 86 (1953), 45-63.

————— "Le leggi *De Iudiciis Repetundarum* fino alla Guerra Sociale," *Athenaeum,* 31 (1953), 5-100, 396.

————— "Lo sviluppo del latifundo in Italia dall' epoca graccana al principio dell' Impero," *Relazioni del X Congresso Internazionale di Scienze Storiche,* 2 (1955), 235-292.

Toynbee, A. J. *Hannibal's Legacy: The Hannibalic War's Effects on Roman Life.* Vols. I-II. London, 1965.

Valgiglio, E. *Plutarco, Vita di Mario.* Florence, 1956.

————— *Silla e la Crisi Repubblicana.* Florence, 1956.

Volterra, E. "Il preteso tribunale domestico in diritto romano," *Riv. Ital. Scienz. Giurid.,* 2 (1948), 103-153.

Vonder Mühll, F. *De L. Appuleio Saturnino Tribuno Plebis.* Basel, 1906.

Vretska, K. "Studien zu Sallusts *Bellum Jugurthinum,*" *SBWien,* 229 (1955), 1-169.

Walsh, P. G. "Massinissa," *JRS,* 55 (1965), 149-160.

Warmington, E. H. *Remains of Old Latin.* Vol. III. London, 1958.

Westermann, W. L. *The Slave Systems of Greek and Roman Antiquity.* Philadelphia, 1955.

Willems, P. *Le senat de la république romaine. Sa composition et ses attributions,* Vols. I-II. Louvain and Paris, 1878-1883.

Wiseman, T. P. *"Viae Anniae,"* *PBSR,* 32 (1964), 21-37.

————— "Lucius Memmius and his Family," *CQ,* 17 (1967), 164-167.

Yarnold, E. A. "The Latin Law of Bantia," *AJP,* 78 (1957), 163-172.

Yeo, C. "The Overgrazing of Ranch-Lands in Ancient Italy," *TAPA,* 79 (1948), 275-309.

————— "The Development of the Roman Plantation and Marketing of Farm Products," *Finanzarchiv,* 13 (1952), 321-342.

Ziegler, K. "L. Caecilius Metellus Diadematus," *Gymnasium,* 63 (1956), 483-486.

Zumpt, A. W. *Das Criminalrecht der römischen Republik.* Berlin, I.2, 1865; II.1, 1868; II.2, 1869.

———— *Der Criminalprocess der römischen Republik.* Leipzig, 1871.